iPhone® 4S
ALL-IN-ONE
FOR
DUMMIES®

by Joe Hutsko and Barbara Boyd

WILEY

John Wiley & Sons, Inc.

iPhone® 4S All-in-One For Dummies®

Published by
John Wiley & Sons, Inc.
111 River Street
Hoboken, NJ 07030-5774

www.wiley.com

Copyright © 2012 by John Wiley & Sons, Inc., Hoboken, New Jersey

Published by John Wiley & Sons, Inc., Hoboken, New Jersey

Published simultaneously in Canada

For general information on our other products and services, please contact our Customer Care Department within the U.S. at 877-762-2974, outside the U.S. at 317-572-3993, or fax 317-572-4002.

For technical support, please visit www.wiley.com/techsupport.

Wiley publishes in a variety of print and electronic formats and by print-on-demand. Some material included with standard print versions of this book may not be included in e-books or in print-on-demand. If this book refers to media such as a CD or DVD that is not included in the version you purchased, you may download this material at http://booksupport.wiley.com. For more information about Wiley products, visit www.wiley.com.

Library of Congress Control Number: 2011946311

ISBN: 978-1-118-10119-3

ISBN: 978-1-118-22382-6 (pbk); ISBN: 978-1-118-23714-4 (ebk); ISBN: 978-1-118-25839-2

Manufactured in the United States of America

10 9 8 7 6 5 4 3 2 1

WILEY

About the Authors

Joe Hutsko is the author of *Green Gadgets For Dummies, Flip Video For Dummies* (with Drew Davidson), and *Mac All-in-One For Dummies* (with Barbara Boyd). For more than two decades, he has written about computers, gadgets, video games, trends, and high-tech movers and shakers for numerous publications and websites, including the *New York Times, Macworld, PC World, Fortune, Newsweek, Popular Science, TV Guide,* the *Washington Post, Wired,* Gamespot, MSNBC, Engadget, TechCrunch, and Salon. You can find links to Joe's stories on his blog, JOEyGADGET.com.

As a kid, Joe built a shortwave radio, played with electronic project kits, and learned the basics of the BASIC programming language on his first computer, the Commodore Vic 20. In his teens, he picked strawberries to buy his first Apple II computer. Four years after that purchase (in 1984), he wound up working for Apple, where he became the personal technology guru for the company's chairman and CEO. Joe left Apple in 1988 to become a writer and worked on and off for other high-tech companies, including Steve Jobs' one-time NeXT. He authored a number of video game strategy guides, including the bestsellers *Donkey Kong Country Game Secrets: The Unauthorized Edition,* and *Rebel Assault: The Official Insiders Guide.*

Joe's first novel, *The Deal,* was published in 1999, and he recently rereleased a trade paperback edition of it with a new foreword by the author (`tinyurl.com/hutskodeal`).

Barbara Boyd writes about food, gardens, travel, and technology. She's written for *ChilePepper Magazine, Islands,* and *BeeCulture. iPhone 4S All-in-One For Dummies* is her first *For Dummies* book. With Joe, she's currently working on the third edition of *Macs All-in-One For Dummies.*

Barbara worked at Apple from 1985 to 1990, beginning as Joe's assistant and the first network administrator for the executive staff. She then took a position as an administrator in the Technical Product Support group. Barbara recalls working with people who went on to become top names in technology — it was an exciting time to be in Silicon Valley and at Apple in particular. That experience instilled a lifelong fascination with technology and Apple products. Her interest and experience led to subsequent jobs in marketing and publishing at IDG (International Data Group) and later for a small San Francisco design firm. In 1998, she left the corporate world to study Italian, write, and teach.

Presently, Barbara stays busy writing, keeping up with technology, growing olives, and beekeeping. (She's a certified honey taster.) Her next writing project — barring any unforeseen *For Dummies* books — will be a memoir of building a farm and house in Italy. Barbara divides her time between city life in Rome and country life on an olive farm in Calabria, which she blogs about at `honeybeesandolivetrees.blogspot.com/`.

Dedication

Joe Hutsko: I dedicate this book to my fabulously thoughtful, kind, caring, smart, creative, beautiful, and amazing co-author — and lifelong friend (and karmic life preserver) — Barbara Boyd.

Barbara Boyd: I dedicate this book to: My sweet, patient husband, Ugo de Paula. He appreciates my inner geek and gave me my first iPhone for Christmas in 2008. He keeps me on my toes by asking complicated and challenging technical questions. Most of all, he never complains when I have to work while he's on vacation and is always ready to share shopping and cooking duties. Ti amo tesoronemio.

Authors' Acknowledgments

You see the author's names on the cover, but these books (like any book) are really a collaboration, an effort of a many-membered team. Thanks go to Bob Woerner at Wiley for trusting Joe's judgment and taking a chance on an unknown author. We couldn't have completed this book without our fabulous project editor, Linda Morris, who pulled everything together and gently nudged us to stay on schedule. A big hats-off to Dennis R. Cohen for his insightful and accurate technical editing and witty comments that often made us laugh out loud during author review. Thanks, too, to the anonymous people at Wiley who contributed to this book — not just editorial, but tech support, legal, accounting, and even the person who delivers the mail. We don't know you but we appreciate the job you do; it takes a lot of worker bees to keep the hive healthy, and each task is important to the whole.

We want to thank our agent, Carole Jelen, for her astute representation and moral support.

Thanks to the folks at Apple who developed such a cool product, and specifically to Keri Walker for her ongoing editorial product support. A big, couldn't-have-done-it-without-you thank you to Maxim Laskavy at the Apple Store Philadelphia for coming through with sales support at the eleventh hour.

Also, a special thanks to the app developers who shared their products and their time — their names are too many to list here, but please take our word for it when we say this book wouldn't have been complete without your support.

Joe adds: Major thanks to my dear, long-time friend Barbara Boyd, who stepped up to the plate as co-author on both this book and *Macs All-in-One For Dummies* when my life and work focuses shifted to other time-sensitive projects and matters; writing and making deadlines on both books would have been impossible without Barbara's contribution. I mean it quite literally when I say both books are more Barbara's than mine, from total word count, attention to detail, and commitment perspectives. Lastly, I am pleased to see Barbara managed to slip in a reference to her beloved bees in the Acknowledgments.

Barbara adds: Not a day goes by that I'm not grateful to my dear, long-time friend, and co-author, Joe. I love my job and working with him is a joy, but the real reason is that by asking me to write this book, I've gotten back in the habit of writing every day and there aren't enough thanks for that. Through the years, I've gotten several jobs by following in Joe's footsteps, but this one is by far the best. A heartfelt "thank you" to my sister, Bonnie, whose enthusiasm was perhaps more than my own about writing this book. She's my biggest fan and personal cheerleader.

Publisher's Acknowledgments

We're proud of this book; please send us your comments at http://dummies.custhelp.com. For other comments, please contact our Customer Care Department within the U.S. at 877-762-2974, outside the U.S. at 317-572-3993, or fax 317-572-4002.

Some of the people who helped bring this book to market include the following:

Acquisitions and Editorial

Project Editor: Linda Morris

Executive Editor: Bob Woerner

Copy Editor: Linda Morris

Technical Editor: Dennis Cohen

Editorial Manager: Jodi Jensen

Editorial Assistant: Amanda Graham

Sr. Editorial Assistant: Cherie Case

Cover Photo: ©istockphoto.com / Ola Dusegard (background); ©istockphoto.com / Muharrem Öner (image of hand)

Cartoons: Rich Tennant (www.the5thwave.com)

Composition Services

Project Coordinator: Katie Crocker

Layout and Graphics: Joyce Haughey, Christin Swinford

Proofreaders: Melissa Cossell, Evelyn Wellborn

Indexer: BIM Indexing & Proofreading Services

Publishing and Editorial for Technology Dummies

    Richard Swadley, Vice President and Executive Group Publisher

    Andy Cummings, Vice President and Publisher

    Mary Bednarek, Executive Acquisitions Director

    Mary C. Corder, Editorial Director

Publishing for Consumer Dummies

    Kathleen Nebenhaus, Vice President and Executive Publisher

Composition Services

    Debbie Stailey, Director of Composition Services

Contents at a Glance

Bonus Online Content: Apps for Every Type of Task ... Online

Table of Contents

Introduction

Apple has built its reputation on creating user-friendly products. Browsing the FingerTips guide that comes with your iPhone or even reading the more extensive iPhone User's Guide gives you enough information to use a portion of your iPhone's capabilities. We think that's kind of like using 10 percent of your brain: You get by, but you're not living up to your maximum potential.

We wrote this book to take your iPhone use to a higher level. This book probably covers some apps or functions that just don't interest you or are unnecessary for the way you use your iPhone, so it's unlikely that you'll reach 100 percent, but we'll be really and truly happy if you up your percentage just a bit, say, to 75 or 80 percent. It'd be plain wasteful to use your iPhone as a simple phone when it's so much more.

About This Book

To write this book, we looked into every nook and cranny of iPhone. Short of telling you how to take it apart, which would void your warranty, we believe we get pretty darn close to telling you all there is to know. That said, Apple releases iOS updates frequently and we encourage you to keep your iPhone and app software up to date and stay informed as to how to use features that may be added with updates.

Book I of this book explains iPhone basics: what your iPhone can do, how your iPhone is organized, and how to use the multitouch screen and voice-recognition interface. Subsequent minibooks are divided by task: adding apps and accessories, and using your iPhone to communicate, to manage your business affairs, and to be entertained. The final minibook takes a look at third-party apps that enhance your iPhone.

We're not perfect, so we undoubtedly missed something. Let us know. Your comments, questions, and compliments help us to improve future editions. Drop a note to Joe at jhutsko@gmail.com or Barbara at babsboyd@me.com.

Conventions Used in This Book

To help you navigate this book efficiently, we use a few style conventions:

- Website addresses, or URLs, are shown in a special monofont typeface, like this.
- Numbered steps that you need to follow are set in **bold**.

✔ Sequential commands are shown as Settings⇨General⇨Network, which means tap Settings, tap General, and then tap Network on your iPhone. Store⇨View My Account means to click the Store menu and drag to click the View My Account option on your computer.

✔ The first time we mention a button or icon we show you what it looks like in the margin so you can find it more easily on your iPhone. The same button may be used in different apps and tapping it elicits the same function regardless of the app it's in.

✔ Sidebars present technical information that you don't have to know but that might interest those of you who want to understand the technology behind the function.

What You're Not to Read

This book doesn't have to be read cover to cover — you can pick and choose the chapters that pertain to how you use your iPhone. However, even if you are familiar with iPhone, we recommend you skim the beginning chapters. That way, you'll understand the commands we use in later chapters.

You don't have to read sidebars. Reading the sidebars can increase your iPhone knowledge, but skipping them won't inhibit your iPhone use. Same goes for Technical Stuff blips: They contain fun information, but they're not life-threateningly necessary.

Foolish Assumptions

We made a few assumptions about you when writing this book. To make sure we're on the same page, we assume that

✔ You know something, but not necessarily a lot, about cellular phones and you want to learn the basics and more about iPhone.

✔ You have at least a general concept of how to use the web and e-mail.

✔ You'll read through the introductory chapters if you find yourself scratching your head when you see terms like *tap, swipe, and flick,* or anything else that we think you should know but you don't.

✔ You acknowledge that it's up to you to go on the web to find updated information about the products described throughout this book.

✔ You know that technology is changing faster than we can keep up and even geeks like us can't stay on top of everything. You will, therefore, let us know about cool stuff you find along the way of your iPhone journey so we can consider it for future editions of this book.

✔ You're not all work and no play. You want to have some fun with your iPhone and maybe even be entertained while you're learning how to use it.

How This Book Is Organized

This book is divided into mini-books, which are further divided into chapters. You can read it cover to cover, but we recommend you familiarize yourself with iPhone basics in Book I, and then skip to the book or chapters that talk about the functions or apps that you use most or are most interested in using. We think you should also take a look at functions you doubt you'll use because you might find you like those functions.

The more you use your iPhone, the more you begin to understand the basic commands and techniques used across the iOS platform. We take you beyond the basics in the books and chapters that follow, giving you tips and showing you advanced settings throughout.

Book 1: Meet iPhone

This minibook explains the functions you need to know to use your iPhone: basics like turning it on and off, adjusting the volume, charging the battery, and how to use the multitouch and voice-recognition (also known as Siri) interfaces. Buttons, icons, notifications, and badges that you might encounter are introduced. We give you an overview of the built-in apps and explain iPhone's settings in detail so you can customize them to your liking. This is also where you can find a troubleshooting question-and-answer guide and tips for avoiding problems.

Book II: Stocking iPhone with iTunes Apps and Add-ons

This minibook explains the concept of syncing (that is, having the same information in two places and have changes made in one place appear automatically in another). Your iPhone uses iCloud to sync with your computers and any other iOS devices you have. Also in this minibook, you learn about the App Store and how to shop for other Apple and third-party apps, and Newsstand and how to subscribe to and read newspapers and magazines on your iPhone The last chapter discusses hardware accessories that enhance your iPhone, such as speakers and protective cases.

Book III: Communications Central: Calls, Messages, and the Web

This minibook gets to the core communications functions of your iPhone. It explains everything about making phone calls, checking voicemail, using iPhone's video chat app FaceTime, sending text and e-mail messages, exchanging messages with other iOS devices with iMessage, and surfing the Internet with Safari, iPhone's web browser.

Book IV: Making iPhone Your Personal Assistant

Contact management, time management, getting directions, taking notes, and reminding you when to be somewhere to meet someone to do something — your iPhone can do it all and we explain it in this minibook. This minibook covers the unexpected iPhone apps like Maps and Compass, Weather, Stocks, and Calculator as well as the basic PDA apps: Contacts, Calendar, Notes, Voice Memos, and the new addition, Reminders.

Book V: Letting iPhone Entertain You: Photos, Videos, Music, and More

This minibook is about having fun with your iPhone. Amateur photographers and videographers will like using iPhone as a still and video camera and for sharing images. This minibook also gives all the details for having the best experience when listening to music, watching movies and TV shows, reading books, and streaming podcasts.

Bonus Content Online

In this online bonus content, you learn how to expand your iPhone beyond the standard Apple apps. Each chapter presents a selection of apps that add a feature or function to your iPhone, or enhance something it already does. For the business user or busy household manager, there are budgeting, task management, and faxing apps. For the social butterfly, there are communications and networking apps. Quiet types might enjoy e-reader and radio apps. There's something for everyone in the leisure, fitness, health, home, and travel apps. Find the bonus content online at www.dummies.com/go/iphone4SAIO.

Icons Used in This Book

To help emphasize certain information, this book displays different icons in the page margins.

The Tip icon points out bits of information that can help you do things better and more efficiently or tells you something useful that you might not know.

This icon highlights interesting information that isn't necessary to know but can help explain why certain things work the way they do on your iPhone. Like Sidebars, you can skip this information if you're in a hurry. On the other hand, you might find something helpful.

This icon gives you a heads up about something that can go wrong if you're not careful. Be sure to read the Warning fully before following related instructions.

This icon points out information that's been mentioned somewhere else in the book but is related to the topic nearby. If you ignore it, you won't cause problems. but you could miss something useful.

Where to Go from Here

As Julie Andrews sang in the *Sound of Music*, "Let's start at the very beginning, it's a very good place to start."

If you're new to iPhone, closely read the first few chapters to get an understanding of how your iPhone works, the command conventions it uses, and how to perform the basic functions. Then move on to chapters that interest you, perhaps starting with the phone and messaging functions before moving up to Internet access, and lastly looking at the multimedia apps like Music, Videos, and Camera.

If you're familiar with your iPhone already, skim through the opening chapters to learn about the recent iOS 5 changes, and then go where you wish, to a chapter on a function you haven't used before, which might be the video camera or the compass or to a function you use a lot but would like to know better.

No matter where you begin, our goal is to give you the tools to get the most out of your iPhone and encourage you to expand your knowledge and explore the many ways of iPhone.

Occasionally, we have updates to our technology books. If this book does have technical updates, they will be posted at `dummies.com/go/iphone AIOupdates`.

Book I
Meet iPhone

The 5th Wave — By Rich Tennant

"You ever notice how much more streaming media there is than there used to be?"

*i*Phone is so much more than a phone. The first chapter of this minibook presents an overview of all the tasks your iPhone can do. Each of these tasks is explained in depth in dedicated chapters throughout the book. In Chapter 2, we explain the icons and messages you see on your iPhone's screen, and how to connect your iPhone to an electrical outlet, a computer, a printer, and a television. In Chapter 3, we explore the multitouch interface. This chapter is crucial to understanding how to use your iPhone, and here we define commands that will be used throughout the other chapters of this book. We introduce the apps that came with your iPhone in Chapter 4 and take a look at the basic settings. We think of the last chapter of this minibook as the preventive maintenance chapter. Chapter 5 gives you a heads up for some common problems you might encounter. We think if you read about these potential snags before they happen, you'll be calmer and better prepared to fix them — if they happen.

If you're on your second, third, or even fifth iPhone, you can probably skim (or even skip) this chapter. If you're an iPhone newbie, this minibook is for you.

Chapter 1: Exploring the Many Faces of iPhone

In This Chapter

- ✓ **Considering iPhone carriers**
- ✓ **Making phone calls**
- ✓ **Sending messages**
- ✓ **Surfing the web and playing games**
- ✓ **Taking photos and video**
- ✓ **Being entertained**

*Y*ou bought this book, so you probably already have an iPhone. Maybe you even took it out of the box (who could resist?) and made a few phone calls or sent a text message. We're here to tell you there's a lot more.

This is the "whet your appetite" chapter. We look at the hardware, software, and a few unseen secrets of your iPhone. We just want to start you thinking about how you can get the most out of your iPhone. We introduce you to all your iPhone can do, and then you can pick and choose the topics and tasks where you want to dive deeper and go to those chapters for the details. Sticking with our appetite metaphor — or is it a simile? — if this chapter is the hors d'oeuvres, the following minibooks and chapters are the main courses, side dishes, and dessert. *Bon appétit!*

Looking at Your iPhone from Every Angle

Unless you lived a solitary, monastic life in a cave for the past few years (and if you did, we admit to being a bit envious), you saw ads for iPhone before you bought one. Just seeing the sleek design and the cool things it can do probably nudged you toward getting one. Like the difference between seeing a car ad and taking the car for a test drive, holding iPhone in your hands probably cinched the deal. Here we take a look at the hardware and then a closer look at what's inside.

Front, back, top, bottom

The first thing you notice is the glass — yes, glass — screen. The front and back of your iPhone are coated with a scratch-resistant, fingerprint-resistant aluminosilicate glass. You might think that makes your iPhone rather delicate, but this glass is the same stuff helicopter windshields are made of. Bet you don't think *they're* delicate.

Around the edges of your iPhone you see a metal band. It's a beautiful design element, but it also functions as an antenna (or as two antennae on the 4S).

Notice the buttons and holes around the edges and on the front and back, which have the following functions:

- On/off sleep/wake switch
- Microphone
- Dock port
- Volume buttons
- Silent/ring button
- Two video/still objective lenses
- LED light
- SIM tray
- Speaker
- Home button

We explain all of them in Book I, Chapter 2.

What you don't see can help you

Your iPhone has antennae and sensors. One is the metal band around the outside that performs antenna functions for connecting to the cellular network. iPhone 4S actually switches between two antennas to receive and transmit, which increases data transfer speeds and call quality. Like your brain that tells your lungs to breathe without you having to consciously think about it, the sensors give your iPhone information to perform functions without you having to give the command:

- **GPS:** Finds your location, gives you directions in Maps, and geotags your photos. In Book V, Chapter 1, we explain how geotagging identifies your location when you take a photo.
- **Wi-Fi:** Connects to available Wi-Fi networks.

- **Cellular antenna:** Connects you to EDGE, GPRS, UMTS, HSUPA, or 3G networks. We explain the different types of cellular networks in Book I, Chapter 2.

- **Gyroscope:** Used to find your location when GPS isn't accessible.

- **Magnetic-field sensor:** Positions the Compass.

- **Proximity sensor:** Turns the touchscreen off when you hold the phone close to your ear, so you don't accidentally tap the mute button while you're in the middle of a conversation. As soon as you move iPhone a few 16ths of an inch from your head, the screen is activated.

- **Tilt sensor:** Senses motion, particularly useful when playing games that involve driving or flying.

- **Accelerometer:** Allows for landscape display.

- **Bluetooth:** Connects to other Bluetooth enabled devices.

- **Light sensor:** Adjusts the screen when you're using your iPhone in low or bright light situations.

- **Backside illumination sensor:** Adjusts the exposure for better photos.

- **Moisture sensor:** Lets Apple know if your iPhone has gone for a swim if you try to have it replaced under AppleCare as a defective iPhone. (Tsk, tsk, tsk! That's not covered under the warranty.) Learn about AppleCare in Book I, Chapter 5.

Other stuff in the box

Your iPhone comes with a few nice accessories too. Here's what you'll find when you open the box:

- **Headset:** Stereo earphones with a built-in microphone and volume control buttons.

- **USB cable connector:** Connects your iPhone to a USB port on your computer, in your car, and on the USB power adapter.

- **USB power adapter:** Connects to the USB cable connector and plugs into an outlet to charge your iPhone's battery.

- **Finger Tips guide:** Apple's quick guide to iPhone functions and features.

- **Product info:** Legal and technical information.

- **SIM eject tool:** Opens the SIM tray where the SIM card from your cellular provider is inserted.

iPhone lineage: Since the beginning of iPhone time

Just as the Mac changed computing in 1984, iPhone changed the way we think about and use cellular phones with its release in 2007. Just for fun, here's a quick timeline and the changes that have taken place in the last four years:

January 9, 2007: After what some say were ten full years from concept to production, iPhone was announced at Macworld.

June 11, 2007: At Worldwide Developers Conference, Steve Jobs announced that iPhone would run applications — quickly dubbed "apps" — created by third-party developers.

June 28, 2007: The day before the official iPhone release, all Apple employees who'd been with the company at least one year received an iPhone.

June 29, 2007: Hordes of Apple fans waited to purchase one of the first iPhones. This revolutionary "smartphone" ran iPhone OS 1.0 and had 128MB of memory, a 3.5 inch display with 480X320 pixel resolution, and a 2.0 megapixel, fixed focus camera. There were two options for storage: 4GB or 8GB.

September 5, 2007: The 4GB model was discontinued.

November, 2007: iPhone was released in the U.K., France, and Germany.

February 5, 2008: The 16GB version was made available.

Spring 2008: IPhone was released in Ireland and Austria.

June 9, 2008: iPhone 3G was introduced at the Worldwide Developers Conference. It offered increased connectivity, an accelerometer and a proximity sensor, an ambient light sensor, and GPS. iPhone 3G was released with iPhone OS 2.0.

July 10, 2008: The App Store launched with 500 apps.

June 8, 2009: Eleven months after the App Store opening, apps had increased one hundred-fold to 50,000 available apps. More than 1 billion downloads had been processed. IPhone 3GS announced.

June 17, 2009: iPhone OS 3.0 was released and, among other improvements, it offered the long-awaited copy and paste functions.

June 19, 2009: iPhone 3GS released with twice the memory of the earlier versions, 256MB, and the option for 8, 16, or 32GB storage. The 3.2 megapixel camera had autofocus and recorded video. The first generation of voice control was released. In the time since the original iPhone release, other companies had developed smartphones, but iPhone 3GS was the first to have a real compass and an oleophobic coating to resist fingerprints.

April 29, 2010: The App Store boasted 200,000 apps and 4.5 billion downloads.

June 2, 2010: iPhone 4 announced.

June 24, 2010: iPhone 4 released with iOS 4.0, the operating system that would be used on iPod touch and iPad as well as iPhone. Memory was again doubled, to 512MB. The screen resolution was increased to 960 x 640 and offered an 800:1 contrast. IPhone 4 featured two cameras: a 5 megapixel autofocus and HD video recording camera with LED flash on the back and a 1.3 megapixel VGA-quality photo and video camera on the front for videochat with an app called FaceTime. An additional microphone offered noise reduction for phone calls in busy places and an internal gyroscope helped determine where you were at all times.

June 4, 2011: iOS 5 announced at the Worldwide Developers Conference. PC-free activation and iCloud meant iPhone could be activated and backed up without a computer. Notifications were given their own screen.

Magazine and newspaper subscriptions were sold in the App Store. They can be read in Newsstand on your iPhone.	October 4, 2011: iPhone 4S announced. October 12, 2011: iOS 5 and iCloud released. October 14, 2011: iPhone 4S shipped.

Considering iPhone Carriers and Configurations

When iPhone was first released, only one cellular service provider was available in the U.S.: AT&T. The situation was similar in other countries — only one cellular service provider supported iPhone. With subsequent releases, many carriers now support iPhone and that's made the situation both more convenient and more confusing for the consumer. Verizon and Sprint joined AT&T in offering cellular service contracts that include iPhones. In Europe, Vodafone is popular, although many countries also have country-specific carriers with competitive pricing.

Unlocked iPhones, which are iPhones you purchase outright without a service contract, work with carriers who use the GSM standard (see the following paragraph). In the U.S., AT&T, T-Mobile, and 30 or so regional carriers use GSM, as do most of the carriers outside the U.S. A customer in good standing can request that his CDMA carrier unlock his iPhone so it can access the GSM networks overseas, but nonetheless remains tied to the national and roaming costs associated with the cellular service contract.

GSM (Global System for Mobile) and CDMA (Code Division Multiple Access) are the telecommunications standards used for cellular networks. GSM, as its name implies, is the worldwide standard, whereas CDMA is limited to America and parts of Asia. CDMA offers slightly better data transfer, although GSM is steadily improving. The GSM standard stores your phone number and account information on a SIM card, whereas in the CDMA standard, the phone number and account information is programmed in the phone itself. Some CDMA networks require a SIM in order to connect to a GSM network outside the U.S. Sprint offers one so you can access the GSM network used by Sprint's partners in Europe. iPhones come with either GSM (with an AT&T contract or unlocked) or CDMA (Verizon or Sprint contracts).

Rates and offers change frequently and we're not in a position to advise you as to which carrier to choose. Here are a few things to consider so you can compare plans from different carriers and make an informed decision:

✔ **How much time do you spend on the phone?** Do you make many calls or just check in now and then? Three hundred and sixty minutes is 12 minutes a day, whereas 1,000 minutes is just over a half hour a day. If you're thinking about replacing your landline with a cell phone, 1,000 minutes may not be enough.

✓ **When do you use your phone?** Some plans offer lower nighttime and weekend rates. If you spend your weekdays at your office, you probably won't be using your cell phone much anyway.

✓ **Who do you call?** Some plans offer a you-and-me or family discount for one number or a group of numbers that you call more than any other.

✓ **Where do you use your phone?** If you travel around the country, you probably want a call plan with nationwide coverage. If you're a homebody, a regional plan is probably just fine.

✓ **Do you travel overseas?** If you do, shop around for the best roaming rate or, if you frequently go to the same country, consider getting a local, rechargeable SIM card and using that in your iPhone when you're out of the U.S.

✓ **Do you send text messages?** Text messages may be billed at a per-message rate or your plan may include a limited number and you pay a per-message rate if you exceed the limited number. iMessage lets you send text messages for free to other iPhone, iPad, and iPod touch users.

✓ **How much cellular data usage do you need?** Wi-Fi is widespread in the U.S. Even the smallest one-café town seems to offer free Wi-Fi if you buy a cup of coffee, which makes cellular data less necessary. Most plans these days offer unlimited Internet access, although 20MB is the file size limit for downloading over a cellular network.

The Big Picture: It's All That and More!

Your iPhone is so much more than a cellular phone. Even the *smartphone* label seems limiting. With each new generation, iPhone has added more functions and features. IPhone itself is the hardware and the iOS and apps are the software that let you do so many things. In the next few sections, we give you the proverbial taste of what you can do.

Phone

Clearly, iPhone is a cellular telephone (see Figure 1-1) that makes voice calls and offers text messaging. Nothing extraordinary there. The standout functions include multimedia messaging with active links in messages you send and receive. Consider visual voicemail that displays a list of messages so you can listen to the most important ones first rather than go through them in chronological order. You have two ways to communicate cost-free with other iOS device owners: FaceTime lets you communicate via video chat and iMessage gives you SMS-type message exchanges. We explain the ins and outs of phoning and messaging in Book III, Chapters 1 and 2.

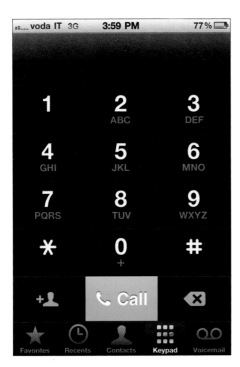

Figure 1-1: iPhone as phone.

Music and videos

This is not your standard MP3 player. With its peerless screen and excellent stereophonic output, your iPhone plays music, movies, podcasts, and more with crisp, clear sound and images. From iTunes, you can download music, movies, TV shows, podcasts, courseware, and audiobooks. Watch and upload videos to YouTube. Connect your iPhone to a monitor or television with a cable or via AirPlay or Apple TV and watch everything on a big screen. All you have to do is pop the popcorn. Check out Book V, Chapters 2, 3, and 4 to learn all about the iPod, iTunes, and audio and video functions.

Camera and video camcorder

Eight megapixels make the digital still camera on iPhone 4S one of the best smartphone cameras on the market. And iPhone 4S video cameras capture high-definition video in 1080 rows of pixels. The LED flash next to the objective lens on the back of your iPhone illuminates both still photos and videos. iOS 5 added a few editing options to the Photos app, which you use to organize and view your photos and videos after you capture them. Go to Book V, Chapter 1 for detailed information.

Personal digital assistant

iPhone 4S becomes a true personal digital assistant (PDA for short) with the addition of Siri, the voice-recognition interface. Just speak your commands to Siri and it (she?) does what you ask, such as typing and sending a dictated e-mail, finding a florist, or changing your dentist appointment. We explain how to use the Siri interface in Book I, Chapter 3.

Don't let Siri steal the limelight from iPhone's other PDA features. Barbara got her first iPhone about the same time she and her husband downsized to a smaller apartment that didn't have an extra room for a home office. That change, combined with a desire to make the absolute most of iPhone, led her to relying on iPhone's PDA features. Contacts eliminated the need for a paper address book. Calendar replaced the little black Filofax she'd coveted for years, and Notes made all those scraps of notes and grocery lists obsolete. The addition of Reminders in iOS 5 makes sure no task or appointment is forgotten. We show you how to use your iPhone's PDA apps along with Voice Memos, Clock, and Calculator in Book IV.

Internet communicator

You start to see the real power of your iPhone when you go online. Able to access the Internet via either your cellular network, 3G, or Wi-Fi, you never have to miss another time-sensitive e-mail or tweet. You can search the Internet with Safari as you would on any computer. For example, you can search for movie times, book airline tickets, settle bets with Wikipedia, and read the news from your favorite news outlets. Safari's Reader function isolates an article from the noise around it, making for easier reading. Book III, Chapter 3 explains Safari.

You access your e-mail accounts through Mail. If you have multiple accounts, you can sync them all with Mail and see them individually or all together. Learn all about Mail in Book III, Chapter 4.

Your iPhone comes with some specific apps that gather information from the Internet, as shown in Figure 1-2. Stocks lets you follow international investment markets as well as your personal investments. Weather leans on Yahoo! to bring you the weather forecast for cities you want to know about. We take you through these apps in Book IV, Chapter 3.

Personal GPS navigator

Between the Compass and Maps apps and the GPS, Wi-Fi, and cellular sensors, 99 percent of the time your iPhone can tell you where you are and tell you how to get where you want to go. What's more, Maps and Siri can give you suggestions for vendors and services, like bookstores and restaurants, based on your location. The links in Maps are active — as they are in most iPhone apps — so you just click on the suggested vendor and the website for that vendor opens in Safari. We explain how to use Maps and Compass in Book IV, Chapter 3.

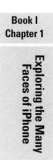

Figure 1-2: iPhone's great graphics make reading websites easy on the eyes.

E-book and document reader

E-readers and tablets are all the rage and we admit the larger screen does make reading easier on an e-reader than on your iPhone, however, your iPhone is a fine e-book and document reader in a pinch. We talk about iBooks, the Apple app for electronic books, and Newsstand, the folder that organizes and updates your magazine and newspaper app subscriptions, in Book I, Chapter 4. You can download books directly from iTunes to your iPhone.

You can also read many types of documents on your iPhone. If a colleague sends you a PowerPoint presentation or a PDF document as an e-mail attachment, just tap on the attachment and your iPhone opens it so you can review it. You can't edit the document (without an additional app), but you can print the document from your iPhone with AirPrint, if there's an AirPrint-enabled printer on your wireless network. We mention a few third-party apps in the online bonus content, Bonus Chapter 2, which give you editing and printing options. (For more information on how to access the online bonus content, see this book's Introduction.)

Personal fitness trainer

In Book I, Chapter 4, we talk about the Nike+ iPod app, which tracks the distances and times of your runs or walks by receiving information from a sensor in certain models of Nike running shoes.

That's not the only app that helps you stay fit. The App Store boasts dozens of apps that create workout routines or track your progress toward fitness goals. Browsing YouTube turns up aerobic, Pilates, and yoga videos for every level and taste, and you can watch them in streaming on your iPhone.

Pocket video game console

With all the ruckus, you might think Angry Birds is the only game in town. Actually, the App Store boasts more than 100,000 games, and many are free. Take that, Nintendo DS! With iPhone, you have a video game console with you at all times, as shown in Figure 1-3, and with Game Center, you can play against friends online and see who has the highest score.

Figure 1-3: Your iPhone is also a tiny game console.

Systemwide functions

The keyboard used in any app where typing is involved supports 21 languages. Voice Control can initiate phone calls, control Music, and tell you what time it is. Accessibility settings make iPhone easier to use with features like enlarged font sizes, custom vibration signals for incoming calls, and spoken text.

Notifications, such as text messages, calendar requests, and voicemails, come in while you're doing other things and you get a small indication at the top of the screen. When it's convenient, you can see them all together on the Notifications screen and choose to which and when you want to respond.

If you use Twitter, knowing you can tweet directly from Safari, Photos, Maps, and YouTube on your iPhone might make you downright chirpy. We explain how to use Twitter on your iPhone in Book I, Chapter 4.

If you want to find something, Spotlight searches from within many of the apps on your iPhone, and you can search Wikipedia and the web directly from Spotlight.

And a thousand other things!

Even if you never add another app to your iPhone, it would do a lot, but adding third-party apps ups the potential. In the online bonus content, we try to knock your socks off by introducing some of the newest, most innovative, and problem-solving apps available. The mini-book is divided into six chapters ranging from practical business solutions and creativity tools to apps for sports, cooking, and travel. We certainly found apps we never imagined existed when we were researching them for this book, and hope this nudges you to do some research on your own.

With that, dear reader, you should have some idea of where you want to go.

Chapter 2: Operating Your iPhone: The Basics and Beyond

In This Chapter

✔ Turning iPhone on and off

✔ Activating your iPhone

✔ Adjusting the volume

✔ Touring the multitouch screen

✔ Charging the battery

✔ Making connections

✔ Printing with AirPrint

✔ Streaming music and video

✔ Adjusting Accessibility options for easier operation

*I*n Chapter 1 of Book I, we gave you the "big picture" view about everything iPhone can do. In this chapter, we tell you how to start using iPhone and take advantage of all the things it can do. We begin with the most obvious tasks: turning your iPhone on and off, activating your iPhone, and adjusting the volume level. Then we review the basic layout and features of iPhone's multitouch interface: things like the Home screen, status bar icons, notifications, and badges. Next, we explain a few nifty, not-so-basic features like printing and streaming media from your iPhone to your TV or sound system. At the end of the chapter, we take a look at some of the ways you can modify your iPhone to make it easier to use if you have vision challenges — helpful things like adding voice commands and voiceover descriptions, and enlarging the text within some of the apps.

Turning iPhone On and Off

The first thing you have to do to use your iPhone is . . . turn it on. Although your iPhone has few external buttons, if you're new to iPhone, knowing which button is the power switch may not be so obvious. Take a look at Figure 2-1, which details the external parts of iPhone. For turning iPhone on and off, note the On/Off Sleep/Wake button and the Home button. Here's how they work:

Figure 2-1: External switches turn iPhone on and off, control the volume, and take photos.

✔ **On/Off Sleep/Wake Button:** This button is on the top of iPhone, to the right, and it does two things. When pressed and held, it turns iPhone on or off, and when tapped, it wakes iPhone from sleep or puts iPhone to sleep.

- To turn iPhone on, press and hold the On/Off Sleep/Wake button. The Apple logo appears in the center of the screen. After 30 seconds or so, the lockscreen appears with a bar at the bottom of the screen and the helpful words "slide to unlock." Drag your finger from left to right across this bar and the home screen opens. If you have a Subscriber Identity Module, better known as a SIM card with a PIN or Personal Identification Number, or have set up a security passcode, a message comes up with two buttons: OK and Unlock. Tap the right button to open a keypad where you enter the PIN code of your SIM card to unlock it. Tap the left OK button, and you can use iPhone apps but not any of the phone, message, or Internet features. (We explain security passcodes in Book I, Chapter 4.)

- To turn iPhone off, press and hold the On/Off Sleep/Wake button until the red bar appears with the message Slide to Power Off. Drag your finger from left to right across this bar to turn iPhone off. Tap the Cancel button at the bottom of the screen if you change your mind.

- To put iPhone to sleep, press the On/Off Sleep/Wake button once. To wake or unlock iPhone, press either the On/Off Sleep/Wake button or the Home button, which is the round button below the screen that we explain in a couple of paragraphs. A slider appears at the bottom that reads Slide to Unlock. Slide your finger across this slider, and the Home screen opens.

- iPhone goes to sleep or locks (not to be confused with the SIM lock) automatically when you don't touch the screen for one minute. You can change this setting to up to five minutes or never in Settings⇨ General⇨Auto-Lock. This saves battery power and keeps you from unintentionally opening an app or making a call by accidentally touching the Home screen. When iPhone is asleep or locked, you still receive phone calls and messages and can listen to music. You can also adjust the volume of a call or music with the volume buttons on the side of the phone.

Tap the On/Off Sleep/Wake button once to silence an incoming call. The caller will hear four rings before going into voicemail. Tap twice and the call is sent directly to voicemail.

✔ **Home Button:** This is the round, central button on the front of iPhone, below the screen.

- Press this button once to return to the Home screen at any time from any app. Pressing this button once when iPhone is locked wakes iPhone the same way as the On/Off Sleep/Wake button does.

- Press once from the first Home screen to open Spotlight Search (which we explain in Book I, Chapter 3).

- Press once from any Home screen other than the first one to return to the first Home screen.

- Quickly press the Home button twice, also known as a double-click, to open the multitasking bar and switch from one app to another, more about that in Book I, Chapter 3.

- If iPhone is sleeping, double-click the Home button to open both an on-screen Camera button and on-screen iPod commands to pause, play, fast-forward, or rewind. We explain everything about the Camera in Book V, Chapter 1, and about the iPod on iPhone in Book V, Chapter 3.

Adjusting the Volume

When you're on a crowded bus and your iPhone is swimming in the bottom of your gym bag, you might want to have the ringer at full volume. On the other hand, if you're in a meeting but waiting for an important call, you may want to keep your iPhone silent and choose to respond only to that one not-to-be-missed call. Here we explain how the three buttons on the left of your iPhone control volume:

✔ **Volume Buttons:** You find the volume buttons — two round, slightly raised buttons — on the left side of iPhone. The button on top with the plus sign increases volume; the lower button with the minus sign lowers volume. When you are engaged in a call or using an app that has volume, be it music, a video, or a game, these buttons control the volume of the thing you are listening to, watching, or playing. When iPhone is awake, but not otherwise engaged in a noisy activity, these buttons control the volume of both the ringer and alerts, unless you've turned that feature off within the sound settings, as we explain in Book I, Chapter 4.

The button used for increasing volume doubles as a shutter button for the Camera. (Refer to Book V, Chapter 1 to learn about using your iPhone's camera and video recorder.)

✔ **Silent/Ring Switch:** The switch above the volume buttons is a mute button. Push it to the left and you see a red bar. This is the off or silent position. Pushed to the right is the On or ring position. When iPhone is in silent mode, it will vibrate when calls or alerts come in. If your iPhone rings and you prefer not to answer, you can turn the Silent/Ring switch off. Your caller will continue to hear the phone ring until he decides to hang up or leave a voicemail message, but your iPhone will be silent.

When iPhone is in silent mode, alarms are still audible. The audio for Music and some games will be heard through the speaker or earphones, if you happen to have those plugged into your iPhone (and into your ears, of course).

Activating Your iPhone

You can't use the phone services of your iPhone until it's connected to a cellular network through your cellular service provider. You can purchase an iPhone with a cellular network contract or without a contract, which is called an *unlocked* iPhone. Here's the difference:

- ✔ **Contract:** iPhone is activated when you sign up for a service plan with an iPhone service. In the U.S., your cellular network carrier choices are AT&T, which uses the GSM (Global System for Mobile Communications) cellular communications protocol, Verizon, and Sprint, which use the CDMA (Code Division Multiple Access) cellular communications protocol. We explain both GSM and CDMA in the "Making Connections" section of this chapter. You register your phone with the network and pick a plan for the number of calling minutes, SMS messages, and Internet service usage you want.

- ✔ **Unlocked:** iPhone arrives without a micro-SIM (that's the little chip inside that gives you access to the cellular network). You purchase a micro-SIM from a service provider and then purchase prepaid calling minutes in a pay-as-you-go option. Cellular broadband Internet access is sold separately. You can use an unlocked iPhone with a contract; in that case, you bought iPhone outright so the monthly contract should be less than iPhone plus a cellular service fee. T-Mobile provides national pay-as-you-go service and there are about 30 regional carriers who offer pay-as-you-go service. Unlocked iPhones work only with carriers who use the GSM cellular communications standard (AT&T and T-Mobile in the U.S.). If you spend a lot of time overseas, say in France, you can purchase a prepaid SIM in France, which you put in your iPhone when you're there. When you're in the U.S., you put the U.S.-based SIM in your iPhone.

If you bought your iPhone with a cellular service contract, it will have already been activated when you bought it; if, for example, you bought it at an Apple Store, an AT&T store, or other retail outlet such as Wal-Mart or Best Buy. If you bought your iPhone through the online Apple Store and selected a carrier, you only need to turn your iPhone on and follow the onscreen instructions.

If you bought an unlocked iPhone, you must purchase and insert a GSM micro-SIM. To insert the micro-SIM, do the following:

1. **Insert the SIM eject tool that came with your iPhone, or a paper clip, into the hole on the SIM card tray on the right side of your iPhone.**

   The SIM card tray pops open.

2. **Place the SIM card in the tray, matching the cut corner of the SIM card to the cut corner in the tray.**

3. **Push the SIM card tray closed.**

When you turn on your iPhone for the first time, the Setup Assistant takes you through a series of screens where you type in the requested information and tap Next or Done. The Setup Assistant activates the following features:

✔ **Sign in or create an Apple ID:** Your Apple ID lets you

- Store your iPhone backup on iCloud, Apple's remote storage site.

- Make purchases from the iTunes Store and the App Store.

- Sign in to FaceTime.

    If you have an iTunes ID, you can use that. However, iCloud requires ID with an e-mail format, such as `babsboyd@me.com`, so you may have to create a new account anyway to activate iCloud. The Setup Assistant asks you to create an ID and password and set up a security question — a question only you know the answer to that Apple asks if you forget your password.

✔ **Wi-Fi Setup:** We explain this in detail later in this chapter in the "Making Connections" section. Briefly, a list of available Wi-Fi networks appears, you click the one you use and type in the password.

✔ **iCloud Setup:** We've dedicated Book II, Chapter 1 to backing up and syncing your iPhone with your computer, and iCloud is a big part of that. Essentially, the Setup Assistant asks which data on your iPhone you would like backed up to iCloud.

You have to have a Wi-Fi or cellular network data connection to complete activation; otherwise, you must connect your iPhone to your computer with the USB connector cable.

Getting Touchy-Feely

The original iPhone's most revolutionary feature was the touchscreen — also known as the *multitouch* screen, where you tap on-screen buttons instead of tapping real, physical buttons. iPhone goes beyond mere buttons, adding sliders, press and hold, pinch and flick — and enough other gesture-based moves to warrant their very own chapter: Book I, Chapter 3.

iPhone 4S went over the top with the addition of Siri, a voice-commanded assistant. You can ask Siri to change appointments, make phone calls, even write e-mails and find restaurants — all by speaking into your iPhone. We explain Siri in Book I, Chapter 3, too.

For the parts we explain here, you just have to touch or tap. Oh, and there's one flick.

Home screen

The point of departure for everything iPhone is the Home screen, which features three basic parts (or zones), as you can see in Figure 2-2. At the very top is the *status bar*, which we get to in just a few paragraphs. The bulk of the screen holds 16 app buttons or folders, which can hold up to 20 apps and folders (we talk about folders in the next chapter). Four of the Home screen's apps stay tacked at the bottom of the screen in what's called the *dock*, which makes it easy to get to your four most-favorite apps no matter which Home screen you're viewing.

Between the last row of apps and the dock is a tiny magnifying glass and a line of dots, one of which is white, the others are gray. These represent the Spotlight Search screen (the magnifying glass) and the number of Home screens you have. You may have up to 11 Home screens plus the Spotlight Search screen. The white dot tells you which of the Home screens you're on. In Figure 2-2, you see the first dot is white followed by seven gray dots, which means this is Home screen one of eight. Flick the current Home screen to the left, and the screen moves one screen to the left; flick the Home screen to the right, and the screen moves one screen to the right. Touch the dots toward the left, and the screen moves one screen to the left; touch the dots to the right, and the screen moves one screen to the right.

Figure 2-2: The Home screen is the point of departure for iPhone.

Tap any of the app icons on the Home screen, and the associated app opens. If you tap a folder, it opens. Then you tap the app inside the folder that you want to launch. Double-click the Home button and the apps that are open appear in the multitasking bar.

Shining a light on Spotlight searches

Spotlight is iPhone's search feature for finding things stored on your iPhone or on the web. To access Spotlight from the first Home screen, click the Home button once or flick the Home screen from left to right to display the Spotlight screen, as shown in Figure 2-3. To find something you're looking for, type a word or phrase in the field next to the magnifying glass. Your search criteria can contain numbers, so you can search for a phone number, date, or address. Spotlight searches all the apps on your iPhone for the word, phrase, or number you type. For example, if we type in the name Bonnie, a list appears showing all the places where that name was found: contacts named Bonnie, songs by Bonnie Raitt, the Burl Ives song "Wee Bonnie Lass," e-mails exchanged with anyone named Bonnie, appointments with Bonnie or Bonnie birthdays, and any notes we may have jotted down about Bonnie. The last two options on the list for any search are Search Web and Search Wikipedia. Tap either of those to open Safari and search the Internet and display general web search results or Wikipedia search results, depending on which option you tapped.

Figure 2-3: The Spotlight screen, to the left of the Home screen, searches all the apps on iPhone for occurrences of a word or phrase.

You also have access to Spotlight within many apps using the Spotlight search field at the top of an app's screen. We tell you more about Spotlight in Book I, Chapter 3.

If you don't see the Spotlight search field — on app screens that support Spotlight — tap the status bar at the top of iPhone's screen to make the Spotlight search field appear. Dragging the app screen down is another way to unhide the Spotlight search field when you don't see it.

To search for something within an app, do the following:

1. **Tap in the Spotlight field.**

   The blinking cursor appears and the keyboard opens.

2. **Type in your word or phrase and then tap Search.**

   Spotlight searches within the app you're using and displays any items that match your search criteria.

3. **Tap an item in the list to view that item's contents.**

You find an in-depth explanation of Spotlight in Book I, Chapter 3.

Tapping into basic Keyboard features

Using Figure 2-3 of the Spotlight screen as a reference, we want to mention a few things about the keyboard. Anytime you want to type something into a field, two things happen when you tap in that field:

- A blinking cursor appears in the empty field.
- The keyboard opens in the bottom half of the screen.

The keyboard has the classic QWERTY format that you may have learned in high school typing class — that's where we learned how to touch type. (Or your keyboard may display a different layout you chose in Settings⟹General⟹ International⟹Keyboards.) Unless you have teeny, tiny fingers, touch-typing is next to impossible on iPhone's on-screen keyboard, but familiarity with the position of the keys definitely helps make you a faster thumb or forefinger typist. We explain all the keyboard tricks in Book I, Chapter 3. For now, noting the Shift key to the left of the Z, the 123 key that changes the keyboard display to numbers and symbols, and the Backspace/Delete key should get you on your way.

Staying informed with status bar icons

The status bar runs across the very top of your iPhone in either portrait or landscape view and the icons there give you information about your cellular and/or wireless network connection, battery life, and auxiliary functions you may have turned on, such as the iPod and alarm clock. Here is an explanation about each one, although you won't see them all at once on your iPhone, and some you may never see.

✔ **Airplane Mode:** You see this icon if you've turned Airplane mode on in Settings. Airplane mode turns off all connections to your cellular network, Wi-Fi, and Bluetooth. You can still listen to music, watch videos, and play games. You can also reread e-mail or SMS messages that have been downloaded. In some countries, you may turn on Wi-Fi while your iPhone is in Airplane mode. See Book I, Chapter 4 for more details on Airplane Mode.

✔ **Alarm:** Appears if you set an alarm using the Clock app, we explore the Clock app in Book IV, Chapter 2.v

✔ **Battery:** Indicates how much charge remains on the battery. It's green if the battery is between 100 and 20 percent charged. It changes to red and shows just a tiny portion on the left when less than 20 percent charge remains. It has a lightning bolt on it when the battery is being charged. You can read more about charging the battery later in this chapter.

✔ **Bluetooth:** Shows that Bluetooth is turned on. When it's blue or white, you are connected to another Bluetooth device such as a headset. When it's gray, Bluetooth is on but no device is connected. If you think Bluetooth is Bluebeard's brother, read more about this connection protocol in the "Making Connections" section of this chapter.

✔ **Call Forwarding:** On GSM models (an unlocked Apple iPhone or an AT&T iPhone, refer to the "Considering iPhone Carriers and Configurations" section in Book I, Chapter 1), appears when you've forwarded your calls to another phone number. The call forwarding settings are explained in Book III, Chapter 1.

✔ **Cell Signal:** Indicates the strength of the cellular signal your iPhone is connected to. If you have no bars or just one, the signal is weak — more bars, stronger signal. *No Service* appears when iPhone is unable to pick-up a signal from your cellular provider. If Airplane Mode is turned on, you see the airplane icon instead of the cell signal bars.

✔ **EDGE (E):** Appears when iPhone is connected to your cellular provider's EDGE data network for accessing the Internet. GSM models support EDGE networks. Read more about Internet access later in this chapter.

✓ **GPRS/1xRTT:** GSM models use the GPRS (General Packet Radio Service) network and CDMA models use the 1xRTT (1x Radio Transmission Technology) network to access the Internet when those networks are available. Read more about Internet access in the "Making Connections" section later in this chapter.

✓ **Location Services:** When you see this icon, an app, such as Maps, is tracking your current location coordinates in order to provide you with nearby information or other services, such as the closest cafe or directions to the pet supply store across town.

 ✓ **Lock:** This icon indicates iPhone is locked. Tap the On/Off Sleep/Wake button to unlock.

✓ **Network Activity:** Spins when iPhone is accessing a cellular or Wi-Fi network for any app that uses the Internet, such as Safari, YouTube, or the App Store. It also appears when iPhone is syncing MobileMe information over-the-air, or sometimes when an app is performing other data-related activities.

✓ **Personal Hotspot:** This icon is active when you've connected to another iPhone that is providing a Personal Hotspot.

✓ **Play:** Appears when you're listening to music or audio using iPod, or when you're listening to other audio, such as a streaming radio program.

✓ **Orientation Lock:** This reminds you that you've turned off the landscape view feature. You can turn your iPhone every which way, but the screen remains in portrait position.

✓ **Syncing:** Indicates that your iPhone is syncing with iTunes.

✓ **TTY:** Indicates your iPhone is configured to work with a Teletype (TTY) machine.

 ✓ **UMTS/EV-DO (3G):** Indicates when GSM models are connected to the UMTS (Universal Mobile Telecommunications System) network, or CDMA models are connected to the EV-DO (Evolution-Data Optimized) network to access the Internet when those networks are available. Read more about Internet access in the "Making Connections" section later in this chapter.

✓ **VPN:** Indicates iPhone is connected to a VPN (Virtual Private Network).

Wi-Fi: Indicates iPhone is connected to a Wi-Fi network. The more bars the merrier — we mean, faster — the connection. Read more about wireless connections further along in this chapter.

Noticing notification messages and badges

On iPhone, badges are the white numbers inside a red circle that appear in the corner of certain app icons, such as Mail and Messages. The number indicates how many unread messages await you in those apps. You can see a couple of badges in Figure 2-2 next to the App Store, Phone, and Mail icons.

There are two kinds of notification messages. The first kind is when you want to do something but iPhone needs something else to happen before it can complete the task. These messages appear in rectangular boxes in the middle of the screen and typically display buttons you can tap to respond to with a certain action. In the example in Figure 2-4, for instance, you have the choice of acknowledging the notification message by tapping OK, or by tapping Settings and turning off Airplane mode.

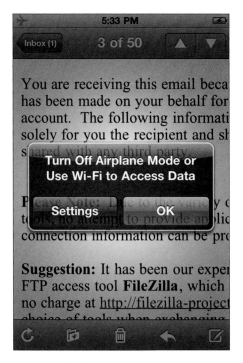

Figure 2-4: Notification messages often have buttons that give you a choice of actions to take.

The second kind of notification is when you're doing one thing, say having a phone conversation, and another thing happens, say, you get an incoming e-mail. You see a notification banner across the top of your iPhone's screen. You can choose to respond or ignore it. If you ignore the banner, it disappears in a few seconds. iPhone saves all your notifications in the Notification Center, as shown in Figure 2-5, which you can see by swiping down from the top of the screen. Notifications are divided by type: Phone, Reminders, Mail, and Weather. You manage the Notification Center in Settings, which we cover in Book 1, Chapter 4.

Figure 2-5: iPhone keeps all your notifications in one place, the Notification Center.

Charging Your iPhone Battery

How long the battery charge lasts is a frequent concern for anyone who uses electronic devices, be it a cell phone, notebook computer, electronic reader, portable game console, or MP3 player. Our experience is that our iPhone battery charge lasts about a day. We frequently check e-mail and surf the web; however, we frequently connect via Wi-Fi, but not often via Bluetooth.

Games, Music, Video, and Wi-Fi or 3G connections consume juice. A few levels of Angry Birds and the battery power notification message comes up. The good news is that iPhone recharges in less than an hour, and you can charge the battery in several ways, which we describe here. We outline tips for obtaining a longer battery charge in Book I, Chapter 5.

The battery icon in the status bar indicates how much battery power you have. If you want a specific percentage to show, go to Settings⇨General⇨Usage and turn on the Battery Percentage switch.

Plugging into the USB charger

Your iPhone comes with a USB connection cable and a USB power adapter. To charge the battery, plug the dock connector — the larger, flatter end — into the dock port at the base of your iPhone, and plug the USB end into the USB power adapter. Plug the power adapter into an electrical outlet. iPhone beeps, which lets you know it's actively charging.

The power adapter automatically adjusts to 110 or 220 voltage, based on the voltage for the location you're plugging into. If you are using your iPhone outside the U.S., you have to purchase an adapter that changes the plug conformation to meet the outlet style of the country you're visiting. You can find a kit at the Apple Store (`store.apple.com/us`) or single adapters at TravelProducts.com (`www.travelproducts.com/`). Or you can charge your iPhone with your computer's USB port as we explain next.

Charging with your Mac or PC's USB port

You can also charge your iPhone battery by connecting it directly to a USB port on your computer. Again, iPhone beeps, which lets you know it's being charged. If your computer is turned off or is sleeping, your iPhone battery may drain instead of charge, so make sure your computer is on if you want to charge your iPhone with it.

The battery icon in the status bar has a lightning bolt on it when the battery is being charged, either with the USB cable connected to your computer or to an electric outlet.

Although plugging your iPhone into any recent or new Mac can charge your iPhone, the same isn't necessarily true for recent or new Windows desktop and notebook computers or older Macs. Apple claims that's because the USB ports on certain of those models aren't powerful enough to charge your iPhone; however, we wonder if the supposed powerlessness isn't really a ploy to get Windows users to switch to Mac, or Mac users to upgrade. Hmm . . . anyway, if connecting your iPhone to your USB port doesn't yield a charge, try plugging into a powered USB port dock. If that doesn't work, you'll have to plug into a charger to charge your iPhone.

Either way you charge, if your iPhone is locked or sleeping and you tap the Home key, a big battery symbol displays your iPhone's current charge level, as shown in Figure 2-6. When it's completely charged, the battery is entirely green.

Figure 2-6: When the battery is charging, you see this screen when you wake or unlock your iPhone.

If iPhone's battery charge drops very low or runs down completely, your iPhone automatically shuts itself off. To bring your iPhone back to life, you must attach the USB cable to a power source (your computer or an electrical outlet). When your iPhone shuts itself off because the battery charge is too low or nearly empty, you won't be able to use your iPhone until the battery reaches a minimal charge level. Usually you only have to wait a few minutes before your iPhone turns itself on again.

Apple and other third-party vendors make charging accessories. One is an iPhone dock, which is a type of base that you set your iPhone in to charge the battery. There are battery packs that you attach to your iPhone to get a longer charge. If you spend a lot of time in your car, another option is a USB adapter that plugs into the cigarette lighter to charge your iPhone. Some newer car models also have a built-in USB port.

Don't pull the cable to detach your iPhone from your computer. Always grasp the hard, square part of either end of the USB cable to remove it.

Although iPhone's battery is rechargeable, all batteries have a limited lifespan. When your iPhone battery eventually gives up the ghost, you must seek the services of an authorized Apple service provider to replace your iPhone's dead battery with a new one. Refer to Book I, Chapter 5 for tips on extending your battery life.

Making Connections

One of the biggest advantages of iPhone is the ability to connect to a variety of signal sources: to the Internet via your cellular carrier's data network or via a Wi-Fi network, or to other devices like printers, keyboards, and hands-free headsets using Bluetooth. Did you know your iPhone has ten built-in antennas? To help you understand all of your iPhone's many connection options, we've organized those options into three sections: cellular and wireless connections; Personal Hotspot and tethering, and lastly, Bluetooth and GPS connections.

Cellular

When you activate your iPhone with a carrier, you gain access to that carrier's cellular voice and data network. iPhone uses two types of cellular connection protocols: the CDMA type used by Sprint and Verizon in the U.S., and the GSM type used by AT&T in the U.S. and in most countries outside the U.S. Without boring you with too many technical details, your iPhone typically connects using one or more of the following protocols:

✐ **GSM (Global System for Mobile Communications) models**

✐ **3G/UMTS:** 3G is the third generation protocol standard that uses the UMTS (Universal Mobile Telecommunications System) cellular frequency. This protocol is faster than EDGE, but consumes more battery power. Try using Safari or Mail with 3G on and off to note any connection speed differences. If 3G is on but unavailable, iPhone defaults to EDGE.

- **EDGE:** Enhanced Data for GSM Evolution is the first generation protocol standard for connecting to the Internet over the cellular carrier network. EDGE will often offer a more stable, albeit slower, connection than 3G because it offers wider network coverage.

- **GPRS:** General Packet Radio Service supports both second (2G) and third (3G) generation cellular telephony. Usage is based on volume rather than time. If neither EDGE nor 3G is available, iPhone defaults to GPRS.

✓ **CDMA (Code Division Multiple Access) models**

- **EV-DO:** The Evolution-Data Optimized is a 3G or third generation protocol, similar to UMTS for access speed.

- **1xRTT:** 1x Radio Transmission Technology is an alternative 3G protocol.

Unlike GSM-model iPhones, if you have a CDMA iPhone and are actively transferring data over your carrier's cellular network — to check your e-mail or browse a web page, for instance — you cannot also engage in an active phone call while those data-related activities are underway. Any calls you may receive while using your cellular carrier's data connection are sent directly to your voicemail. You can make and receive calls while doing those data-related things on your CDMA iPhone if you are connected to a Wi-Fi network.

When your iPhone is connected to the Internet with one of these protocols, the associated icon appears in the status bar, as mentioned earlier in this chapter.

If you happen to be outside your carrier's network, you can try to access the Internet through another carrier. This is called Data Roaming and is enabled by going to Settings⇨General⇨Network and flipping the Data Roaming switch to On. Be warned, however, that Data Roaming, especially if you're out of the country, can rack up sizeable surcharges. Check with your carrier for Data Roaming fees before being surprised with a whopping bill at the end of the month. Out of curiosity, Barbara turned Data Roaming on when she was overseas and checked her e-mail — and wound up getting socked with a $12 fee for a measly 30 seconds of Internet time!

If your cellular carrier contract has a data transfer limit, you can monitor your cellular data usage by opening Settings⇨General⇨Usage. Using Wi-Fi for data access is an alternative if you have free or low-cost Wi-Fi service in places where you use your iPhone.

Wi-Fi

You may want to say that cellular is wireless, and you'd be right. But Wi-Fi is wireless, only better. Connecting to the Internet using iPhone's Wi-Fi feature is almost always the fastest — and cheapest — way to connect to the Internet. Wi-Fi networks blast their typically close-range signals from a device known as a *wireless router*, which is connected to a broadband modem, which in turn is typically connected to your cable or phone company's broadband Internet service (or whatever the Wi-Fi router you tap into is connected to, be it at your favorite cafe, in a jetliner, or a public library, for example). Other people can connect their Wi-Fi enabled devices as well, making the group of you a network, as opposed to a single connection. You may need a password to access a Wi-Fi network, and some Wi-Fi services charge an hourly or daily fee to access their networks.

To join a Wi-Fi network, follow these steps:

1. **Tap Settings on your Home screen, and then tap Wi-Fi.**

   The Wi-Fi Networks screen opens.

2. **Tap the toggle switch to turn Wi-Fi on.**

   The screen expands to give you the option to Choose a Network, as seen in Figure 2-7. iPhone detects servers in the area and the Wi-Fi symbol indicates how strong the signal is. Servers that require a password have a closed lock icon next to them.

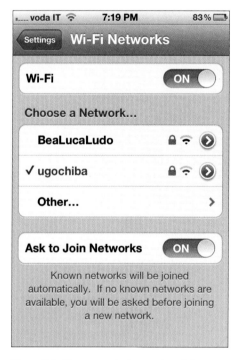

Figure 2-7: Choose a wireless network from the list of visible servers.

If you know the name of the network you want to join and it's not in the list, do this:

1. **Tap Other.**

   The Other Network pane opens.

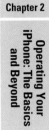

2. Type in the name of the network in the Name field.

3. If the network has a password, tap Security.

   The Security screen opens, as shown in Figure 2-8.

4. **Choose the type of password this network uses and tap the back button that reads Other Network.**

   The Other Network screen reopens, and the cursor is blinking in the Password field.

3. Type in the password.

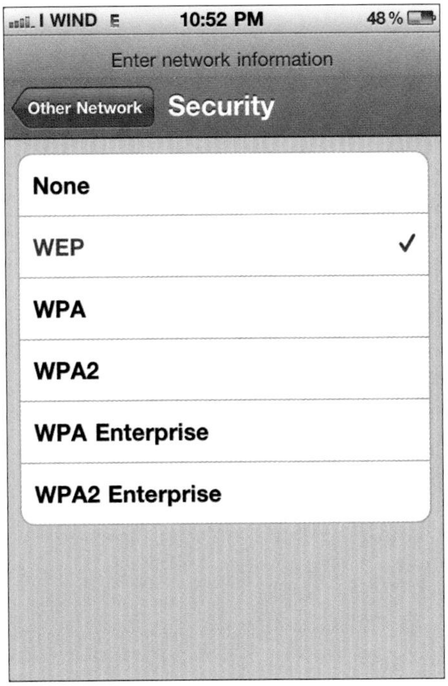

ᴖᴖᴖ I WIND E	10:52 PM	48%

Enter network information

< Other Network   **Security**

None

WEP   ✓

WPA

WPA2

WPA Enterprise

WPA2 Enterprise

Figure 2-8: Choose the type of password your desired Wi-Fi network uses and then type it in on the previous screen.

4. Tap the Join button.

   You return to the Wi-Fi Networks screen. A checkmark appears next to the highlighted name of the network you've joined. iPhone automatically remembers any Wi-Fi network you've joined and connects to it whenever you're in its range.

The Wi-Fi icon in the status bar shows iPhone's connection status and the strength of the signal.

Personal Hotspot and tethering

When another device uses your iPhone's Internet connection to connect to the Internet, that's called *tethering*. Tethering essentially turns your iPhone into a miniature Wi-Fi router that broadcasts a signal that you or a few others can tap into with your notebook computer, your iPad, or most any other Wi-Fi enabled gadget. On your iPhone, this feature is called Personal Hotspot. (A Wi-Fi network you can connect to is typically referred to as a *hotspot*.) You can also connect your computer to iPhone's Personal Hotspot feature using a USB cable or Bluetooth, rather than connect using Wi-Fi.

To use iPhone's Personal Hotspot feature, you must pay your cellular service provider a separate fee in addition to your existing cellular service plan. Contact your provider for details.

To share an Internet connection using your iPhone's Personal Hotspot feature, follow these steps:

1. **Tap Settings on the Home screen.**

2. **Choose Personal Hotspot.**

   If Personal Hotspot isn't in the top level of Settings, tap General⇨ Network⇨Personal Hotspot.

3. **Tap On.**

   Choose one of the options below to connect:

   • **To connect a computer using the Personal Hotspot feature's direct cable option, connect iPhone to your computer with the USB cable.**

   In Network preferences, choose iPhone. Follow the onscreen instructions to configure the connection if this is the first time.

   • **To connect a computer or other device (such as an iPad, another iPhone, or an iPod touch) using that device's built-in Wi-Fi feature, choose iPhone (or whatever you named your Personal Hotspot network) from the list of Wi-Fi networks that appears on the device's list of nearby Wi-Fi networks.**

   Type the Wi-Fi password you created.

4. **A blue band appears at the top of your iPhone screen whenever a device is connected.**

The Personal Hotspot icon appears in the status bar when your iPhone is connected to another iPhone's Personal Hotspot, not when your iPhone is the Personal Hotspot.

Bluetooth

Bluetooth is a short-range (up to 33 feet or ten meters) wireless protocol used to attach, or pair, devices to your iPhone. Unlike Wi-Fi, which broadcasts its availability continuously, Bluetooth has to be turned on to make your iPhone or other device discoverable so that they can see each other. A passkey or PIN (Personal Identification Number) is used to make that connection private.

One of the most common devices paired with iPhone is a wireless headset. This small device is either inserted in your ear or wrapped around it and has both a speaker to hear the person you're talking to and a microphone so they can hear you. You can have phone conversations without risking strangulation by earphone cord or, worse yet, catching the cord on something, resulting in your iPhone flying through the air and smashing on the floor. (Yeesh, just writing that makes us shudder.)

Other devices that you might want to pair with your iPhone are earphones for listening to music, a life-size keyboard, or your car so you can answer calls by tapping a button on the steering wheel or radio. If you pair two iPhones or your iPhone and your computer, you can share photos, files, and even an Internet connection between them. To connect devices to your iPhone via Bluetooth:

1. **On your iPhone, go to Settings⟹General and tap the Bluetooth button on.**

   The Bluetooth screen opens, as shown in Figure 2-9. Tapping on makes your iPhone discoverable, which means other devices with Bluetooth turned on can see your iPhone. The Bluetooth icon appears in the status bar.

2. **Turn on Bluetooth on the device you want to connect so it too is discoverable.**

   If the device is another iPhone or computer, you have to turn on Bluetooth on that iPhone or computer too. Active devices show up in a list on the Bluetooth screen on your iPhone.

   A Bluetooth headset only needs to be turned on. Obviously a headset doesn't have a keypad to enter a passkey but it comes with an assigned passkey, which you need to pair it with your iPhone. Check the instructions that came with the headset for the passkey code.

3. **In the list, tap the device you want to pair with your iPhone.**

4. **Enter the passkey on the keypad that appears on your iPhone, if requested.**

   The two devices can now communicate across the Bluetooth connection.

5. **To turn Bluetooth off and make your iPhone undiscoverable, tap Settings⟹General⟹Bluetooth⟹Off.**

Figure 2-9: Bluetooth lets you connect devices to your iPhone.

If you want to listen to music through a headset that you've paired with your iPhone, you have to adjust the speaker settings in iPod. While you're listening to a song or podcast, tap the Bluetooth button in the lower right corner. Buttons appear giving you the option to choose which device you want iPod to play through. Tap the button for your headset.

Bluetooth is one of the features that drains battery power, so don't leave it on if you aren't using it.

GPS

iPhone's built-in GPS or Global Positioning System sensor determines your location. Apps like Compass use GPS to find true north, and Maps pinpoints where you are in relation to where you want to go, or where you came from. The Camera uses GPS to do geotagging, which is adding the location to a photo when it's taken. The GPS is accessed when you check-in to some third-party apps or social networks. If you add a navigation app to your iPhone, it will use the GPS sensor to dictate directions to you. To learn more about using the Compass and Maps apps, go to Book IV, Chapter 3. We explain everything about the Camera in Book V, Chapter 1. We explore navigation apps in the online bonus content, Bonus Chapter 6.

To turn the GPS sensor on

1. **Tap Settings on the Home screen.**

2. **Tap the Location Services button in the first block of choices.**

3. **Tap the toggle switch to turn Location Services on.**

   The screen displays a list of the apps that find Location Services useful. You can select which apps you want to give that option to, as shown in Figure 2-10.

Figure 2-10: The Location Services list displays apps that use the GPS sensor.

 The Location Services icon appears next to apps that have used it in the last 24 hours.

The Location Services icon appears in the status bar when you are using an app that uses it.

Printing from your iPhone

The utopian idea of a paperless society may be near, but it hasn't arrived yet. Words and images on a piece of paper are sometimes necessary. AirPrint enables your iPhone to print directly to an AirPrint-enabled printer. Many types of files can be printed: e-mail messages and any readable attachments, photos, web pages, even PDFs. Apps you download from the App Store may also support AirPrint. AirPrint couldn't be easier. Here are the steps to take:

1. **Make sure the printer you want to use is on the same Wi-Fi network that your iPhone is connected to.**

2. **On your iPhone, open the document you want to print.**

3. **Tap the forward or action button, depending on which app you want to print from.**

    The screen as shown in Figure 2-11 opens.

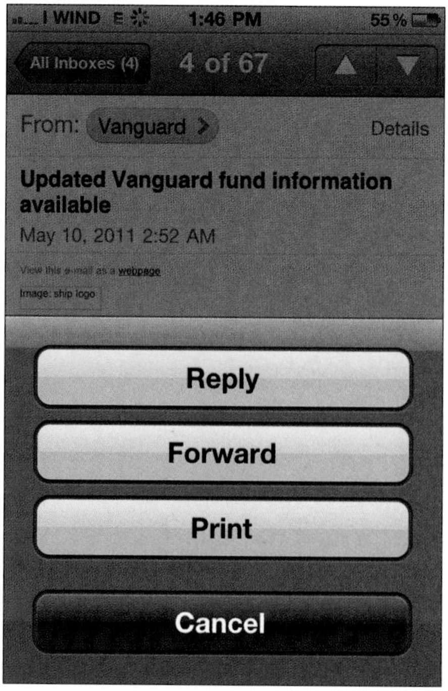

Figure 2-11: Tapping the Forward or Action button gives you several options.

4. **Tap the Print button.**

   The Printer Options screen opens, as you can see in Figure 2-12.

>   voda IT 🔋   7:46 PM   ⚡ 79% 🔋
>
>   [Cancel]   **Printer Options**
>
>   **Printer** Photosmart B110 serie... ❯
>
>   **1 Copy**   —   +
>
>   **Print**

Figure 2-12: Choose your printer and the number of copies from the Printer Options screen.

5. **Tap the Printer button to select the printer you want to use.**

   Another screen opens, showing the printers that are available in the Wi-Fi vicinity.

6. **Select the number of copies you want to print.**

   Depending on the app and the printer, you may also have the option to choose double-sided printing and/or a range of pages.

7. **The Print Center app appears on the Home screen and a badge indicates how many documents are waiting to be printed.**

8. **Tap the Print Center button on the Home screen to see a list of queued documents.**

   Tap a document in the list to see its status. Tap the cancel printing button if you've changed your mind.

Connecting to a Monitor and Streaming Media

Sometimes you want to share media from your iPhone on a larger scale. Sure you can send e-mail with attachments or connect two iPhones via Bluetooth, but what if you want to listen to music from Music throughout your house or stream a YouTube video on your television? Specific Apple cables, AirPlay, and Apple TV let you do just that. AirPlay connects your iPhone to speakers, AV receivers, and AppleTV so you can stream music from Music or video from YouTube or Videos. Here we show you how to display photos and stream music and video from your iPhone to an output device (that's geek speak for speakers and monitors). For even more about photos, video, and music, refer to the chapters in Book V.

Streaming is when you are connected to the Internet, or your home or office network, and watch media as you access it. The media remains on the Internet when you use streaming. If you download music or video, it is resident on the device where you downloaded it; for example, your iPhone or computer.

Connecting iPhone to an HDTV or display

Granted, iPhone has a beautiful monitor. With the increased pixel display from iPhone 4 forward, images are crisp and colors are vibrant. The only drawback is the size. It's great if you are alone or with one other person, but what if you want to show your photos of your vacation in Jamaica after Thanksgiving dinner? Passing your iPhone around the table isn't the ideal solution. You can connect your iPhone to a high-definition television or a display and watch photos, slideshows, and videos.

To attach your iPhone to a television, you need one of the following cables:

- ✐ **Apple Component AV Cable:** This connects to your iPhone dock at one end and your television's component port on the other. Newer televisions usually have component connections.

- ✐ **Apple Composite AV Cable:** This connects to your iPhone dock at one end and your television's composite port on the other. Older televisions usually have composite connections.

- ✐ **Apple Digital AV Adapter and an HDMI cable (iPhone 4 or 4S):** Attach the adapter to your iPhone and then connect an HDMI cable from the adapter to your television.

- ✐ **Apple VGA Adapter and a VGA cable:** This setup connects your iPhone to a VGA-compatible television, monitor, or projector.

To play your slideshow or video:

1. Connect the cable to both your iPhone and your television or monitor.

2. **On your television, select the input device.**

   Refer to the instruction booklet for your television if you don't know how to do this.

3. **Play the video or slideshow as you normally would on your iPhone.**

   You see the images on your television.

Streaming video with AirPlay

You can also stream video and images from the Internet across your iPhone and onto your television if you have an AppleTV. To do this:

1. **Tap Photos on your Home screen.**

2. **Open the Album where your video or photos reside.**

3. **Tap the AirPlay button.**

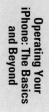

4. **Choose Apple TV from the list.**

   If Apple TV doesn't appear on the list of AirPlay devices, check that both your iPhone and Apple TV are on the same wireless network.

5. **Tap the Play button.**

   The video or slideshow plays on your television.

6. **To switch back to play on your iPhone, tap the AirPlay button again and then choose iPhone.**

Listening to music with AirPlay

AirPlay is Apple's wireless technology that is integrated into speakers and stereo systems from selected companies that include Denon and JBL. You can choose to broadcast music from your iPhone to speakers in different rooms of your house. You can also use AirPlay to stream audio to an AppleTV or to speakers that are connected to an AirPort Express Wi-Fi router or an AirPlay-enabled stereo (such as the Denon AVR-991). Go to Book V to learn all about music management on your iPhone. For a quick setup, follow these steps:

1. **Tap Music on your Home screen.**

2. **Open the song, album, or podcast you want to hear.**

3. **Tap the AirPlay button.**

4. **Choose the speakers you want from the list.**

   If the speakers don't appear on the list of AirPlay devices, check that both your iPhone and speakers are on the same wireless network.

5. **Tap the Play button.**

The music plays on the speakers you've chosen.

6. **To switch back to play on your iPhone, tap the AirPlay button again and then choose iPhone.**

Adjusting Accessibility Options for Easier Operation

With the Accessibility settings, Apple addresses the physical challenges that some users might have with iPhone's interface. They've created optional features that customize the interface to make iPhone more accessible. From the Home screen, tap Settings⟐General and then scroll down to Accessibility. You see the screen in Figure 2-13. We recommend that you consult Chapter 31 of iPhone's User Guide (`manuals.info.apple.com/en_US/iphone_ user_guide.pdf`) for complete instructions on how to get the most out of the Accessibility features. The features are divided into three categories: Vision, Hearing, and Physical & Motor. Here we briefly explain each feature:

Figure 2-13: Customize Accessibility functions to make the most of your iPhone user experience.

✒ **VoiceOver:** Turn this setting on to hear an audible description of the buttons on the screen. With some practice, vision-impaired iPhone users can learn the tapping, double-clicking, and flicking movements necessary to use apps. Within VoiceOver, you can adjust the speaking rate, attach a Braille device, select which parts of a web screen you wish to have read, and which language you want VoiceOver to speak.

✔ **Zoom:** The Zoom feature enlarges the entire iPhone screen when you double-tap with three fingers. Use three fingers to move from left to right on the screen and one finger to move the screen up and down. Double-tap again with three fingers to return to normal size.

You can't use VoiceOver and Zoom simultaneously.

✔ **Large Text:** Tap the Large Text switch and a list of text sizes from 20 point to 56 point text appears. Tap the size you wish to use. Your choice is reflected in Calendar, Contacts, Mail, Messages, and Notes.

✔ **White on Black:** Turn this feature on and all color on the display is inverted, like a photo negative.

✔ **Speak Selection:** Turn this feature on to have iPhone read selected text out loud, even if VoiceOver is turned off.

✔ **Speak Auto-text:** Corrections iPhone makes automatically while you're typing are spoken out loud if this function is turned on.

✔ **Hearing Aid Mode:** For those who use a hearing aid, turning this feature on may reduce interference.

✔ **Custom Vibrations:** Create a unique vibration pattern for individual contacts in Contacts. Refer to Book IV, Chapter 1 to learn about the Contacts app.

✔ **LED Flash for Alerts:** When this feature is turned on, the LED next to the camera lens on the back of your iPhone flashes when iPhone is locked or asleep. It works whether the ring volume is on or not.

✔ **Mono Audio:** This feature changes the left and right sound channels into a mono channel that comes through both sides so those who can hear with only one ear hear both parts.

✔ **AssistiveTouch:** Lets you use an adaptive accessory, such as a joystick, to control your iPhone. You can also adjust tracking speed or create custom gestures to make them easier.

✔ **Incoming Calls:** Lets you designate the headset or speaker as the default device for incoming calls.

✔ **Triple-click Home:** You can choose to associate a triple-click of the Home button with one of three Accessibility functions: VoiceOver, Zoom, or White on Black.

Other Accessibility Features

While the functions controlled by the Accessibility settings are reflected across iPhone, some apps contain accessibility features that are specific to those apps. Here are some:

- ✔ **Closed Captioning:** Go to Settings⇨iPod⇨Video and turn on Closed Captioning.

- ✔ **Voice Control:** Press and hold the Home button on your iPhone, the center button on iPhone's headset, or the button on a Bluetooth headset to open Voice Control. You can ask iPhone to call a person, tell you what time it is, or play a song in Music. On a 4S, Siri, if enabled, performs the Voice Control functions.

- ✔ **Visual Voicemail:** This feature is explained more in Book III, Chapter 1. In a nutshell, iPhone adds pause and playback functions to voicemail messages and allows you to check your messages in any order you wish.

- ✔ **Minimum Font Size for Mail Messages:** With the settings for Mail, you can establish a minimum font size to make Mail messages easier to read.

- ✔ **TTY Support:** You can add a TTY adapter to attach a Teletype machine to your iPhone.

Adjust the Accessibility settings from iTunes by connecting your iPhone to your computer with the USB cable. Open iTunes and click the Configure Universal Access button under Options.

Chapter 3: Controlling the Multitouch and Voice Recognition Interfaces

In This Chapter

✓ **Learning the moves: tapping, flicking, and zooming**

✓ **Leaving Home and going Home again**

✓ **Organizing apps and folders every which way you can**

✓ **Commandeering the keyboard**

✓ **Searching here, there, and everywhere**

✓ **Talking to your iPhone**

The original iPhone multitouch gestures — pinch and spread zooming and tapping — were revolutionary for a mobile phone at the time. With the release of iPhone 4S, Apple's gone one step farther into the future with Siri, the digital assistant that recognizes and executes your spoken commands. You've probably already tried your hand at iPhone gestures, and you've no doubt used the keyboard and tried to tap in information with your fingertips. Maybe you've even started talking to Siri.

In this chapter, we formally introduce you to all of iPhone's gestures, and show you how they work. We give you examples of when and where to use them. Then we explain how to organize apps and folders on the Home screen. We also introduce you to the keyboard. And we give you some tricks that can make typing and editing easier. We wrap up by telling you how to tell your iPhone to search for things, play music, or dial phone numbers using your iPhone's awesome Voice Control feature and, for those of you who have an iPhone 4S, we introduce you to Siri, your new assistant.

Learning the Moves

You've probably noticed iPhone is different than a standard mobile phone. There's no keypad or keyboard, the beloved tools we're accustomed to using for making phone calls, typing missives, and navigating the Internet. There's only that flat multitouch screen. But that's okay. You need just a few good moves to make iPhone do all the things you're used to doing and more. These are the finger gestures that control everything on your iPhone:

- **Tapping:** A tap is lighter than pressing a button. It's a quick touch without any holding. Tap an app button on the Home screen to open the app. Tap an item in a list to select it. Variations on tapping are

  - **Double-tap:** Two quick taps zoom in and zoom out of a web page, e-mail message, or photos. A double-tap also changes the Shift key to a Caps Lock key if you enable that function in Settings⊏⟩General⊏⟩ Keyboard. A single tap zooms in on a map, but to zoom out on a map, you need to do the . . .

  - **Two-finger tap:** On a map in the Maps app, a two-finger tap zooms out of the map; tap twice with a single finger to zoom in again.

- **Scrolling:** Scrolling is a dragging motion done with one finger. Touch the screen and drag up or down. In some apps and websites, you can scroll left or right too. Scrolling is most often used to go through a list, such as Contacts, or to rotate a rotor like the one used to set the alarm clock, which we explain in Book IV, Chapter 2. Scrolling doesn't select or open anything, it only moves the list. You must tap to select.

- **Flicking:** Touch your finger to the screen and quickly flick it up, or left, or right, and away. Flicking left and right on the Home screen moves to the next or previous screen. Flicking in a list, instead of scrolling, moves the list up and down more quickly. You can wait for it to stop or tap when you see what you're looking for, and then tap the item you want to select.

Apple has added a lot of options to make iPhone gestures easier for people with visual, auditory, or manual dexterity challenges. You adjust those settings by going to Settings⊏⟩General⊏⟩Accessibility. Read about them in Book I, Chapter 2.

- **Zooming in and out:** Pinch and spread (unpinch) two fingers together or apart to zoom out and in on photos, web pages, and other elements.

- **Sliding:** Slider bars show up when you want to turn your iPhone on or off or wake it from sleep. They also appear on the lock screen when your iPhone rings, as shown in Figure 3-1. Touch and hold the slider bar on the arrow on the left and slide your finger across the bar to the right. The action listed on the slider bar happens.

Figure 3-1: Use the sliding move on slider bars, mostly to unlock your iPhone.

✓ **Pressing:** Press the physical buttons on your iPhone: the Home, the On/Off Sleep/Wake, or the volume buttons. You switch the Silent/Ring button on and off. We explain these buttons in Book I, Chapter 2.

✓ **Double-clicking:** Double-clicking the Home button reveals the multitasking bar at the bottom of the screen, which shows apps that are running. You can then tap the app you want to switch to.

Home, Away from Home, and Home Again

Home is the equivalent of the desktop on your computer. The round, slightly depressed button centered beneath the screen is the Home button. When you press this button, you return to the Home screen. If your iPhone is sleeping or locked when you press the Home button, a slider bar appears that reads Slide to Unlock. Refer to Figure 3-1. Touch the arrow and slide your finger across this slider in the direction the arrow is pointing, and the last screen you were viewing appears. It could be a Home screen or a running app.

The Home screen is actually more than one screen. You move between one Home screen and the next by flicking left to go to the next screen to the right and flicking right to go back. You can have up to eleven Home screens.

Going from top to bottom, the Home screen has a status bar that tells you about the various connections your iPhone is tapped into at the moment, as well as the current time of day. We explain the status bar icons in Book I, Chapter 2. Below the status bar are 16 spaces for apps or app folders. We go over folders in the Organizing Apps and Folders section later in this chapter. At the bottom of the screen, you see up to four more app buttons. This area is known as the *dock*. Place four app buttons you use frequently there, and they appear in a fixed position at the bottom of every Home screen. Figure 3-2 shows the first and second Home screen on Barbara's iPhone. Notice that both screens have Phone, Mail, Safari, and Music in the dock.

You can also create a URL icon while browsing a specific web page in Safari and place that icon in the dock. Refer to Book III, Chapter 3.

Figure 3-2: The four apps in the dock remain in the same position when you move from one Home screen to another.

There's one other part to the Home screen. Those tiny gray and white dots floating just above the dock indicate how many Home screens you have. The white dot tells you which screen you're on. See how it moves from the first to the second position in Figure 3-2. If you look closely, you see a teensy magnifying glass to the very left of the dots. This represents the Spotlight search screen. Flick to the right from the first Home screen and a search screen opens. We explain searching in the section "Searching Here, There, and Everywhere with Spotlight" later in this chapter.

Pressing the Home button once takes you to the Home screen from whatever app you happen to be using. You return to the last Home screen you were on. If you launch an app from the third Home screen and then press the Home screen while you're using the app, the third Home screen appears. Pressing the Home button once from a Home screen takes you to the previous Home screen or to Spotlight Search from the first Home screen.

Launching and Managing Apps

Apps, short for applications, are the programs on your iPhone. Book I, Chapter 4 covers the apps that come with your iPhone. The online bonus content presents some third-party apps we think you'll like. Here, we tell you how to launch and close apps, and how to organize the app buttons on your Home screen.

Launching apps

To launch or open an app on the Home screen, tap the app icon. You may see icons that have a white outline border; these are folders, which can contain up to twelve apps. An iPhone running iOS 4.3 or higher when you bought it has a Utilities folder. If you updated your iPhone from 4.2 to a later iOS, you won't see folders until you create them. To launch an app that resides in a folder, tap the folder. It opens. Tap the app button you want to launch. To close the folder, tap it or the Home screen.

Switching between apps

Instead of opening an app, closing it, returning to the Home screen, and then opening another app, you can have multiple apps open at the same time — although you just see one app at a time on your screen. When you double-click the Home button, the screen shifts up, as in Figure 3-3. Four app buttons appear beneath the active screen in the multitasking bar. These are the apps that you most recently used. Although you see four at a time, up to 50 can be open. Flick left and right to move through the app buttons. Tap the button for the app you want to switch to or tap the screen to return to the active app. Flick left to right from the first screen to reveal the orientation lock button and music and video playback controls.

Closing apps

To quit apps and remove them from the multitasking bar, press and hold one of the app buttons in the multitasking bar. All of them start to wiggle and shake, and a minus sign in a red circle appears on the left shoulder of each app icon. Tap the minus sign and the app closes. The remaining app buttons shift to fill in the space. Press the Home button when you've finished closing apps and they stop wiggling.

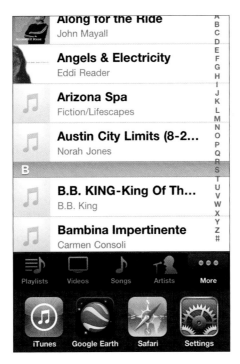

Figure 3-3: The multitasking bar list lets you switch between open apps without returning to the Home screen.

Although Apple insists you don't need to quit apps you're no longer using, some apps — like the National Public Radio (NPR) app, for instance — do continue using some of iPhone's available memory and processing brainpower when it's in the multitasking bar, even when you aren't using it. Call us obsessively compulsive, but both authors regularly double-click the Home button and close apps we aren't using.

Organizing Apps and Folders

Your iPhone comes with the first Home screens displaying the included apps, which we review in Book I, Chapter 4. You may want to rearrange the apps so that the ones you use most frequently are at the top of the Home screen, or you may want to change the apps that are in the dock. As you add new apps, you'll want to arrange them in a way that makes sense to you, and you may want to group some together in a folder. You can move apps around on your iPhone and from iTunes.

Organizing apps on your iPhone

To organize apps from your iPhone, follow these steps:

1. **Press and hold any app button on your Home screen.**

   Barbara loves this part. Sometimes she does it just to brighten the day because the apps start wiggling. Unfortunately, this isn't a video book, but you've got to see this. Try it — we'll wait.

2. **Any of the apps that have circled Xs on the upper left corner can be deleted. Just tap the circled X.**

   A message opens asking if you really want to delete that app, as shown in Figure 3-4. Tap the appropriate button: Delete, if you want to delete that app, or cancel, if you tapped the circled X by mistake.

   Don't worry — if you delete an app by mistake, iTunes maintains a copy of all your apps so you can reload it.

Figure 3-4: A notification message asks for confirmation before deleting an app.

3. **Touch and drag the app buttons around to arrange them in a way you like, even from one Home screen to another.**

   The Photos app button is being moved in Figure 3-5.

Figure 3-5: Drag the app icon to the position you want.

4. **To change the four apps that are in the dock, you first have to drag one out, and then you can replace it with another app.**

   You don't have to have four apps in the dock. If you prefer three or two or none, you can move the buttons out of the dock onto a Home screen.

You can have up to four folders on the dock instead of single apps and each of those folders can have up to 12 apps inside.

Folders

Folders give you the option of putting like-minded apps together in one place so you can find them quickly and easily.

Adding folders

To add a folder, press and hold your finger on an app on the Home screen until they start a-wigglin' and a-jigglin'. Then, follow these steps:

1. **Lift your finger.**

2. **Touch and drag one app button over another app button.**

   A square is formed around both apps and their icons are greatly reduced. The folder opens beneath the square, as shown in Figure 3-6.

3. **If you want to add another app to the folder, tap the folder.**

   The folder closes.

4. **Touch and drag another app into the folder.**

5. **Tap the Home button to save the new folder.**

Figure 3-6: Drag one app over another to create a folder that holds up to 12 apps.

If a folder has already been created but you want to add apps to it, press and hold an app to make them wiggle then drag the app you want into the folder. To remove apps, while the apps are wiggling, double-tap the folder you want to change to open it. Drag apps out of the folder onto the Home screen. A folder is automatically deleted when all apps are moved out and it's empty.

Renaming folders

iPhone assigns a name it thinks is appropriate by default, such as Utilities or Productivity, based on the kinds of apps you put in the folder, but you can change the name with these steps:

1. **Press and hold an app on the Home screen.**

2. **Tap the wiggling folder whose name you want to edit.**

3. **Tap the circled X on the right of the field where the name is written.**

   The field is erased. A cursor appears at the beginning of the field and the keyboard opens.

4. **Tap out the name you wish to give this folder.**

5. **Tap the Done key on the bottom right of the keyboard.**

6. **Tap outside the folder to close it.**

   The buttons are still wiggling.

7. **Tap the Home button to save the renamed folder.**

Each Home screen can hold 16 apps or app folders. Each app folder can hold up to 12 apps. Add four app folders containing 12 apps each on the dock, and some quick multiplication and addition results in the possibility of 2,160 apps on your iPhone! Actually, that's how many app icons you can have on your iPhone. You can continue to add apps to your iPhone and find them with Spotlight.

If your apps folder has a badge on the upper right corner, the number on the badge is a cumulative number of items that need attending to, such as unread messages, app updates, or information updates.

Organizing apps and folders using iTunes

When you have a lot of apps and folders, moving them around from screen to screen can be tedious. Luckily, you can also organize your Home screens, apps, and folders in iTunes. Follow these steps:

1. **Connect your iPhone to your computer with the USB connector cable or connect both your iPhone and your computer to the same Wi-Fi network.**

   See Book II, Chapter 1 to learn about syncing.

2. **Open iTunes.**

You should see your iPhone in the Devices list on the left.

3. **Click the name of your iPhone in the list.**

   iPhone's Summary window opens.

4. **Click on Apps at the top of the window.**

   You see a list of the apps iTunes has in its Apps category (some may not be on your iPhone), and a copy of your Home screens, like in Figure 3-7.

5. **Drag the app from the list to the Home screen where you want it to reside or click and drag the app icons around the Home screens.**

6. **Create, move, and rename folders using the same techniques as you would to do the same on your iPhone.**

7. **To delete an app, click on the X in the corner that appears when you drag the pointer over the app icon or de-select it from the apps list.**

   Even if you choose to delete an app from your iPhone, it remains in iTunes. You never know if you might want to use removed apps at a later date.

8. **After you make your changes and the Home screens are organized, click the Sync button to sync your changes with your iPhone.**

Figure 3-7: Organize your apps and folders via iTunes.

Switching Between Portrait and Landscape Views

You might have noticed that if you rotate your iPhone 90 degrees to the left or right, the screen rotates too. This is considered switching between a portrait, or vertical, view and a landscape, or horizontal, view. Many games, as well as movies viewed in Videos or YouTube, work only in landscape view. Some apps and the Home screen work only in portrait view. The supplied apps that can be viewed in both portrait and landscape are Mail, Safari, Messages, Notes, Contacts, Stocks, Photos, Camera, Calculator (changes to a scientific calculator in landscape view), Calendar (changes to a weekly calendar in landscape view), and Music in playback mode.

You can lock your iPhone so it stays in portrait view by doing the following:

1. **Double-click the Home button to open the multitasking bar.**

2. **Flick to the right to go beyond the first set of four app buttons.**

   Two controls open: the Portrait Orientation Lock button and the media playback controls. See Figure 3-8.

3. **Tap the Portrait Orientation Lock button.**

   A lock appears to show that Portrait Orientation Lock is on and the same icon appears in the status bar to remind you it's on.

4. **Repeat the steps to turn Portrait Orientation Lock off.**

Portrait Orientation Lock

Figure 3-8: The Portrait Lock and media playback controls are to the left of the first multitasking bar.

Commandeering the Keyboard

For many iPhone users, the keyboard is the hardest thing to get used to. You may think the keys are too small for your fingers. However, with a little practice, the keyboard becomes second nature in no time. Any time you tap in a blank field, the keyboard opens in apps like Mail, Messages, Notes, or when you're filling out a form on a web page in Safari (and when you're adding contacts and calendar entries when using those respective apps).

Keyboard settings

The default keyboard settings are probably fine for your typing needs. If you write in a language other than English, however, you'll want to select the keyboard that reflects the language you want to type in — and recognizes words in that preferred language. You'll get crazy suggestions if you type in Pakistani with an English keyboard and dictionary. Read below to learn about your options and follow these steps to change them:

1. **Tap Settings on the Home screen.**

2. **Tap General⟳Keyboard.**

   The screen shown in Figure 3-9 opens.

3. **Tap the toggle switch to turn the function on or off.**

   - **Auto-Capitalization:** Automatically capitalizes the letter "I" when it stands alone and capitalizes the first letter after any punctuation that iPhone recognizes as a new sentence.

   - **Auto-Correction:** Automatically corrects words as you are typing using iPhone's built-in dictionary. For example, as in Figure 3-10, if you type **thr**, "the" appears in a box beneath the word. If you tap the space bar, the return key, or a punctuation key, the suggestion is accepted; tap the X on the box and your typed word remains. The dictionary automatically adds names from Contacts so it recognizes many names you type. Your iPhone learns your idiosyncrasies, adding words you type frequently, that it doesn't know, to the dictionary.

   - **Check Spelling:** iPhone underlines words it thinks are spelled wrong. Double-tap on the underlined word and iPhone gives you a suggestion. Tap the suggestion to accept it or the X to decline. If iPhone thinks the word is spelled wrong but doesn't have a suggestion, you have to correct the word, if necessary, on your own.

     Auto-Correction and Check Spelling are on by default. Check Spelling only works when Auto-Correction is turned on.

   - **Enable Caps Lock:** When on, you can quickly tap twice on the shift key and it changes to a caps lock key.

- **"." Shortcut:** Double-tapping the space bar inserts a period then one space. This feature is very handy as you tap the same key — the space bar— twice rather than changing the keyboard layout, tapping the period, changing the keyboard back again, and then tapping the space bar.

Figure 3-9: The Keyboard settings let you control automatic keyboard functions.

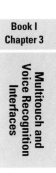

Figure 3-10: Turn Auto-Correction on to get suggestions for presumed typing errors.

4. **To change the keyboard layout or add a keyboard for another language, tap International Keyboards.**

   The screen shown in Figure 3-11 opens.

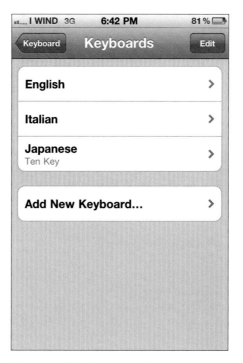

Figure 3-11: The International Keyboard option lets you add keyboards of different languages.

5. **Tap English or whichever language's keyboard you wish to edit.**

   The screen opens (refer to Figure 3-12) and displays options for the Software Keyboard Layout, that is the keyboard on your iPhone, and for a Hardware Keyboard Layout, which is a peripheral keyboard that you use with your iPhone. You can choose the Software Keyboard Layout you're used to using. Choose the Hardware Keyboard Layout that corresponds to the type of peripheral keyboard you use with your iPhone. Learn about using peripheral accessories in Book I, Chapter 4.

6. **Tap Add New Keyboard to add another language-specific keyboard.**

   A list of languages opens.

7. **Tap the language you want to add.**

   It automatically appears in the list of keyboards.

8. **Tap Add New Shortcut.**

   Shortcuts let you type a few letters that your iPhone interprets and expands into a longer phrase. For example, type **omw** in a message and it becomes "On my way!" Type your text in the Phrase and Shortcut text fields and then tap Save.

....I WIND E	12:51 PM	83% 🔋
◀ Keyboards	**English**	

Software Keyboard Layout

QWERTY	✓
AZERTY	
QWERTZ	

Hardware Keyboard Layout

U.S.	✓
Dvorak	
U.S. International - PC	
U.S. Extended	

Figure 3-12: Choose the Software Keyboard Layout that suits you; the Hardware Keyboard Layout should match that of the peripheral keyboard you use.

TIP

If you add a word or phrase to Shortcuts without typing in the shortcut, the word or phrase is added to your Personal Dictionary and iPhone won't make suggestions for correcting it.

TIP

Both Japanese and Chinese have multiple options for the keyboard layout you want to use. Chinese also has a handwriting option in which you use your fingertip to draw the characters.

To switch between keyboards of different languages, when the keyboard opens, a globe button appears at the bottom of the keyboard. Tap the globe button to switch between languages. Tap and hold the globe button to see a pop-up list of languages you added and then slide to select the language.

Typing tips

Apple suggests, and we concur, that you begin typing with one index finger, probably that of your dominant hand, and gradually move up to two-finger or two-thumb typing. When you tap a key, the letter appears enlarged on the screen so you know which key you actually hit. If it's the letter you want, just lift your finger and that letter appears on the message, note, or field you're typing in. If it's not the letter you want, without lifting your finger, slide your finger to the key of the letter you want. As you slide, the enlarged letter changes to show which key your finger is on.

As you become familiar with the tap typing technique with your index finger, you may want to try putting iPhone on a flat surface and typing with two index fingers. In the landscape position, you can hold your iPhone with both hands, placing your thumbs at the bottom and your middle fingers at the top. Use both index fingers to type.

For thumb-typing in either portrait or landscape position, cradle your iPhone in both hands, keeping them slightly relaxed, and use your thumbs to type. Say you're standing on a moving bus and have to hold on, leaving only one hand free to type an urgent message. With practice, you can cradle your iPhone in one hand and type with the cradling hand's thumb.

Turning your iPhone to landscape orientation makes the keyboard wider and the keys slightly bigger; however, the field where you are typing is smaller.

After you get going, iPhone uses an algorithm to predict the word you are typing so zones of letters imperceptibly increase in size to increase the probability that you hit the letter you want.

Dictating

The easiest way to avoid typing is to dictate text. On iPhone 4S, Siri takes dictation. (With an iPhone 3GS or 4, you can use a dictation app, which we mention in the online bonus content, Bonus Chapter 1.) To dictate messages with Siri, do the following:

1. **Open the app you want to use, such as Mail, Messages, or Notes.**

2. **Tap the microphone key on the keyboard, which looks like a microphone.**

3. **Dictate your message or note.**

4. **Tap Done.**

   Tap the microphone key again to make corrections or type them.

Keyboard layouts

Looking at the keyboard in Figure 3-13, moving top to bottom, left to right, you see the letters of the alphabet, the shift key, the delete key, the ABC/123 key, the globe key (if you've added a language), the microphone key (if you have an iPhone 4S), the space bar, and a return key. The keyboard changes slightly depending on what function you want to perform. When you are in a To field in Mail or in the URL field in Safari, the space bar shrinks to allow two more buttons in next to it: an at (@) button and a dot (.) button. This makes typing an e-mail or website address easier. The Return key becomes the Search button in Spotlight and a Go button in Safari. In addition to these visible changes that make typing easier, there are some invisible shortcuts:

ABC/123   Microphone   Delete

Shift   Globe

Figure 3-13: Familiarizing yourself with the keyboard layouts makes typing faster and more efficient.

- Double-tap the shift key to turn it into a caps-lock key so you can type in ALL CAPS. You have to turn this option on in the Keyboard settings.

- Tap the delete key once to delete one character to the left. Tap and hold the delete key and it begins deleting one letter after another. If you continue holding, it deletes whole words at once.

- Hold the ABC key and slide your finger to the symbol or number you wish to type. The character is typed but the keyboard reverts to letters.

- When the cursor is in the To field and you have the space, at, and dot buttons, touch and hold the dot key and a small window opens offering an assortment of the most common web suffixes: .com, .net, .edu, .org, and so on. If you've added an international keyboard, the local suffixes are included, for example .it for Italy and .eu for European Union.

- Tap the 123 key to change the keyboard to show numbers, as seen in Figure 3-14. The shift key changes to a symbols key; the 123 key changes to an ABC key. Tap the symbols key and the top row of the keyboard where the numbers were changes to show more symbols, as shown in Figure 3-14. Tap the ABC/123 key to return to the alphabet keyboard; tap the symbols key to switch between numbers and symbols.

Figure 3-14: The letters change to numbers when you tap the ABC/123 key and the numbers change to symbols when you tap the symbols key.

Some of the letters, when held, give non-English options, and some of the numbers and symbols give multiple options as well, as shown in Table 3-1.

Table 3-1	Special Characters and Symbols
Key Pressed	*Special Character*
A or a	à á â ä æ ã å ā
C or c	ç ć č
E or e	è é ê ë ē ė ę
I or i	Ì į ī í ï î
L or l	ł
O or o	õ ō ø œ ó ò ö ô
N or n	ń ñ
S or s	ß ś š
U or u	ū ú ù ü û
Y or y	ÿ
Z or z	ž ź ż
Period	Ellipsis (…)
Question mark (?)	Upside down question mark
Exclamation point (!)	Upside down exclamation point
Apostrophe (')	Smart single quote and simple single quote
Hyphen/minus sign (–)	Em dash (—)
Dollar sign ($)	¥, €, ¢, £, ₩
Ampersand (&)	§
Quote (")	Left bracket, right bracket, lower quote, left and right smart quotes, simple quote
Percentage (found when you tap the symbols button after tapping the numbers button) %	‰

Editing Your Text

Writing messages on a cell phone used to be time-consuming and the character limit often forced us to write telegraphic messages. On your iPhone, you have a full keyboard with multiple languages and many characters, along with character-limit-free SMS and e-mail functions. You can type longer, more complex communications, but this means you make mistakes, change your mind, want to move sentences around — in other words, you want to edit your text. iPhone has the basic editing capabilities of copy, cut, and paste, select or select all, even undoing and redoing. We show you how to do each of these tasks in the following sections.

Selecting

You can tap once to insert the cursor somewhere in the middle of your text, then make changes letter by letter or you can select a word, phrase, paragraph, or the entire text and make changes with this procedure:

1. **Tap the text you want to edit.**

   The keyboard appears and the cursor blinks more or less where you tapped.

2. **Press and hold your finger in the general area where you want to insert the cursor.**

   A magnifying loupe appears over the text with the cursor in the center.

3. **Drag your finger over the text until the cursor is at the point where you want it.**

4. **Lift your finger.**

   Two buttons appear: Select and Select All.

5. **Tap once to edit with the delete key and keyboard.**

   Select and Select All disappear and the cursor is where you put it.

6. **Tap Select to select the word or portion of the text; tap Select All to select the entire text.**

   The word is highlighted in blue and there are blue grab points on the upper left and lower right corner. (Refer to Figure 3-15.)

   If you select just one word, you can *cut* or *copy* that word, or iPhone can *suggest* synonyms or *define* the selected word — just tap the appropriate button.

7. **To select a portion of the text, touch and drag the blue grab points to select the text you want to cut or copy.**

8. **If you want to delete, press the cut button. If you want to copy or cut, and paste in another location, read on.**

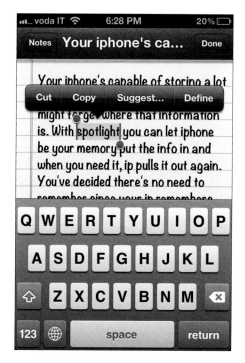

Figure 3-15: Use blue grab points to select the text you want to copy, cut, or replace with a suggested synonym.

Cutting, copying, and pasting

What if you want to copy something from an e-mail message you received and paste it onto an existing list in Notes for future reference? Here's how to copy and paste into an existing document:

1. **Following the previous steps to select the text you want to copy.**

   After you've tapped Select or Select All, a Copy button appears above the highlighted text.

2. **Open the document in the app where you want to place the copied text.**

   If, from our example, Notes is already open, double-click the Home button to open the multitasking bar, and then tap the Notes button. Otherwise, press the Home button to open the Home screen and tap Notes from there.

3. **Tap and hold on the screen where you want to insert the copied text.**

   The magnifying loupe appears, allowing you to move the cursor precisely where you want it.

4. **Lift your finger.**

   A Paste button appears.

5. **Tap the Paste button.**

   Your copied text is now in a new spot.

Copying and pasting isn't only for text within apps like Notes and Mail. You can copy a portion of a web page and paste it into an e-mail. Press and hold the part of the page you want to copy and the blue grabbers come up, along with a Copy button. Drag the grab points to select everything you want to copy, and then tap the Copy button. Open the app where you want to paste the selection. Press and hold until you see the Paste button. Tap Paste.

Undoing and redoing

To undo your edit, shake your iPhone. A message opens with the option to undo the last action or cancel. Tap the Undo button and you're home free. And if you want to redo what you thought you wanted to undo? Just shake your iPhone again and the buttons ask if you want to redo or undo or cancel, as shown in Figure 3-16.

Figure 3-16: Shake your iPhone to undo and redo the last edit you did.

Searching Here, There, and Everywhere with Spotlight

Q iPhone's search function, Spotlight, helps you find things on your iPhone or the Internet. You can access Spotlight from the screen before the first Home screen or from within many apps. First, we show you how to use the main Spotlight screen, and then we show you how to use it from different apps.

From the first Home screen, press the Home button. Spotlight opens, as shown in Figure 3-17. When you search from this Spotlight screen, your search — defined by a word, phrase, or number — encompasses all the apps that are on your iPhone: e-mail, notes, contacts, calendars, and so on. Moreover, you can search the web or Wikipedia. Follow these steps to search from the Spotlight screen:

1. **Type your word or phrase in the blank field at the top of the screen.**

2. **Tap Search.**

   Spotlight searches your iPhone and displays any items that match your search criteria.

3. **Tap an item in the list to view that item's contents.**

   or

   Scroll down the list to where you see Search Web and Search Wikipedia.

4. **Tap either one.**

   iPhone opens Safari, searches the Internet, and displays general web search results or Wikipedia search results, depending on which option you tapped.

5. **Tap the item you wish to view from the results list.**

You also find Spotlight within many apps on iPhone. In the Mail, Messages, or Contacts apps, tap the status bar to open Spotlight. In other apps, any time you see the magnifying glass icon, you can tap it to open Spotlight. Dragging the app screen down is another way to unhide the Spotlight search field when you don't see it. Then do the following:

1. **Tap in the Spotlight field.**

   The cursor appears there and the keyboard opens.

2. **Type in your word or phrase and then tap the Search button.**

   Spotlight searches within the app you're using.

3. **Tap the item in the list that you were searching for.**

   A screen with that item opens.

Figure 3-17: The Spotlight screen, to the left of the Home screen, searches all the apps on iPhone for occurrences of a word or phrase.

When you search from within an app, iPhone searches only in that app — in Mail that means the sender, recipient, and subject line only, not within the messages, and first, last, and company names in Contacts.

In Safari, which we write about in Book III, Chapter 3, do the following:

1. **Tap in the search field (where the name of your search engine — Google, Yahoo!, or Bing — is displayed in gray letters).**

2. **Type in the word or phrase you wish to search for on the Internet.**

3. **Tap the blue Search button on the bottom right of the keyboard.**

   A list of matches found on the Internet appears.

4. **Tap the item in the list you wish to view.**

   Safari opens that web page.

You can alter the Spotlight settings to limit your searches to certain apps or priority order in which the apps are searched. To change Spotlight settings,

1. **Open Settings⟳General⟳Spotlight Search.**

   The Spotlight Search list opens, as seen in Figure 3-18.

2. **Tap the name of the app in the list to make the checkmark on the left appear or disappear.**

   A checkmark means Spotlight will search that app when looking for something from the Spotlight search screen or within that app.

3. **To change the order of the apps, press and hold the re-order icon to the right of the app, and then drag up and down to move it.**

   Spotlight searches in the apps at the top of the list first when doing a search.

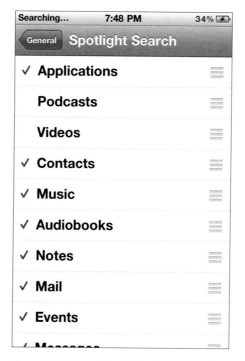

Figure 3-18: Change the priority of your searches in the Spotlight Search settings.

Talking to Your iPhone

Sometimes you have to do two things at once and your hands aren't free to search through Contacts to find a phone number, let alone dial it. Or maybe you need to change an appointment or find a restaurant in an unfamiliar city. You'd like to listen to a song or playlist, but you have so many songs in the iPod app that it takes longer to find what you want to hear than actually listen to it. You have two options for talking to your iPhone and asking it to do things for you:

- ✓ **Siri,** which — or should we say "who" — does everything Voice Control does, plus takes dictation and does tasks for you. Siri works only on iPhone 4S and only when you have an Internet connection.

- ✓ **Voice Control,** which follows simple commands such as "Call Joe" or "Play songs by Joni Mitchell." Voice Control functions on iPhone 3GS, 4, and 4S. On the 4S, Siri performs the Voice Control functions unless it is disabled. If you don't have Internet access but want to use Voice Control, go to Settings➪General➪Siri and tap Off.

When you ask Siri to do something for you, the request is sent to the remote Siri server, which interprets your request and sends the answer back. All of this happens in the blink of an eye because of the superfast A5 dual-core processor (the brain, if you will) inside iPhone 4S.

Telling Siri what to do

We can't help but wonder what Bunny Watson (Katherine Hepburn in the classic movie *Desk Set)* would think of Siri. (If you haven't seen this film, watch it soon.) Bunny set out to prove that a computer couldn't replace a human researcher. We're not placing bets on whether Siri can replace a human assistant, but "she" certainly comes close. Like any good assistant, Siri takes dictation, finds information, and does many tasks for you. Tap Settings➪General➪Siri➪On to turn Siri on. To talk to Siri, do the following:

1. **Press and hold the Home button, the center button on the earphones, or the button on your Bluetooth headset, until the Siri screen opens.**

   You can do this from the Home screen or from within an app. Siri knows what you're doing and responds appropriately.

2. **A tone lets you know Siri is ready to listen. Following are examples of how Siri uses the apps on your iPhone. You don't have to open the app — just speak when Siri's ready:**

   - *Phone:* Make a phone or FaceTime call. Say "Call Joe Hutsko" or "FaceTime Barbara Boyd."

   - *Messages:* Read and send SMS and iMessages text messages. Say "Tell Darrin Smith I'm on my way."

   - *Mail:* Search and send e-mail. Say "E-mail Joe Hutsko about deadline."

   - *Calendar:* View and create events. Ask "Where is my 9 o'clock meeting?" or "Make appointment with Bill Jones for 10 am."

   - *Contacts:* Ask for information about your contacts. Ask "What's Jim Rose's address?" If you refer to someone by first name only, Siri looks for matches in Favorites in Contacts and in Conversations in

Messages, and then repeats the first and last name asking if it's the correct contact. It's quicker and easier to use both first and last names. Enter names of related people on your info card so Siri knows who "Mom" or "sister" are. Book IV, Chapter 1 is about Contacts.

- *Reminders:* Create, search, and change reminders. Say "Remind me to take book to Jen when I get home."

- *Notes:* Create, search, and edit notes. Say "Note tablecloth is 104 by 84."

- *Maps:* Get directions, find addresses. Ask "Where is the nearest Apple Store?"

- *Clock:* Set alarms, start the timer, find out the time in another city. Say "Set timer for 25 minutes."

- *Music:* Play artists, albums, playlists, or songs. Say "Play Blue."

- *Weather:* Ask for forecasts. Ask "What is today's weather?"

- *Stocks:* Obtain stock info. Ask "What is the stock price for Apple?"

- *Safari:* Search the web. Say "Search the web for cold remedies."

- *WolframAlpha:* Answer factual, statistical, and mathematical questions. Ask "How fast is the speed of light?"

3. **Siri makes an audible response and displays what was done on your screen, as shown in Figure 3-19.**

Siri understands different ways of saying the same thing; however, if it's unsure of a command, Siri asks for clarification.

Figure 3-19: Siri reads and displays the response to your request.

4. **If Siri doesn't understand what you say, you can make corrections by doing the following:**

   • Type corrections in the bubble onscreen that shows what Siri understood or tap the microphone and dictate the correction. Tap Done when you finish.

   • If a word is underlined in blue, tap the word and then choose an alternative from the choices or tap the microphone to dictate the correction.

   • Tap the microphone to speak to Siri and clarify your request.

   • To correct a message or e-mail before sending, dictate the changes or say "Send it" when it's correct.

5. **To cancel a request, say "Cancel," tap the microphone button, or press the Home button.**

Any time you want to dictate instead of type, tap the microphone key on the keyboard, dictate, then tap Done when you finish.

Using Voice Control

With Voice Control, you can ask your iPhone to perform simple tasks such as calling someone or playing an album from your Music collection. Voice Control doesn't work if Siri is turned on, but Siri performs all the functions of Voice Control, so you aren't missing out on anything. Voice Control is independent of the Internet, so if you're in an area without Internet service, you may want to turn Siri off (tap Settings➪General➪Siri➪Off) and use Voice Control. Here's how to use Voice Control:

1. **Press and hold the Home button, the center button on the earphones, or the button on your Bluetooth headset, until the Voice Control screen opens, as shown in Figure 3-20.**

   The words that float across the Voice Control screen are suggestions for commands you can give.

   Two quick beeps let you know that Voice Control is ready to listen to your command.

2. **Speak the name of the person you want to call (or the artist you want to hear).**

   Voice Control replies with the name it understood. If it found more than one match, it reads off a list of the options. Repeat the option you want.

   If you asked for music, iPhone responds with "Playing songs by *artist's or album name*," and begins playing.

Figure 3-20: You can command your iPhone to call someone, play a song, or tell the time with Voice Control.

3. Repeat the option that you want.

4. iPhone dials that person.

If Voice Control offers an option you don't want, say "No" or "Cancel." Voice Control closes and you have to start over.

Voice Control also tells time. Press and hold the Home button. When Voice Control opens, ask "What time is it?" Voice Control tells you.

Chapter 4: Touring iPhone's Built-in Apps and Settings

In This Chapter

✏ **Getting acquainted with built-in apps**

✏ **Downloading extra Apple-created apps**

✏ **Adjusting basic settings to suit your style**

✏ **Invoking iPhone's security and privacy features**

✏ **Restricting access to kid-sensitive apps and content**

✏ **Averting panic in case your iPhone is lost or stolen**

*F*rom placing and answering calls with iPhone, to browsing the web and juggling e-mail with Safari and Mail, your iPhone has a lot of great apps. This chapter introduces you to those apps, as well as every other built-in app. We show you how to download a pair of free iPhone apps — iBooks and Find My iPhone — that don't come preloaded on your iPhone (although they might as well have). We also introduce you to a few additional apps you can download to complete your collection of Apple-branded iPhone apps.

In this chapter, we also show you how to adjust your iPhone's basic settings to suit your personal style, explain how to activate security features for protecting your iPhone from prying eyes, and introduce you to steps you can take to track down your iPhone (and even remotely erase your personal information) if your beloved gadget is ever lost or stolen.

YOUR TOTAL MILES

9.27m

🏃3   ⏱ 13'36"   ⏲ 2:06:06
RUNS   AVG PACE   DURATION   CA

Start a New Run

Tapping into iPhone's Built-in Apps

Right out of the box, your iPhone is preloaded with a gaggle of   ¬hallenge Me
great apps that can do just about everything under the sun. (Okay, maybe not everything, like fold your laundry or take your dog for a walk, but practically anything you can imagine you'd want to do with an incredibly versatile all-in-one gadget that fits in the palm of your hand.) Getting acquainted with the basic purpose and features of iPhone's apps can help you choose which apps you want to use right away.

When you turn on your iPhone for the first time, you see iPhone's apps arranged on the main and second Home screen pages in a way Apple's iPhone designers figured probably makes sense for most people, as shown in Figure 4-1.

Figure 4-1: iPhone's main Home screens display built-in apps and app folders.

 If, like me, you like to think of yourself as unlike most people (wait, doesn't that actually make us alike?), you can organize your iPhone's app icons in whatever way makes the most sense to you. We write about how to organize the Home screen any which way you want, in Book I, Chapter 3.

Here's a roll-call rundown of your iPhone's apps, with bite-size descriptions of what each app can do, and pointers to the chapters you can read to learn more about each app:

- ✔ **Messages:** Use this app to send, receive, and manage SMS (Short Message Service) text messages, MMS (Multimedia Message Service) messages, and iMessages messages that can include photos, videos, contact information, web links, and map locations. (See Book III, Chapter 2.)

✔ **Calendar:** Create, manage, and search events that you can keep in sync with calendars you maintain on your Mac or Windows PC, and with any online calendars you access using Microsoft Exchange, Google Calendar, and iCloud accounts. (See Book II, Chapter 1, and Book IV, Chapter 2.)

✔ **Photos:** View, share, and manage photos and videos captured with your iPhone, copied from your computer, saved from other apps, or downloaded from Photostream. Printing photos, viewing photos as a slideshow, assigning a photo to a contact card, or choosing a photo as your iPhone's wallpaper are just a few things you can do with Photo. (See Book II, Chapter 1, and Book V, Chapter 2.)

✔ **Camera:** Take photos and record videos, share them with others via MMS, iMessage, Twitter, and e-mail messages, assign a snapshot to a contact card, and trim and upload videos directly to YouTube and FaceBook. (See Book II, Chapter 1, and Book V, Chapter 1.)

✔ **YouTube:** Search, watch, review, and upload YouTube videos; e-mail a link to a video you want to share. (See Book V, Chapter 5.)

✔ **Stocks:** Stay on top of stock prices, track trading summaries, and view detailed market data and news. (See Book IV, Chapter 3.)

✔ **Maps:** Locate and view your current location on a map, search for worldwide locations, show traffic conditions, view information about a location, bookmark it or save it as a contact, call a location's phone number (if it's listed), get directions, and share a location in an e-mail or SMS text message, iMessage, or Twitter. (See Book IV, Chapter 3.)

✔ **Weather:** View current weather conditions and a six-day forecast for one or more locations around the world. (See Book IV, Chapter 3.)

✔ **Notes:** Create, view, and manage text notes you can sync with your computer using iTunes, or over the air using your iCloud, Gmail, Yahoo!, or Microsoft Exchange. Copy and paste text to and from notes and send e-mail from Notes. (See Book II, Chapter 1 and Book IV, Chapter 4.)

✔ **Utilities (folder):** Not an app, the Utilities icon is actually a folder containing other apps, as shown in Figure 4-2. The following apps may be in the Utilities folder or on the Home screen:

✔ **Clock:** View the current time in your present location and other locations with World Clock; use Alarm to wake you up or remind you of an upcoming event; tap Stopwatch to track a timed event, and use Timer to countdown the hours, minutes, and seconds remaining 'til the cows come home. (See Book IV, Chapter 2.)

✔ **Calculator:** Add, subtract, multiply, and divide with the basic keypad, or turn iPhone sideways to reveal a wider-ranging scientific calculator keyboard; copy and paste numbers to and from the calculator display. (See Book IV, Chapter 3.)

✔ **Compass:** Find out which direction you're facing, view your longitude and latitude coordinates, switch between True North and Magnetic North bearings. (See Book IV, Chapter 3.)

✔ **Voice Memos:** Record, replay, and manage spoken or other in-the-moment sounds you want to capture and listen to again (like a friend's live band performance); send your recorded ramblings as e-mail or SMS text messages, and copy them to your computer with iTunes. (See Book II, Chapter 1 and Book IV, Chapter 4.)

✔ **iTunes:** Browse, search, preview, and purchase music, movies, TV shows, ringtones, and audio books; rent movies; listen to and watch audio and video podcasts and iTunes U educational programs; use Ping to share your favorite selections with friends; Genius makes recommendations for music, movies, and TV shows. (See Book V, Chapter 3.)

✔ **App Store:** Search, browse, and read reviews of thousands of apps that you can download for free or a fee. Review and download updates to installed apps you already own. (See Book II, Chapter 2.)

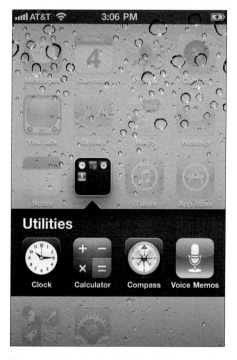

Figure 4-2: Tapping the Utilities folder reveals more apps stored inside the folder.

✔ **Game Center:** View and compare your game score rankings and achievements with friends and leaderboard top scores; invite friends and new opponents from around the world to compete in multiplayer games; and find Game Center-savvy games to play. (See Book IV, Chapter 3.)

✔ **Phone:** Use this app to place and answer calls; create, search, and edit Contacts, record your voicemail personal greeting and listen to, reply to, and manage voicemail messages; make and manage conference calls and FaceTime video chat calls. (See Book III, Chapter 1.)

✔ **Mail:** Send, receive, and manage e-mail messages for multiple e-mail account types, including Gmail, Yahoo!, AOL, and Hotmail. Access and stay in sync with iCloud and Microsoft Exchange e-mail, calendar, and contacts accounts; view, save, and print photo and document attachments; view and save video file attachments. (See Book III, Chapter 2.)

✔ **Safari:** Access and view websites; create a reading list that you can return to when you have more time; read without distraction in Reader; switch between web page windows; create and manage bookmarks, and sync your bookmarks between iPhone and Safari or Internet Explorer on your computer; view, save and print web pages, photo files, PDF and other document files. (See Book III, Chapter 3.)

✔ **Music:** Listen to your music, audio books, and audio podcasts through your iPhone speaker, earphones, or external speakers connected to your iPhone. (See Book II, Chapter 1, Book V, Chapters 2 and 3.)

✔ **Videos:** Watch and listen to music videos, movies, TV shows and video podcasts and iTunes U educational programs; stream video content to your AppleTV, or connect directly to your TV using the appropriate connector cable. (See Book II, Chapter 1, Book V, Chapters 2 and 4.)

✔ **Contacts:** Contacts helps you create, view, and manage contact information to keep track of people and company names, addresses, phone numbers, e-mail addresses and instant messaging account names, birthday and anniversary dates, and other contact-related bits of information. (See Book II, Chapter 1 and Book IV, Chapter 1.)

✔ **Reminders:** Create and manage an interactive to-do list. Add deadlines and locations, even link to events on your calendar and set up alerts so you know when you have to be somewhere. (See Book IV, Chapter 2.)

✔ **Newsstand:** Keep your magazine, newspaper, and journal subscriptions in one place. Connect to the Newsstand store to download the periodical's app and then subscribe in-app. (See Book II, Chapter 4.)

✔ **Nike + iPod:** This app icon won't appear until you turn on the Nike + iPod feature in Settings (tap Settings ➪ Nike + iPod, and then tap the On/Off button); use this app to record and monitor your walking and running workouts when linked to the Nike + iPod sensor tucked into the foot bed of your Nike+ running shoes (sensor and shoes sold separately); Upload your workout data to the Nike+ website to view past workouts and track progress toward your running goals. (See the online bonus content, Bonus Chapter 6.)

Want the same Nike + iPod workout goodness, minus having to spend big bucks to buy the sensor and sneakers? Head over to iPhone's App Store and purchase the "Nike+ GPS" app ($1.99), shown in Figure 4-3, which uses your iPhone's built-in GPS feature to track your location, pace and distance instead of relying on the Nike+ sensor and shoe combo. Though math was always Joe's worst subject, the way he sees it is that if $E = MC^2$, then Nike+ GPS = Nike + iPod - $100 = :-).

Figure 4-3: The Nike+ GPS app tracks your performance so you don't have to.

Downloading Extra Apple iPhone Apps

Besides the handy assortment of apps that come preloaded on your iPhone, Apple has a few other nifty apps up its proverbial sleeve that are definitely worth considering. Most of these extra Apple apps are free (or sort of free, which we explain in a moment), whereas one of them — iMovie — costs you $4.99.

We write about finding, browsing, installing, and updating apps with App Store in Book II, Chapter 2.

The following is a rundown of extra Apple apps you can find and download using your iPhone's App Store app:

✔ **iBooks:** The first time you use the App Store app, a notification asks "Would you like to download your free copy of iBooks now?" so you may already have it. If not, you can download iBooks later from the App Store, as shown in Figure 4-4. iBooks acts as your virtual doorway to Apple's iBookstore, where you can download free classics in e-book form, like *Great Expectations* and *War and Peace*, as well as purchase the latest bestsellers and other e-books. You can also read PDF and other e-pub documents downloaded from other sources such as Project Gutenberg (`www.gutenberg.org/`). (See the online bonus content, Bonus Chapter 5.)

✔ **Find My iPhone:** In the unhappy event your iPhone is lost or stolen, all may not truly be lost if you have the Find My iPhone feature turned on. The Find My iPhone app is not required to use the Find My iPhone feature, but lets you manage and track other iPhones or iPads. It's just so handy to have on hand to see those other gadgets, or to help a friend who may have misplaced or lost his iPhone. We tell you how to use the Find My iPhone feature and app at the end of this chapter.

Figure 4-4: Apple's campaign against e-illiteracy: "Just say yes" to iBooks!

✔ **Apple Store:** Browse and order Apple products online and have them shipped to your doorstep — or reserve them at your nearest Apple Store and then drop in to fetch your new goods in person, with directions to the store brought to you by your iPhone's own Map app. The Apple Store app also lets you make a date for One on One training, or reserve a seat at the genius bar or at upcoming events and training workshops.

✔ **Remote:** Taps into your home Wi-Fi network to turn your iPhone into a remote control for browsing and playing content stored in your computer's iTunes library or controlling AppleTV.

✔ **iMovie:** Turn videos you record using the Camera app into mini-movies, complete with titles, fade-ins, and fade-outs, music, and sound effects. The iMovie app is a scaled down version of iMovie for Mac, so you may prefer using your Mac to edit video captured on your iPhone. iMovie is a universal app, so you can download it once and use it on your iPad, too.

Adjusting iPhone's Basic Settings

In browsing through the apps that came with your iPhone, you probably noticed a button called Settings. In Settings, you adjust iPhone's numerous settings to suit your style, including date and time, screen brightness, ringtone, and background wallpaper image options (to name a few). Turn Wi-Fi, cellular, and Bluetooth networking features on and off; tweak individual app settings and choose which ones can access your location or send you notification messages; create and manage e-mail, contacts, calendar, and notes accounts and settings; and view information about your iPhone's system software, usage, and capacity. Settings is command central for just about everything your iPhone does.

On your journey through this book's many minibooks and chapters, we show you how to access and adjust iPhone's individual app settings on a need-to-know basis. For instance, in Book II, Chapter 2, we show how to adjust iPhone's Phone settings to turn on (or off) features like call forwarding and whether your Caller ID is displayed when you place calls to others.

Some settings, such as the image that appears behind the buttons on the Home screen — referred to as *wallpaper* — can be changed in more than one way. For instance, when you capture a photo with Camera, you can then choose that snapshot as your Home screen or Lock screen (or both) wallpaper image. Using the Photos app to browse images you copied from your computer is another way to change iPhone's wallpaper setting.

In the rest of this chapter, we show you how to change the basic settings you may want to change now or later, straight up, no stumbling-upon necessary.

You can extend your iPhone's battery charge by turning off or adjusting certain settings to minimize battery drain. To learn which settings to tweak and other iPhone energy saving tips, check out Book I, Chapter 5.

Tap Settings to display iPhone's list of settings, as shown in Figure 4-5, and then scroll up and down the list and tap on one you want to change. We go through each setting here in order of appearance.

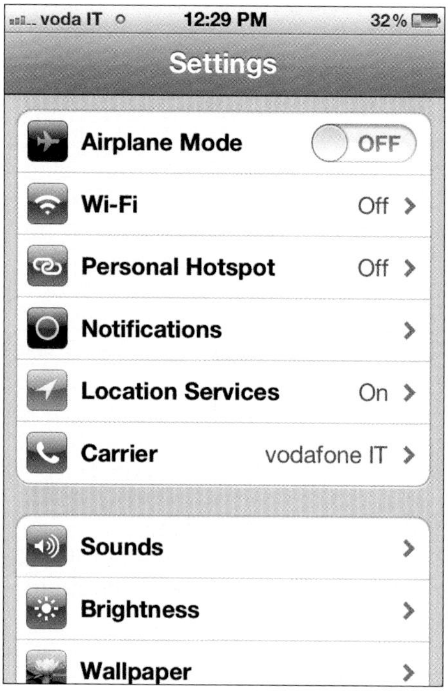

Figure 4-5: Tapping into iPhone's list of Settings.

Airplane Mode

Airplane Mode is your iPhone's only top-level setting featuring a single On/Off button rather than the > symbol that, when tapped, displays the selected setting's individual options (and, in some cases, additional sub-settings options for that selected top-level setting).

Think of the Airplane Mode setting as your one-stop, instant-cut-off switch for immediately disconnecting every one of your iPhone's wireless connection "cords" in one fell swoop.

When turned on, the airplane icon appears in the status bar, indicating Airplane Mode's "no fly" zone is in effect.

This setting is called Airplane Mode because nearly every airline requires that you turn off all wireless devices while your journey is underway. In the case of your iPhone, hitting the Airplane Mode switch turns off the following wireless connection features:

- ✔ **Cellular voice and data**
- ✔ **Wi-Fi**
- ✔ **Bluetooth**

When Airplane Mode is on, you can't make or receive phone calls or messages, or browse the web or check your e-mail. Nor can you use wireless Bluetooth accessories like Apple's Bluetooth Wireless Keyboard, headsets, and headphones.

But that doesn't mean you can't use your iPhone to do things like listen to music or watch a movie (with wired earphones so as not to disturb fellow passengers, of course), read an e-book in iBooks, or play a favorite game.

Although most airlines require you to turn off wireless features on devices like notebook computers and smartphones like your iPhone, some airlines that offer in-flight Wi-Fi networks do let you turn on your gadget's Wi-Fi option to connect to the network while you're high in the sky. In those instances, you can turn on Airplane Mode to turn off most of your iPhone's wireless features, and then turn on the Wi-Fi setting.

Wi-Fi

As we mention in Chapter 2 of this minibook, Wi-Fi almost always provides the fastest connection for doing all things Internet, including browsing the web, sending and receiving e-mail, or finding and watching YouTube videos. The only times Wi-Fi might actually operate slower than your cellular network carrier's wireless data capabilities is when the Wi-Fi network you connect to has a very weak signal, or when too many people are tapping into the same Wi-Fi network connection at the same time (like in a Manhattan cafe packed with notebook and smartphone users).

Tap Wi-Fi to turn Wi-Fi off or on and, when turned on, display a list of nearby networks, as shown in Figure 4-6. Available Wi-Fi networks are listed based on signal strength, as indicated by one, two, or three waves in the Wi-Fi signal to the right of the Wi-Fi network's name. The more waves, the stronger the signal.

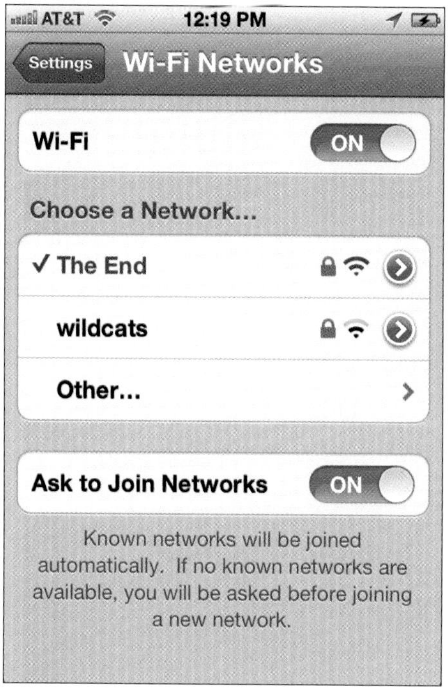

Figure 4-6: Wi-Fi networks are sorted by strongest to weakest signal strength.

Wi-Fi networks marked with a padlock icon indicate secured networks that require a password to connect to them. Wi-Fi networks without the padlock icon are unsecured networks, which don't require a password.

Tap a Wi-Fi network to connect to it. If prompted, type in the network's password, and then tap the Join button to connect to the Wi-Fi network.

A checkmark appears to the left of the Wi-Fi you're currently connected to (refer to Figure 4-6).

iPhone remembers Wi-Fi networks you previously connected to and automatically reconnects whenever you're in range of those Wi-Fi networks.

Some Wi-Fi networks may require you to agree to the provider's terms before you can use the network. In those cases, a prompt appears, asking for your permission to launch Safari to view the provider's web page, where you typically tap a checkbox indicating you agree to the legal mumbo jumbo listed on the web page. In other cases, you have to type in a user name and password in order to agree to the provider's terms.

Tap the Other network choice at the bottom of the available Wi-Fi networks list if you want to connect to a Wi-Fi network that you know is available, even though the network doesn't appear in the list of available Wi-Fi networks. The Other Network settings screen, as shown in Figure 4-7 opens. Type in the name of the hidden network you want to connect to, and then tap Join if the hidden network isn't protected with a password.

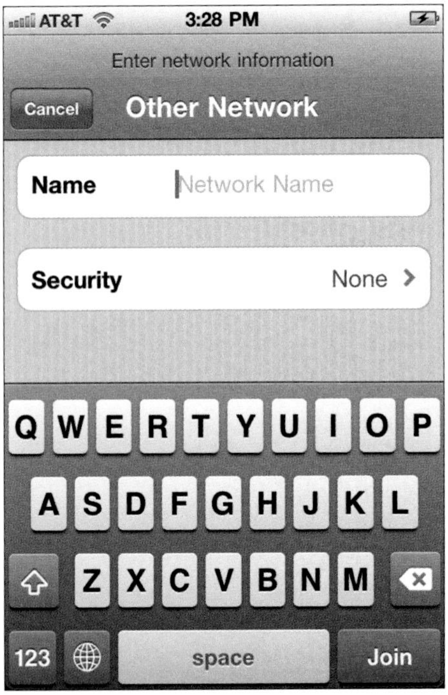

Figure 4-7: Connecting to hidden Wi-Fi networks is easy — if you're in on the secret.

If the hidden network you want to connect to is protected with a password, tap the Security button to display the Security settings screen, tap the type of security protection the hidden network employs, and then tap the Other Network button to return to the previous screen. Type in the hidden network's password, and then tap Join to complete the connection.

A savvy Wi-Fi network administrator typically chooses to hide their private network so only those who already know it exists can connect to the network, usually with a password.

Turning on the Ask to Join Networks option tells your iPhone to continuously "sniff" for any available Wi-Fi networks in the area and alert you with a prompt offering to connect to Wi-Fi networks it discovers, as shown in Figure 4-8. Although this may seem like a handy feature to keep turned on, it can become annoying if you're in a heavily populated area where there are tons of Wi-Fi networks vying for your iPhone's attention. What's more (or less, actually), all of that ceaseless searching for nearby Wi-Fi networks drains your iPhone's battery more quickly.

Figure 4-8: Automatically finding nearby Wi-Fi networks is handy — and battery draining.

Tap the > button to the far right of a Wi-Fi network name to display additional information and options for that network, as shown in Figure 4-9.

Tap the Forget this Network button to immediately disconnect from a Wi-Fi network you're connected to. Tapping this option also erases any password or other information you may have typed in to connect to the Wi-Fi network.

AT&T	3:38 PM	

Wi-Fi Networks **Crashproof**

Forget this Network

IP Address

DHCP	BootP	Static

IP Address	10.0.1.102
Subnet Mask	255.255.255.0
Router	10.0.1.1
DNS	10.0.1.1
Search Domains	hsd1.pa.comcast.net.
Client ID	

Figure 4-9: Taking a peek at additional Wi-Fi network options and settings.

To reconnect to a Wi-Fi network after choosing Forget this Network, tap the network's name on the previous list of Wi-Fi networks and, if prompted, type in the network's password to complete the connection.

Information about and configuration options for the Wi-Fi network you're connected to appear beneath the Forget this Network button. Scroll down the list to see the Wi-Fi network's information and configuration options, as shown in Figure 4-10.

Chances are you'll probably only view or change these additional Wi-Fi network settings if the tech folks at the company or organization that operates the network tell you that you need to and provide you with the necessary details you must type in to make the connection.

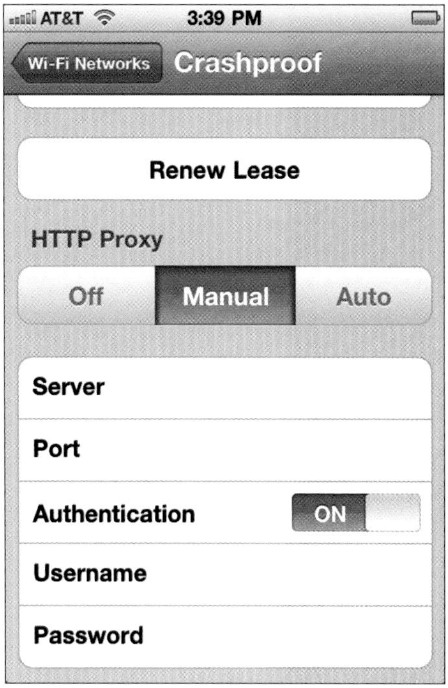

Figure 4-10: Still more Wi-Fi settings you can fiddle with.

Personal Hotspot

Personal Hotspot lets another device such as a computer, iPod touch, iPad, or another smartphone use your iPhone's cellular data connection to access the Internet. You can connect any of these devices using Wi-Fi, and you have the option of connecting a computer with a USB connector cable or pairing your computer with your iPhone via a wireless Bluetooth connection.

Tap Settings⇨Personal Hotspot and then tap the switch to On, as shown in Figure 4-11. Go to the network or Wi-Fi settings of the other device and choose the name of your iPhone in the list of available networks, and then type in the Wi-Fi password shown on the Personal Hotspot screen of your iPhone. We have to warn you, however, that Personal Hotspot is slower than tin-can-on-a-string communications.

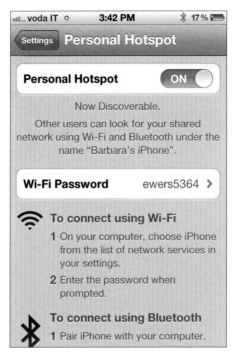

Figure 4-11: Personal Hotspot lets other devices use your iPhone's Internet connection.

Using a Personal Hotspot is also referred to as *tethering*, and may not be included in your cellular data service plan. In fact, if you try to use Personal Hotspot and it isn't included, your cellular service provider may send you a friendly message letting you know the service is not part of your plan.

Notifications

Notifications offer a combination of sounds, alert messages, and badges that can appear on particular app icons to indicate you've received new messages or other kinds of updated information. The great thing about notifications is they grab your attention even if the app that's doing the attention-grabbing isn't running, as illustrated by Figure 4-12.

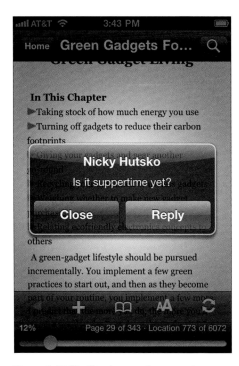

Figure 4-12: Notifications update you about apps even when you're using other apps.

The downside of notifications is they can be distracting, not to mention annoying, if they are a source of constant interruptions. With iOS 5, you can choose which apps alert you with notifications, and what kind of notification each uses: badges, banners, alerts, and, for some, sounds. Your iPhone also has a Notification Center, a central location where all notifications are saved until you remove them.

The Notifications Center (see Figure 4-13) appears when you swipe down from the top of the screen from any Home screen or app. If the app is in landscape view, swipe down from the top of that view. See Book I, Chapter 2 for more information about the Notifications Center.

Figure 4-13: The Notifications Center keeps all your notifications in one place.

Tap Settings and then Notifications to display a list of apps that offer notification options, as shown in Figure 4-14. Tap the Edit button and drag the apps to rearrange the order they appear, and then tap Done.

Tap either Manually or By Time in the Sort Apps section to choose how notifications are sorted in the Notification Center.

The list of apps is divided into two groups: In Notification Center and Not In Notification Center. Tap the name of each app in the list to choose if and how you want that app to send you notifications. A screen similar to the one in Figure 4-15 opens. Apps with Notifications On are in the first group.

Figure 4-14: Notification settings on a per-app basis.

Tap Notification Center On if you want to receive notifications from the app and choose how many recent items you want to appear in the Notification Center. Notification Center Off means you don't receive alerts but you can have badges On.

Choose the Alert Style you wish the app to use:

✔ **None** means you don't want any alerts from this app.

✔ **Banners** appear across the top of the Home screen or app you are using, and then automatically disappear after a few seconds (to be found in the Notifications Center if you turned that feature on for this app).

✔ **Alerts** appear in the center of the screen and require an action before they disappear.

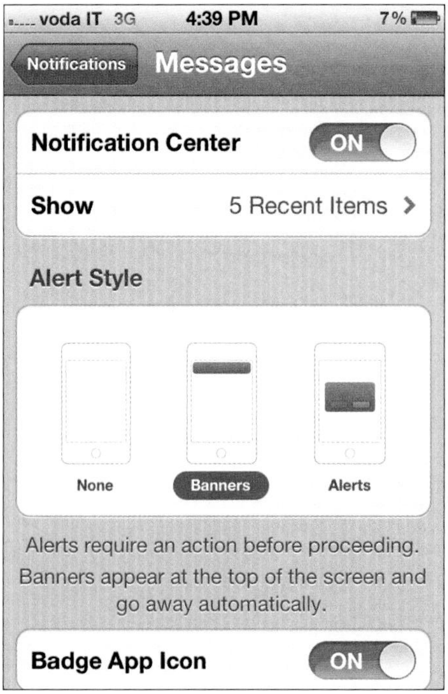

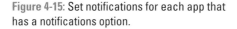

Figure 4-15: Set notifications for each app that has a notifications option.

Tap the Badge App Icon On if you want to see the numbered badge on the right shoulder of the app's icon on the Home screen. Those numbers tell you, for example, how many unread e-mail messages you have in Mail or how many missed calls and unprocessed voicemails you have in Phone.

You can't turn the badge off for the App Store, which indicates how many app updates are waiting for you. Book II, Chapter 2 is about the App Store.

Scroll down to see other Notifications options, which can vary from app to app. For example, Messages and Mail have a Show Preview option, which when turned On, displays a few lines of the message in the notification. Some apps have sound options so you are both audibly and visually alerted.

The last option is View in Lock Screen. When this option is turned on, you see notifications on the screen even when your iPhone is locked.

Sometimes you can uncover even more notification-related settings for fine-tuning your notification options for a particular app, such as Facebook.

To find out if certain apps offer additional notification settings options, tap Settings, and then scroll down the list of apps and tap the one you want to review. Tap on or off any individual notification settings options. Figure 4-16 shows the additional Facebook notification options; tapping Push Notifications reveals even more notification settings, as shown in Figure 4-17.

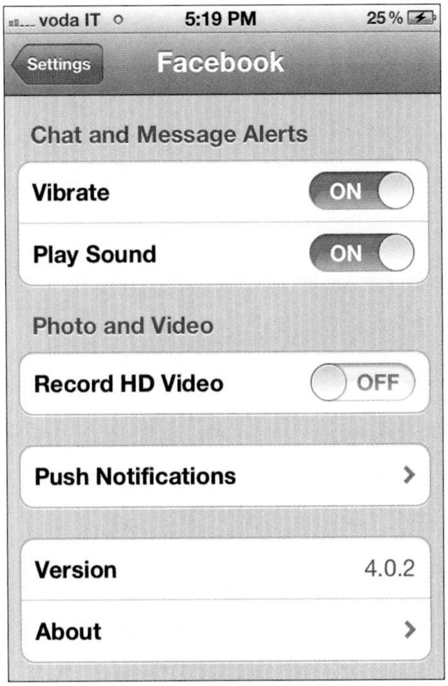

Figure 4-16: Apps listed in Settings may offer additional notification options.

Location Services

Many apps, like Weather and Maps, tap into your iPhone's Location Services feature to pinpoint your current location to provide current weather conditions, or give you step-by-step directions to the nearest taco joint.

Tap Settings and then Location Services to display the main Location Services setting switch and a list of all the apps that tap into your iPhone's Location Services features, as shown in Figure 4-18. Tap the On/Off button to turn your iPhone's Location Services feature on or off. (The app list disappears when you turn the main Location Services feature off, and reappears when you turn Locations On again.)

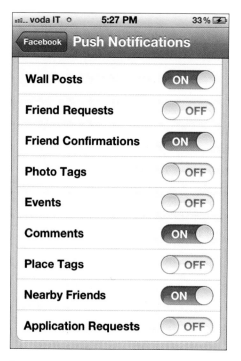

Figure 4-17: Some apps have second level settings.

Scroll down the list of apps and tap the switch to turn an app's Location Services setting on or off.

If you spot the Location Services icon beside certain apps in the app list, that means the app tapped into your iPhone's Location Services sometime over the last 24 hours (refer to Figure 4-18).

Carrier

This setting appears on GSM models (such as the AT&T iPhone or an unlocked iPhone) when you are outside your service provider's network. Tap Carrier and choose the network you want to use. You may incur Roaming Charges when you use a different network.

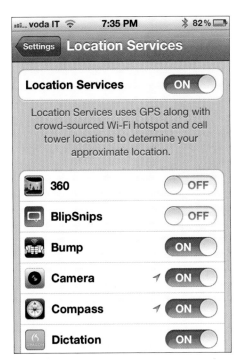

Figure 4-18: Location Services helps your iPhone find its way — and yours.

Sounds

By default, your iPhone is set to vibrate when the Ring/Silent switch is set to Silent, as shown in Figure 4-19. Turn the feature off if you'd rather not feel a tiny tremor every time someone reaches out and touches you when you're iPhone is in Silent mode.

Dragging the volume slider left or right to decrease or increase ringtone and alert message sounds has the same effect as pressing your iPhone's actual volume buttons up or down. Turn off Change with Buttons if you don't want your iPhone's physical buttons (or, if plugged in, headset volume buttons) to change ringtone and alert volume levels. (The volume buttons will still let you increase or decrease the volume level of other sound-related output, such as music you're listening to, videos you're watching, and games you're playing as well as the voice of anyone you're speaking with on the phone.)

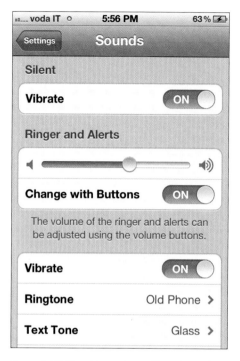

Figure 4-19: Checking out your Sounds settings options.

Tap the other sound settings options to turn them on or off, or to change choices such as the ringtone or text alert sounds you hear when someone calls or sends you a message, and whether you want to hear a typing sound effect for every key you tap when you're using the onscreen keyboard.

Brightness

Drag the slider left or right to decrease or increase your iPhone's screen brightness. Turn Auto-Brightness on if you want your iPhone to automatically (and only slightly) increase or decrease your iPhone's brightness level based on your environment.

Wallpaper

Wallpaper is the term used to describe the screen you see when your iPhone is locked, and the background image displayed behind app icons on the home screen. You can choose the same image for both wallpaper choices, or you can choose a unique image for each choice, as shown in Figure 4-20.

Figure 4-20: Wallpaper choices you can live with.

Tap Wallpaper, and then tap the big double-thumbnails button showing your current wallpaper choice to display the locations you can choose to pick your new wallpaper. Tap one of the categories to see the images stored in that category. Wallpaper contains pretty pictures that came preloaded on your iPhone. Camera Roll is where you find any snapshots you captured using Camera, or any images you may have saved from web pages, e-mail, or text messages. Photo Library holds photos and images you may have copied from your computer using iTunes. (See Book V, Chapter 1.)

Tap an image to preview what your choice will look like as a wallpaper image, and then move or zoom the image in or out to adjust the image to your liking. Tap Cancel if you don't want to use the image and return to your choices. Or tap Set to choose the image, and then tap Set Lock Screen, Set Home Screen, or Set Both to set the image as your wallpaper of choice for either or both screens, as shown in Figure 4-21.

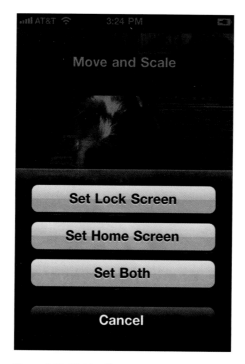

Figure 4-21: Picking the one or two screens to display your wallpaper.

General

The General setting shown in Figure 4-22 is actually a catch-all for more than a dozen individual settings — most of which we write about in greater detail in the chapters where those settings are called into play. The following list points you in the right direction for the settings that are fully explained in other chapters and provides details for settings you won't find explained elsewhere in this book:

✓ **About:** Lists detailed information about your iPhone that includes serial number, phone carrier, hardware model and software versions, the number of songs, photos, videos, and applications, the total amount of memory space storing all of those things is gobbling up (and how much memory space remains), a bunch of interesting-looking regulatory logos and glyph-like symbols that are sort of like virtual passport stamps, and page after page of tiny legal gobblygook describing a panic-inducing laundry list of permissions, rules, regulations, warnings, disclaimers, and outright threats that, were you to actually read all of it, would probably scare you so badly you'd wind up ditching your phone contract, selling or giving away your iPhone, and switching to tribal bongos or tin cans connected by a single length of string as your preferred mode of communicating with the rest of the world.

✔ **Software Update:** If a new version of the operating system, also known as iOS, is available, tapping this button downloads and installs it to your iPhone. Make sure your iPhone is connected to a power source while installing.

✔ **Usage:** Lists how much storage each app on your iPhone uses and how much overall storage remains. If you activated iCloud, you see the total and available storage amounts. Discloses how long you've used your iPhone since its last full charge. Tapping the Cellular button at the bottom of the screen opens another screen that shows the number of days and hours you spent on your iPhone during that period and during the total span of your relationship with your iPhone, the amount of data you've shuttled back and forth over your cellular carrier's network, and a button to reset the aforementioned stats so you can start tracking those figures. The most useful button is, perhaps, the Battery Percentage setting. When you turn this setting on, it pins an estimated-percentage-remaining figure alongside your iPhone's pretty vague battery charge level indicator.

▁▃▅ 📶	**2:48 PM**		🔋
◀ Settings	**General**		
About			>
Software Update			>
Usage			>
Siri			>
Network			>
Bluetooth		Off	>
iTunes Wi-Fi Sync			>
Spotlight Search			>

Figure 4-22: Speaking of General settings.

✓ **Siri (Only on iPhone 4S):** Choose how you interact with Siri. Choose the language you use to speak to Siri. Select Handsfree Only if you want Siri to respond audibly only when you're using earphones or a headset (Siri will still do things for you, but will respond only with written responses.) Specify which card in Contacts contains your information, such as your home and work address and the relationships you have with others in Contacts, which Siri uses to do what you ask. Turning Raise to Speak On activates Siri when your iPhone screen is on and you put it to your ear. See Book I, Chapter 3.

✓ **Network:** Your one-stop wireless and networking control central for activating, deactivating and configuring iPhone's 3G, cellular data, data roaming, VPN and Wi-Fi connections. The Personal Hotspot settings here are the same as on the first Settings screen. See Book I, Chapter 2.

✓ **Bluetooth:** Used for turning Bluetooth on or off, and for pairing and unpairing iPhone with wireless Bluetooth-enabled gadgets like a wireless keyboard, headphones or hands-free headsets for easier music listening and phone call juggling, minus tangled wires. See Book 1, Chapter 2.

✓ **iTunes Wi-Fi Sync:** To sync your iPhone with iTunes without using the USB connector cable, tap Wi-Fi Sync and then tap Sync Now. See Book II, Chapter 1.

✓ **Spotlight Search:** For choosing which apps (and app contents) Spotlight searches, and the order in which they will be searched. See Book 1, Chapter 3.

✓ **Auto Lock, Passcode Lock, and Restrictions:** We cover these in the next section, but in a nutshell, you use this trio of settings for choosing the length of time your iPhone waits before automatically locking the screen, for creating a secret passcode that must be keyed in to unlock your iPhone, and for activating and managing a slew of options for blocking (we mean, ahem, restricting) functions with a password.

✓ **Date & Time:** See Book IV, Chapter 2.

✓ **Keyboard and International:** See Book I, Chapter 3.

✓ **Accessibility:** See Book I, Chapter 2.

✓ **Reset:** See Book 1, Chapter 5.

Other Apple and third-party app settings

After the General button, you see a long list of other apps. Those grouped with General are the apps that came with your iPhone, such as iCloud, Phone, Music, Notes, and so on. The group that follows comprises Apple and third-party apps that you downloaded (the oddity here is that Nike + iPod is in this group even though it came with your iPhone). Some apps have settings in Settings; some have settings within the app itself. There's no set rule so you have to poke around when you download a new app — or read the app's instructions either on your iPhone or on the app's website.

Activating iPhone's Security Features

This section is all about taking advantage of your iPhone's security and privacy options to ensure your personal data stays that way — personal, for your eyes only, or for others you may choose to share your iPhone with. To access the settings that follow, tap Settings, and then tap General.

Auto Lock

Locking your iPhone's screen helps conserve power, and prevents against unintentional screen taps, like when you're toting your iPhone in your pocket.

Choose the amount of time you want your iPhone to wait before it automatically locks the screen. Your choices range from one to five minutes, or you can choose Never, which means it's up to you to remember to press the Sleep/Wake button to lock your iPhone.

Even when locked, your iPhone can still receive calls, text messages, and inbound communications, and you can still listen to music or other audio.

Passcode Lock

Requiring a passcode to unlock your iPhone can help prevent others from viewing your personal data or making calls on your dime. Tap Turn Passcode On, type in a four-digit passcode, and then type in the code a second time to verify your code. You can change your secret code anytime by tapping Change Passcode, entering your old passcode then entering a new passcode. Turn Simple Passcode Off to use a more complicated passcode, such as an alpha-numeric combination.

Tap Require Passcode and then tap Immediately if you want your iPhone to require your passcode whenever you unlock it. Or choose one of the timeout options if you want your iPhone to require your code after the chosen amount of time has passed.

Turn on the Voice Dial option if you want to allow your iPhone to respond to your voice using Voice Control even when it's locked.

To protect your personal information in the event your iPhone falls into the wrong hands, turn on the Erase Data option if you want your iPhone to erase everything stored on it if the correct passcode isn't entered after ten tries.

On GSM model iPhones, you can activate and change a PIN (personal identification number) to lock your iPhone's SIM card. When activated, you must type in the PIN code whenever you turn iPhone off then on again. But unlike the Passcode Lock feature, which generously offers up to ten tries in the game of Guess Your Secret Code, the SIM Pin lock feature is less forgiving —

after three failed attempts to crack the SIM code, unlocking the SIM pin may then require a unique Personal Unlocking Key (PUK) code to unlock your iPhone (which rightful owners may obtain by contacting their cellular carrier's customer service department).

Restrictions

If you share your iPhone with another person (or you're a parent or guardian who holds the keys to iPhone's kingdom), you can allow or restrict access to apps and features, or block access to content, such as songs containing explicit lyrics, or movies or TV shows based on their MPA rating.

To activate and adjust iPhone's restriction settings, tap the Enable Restrictions button shown in Figure 4-23, and then type in a secret four-digit code, and then type in the code a second time to verify your code. Tap the apps and features you want to turn off or on. App icons for any apps you restrict disappear from iPhone's Home screen.

Figure 4-23: Pick and choose apps and features you want to block access to.

Though you'd think turning off access to a certain app such as Safari, for instance, totally blocks your iPhone from accessing web pages, that isn't one-hundred percent true. A few caveats to keep in mind when restricting access to the following apps include

✓ **Safari:** Although the app icon disappears from the Home screen and browsing the web with Safari is therefore disabled, certain apps you may have installed on your iPhone may *still* access the web using their own web browser features. For instance, tapping a web page link that appears in the Facebook, Twitter, or Google apps opens those apps' built-in web browsers to display the content of a web page link. You can also use a different general purpose browser instead of Safari.

✓ **YouTube:** The app icon disappears; however, YouTube can still be accessed using Safari — and as we explain in the previous bullet point, turning off Safari doesn't prevent other apps you may have installed on your iPhone from accessing YouTube videos.

Taking Steps if Your iPhone Is Lost or Stolen

Your worst iPhone nightmare: Your beloved iPhone is lost or stolen. Don't panic — even though your iPhone may be gone for good (er, bad), all may not be totally lost. We're speaking of course of the personal data stored on your iPhone, which may be more valuable than your iPhone itself.

On this very personal matter, we have potentially good news, possibly great news, and maybe even fabulous news. First the potentially good news: If you turned on the Passcode Lock feature described in the previous section, who-ever found or "borrowed" your iPhone must type in your secret passcode before they can even unlock your iPhone and start snooping around.

Second, the possibly great news: If, in addition to turning on the Passcode Lock feature, you also turned on the Erase Data option, your iPhone devel-ops a sudden case of permanent amnesia and erases everything stored on it if, after the tenth try, the interloper fails to guess your secret code.

And finally, what may be the best-case-scenario news of all: Before unexpect-edly parting ways, hopefully you configured the Find My iPhone feature we explain here.

To use Find My iPhone, you must have an iCloud account, and then turn on the Find My iPhone option in Settings⊅iCloud, as seen in Figure 4-24.

Figure 4-24: The Find My iPhone setting.

With Find My iPhone activated, you may be able to track down your iPhone's general location on a map using a web browser on your computer or other web-savvy gadget, or by using the Find My iPhone app installed on another person's iPhone, iPad, or iPod touch, which in turn may jog your memory as to where you may have lost or misplaced your iPhone (like between the sofa cushions in the den, or your gym locker).

What's more, you can command your iPhone to play a loud bleating sound to help guide you (or anyone nearby) to wherever it's hiding. You can lock your iPhone with a secret passcode you create on the fly in the event your iPhone wasn't already protected using the Passcode Lock feature before it vanished. And you can send a text message appealing to anyone who may have found or "borrowed" your iPhone to contact you at another number you provide, so you can make arrangements to retrieve what's rightly yours. (Offering a cash reward may further entice would-be do-gooders to do the right thing.)

And finally, if you still can't find your iPhone or your plea goes unheeded, you can issue a "self-destruct" command that instructs your iPhone to erase everything stored on it. That way, you lose only your iPhone — which you can replace — but not your personal data and identity information.

To track down a missing iPhone, tap the Find My iPhone app on a friend's iPhone (or iPad or iPod touch), or visit www.icloud.com with your computer's web browser, and then log in using your iCloud user name and password. A map appears and shows your iPhone's current location, give or take a few — or a few hundred — feet, depending on the service's ability to accurately home in on your missing iPhone. Clicking the > button displays more information and options, also shown in Figure 4-25.

Figure 4-25: Locating your iPhone (left) and weighing your options (right).

Choosing the Remote Lock option is a good first measure in case your iPhone isn't already locked. Next, tap Display Message or Play Sound in the hopes of getting the attention of whoever may have found, or is in the vicinity of, your missing iPhone.

If repeated attempts to reach out and touch someone who may be in possession of your iPhone go unanswered, your last-gasp option is to click the Wipe button to completely erase everything stored on your iPhone.

If you wish to remove an iPhone, iPod touch, or iPad from your account, in the event that you've sold or gifted your device, make sure the device is turned off and use Find My iPhone. It will fail to find the device. Click the X next to your iPhone in the list of devices and a dialog appears, giving you the option of removing the device from your account. (Refer to Figure 4-26.)

The Remove option won't appear if Find My iPhone does in fact find your former iPhone and display its whereabouts. In that case, you'll need to kindly ask the new owner to temporarily turn off iPhone or switch it to Airplane Mode so that the Remove option appears, allowing you to do just that. If you're the type of person who likes pranks, before removing iPhone from your account, you could have a little "fun" with the new owner, by sending a message like the one shown in Figure 4-27.

Mind you, that's not the sort of thing we would do — because we would ask for "One hundred billllllllion dollars!"

Figure 4-26: Use the Remove option to delete an iPhone you purposely got rid of.

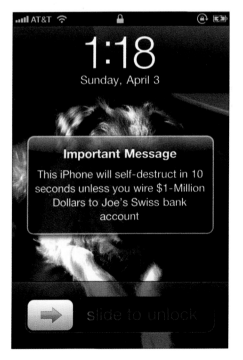

Figure 4-27: Having a little fun with Find My iPhone.

Chapter 5: Anticipating and Tackling iPhone Troubles

In This Chapter

☞ **Keeping the battery charged**

☞ **Avoiding common iPhone problems**

☞ **Troubleshooting Q&A**

*Y*ou might think that near the beginning of a book is a strange place for the troubleshooting chapter. We decided to do things a little differently.

Often, when something goes awry, you panic — it's human nature. No one likes a glitch, or feeling unprepared or stupid. That's why we put this chapter up front. You can skim through the topics so if one of the problems we mention occurs, you won't be surprised or panicked. You'll know where to look to resolve the problem calmly and quickly.

We include some information here to help you avoid problems, along with the traditional troubleshooting question-and-answer format. In each chapter, we include some warnings of things that could happen and tips for how to resolve problems specific to the chapter at hand.

.ery Percentage — ON

Time since last full charge

Usage	4 Hours, 3 Mi
Standby	23 Hours, 24 Mi

'all Time

ᵔeriod   57

Keeping the Battery Charged

When you connect your iPhone to a power source, it charges in record time. Even if you have zero charge, in about an hour, you're up and running at 100 percent. Technically, you should get between 8 and 14 hours of talk time on an iPhone 4S. The lower number reflects use on a 3G network, the higher number on the older EDGE network. Realistically, if you play games and go on the Internet, you probably get less. Here are some tips for keeping the battery charged longer and for maintaining long battery life.

To preserve the overall life, you should cycle the battery on a monthly basis. *Cycling* is letting the battery completely discharge and then charging it fully.

Big battery consumers

The biggest battery consumer on your iPhone depends on how you use your phone. An iPhone action that quickly drains the battery is when your iPhone searches for something it can't find, such as a Wi-Fi or cellular network or when information is being continually pushed from the cloud. Keep these tips in mind for a longer battery charge:

- ✓ **Turn Off Wi-Fi:** If you have Wi-Fi turned on and there's no Wi-Fi network, your iPhone keeps searching and searching and consuming battery power. To turn off Wi-Fi, tap Settings➪Wi-Fi➪Off.

- ✓ **Turn Off 3G:** If 3G isn't available where you are or you don't need to access the 3G network, turn it off. Sometimes this actually improves access to your cellular calling network. It doubles your battery charge. Tap Settings➪General➪Network➪Enable 3G Off.

- ✓ **Turn On Airplane Mode:** If you happen to be out of your network range, say hiking in a remote area, your iPhone consumes a lot of battery power as it continually searches for the cellular network. Eventually the words *No Service* appear instead of the carrier name and your iPhone settles down and stops searching. Consider putting your iPhone in Airplane mode: Tap Settings➪Airplane Mode On.

- ✓ **Use Fetch Instead of Push:** Rather than having your iPhone constantly check for new information with Push, you can set your iPhone to sync with whichever cloud service you use, such as iCloud, Yahoo! Mail, or MS-Exchange, at set time intervals, or sync manually. Tap Settings➪Mail, Contacts, Calendars➪Fetch New Data➪Push Off.

- ✓ **Use Auto-Brightness:** Dimming your screen also improves the length of a charge. The ambient light sensor dims or brightens your screen based on the light it senses. You can turn the automatic adjustment on by going to Settings➪Brightness➪Turn Auto-Brightness On.

Gaming, watching videos, and surfing the web use big chunks of memory. Playing a game helps pass the time on a long trip, but make sure you leave enough battery power to call your ride when you arrive at your destination, or that there's a power source into which to plug your iPhone.

Lesser battery consumers

You can turn off some apps to improve the length of time your battery stays charged. These features consume the battery only when they're being used, but sometimes a little extra charge makes all the difference. For example, Location Services isn't using GPS to constantly look for your location; it only kicks in when an app requests it. These are like leaving a nightlight on during the day. It consumes a little bit, perhaps unnecessarily:

✔ **Bluetooth:** Tap Settings⟐General⟐Bluetooth⟐Off if you don't have any Bluetooth devices connected.

✔ **Cellular Data:** Tap Settings⟐General⟐Network⟐Cellular Data Off. You can still use the phone and Wi-Fi connection.

✔ **GPS:** Tap Settings⟐Location Services Off. As long as your iPhone doesn't need to track your location, this can be turned off.

✔ **Phone:** Yes, your phone. Tap Settings⟐Airplane Mode On. Both cellular and Wi-Fi are turned off, saving a heap of battery juice.

When charging your iPhone with the USB cable connected to a computer, make sure it's really charging — you see a lightning bolt in the battery icon on the status bar — if your computer is turned off or sleeping, it could drain your iPhone battery instead of charging it.

Tracking battery usage

Tap Settings⟐General⟐Usage to see how much time you used your iPhone since the last charge, as shown in Figure 5-1. Usage is how much you've used it. Standby is how much time your iPhone spent sleeping.

▫▫▫▫ voda IT 🛜	12:06 PM	92% 🔋
◀ General	**Usage**	

iCloud

Total Storage	25.0 GB
Available	24.6 GB
Manage Storage	❯

Battery Usage

Battery Percentage	ON ⬤

Time since last full charge

Usage	28 Minutes
Standby	15 Hours, 19 Minutes

Figure 5-1: Usage shows how much you've used your iPhone since the last charge.

Changing the battery

If you keep your iPhone for many years, sooner or later, you'll need to replace the battery. Despite our DIY (do-it-yourself) world, you can't replace the battery yourself. You have to send it through the Battery Replacement Program. For $85 (at the time of publication), you send your iPhone to Apple or take it to an Apple store, the battery is replaced, and Apple takes care of disposing of the old one. This service is covered if your iPhone is still under the one year warranty or you extended the warranty to two years with the AppleCare protection plan, which we explain in the last section of this chapter, "Getting Repairs If You Need Them."

Avoiding Common iPhone Problems

With iCloud syncing, your version of iOS should always be current. Your apps need to be kept current, too. Keep your eye out for a badge on the App Store icon on the Home screen, which lets you know that one or more of your apps have updates available.

Make sure the SIM card is properly installed. If you dropped your iPhone, the SIM card may be slightly dislodged. Carefully insert the SIM Eject Tool, which came with your iPhone, or the end of a paper clip, in the hole of the SIM tray to open the tray. Take out the SIM card and re-insert it and then gently push the tray closed.

Here are a few other things to consider if you have a problem:

The headset is plugged in but you can't hear anything.

Make sure the headset is plugged in all the way — it makes a little "click" when it is. It may not be compatible with the cover or bumper (those colored frames that go around iPhone's outer edge) you use, that is; it doesn't go all the way into the hole. Although 1/8-inch plugs work most of the time, the specifications call for a 3.5 mm plug.

The words *No Service* appear where your carrier's name usually appears.

First, make sure you aren't in Airplane Mode. Then, try turning 3G on or off. Lastly, try turning your iPhone off and on again. Try moving closer to a window or going outside. If you have a weak signal, turning 3G on can bring a stronger signal. If you're in a crowded area with lots of other cell phone users, turning 3G off gives you access to a larger network.

You don't have Internet access.

Assuming you have data service as part of your cellular contract, make sure you have a cellular data signal or are in a Wi-Fi zone. You see the icons in the status bar (see Book I, Chapter 2). Without one of these options, you can't get online. Try these tactics to solve the problem:

- Disconnect and reconnect to the network. Tap Settings⇨Wi-Fi Off. Wait a minute, and then tap Wi-Fi On.

- Try renewing the Dynamic Host Control Protocol (DHCP) lease, which is the access point that allows your iPhone to access a Wi-Fi network. Tap Settings⇨Wi-Fi. Tap the blue and white arrow to the right of the connected Wi-Fi network, and then tap the DHCP tab. Scroll down the screen and tap the Renew Lease button.

- Reset network settings by tapping Settings⇨General, and then scroll down to Reset, which is the last button on the screen. Tap Reset Network Settings.

- Look for interference from devices like walkie-talkies or baby monitors.

- If you know Wi-Fi should be available because, say, you're home, and none of these procedures work, the problem could be with the Wi-Fi router, modem, or incoming DSL line.

✔ **You can't send text messages.**

For SMS and MMS messages, make sure you have cellular service. iMessages require a Wi-Fi or cellular data connection. Check that the recipient's phone number has an area code and that you typed your message in the message field and not the subject line. Refer to Book III, Chapter 2 to find out more about text messaging.

✔ **You can't receive or send e-mail.**

Make sure you have an Internet connection, either through your cellular data network or Wi-Fi.

Try re-entering your password. Tap Settings⇨Mail, Contacts, Calendars⇨Account Name⇨Account. Delete and retype the password. See Book III, Chapter 4 for information about the Mail app.

✔ **Syncing doesn't seem to work.**

If you use iTunes, make sure the USB connector cable is properly inserted in both your computer and your iPhone. If you sync wirelessly with iTunes, make sure your iPhone and computer are on the same wireless network. If you use iCloud, make sure you are signed in: Tap Settings⇨ iCloud⇨Account and enter your Apple ID and password. Refer to Book II, Chapter 1 for full details on syncing.

Troubleshooting Q&A

Here are some of the most common difficulties you may encounter with your iPhone and how to handle them:

Q: An app is frozen on my screen. Nothing closes it, the Home button doesn't work — it just sits there.

A: Force-quit the app. Hold down the Sleep/Wake switch until the Slide to Power Off message appears, and then hold the Home button until the frozen program quits and you return to the Home screen. The app should be fine the next time you open it.

Q: Um, force-quitting the app didn't work.

A: Force-restart your iPhone. Hold down the Home button and the Sleep/Wake switch simultaneously for about 10 seconds. Release when you see the Apple logo, which means your iPhone is restarting.

Q: My iPhone won't turn on.

A: Probably the battery needs to be charged. Connect your iPhone to the USB connector cable and power adapter and begin charging. It takes about ten minutes for a completely dead battery to have enough charge to show signs of life. A lightning bolt appears on the screen, followed by the Apple logo, and you can turn your iPhone on at that point.

If you lock your iPhone in the car with the windows closed on a 100 degree day, you risk overheating your iPhone. Likewise, leaving it out in the cold can send your iPhone into hypothermia. Signs of iPhone heat stroke, or frostbite, are a dimmed screen, weak cellular signal, and in the case of heat stroke, a temperature warning screen as your iPhone tries to cool itself. You cannot use your iPhone — except for an emergency call — when the temperature warning screen is visible. If your iPhone can't cool or warm itself, it goes into a deep sleep, a sort of iPhone coma, until it cools or warms. Put your iPhone in a cooler or warmer location. It will wake up once its internal temperature returns to normal.

Q: The same app or apps keep giving me trouble.

A: Try removing and reinstalling the troublesome app or apps. See Book I, Chapter 3 to learn about removing and installing apps. Connect your iPhone to your computer and open iTunes. Turn off the app you want to remove and sync. Turn it on in iTunes and sync again.

Q: Nope, didn't work.

A: Try resetting your iPhone settings. Tap Settings⟳General⟳Reset⟳Reset All Settings. This takes your settings back to how they were when you took your iPhone out of the box. It doesn't remove any data, but you do have to redo any settings you had altered.

Q: I'm still having problems.

A: Tap Erase All Content and Settings. This does just what it says. This resets all settings and erases all your information and media by removing the encryption key to the data (which is encrypted using 256-bit AES encryption). Make sure you sync and back up before so you can re-sync after.

Q: Nothing seems to work.

A: Restore your phone. Restore erases your iPhone and returns it to the state it was in out of the box, but better than new because the latest iOS version will be installed. All contacts, photos, music, television shows, calendars, e-mails, notes, bookmarks, and third-party apps are deleted. This sounds like a drastic measure, and in a way it is, but it's not as bad as it seems. If you use iCloud to back up, you can restore from your iCloud account. If you use iTunes, try to sync with iTunes before restoring your iPhone. Even if you can't sync, your most recent backup is stored on iTunes on your computer. See Book II, Chapter 1 to learn about backing up with iCloud and iTunes.

Q: iTunes doesn't recognize my iPhone.

A: Do a Device Firmware Upgrade (DFU). DFU wipes out the old OS (but not your content) and installs a new one. You can then sync and restore as explained previously. The DFU procedure is

1. Turn off your iPhone.

2. Connect your iPhone to your computer.

3. Open iTunes.

4. Press and hold the Sleep/Wake and Home buttons for exactly ten seconds.

5. After ten seconds, release the Sleep/Wake button, but continue to hold the Home button for another ten seconds.

6. After ten seconds, release the Home button. iTunes now recognizes your iPhone.

7. Click OK. iTunes asks you to confirm.

8. Click Restore and Update.

Getting More Help

If you have a problem we didn't talk about or none of the previously discussed tactics work, you can still find more help on the Internet. Your first stop should be Apple's iPhone Support page at `www.apple.com/support/iphone`. You can contact Apple's technical support group for personalized attention.

You can also search the discussion forums, as shown in Figure 5-2, where questions and answers are submitted by other iPhone users. Type in a few words that describe your problem and peruse the discussions. If you don't find a discussion pertinent to your problem, you can submit your question and usually an answer from another user is available within a day.

If you still don't find a satisfying answer, type a few key words about your problem in to one of the Internet search engines like Google (www.google.com) or Yahoo! (www.yahoo.com).

Wherever you search, you may be surprised to find that you aren't the first person to have the problem you're having.

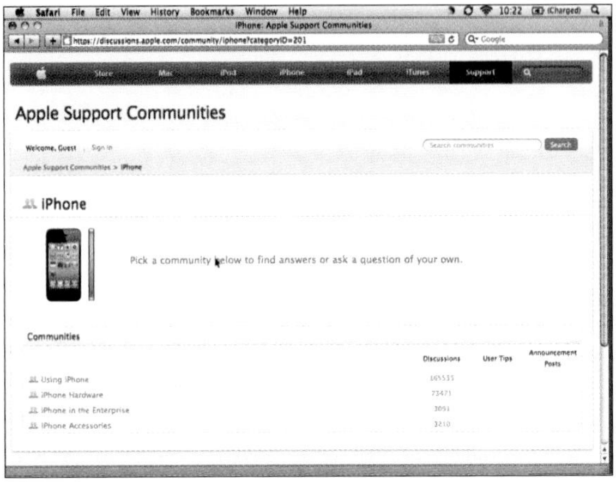

Figure 5-2: iPhone users exchange questions and answers on the discussion forums at the Apple website.

Getting Repairs if You Need Them

We are always impressed with the seriousness and efficiency of Apple's warranty and repair service. Your iPhone includes a one-year warranty and you can get a second year of coverage if you buy AppleCare. If anything (that's not your fault) goes wrong with your iPhone, call Apple or take it to an Apple Store. If you can, back everything up before you leave your iPhone with Apple so you can re-sync on the repaired iPhone. A couple years ago, the Silent/Ring button fell off Barbara's iPhone 3G. Apple sent a shipping pack the next day and a replacement phone showed up two days later.

If you can't be without a cellular phone for two or three days, the Apple Store offers what's called the Express Replacement Service (ERS). If your iPhone is covered under AppleCare, ERS is included. If your iPhone is not covered, you have to pay a fee that's somewhere between the value of your broken phone and the value of a replacement phone. Apple gives you a replacement iPhone, or sends one if you call instead of going to the Apple Store. You just have to insert your SIM card and sync what was on your broken iPhone to the replacement iPhone.

Book II

Stocking iPhone with iTunes Apps and Add-ons

The 5th Wave — By Rich Tennant

"Hold on Barbara. I'm pretty sure there's an app for this."

You could think of this minibook as the iPhone accessory book. The first chapter in this minibook explains how to move your data from your computer to your iPhone. If you're curious about iCloud, Apple's wireless syncing and storage offer, read Chapter 1. The second chapter introduces you to apps — short for applications — and the App Store. Here we show you how to find and install third-party apps on your iPhone. The last chapter presents some pretty nifty hardware accessories — things like bumpers, cases, and speakers.

Chapter 1: Syncing, Backing Up, and Updating Your iPhone

In This Chapter

✓ **Creating an Apple ID**

✓ **Understanding the syncing relationship**

✓ **Syncing with iTunes**

✓ **Syncing with iCloud**

✓ **Backing up your iPhone**

✓ **Updating apps on iTunes and iPhone**

✓ **Upgrading iPhone and iTunes software**

The information in this chapter is essential to using your iPhone. Of all the chapters in this book, perhaps this one is the most important. We explain the theory behind syncing, and then go through, step-by-step, how to sync the data between your iPhone and your computer using iTunes and/or iCloud. We outline how to back up everything on your iPhone and then use the backup should you lose everything on your iPhone. Lastly, we give you the steps you need to keep iTunes, iPhone, and your apps up-to-date with the latest versions.

Creating an Apple ID

You need an Apple ID to do many tasks with your iPhone. Specifically, to download media and apps from iTunes and the App Store, and to use iCloud, you must have an Apple ID. You are asked for your Apple ID when you download software updates. You may have set one up when your phone was activated at the Apple Store or the retailer where you bought your iPhone. If not, you can create an Apple ID from your computer or your iPhone by doing one of the following:

1. **On your computer, open iTunes.**

2. **Click Store⇨Create Account.**

3. **Follow the instructions on the successive screens to create your Apple ID.**

   You will be asked to choose the country where you reside, to accept Apple's terms and conditions, and then type in an e-mail address, which will be your Apple ID, and a password. You also specify a security question and answer, which is used to verify your identity if you forget your password.

If you don't have an e-mail address, or prefer to create an Apple e-mail address for your syncing and shopping tasks, use the following procedure:

1. **On your iPhone, tap Settings⊅Mail, Contacts, Calendars.**

2. **Tap the Add Account button.**

3. **Tap iCloud.**

4. **Tap Get a Free Apple ID.**

   The Create an Apple ID screen opens.

5. **Tap the Location field to select your location from the rotor that appears.**

6. **Tap the Month, Day, and Year fields to enter your birth date.**

7. **Tap the Next button in the upper right corner.**

   A second Create an Apple ID screen opens, as shown in Figure 1-1.

8. **Tap Use An Existing Email Address if you want to use an e-mail address you already have.**

   Or

   Tap Get a Free @me.com E-mail Address, to create an e-mail address that will be your Apple ID and create an iCloud account that has e-mail, contact, and calendar services associated with it. (See Book III, Chapter 4 and Book IV, Chapters 1 and 2, respectively.)

9. **Tap in the E-mail field to type in the e-mail address you would like to use, either an existing e-mail or one you create with @me.com.**

10. **Tap in the subsequent fields to type in your First Name, Last Name, Password, and security question.**

    Your password must be at least eight characters containing one uppercase letter, one lowercase letter, and one number.

    This is your Apple ID password and must meet these requirements. Even if you use an existing e-mail address, the Apple ID password may be different than the password you use with the existing e-mail address to access your e-mail account.

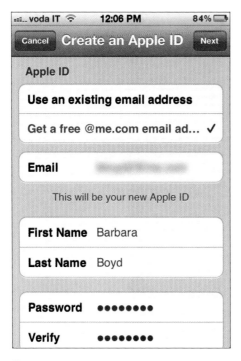

Figure 1-1: Fill in the fields to create an Apple ID.

11. **Tap the Next button.**

    If your chosen e-mail is already in use by another person, a suggestion appears in the E-mail field. Likewise, if your password doesn't meet the password requirements, you are asked to create a different one.

12. **The Welcome to iCloud screen appears.**

    Scroll to the bottom and tap the Agree button. A dialog appears asking if you agree to the terms and conditions. Tap Agree.

13. **The iCloud screen opens.**

14. **Tap Save.**

    The new iCloud e-mail account is added to your Mail accounts. (See Book III, Chapter 4 to learn about using Mail.)

15. **Make note of your @me.com e-mail address and keep your password in a safe place.**

16. **Press the Home button to return to the Home screen.**

Understanding the Syncing Relationship

Syncing, or synchronizing, is keeping the data on two or more devices — your iPhone and your computer and other iOS5 devices such as an iPad or iPod touch — up-to-date and mirrored on either device. You begin using your iPhone by connecting it to your computer and opening iTunes, or you can use iCloud to backup and sync the data on your iPhone with other iOS 5 devices and computers. We give you the details for doing both so you can choose between iTunes and iCloud or use a combination of the two for all your backing up and syncing needs.

Syncing with iTunes

You can use iTunes to copy data from your computer to your iPhone. This data may include contacts, calendars, and e-mail accounts, and media such as songs, videos, and photos. After that initial connection and exchange of information, you use iTunes to keep the data on both devices in sync. You can set up a daily wireless sync, which is called iTunes Wi-Fi Sync, or you can physically connect your iPhone to your computer with the USB connector cable and run the iTunes Sync feature. Although Wi-Fi Sync is more convenient, it is slower than syncing with the USB connector cable.

When you sync your iPhone with iTunes, iTunes evaluates and compares the data on both devices. If two pieces of data are different — for example, say iTunes discovers two different home phone numbers for the same contact — iTunes replaces the older data, (the phone number, in our example) with the more recent one.

You can also choose to sync only some kinds of your data and media but not other kinds, instead of syncing everything. What's more, any music, videos, podcasts, or apps that you download or purchase (rentals follow slightly different rules, see the following bullet on media from your iTunes Library) on iTunes via your computer or iPhone are transferred to the other device when you perform a sync. iTunes syncs the following types of data:

- **Apps:** Downloaded onto either your computer or iPhone.
- **Calendars:** Appointments and events on both your computer and your iPhone.
- **Contacts:** Names, addresses, phone numbers, e-mail addresses, and information from other fields you may use on the compatible contact management program on your computer and in Contacts on iPhone.
- **E-mail:** The account settings, but not the messages. This data only goes from your computer to your iPhone. Accounts set up on your iPhone will not be synced with your computer.

✓ **Media from your iTunes library:** Music and music videos, podcasts, iTunes U lectures, books and audio books, movies, TV shows, photos, and videos. Movies rented on your computer can sync to your iPhone, but movies rented on your iPhone cannot sync to your computer.

✓ **Notes:** From applications on your computer and Notes on your iPhone.

✓ **Web page bookmarks:** From the browser you use on your computer (Internet Explorer or Safari for Windows, or Safari for Mac).

The first sync with iTunes

Now, you're ready to connect your iPhone to your computer and iTunes. Even if you plan to use iTunes Wi-Fi Sync, you must connect your iPhone to your computer one time. The first time you connect your iPhone to your computer, iTunes opens and gives you a chance to name your iPhone and perform your first automatic sync. In this section, we go through those initial operations and then explain how to manually sync by going through the syncing options one by one. We then look at establishing the criteria for future syncing operations.

To begin, follow these steps:

Book II
Chapter 1

1. **Connect your iPhone to your computer with the USB connector cable, using a port that is on your computer rather than one on the keyboard or hub (unless you have a powered hub).**

   iTunes opens. If iTunes doesn't open, open it manually.

2. **Select your iPhone in the source list to the left of the iTunes window, as shown in Figure 1-2.**

   The Setup Your iPhone pane opens.

   If you don't see your iPhone in the list, make sure the USB connector cable is firmly seated in both your iPhone and computer ports and that your iPhone is turned on.

   If you still don't see iPhone in the list, choose iTunes⟳Preferences on a Mac or Edit⟳Preferences in Windows. Click the Devices icon at the top of the window that opens. Deselect the box next to Prevent iPods, iPhones, and iPads from Syncing Automatically. Click OK to activate the new setting.

3. **Click in the Name field and type in the name you want to give your iPhone.**

   Don't worry: You can change the name of your iPhone later if you like. We'll show you how.

Your iPhone name appears here

Figure 1-2: When you connect your iPhone to your computer and open iTunes, the name of your iPhone appears in the Source list on the left side of the iTunes window.

4. Check the box next to Automatically Sync Contacts, Calendars, Bookmarks, Notes, and E-mail Accounts.

Data from those types of programs on your computer are copied onto your iPhone into the corresponding apps, Contacts, Calendar, and Notes. Bookmarks from your web browser are copied to Safari on your iPhone and the account information for any e-mail accounts on your computer is copied into Mail on your iPhone. The messages themselves aren't copied.

If you don't want to automatically sync even one of these apps, (bookmarks, for instance), uncheck the box and proceed with a manual sync, as explained next.

5. Select the check box next to Automatically Sync Applications.

Any iPhone apps you've downloaded to iTunes are added to your iPhone.

Again, if you don't want to automatically sync apps, uncheck the box and proceed with a manual sync.

6. Click Done.

On your iPhone, you see Sync in Progress at the top and a slider bar at the bottom labeled Slide to Cancel. On the iTunes display at the top of the window, the message tells you it's syncing your iPhone and changes as it syncs each part: Contacts, Calendar, and so on. When the sync is complete, the iTunes message reads iPhone Sync Is Complete. OK to Disconnect.

iTunes review

You can use iTunes to manage much of the data and media you use on your iPhone. Here, we have a brief aside from iPhone to explain iTunes. (If you are already familiar with iTunes, you can skip ahead to the section, "Establishing iPhone's Relationship with iTunes.") We run through downloading and installing iTunes and cover the basics involved in adjusting iTunes' settings to suit your needs. To learn about downloading music, videos, podcasts, and more on iTunes, take a look at Book V, Chapter 3.

Downloading and installing (or updating) iTunes

If you don't have iTunes installed on your computer, you have to download and install it before connecting your iPhone. Go to www.apple.com/itunes/ and click the blue Download iTunes button on the upper right side of the window. iTunes comes in both Mac and Windows versions. Scroll down to the bottom of the page under the hardware and software requirements if the version you need doesn't open automatically. Click either the Get iTunes for Windows or Get iTunes for Macintosh link (although it's highly unlikely you would have a Mac without iTunes). When the version you need is active, click Download Now. The download begins automatically. Follow the on-screen instructions to install iTunes on your computer.

If you already have iTunes installed on your computer, make sure you are running the latest version by checking for software updates. Click iTunes⇨Check for Updates. If a newer version is available, run the update for that version, and then check again, until you receive the message, This Version of iTunes Is the Current Version.

The iTunes window

The iTunes window is divided into two main parts: the Source list, which goes down the left side, and the main center zone, which is where you see the things you've clicked on in the Source list. The Source list is divided into the following sections:

- **Library:** The Library shows subheads for the types of media you have — music, video, podcasts, and so on.

- **Store:** Click iTunes Store to open the store or click Purchased or Downloaded to see items you've purchased or are downloading.

- **Devices:** Devices displays the devices you have connected such as your iPhone or an iPod or a CD in your computer's drive.

- **Genius:** iTunes looks at your songs and puts together playlists for you.

- **Playlists:** Playlists are lists of songs that you compile yourself or have iTunes create for you based upon criteria you specify, mixing and matching songs as you like.

In the center of the toolbar that goes across the top of the window is a display that tells you what iTunes is doing while it's doing it. If you are syncing your iPhone, for example, Synchronizing iPhone is displayed. If a song is playing, the name and artist of the song are displayed above a progress bar that indicates how much has been played and how much remains to be played. If you click the progress bar, it changes to a waveform.

Notice that media, such as songs, videos, podcasts, and photos, are not included in this initial sync. We explain that next, along with how to adjust settings and perform a manual sync.

To rename your iPhone, double-click your iPhone in the Devices list. A text box appears around the name. Just type in the name you want to use and press Return or Enter. The name is saved on your iPhone. Anytime you connect this iPhone to another device, you'll see that name. You can also change your iPhone's name by tapping Settings⇨General⇨About and tapping Name. The Name screen opens with a keyboard that lets you type in a new name for your iPhone.

Your syncing options in iTunes

Say you didn't do an automatic sync as outlined in the previous steps, but only named your iPhone and clicked Done. In this section, we go through all the syncing options so you can pick and choose the ones that are right for you. When you have set up the options as you wish, you can click the Sync button (which will be an Apply button if you make changes) and your iPhone will have all the data and media you want it to.

Across the top of the iTunes window are ten tabs: Summary, Info, Apps, Music, Movies, TV Shows, Podcasts, iTunes U, Books, and Photos. We take a look at each of these in the following sections.

Summary

The Summary pane is divided into four sections, as you see in Figure 1-3. The first section, iPhone, tells you about your iPhone, the name and total storage capacity, the version of the operation system you're using, iPhone's serial number, and your iPhone's phone number.

The second section, Version, tells you if your iPhone is up-to-date and when iTunes will automatically check again for an update. The top button, Check for Update, gives you the option of checking for software updates before the date shown. If you know Apple has released an iPhone operating system software update, you can manually check and download that update by clicking this button.

The Restore button is used when you have problems with your iPhone or if you want to reset it to its original factory settings — say when you're giving or selling it to someone. All the contents are erased, and your iPhone wakes up restored as if it were fresh from the factory with the latest iOS.

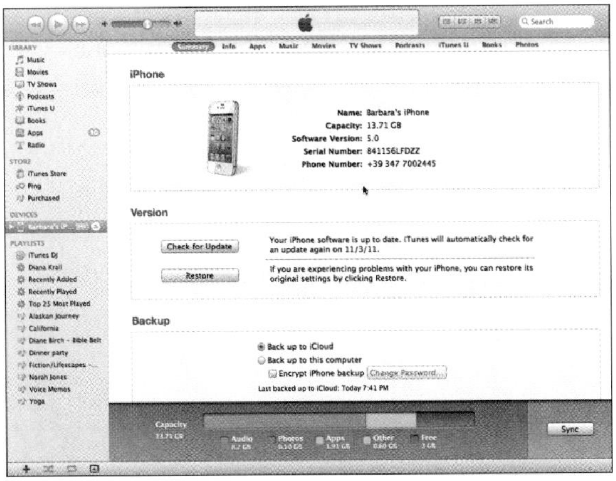

Figure 1-3: The Summary pane gives you information about your iPhone and options for working with iTunes.

The third section, Backup, displays checkboxes next to your backing up options, of which you have to choose one:

✔ **Back Up to iCloud:** Select this choice to use iCloud as your backup destination.

✔ **Back Up to This Computer:** Select this choice if you want to keep your iPhone backup on your computer. You have a subchoice of

✔ **Encrypt iPhone Backup:** Allows you to add a password to your iPhone backup file.

The fourth section, Options, gives you options for how your iPhone interacts with your computer:

✔ **Open iTunes When This iPhone Is Connected:** Automatically launches iTunes and begins syncing when you connect your iPhone to your computer with the USB connector cable. When this box is not checked, you sync manually by clicking the Sync button in the bottom right corner.

If the Prevent iPods, iPhones, and iPads from Syncing Automatically option in the Devices pane of iTunes Preferences (iTunes➪Preferences on a Mac; Edit➪Preferences on a PC) is checked, this option appears dimmed and unavailable.

✔ **Sync With This iPhone Over Wi-Fi:** Your iPhone syncs with iTunes once a day when both your computer and iPhone are connected to the same Wi-Fi network, and iTunes is open on your computer. Apple recommends that your iPhone is connected to a power source and we concur. Although you can sync without power, it significantly drains the battery.

✔ **Sync Only Checked Songs and Videos:** Only songs and videos that you manually check are synced. If you sync a playlist that contains unchecked songs and sync the playlist, the unchecked songs will not be included in the sync. This means going through your iTunes library and manually selecting or deselecting all the songs and videos you have stored on your computer.

✔ **Prefer Standard Definition Videos:** iTunes syncs standard definition instead of high definition videos.

✔ **Convert Higher Bit Rate Songs to 128 Kbps AAC:** iTunes automatically creates smaller audio files so you can squeeze more music onto your iPhone.

Songs purchased from the iTunes store are AAC (Advanced Audio Coding) files with a 256 Kbps bit rate. Converting to a 128 Kbps bit rate cuts them down to about half their size. In real terms, a four-minute song at 256 Kbps takes up almost 8 megabytes of memory; the same song at 128 Kbps is slightly more than 4 megabytes. Unless you have bionic ears or hook your iPhone to some super-duper speakers, you probably won't hear a difference, but you'll be able to store and listen to almost twice as many songs on your iPhone.

✔ **Manually Manage Music and Videos:** Everything else will be automatically synced, but you sync your music and videos manually. You click and drag the music and videos you want from iTunes (or even your computer desktop) to iPhone's icon in the Source list. They are copied to your iPhone. iTunes' Genius feature doesn't work if you manually manage music and video syncing.

The last item in the Options section is the Configure Universal Access button. Click this button to turn on the various Universal Access functions, such as VoiceOver and Speak Auto-Text. We explain Universal Access in Book I, Chapter 2 and also recommend you refer to Chapter 31 of iPhone's User Guide (manuals.info.apple.com/en_US/iphone_user_guide.pdf) for complete instructions on how to get the most out of the Accessibility features.

You can override the automatic syncing on an as-needed basis by launching iTunes before you connect your iPhone to your computer. Press and hold ⌘+Option (Mac) or Shift+Ctrl (PC) and connect your iPhone. Hold the keys until your iPhone appears in the iTunes source list. Your iPhone won't sync automatically, but the settings you previously established remain unchanged.

Info

From the Info pane, you configure the sync settings for your data; that is, contacts, calendars, e-mail accounts, and your web browser. If you use iCloud, Apple's OTA (over-the-air) syncing service, you'll see these options and can even select them, but you will also see a warning that you are syncing your iPhone with iCloud and syncing with iTunes as well may result in duplicates. You still use iTunes for media syncing, so you can skip down to the Music section. If you use Microsoft Outlook on a Mac, you must first turn on Sync Services in Outlook by clicking Tools➪Sync Services and then selecting the items you want to sync, such as Calendar, Contacts, Tasks, and Notes. This syncs anything in Outlook with iCal and Address Book on your Mac, which you then sync with your iPhone with iTunes. Refer to Figure 1-4 for the following settings. You have to scroll down to see the last few:

✏ **Contacts:** You can sync contacts from multiple applications, which might include Address Book (on a Mac), Yahoo! Address Book, Google Contacts, or Outlook. If your contacts are divided into groups, you can choose to sync all your contacts or only subsets or groups of contacts. This is useful if you use your work computer to sync but don't want the company directory on your iPhone. Refer to Book IV, Chapter 1 to learn about the Contacts app.

There is also an option to instruct iTunes what to do if, when syncing, it finds a new contact that's been created on your iPhone but hasn't been assigned to a group. Next to Add Contacts Created Outside of Groups on This iPhone to, choose a location from the pop-up menu.

If you use Yahoo! Address Book or Google Contacts, you configure them from iTunes by checking the box, typing in your name and password, and then clicking Configure. iTunes accesses your Yahoo! or Google information and syncs it with your iPhone.

✏ **Calendars:** You can sync calendars from more than one application including iCal and Microsoft Outlook 2011 (on a Mac), Microsoft Outlook, 2003, 2007, or 2010 (on a Windows computer), and Google Calendar. If you have more than one calendar created, you can pick and choose which to sync with your iPhone. You can also establish a cut-off date for old syncs, such as not syncing events older than 15 days. No sense clogging up your iPhone with the past. Refer to Book IV, Chapter 2 to learn about the Calendar app.

✏ **E-mail:** Only your account settings are synced, not the actual messages. You can choose which accounts you want on your iPhone.

On Mac, when you check the Sync Mail Accounts box, iTunes automatically checks the box next to the first account on the list. You can de-select that one and choose one or more other accounts. Say, for example, that you have an e-mail account for your golf league. You may not want to receive those messages on your iPhone, but just on your computer. Don't check the box next to that e-mail account name in the accounts list.

✔ On Windows, check Sync Selected Mail Accounts From and then choose Outlook or Outlook Express from the pop-up menu.

Your password may or may not be synced with the account information. If you find iPhone asks for your password, you can add it permanently by tapping Settings⇨Mail, Contacts, Calendar. Tap the account name and then type your password in the appropriate field.

Account settings move in one direction only: from your computer to your iPhone. If you set up e-mail accounts on your iPhone (as explained in Book III, Chapter 4), they must be set up manually on your computer, if you want them to be on your computer.

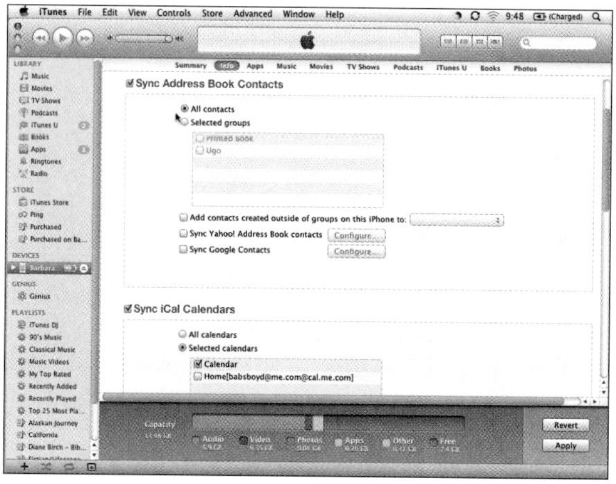

Figure 1-4: Choose your data sync settings from the Info pane.

✔ **Other:** Choose to sync bookmarks that you have in Safari on a Mac, or Safari or Microsoft Internet Explorer on Windows — the check boxes reflect the possible choices. You may want to delete old bookmarks you don't want any more before syncing.

Notes are synced between the Notes app on iPhone and Notes in Mail on a Mac or Microsoft Outlook 2003, 2007, or 2010 on Windows.

✔ **Advanced:** Checking any or all of these boxes will replace, instead of sync, information on your iPhone with the information that's on your computer. Why would you do this? Say you tried to organize your contacts on your iPhone and made a mess. You could rework everything — with a full-size keyboard — on your computer and then over-write everything on your iPhone. Obviously, if you mainly use your iPhone to add or make changes to any of these apps, don't check this box.

Apps

You use the Apps pane, shown in Figure 1-5, not only to sync apps you buy in the Apps Store but also to arrange apps on your iPhone Home screen. In this pane, you can also copy documents between your iPhone and your computer with the Share Files feature.

Figure 1-5: Manage your apps and share files in the Apps pane.

Select the Sync Apps box to sync to your iPhone new apps that you either downloaded to your computer or synced from another device, like an iPad.

On the left side, you see a list of all the apps you have on your computer. Scrolling through the list, notice that it's sorted by kind: iPhone, iPod touch, iPad Apps, and iPhone and iPod touch Apps. With the pop-up menu, you can also sort by name, category, date, or size. Check the apps in this list that you want to sync with your iPhone. Any apps you leave unchecked will be removed from your iPhone, but they remain on your computer so you can re-sync them to your iPhone, or to another device, at a later date.

On the right side is an image of your iPhone's Home screen. You can move the buttons around from screen to screen here, which is a lot easier than doing so on your iPhone when you have a lot of apps and folders. Follow these three steps:

1. **Click and drag the app icons around from Home screen to Home screen or click and drag the icon from the list to the Home screen where you want it to reside, until they are in positions that you like and find useful.**

2. **Create folders by dragging one app icon over another.**

The button is replaced by a highlighted square in which you see two or more tiny representations of the apps inside. A rectangle (the folder) opens beneath showing the apps that are in the folder. iPhone names the folder based on the kind of apps that are in it, but you can rename it by typing in the field.

3. **To delete an app, click on the X in the corner that appears when you drag the pointer over the app icon or de-select it from the apps list so it will be deleted from your iPhone during the next sync.**

If you drag the pointer over the app and an X doesn't appear in the corner, that app cannot be deleted from your iPhone.

4. **After you've made the changes you want and your Home screens are neatly organized, click the Apply button to sync your changes with your iPhone.**

In the lower half of the Apps pane, as seen in Figure 1-6, you see File Sharing, which lets you share documents, created with apps that support file sharing, to and from your computer and iPhone. On the left are the apps you have that support file sharing; on the right are the files on your iPhone. To transfer files from your iPhone to your computer:

1. **Connect your iPhone to your computer and open iTunes, and then click the Apps tab.**

Figure 1-6: Manage file transfers from the Apps pane.

2. **From the list on the left, select the app that supports the document you want to share.**

   A list of available documents appears on the right.

3. **Click on the document or documents you want to transfer from your iPhone to your computer.**

4. **Click the Save to button at the bottom of the list.**

   Select the destination where you want to save the documents.

5. **Click Choose (Mac) or OK (Windows).**

   The file is transferred to your computer.

To transfer files from your computer to your iPhone:

1. **Repeat steps 1 and 2 of the previous list.**

2. **Click the Add button at the bottom of the list.**

   Select the file from your computer that you want to transfer from your computer to your iPhone.

3. **Click Choose (Mac) or OK (Windows).**

   The file is transferred to your iPhone and can be opened with an app that supports that type of document. Select additional files to transfer more than one.

To delete a file from your iPhone, select the file in the list and then tap the Delete key (Backspace in Windows) on the keyboard.

Music

You have three choices for syncing music from iTunes to your iPhone. The first two are selected from the Music pane:

- ✔ You can sync the Entire music library, which is a great and easy choice if you have enough storage on your iPhone to hold your entire music library.

- ✔ You can sync selected playlists, artists, albums, and genres. Make the selections you want in the boxes, as seen in Figure 1-7. This is a good solution if you don't have enough iPhone memory or if you have a lot of music on your computer that you don't want on your iPhone.

You can't create playlist folders on your iPhone, but those created in iTunes will be synced. See Book V, Chapters 2 and 3 for more about using iTunes and managing your media collection.

Figure 1-7: Manage your music from the Music pane.

You have three other considerations on the Music pane:

- **Include Music Videos:** Any music videos you have will be synced to your iPhone from iTunes.

- **Include Voice Memos:** Voice memos from your iPhone are synced to iTunes.

- **Automatically Fill Free Space with Songs:** If you don't have enough storage space on your iPhone for your whole music library, iTunes syncs as many songs as will fit, choosing a selection of music based on your most recent and most frequent listening choices.

The third choice is to sync only checked songs and videos. If you have a lot of music, this can be a long and tedious operation, the upside is that you have exactly the music you want on your iPhone. Here's how to do it:

1. **In the Summary pane, select Sync Only Checked Songs and Videos.**

2. **Click Apply.**

   If iTunes begins syncing, drag the Slide to Cancel slider on your iPhone to interrupt the sync.

3. **Click Music in the Library section of the Source list.**

4. **Check all the songs and videos you want to sync to your iPhone. Uncheck any you don't want to sync, if they are checked.**

   You can also select a playlist from the Source list and check the songs in the playlist.

5. **When you finish your selection, click on your iPhone under Devices in the Source list.**

6. **Click the Sync button on the bottom right corner.**

   Only songs and videos you checked are synced to your iPhone. The selection of checked music completely replaces the music on your iPhone, meaning that if a song is on your iPhone but remains unchecked on iTunes, it is deleted during the sync.

If you have selected Manually Manage Music and Videos on the Summary pane, you can click and drag media — songs, videos, podcasts, or playlists — from your iTunes library to your iPhone (in the Source list). The content will sync immediately. However, if/when someday you deselect Manually Manage Music and Videos, the content you added manually will be removed when you automatically sync. This won't make a difference if the media you manually transferred is included in the automatic sync; however, it is a hassle if you have a lot of music on your iPhone that you copied from other sources.

You can choose to convert songs to 128 Kpbs AAC by selecting that option on the Summary pane.

Movies

With iPhone's increased storage space and fabulous display, watching movies on your iPhone has become a realistic choice. Syncing gives you the option of downloading and beginning to watch a movie on one device and then syncing and watching through to the end on the other device. If you fall asleep watching a movie on your computer in the evening, you can sync it to your iPhone and watch the end during your train commute the next morning. If you click the Movies tab at the top of iTunes, you have a couple of options:

✔ **Click the Sync Movies check box only:** Movies you have on iTunes appear in the Movies box. Manually select the movies you want to sync by selecting the box next to the name of the movie to select.

✔ **Click the Sync Movies and the Automatically Include check boxes:** The pop-up menu is activated as shown in Figure 1-8, which lets you choose

   • All or all unwatched movies

   • A quantity of 1, 3, 5, or 10 watched movies

   • A quantity of 1, 3, 5, or 10 unwatched movies, either the most or least recently released.

An unwatched movie is one that hasn't been seen on either iTunes or your iPhone. After you watch a movie on your iPhone, this information is sent to iTunes during the next sync.

Rented Movies: Click the Move button next to any rented movie you want to sync to your iPhone and it appears on the On iPhone list. Remember, movies rented from iTunes expire in 24 hours from the time you begin watching and in 30 days, even if you don't watch it.

If you have begun watching the rented movie, it picks up where you left off when you open it on your iPhone.

Figure 1-8: The pop-up menu in the Movies pane lets you choose which movies to sync.

Music videos are downloaded and imported into the Movies library of iTunes. If you want the music video in the Music library, click on the video, and then click Get Info. Under the Kind list, choose Music Video, and then click OK. iTunes moves it from Movies to Music, although it will be in Videos on your iPhone.

TV Shows

Who watches TV shows on TV anymore? With iTunes, you can download free or purchased episodes and watch them when you want — on your computer or your iPhone. Watch out, though: A single half-hour episode takes about 250MB of storage, so your iPhone fills up fast if you don't manage the sync process. Alternatively, if you're connected to your Wi-Fi network, you can use Home Sharing to stream the show from your computer to your iPhone. Here's what you need to know:

 1. **Click the box next to Sync TV Shows at the top of the pane to activate the other options.**

2. **Click the box next to Automatically Include and the criteria you choose in the two adjacent pop-up menus will be applied to all the shows you have on iTunes.**

3. **Choose one selection from each of the two pop-up menus:**

   Left menu:

   - All, which includes watched and unwatched

   - All unwatched

   - 1, 3, 5, or 10 of the newest episodes, watched and unwatched

   - 1, 3, 5, or 10 of the most recent unwatched episodes

   - 1, 3, 5, or 10 of the oldest unwatched episodes

   Right menu:

   - Apply your choice to either all shows in your iTunes library or selected shows, in which case the Shows section appears, as in Figure 1-9. Click the box next to the shows you want to apply your choices to.

   Or

4. **To pick and choose manually among the shows you have in your library, deselect the box next to Automatically Include.**

5. **Click Show in the Show box.**

   The episodes appear in the Episodes box on the right.

6. **Select the check box next to the episodes you want to sync to your iPhone.**

Figure 1-9: Choose to sync single episodes of whole series from the TV Shows pane.

You can check the options under Include Episodes in Playlists to sync those found in your Purchased or Recently Added playlists.

If you want to include or exclude a watched or unwatched episode without changing your syncing options, click TV Shows in the Library section of iTunes' Source list. Control+click or right-click on the episode and choose Mark as Unwatched or Mark as Watched (whichever you have already done and want to change).

Podcasts

As with movies and television shows, you can pick and choose the podcasts you want to sync based on whether you've listened to it, the number of podcasts you want to sync, and the newest or oldest of those in your iTunes library. And, like movies and televisions shows, if you begin listening to a podcast on either device and then sync the devices, the podcast picks up where it was stopped, regardless of which device you listen on.

1. **Click the box next to Sync Podcasts at the top of the pane to activate the other options.**

2. **Click the box next to Automatically Include and the criteria you choose in the two adjacent pop-up menus will be applied to all the shows you have on iTunes.**

3. **Choose one selection from each of the two pop-up menus:**

   Left menu:

   - All, which includes played and unplayed podcasts

   - 1, 3, 5, or 10 of the most recent played and unplayed episodes

   - All unplayed podcasts

   - 1, 3, 5, or 10 of the most recent unplayed

   - 1, 3, 5, or 10 of the least recent unplayed

   - All new podcasts

   - 1, 3, 5, or 10 of the most recent new podcasts

   - 1, 3, 5, or 10 of the least recent new podcasts

   Right menu:

   - Apply your choice to either all podcasts in your iTunes library or selected podcasts, in which case a check box appears next to each podcast in the list. Click the box next to the shows you want to apply your played, unplayed, new, 1, 3, 5, or 10 choices to.

OR

4. **To pick and choose manually among the podcasts you have in your library, uncheck the box next to Automatically Include.**

5. **Click on Podcast in the podcast box.**

   The episodes appear in the Episodes box on the right.

6. **Click the check box next to the episodes you want to sync to your iPhone (see Figure 1-10).**

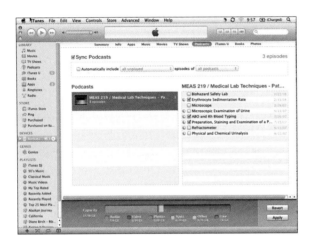

Figure 1-10: Manually select the episodes of a podcast you want to sync.

iTunes U

iTunes U has opened up a universe of knowledge, giving you access to grammar and high school lessons and lectures from universities and colleges around the world. You find videos and audio books, post-graduate seminars, and presentations from museums like the Metropolitan Museum of Art and organizations like the American Society of Clinical Oncology that give lifelong learning a whole new definition. The steps to sync episodes from iTunes to your iPhone are as follows:

1. **Select the check box next to Sync iTunes U at the top of the pane to activate the other options.**

2. **Select the check box next to Automatically Include and the criteria you choose in the two adjacent pop-up menus is applied to all the shows you have on iTunes.**

3. **Choose one selection from each of the two pop-up menus (refer to Figure 1-11):**

   Left menu:

   - All, which includes played and unplayed lectures or episodes
   - 1, 3, 5, or 10 of the most recent played and unplayed episodes
   - All unplayed episodes
   - 1, 3, 5, or 10 of the most recent unplayed
   - 1, 3, 5, or 10 of the least recent unplayed
   - All new episodes
   - 1, 3, 5, or 10 of the most recent new episodes
   - 1, 3, 5, or 10 of the least recent new episodes

   Right menu:

   - Apply your choice to either all collections in your iTunes library or selected collections, in which case a check box appears next to each item in the list. Select the check boxes next to the shows you want to apply your choices to.

   Or

4. **To pick and choose manually among the lectures you have in your library, deselect the box next to Automatically Include.**

Figure 1-11: Choose one selection from each pop-up menu to select items you've downloaded from iTunes U.

5. **Click Episode in the Collections box.**

   The episodes appear in the Items box on the right.

6. **Select the check box next to the episodes you want to sync to your iPhone.**

In Movies, TV Shows, Podcasts, and iTunes U, when you set your sync options using one of the numbered selections (5 most recent unplayed, or 10 least recent unwatched), the selection changes as your download new media to iTunes. If you choose a specific episode or movie, it remains selected for subsequent syncs until you deselect it (or it expires, if it was rented).

Books

Books manages both e-books and audio books. Audio books, which became popular as books-on-tape, have been around for a while. Commuters used to pop a cassette into their car stereos and listen to their favorite author's latest novel while driving to work. Today, the Internet holds myriad titles of every genre, which you can download to your computer.

E-books, or electronic books, have been on the scene for a few years now, too. Your iPhone can function as both an audio book listening device and an e-book reader — cool! You do have to download the iBooks app from Apple or one of the other reader apps to view e-books on your iPhone; we talk about those in the online bonus content. (For more information on how to access the online bonus content, see this book's Introduction.) Syncing media from iTunes to your iPhone to read in iBooks works pretty much the same as for other media, but we show you what to do anyway:

1. **Select the check box next to Sync Books at the top of the pane to activate the other options.**

2. **If you click All Books, all the e-books that you see in the Books box are synced to your iPhone.**

   Or

3. **Click Selected Books, and then set your criteria by choosing from the pop-up menus in the Books section:**

   • **Books and PDF files, Only Books, or Only PDF files**

   • **Sort by Authors or Sort by Title:** This doesn't change your syncing option, but can make finding the books you want to sync easier.

4. **Click the boxes next to the books you want to sync, as shown in Figure 1-12.**

Book II
Chapter 1

Syncing, Backing
Up, and Updating
Your iPhone

Figure 1-12: Make syncing selections for e-books and audio books from the Books pane.

The Audio Books section works the same way:

1. **Click the box next to Sync Audio Books at the top of the pane to activate the other options.**

2. **If you click All Audio Books, all the audio books that you have on iTunes are synced to your iPhone.**

   Or

3. **Click Selected books, which opens the Audio Books and Parts boxes.**

4. **Select the check boxes next to the items you want to sync in the Audio Books and Parts lists.**

Photos

The Photos pane lets you move photos from your computer to your iPhone. (From one computer only; if you try to move photos from a second computer, the originals are erased from your iPhone.)

To do the reverse (that is, move photos from your iPhone to your computer), you use your photo management program such as iPhoto or Photoshop Elements, which considers your iPhone a digital camera or external drive with images. Photos are synced with photo management software. Another option is the Photo Stream feature of iCloud (see the "Syncing with iCloud" section later in this chapter), where your photos are stored in Photo Stream on iCloud and then pushed to your devices, such as your iPhone or your computer.

We talk about Photos and Photo Stream in Book V, Chapters 1. To move copies of photos from your computer to your iPhone, follow these steps (refer to Figure 1-13):

1. **Select the check box next to Sync Photos From and choose the photo management application or folder where your photos reside.**

2. **Click Include Videos at the top if you want videos included in your selection.**

3. **Click All Photos, Albums, Events, and Faces to copy every photo in that application. However, photos that are in format that is incompatible with your iPhone won't be copied.**

   If you choose a single folder, a selected button appears which reads All Folders. You can't deselect this button.

   If you choose a folder that holds other folders, you can choose All Folders or Selected Folders, and then choose from the subfolders from the list that appears.

   Or

4. **Click Selected Albums, Events, and Faces, and Automatically Include.**

   Boxes appear for Albums and Events. Mac users who work with iPhoto or Aperture have the Faces option too.

5. **Define what you want to automatically include by choosing one of the following from the pop-up menu:**

   • **No events:** Only photos you choose from the boxes below will be included. Nothing is synced automatically.

   • **All events:** Selects and syncs all the events in the events box.

   • **The most recent 1, 3, 5, or 10 events:** Selects and syncs from one to 10 of the most recent events, which you see at the very bottom of the Events list. You may have to scroll down to see them.

   • **Events from the last 1, 2, 3, 6, or 12 months:** Selects all events that took place in the time period you select.

6. **In addition to defined events, you can choose albums and faces to sync by selecting them in the corresponding boxes.**

   The number of photos included in the selection appears in gray next to the selection.

**Book II
Chapter 1**

**Syncing, Backing
Up, and Updating
Your iPhone**

iPhone supports many common image file types including GIF, PNG, JPG, although iTunes doesn't sync exact copies of your photos but files that have been converted to fit iPhone's screen size. This conversion gives you better viewing quality and uses less storage space on your iPhone.

Figure 1-13: Move photos from your computer to your iPhone in the Photos pane.

iTunes works with the latest versions of the iPhoto and Aperture photo management apps on the Mac and Photoshop Elements and Photoshop Album on Windows. Consult the Apple iTunes web site to determine if older versions are compatible.

The iTunes sync

Now that you've set the criteria for your sync, all that remains is to click the Sync or Apply button in the bottom right corner. Sync changes to Apply when you make changes to your Sync options.

When you connect your iPhone to your computer in the future, you only need to click Sync to perform a sync that uses the same criteria.

When you tap Sync (or Apply), iTunes syncs the categories where you have selected the Sync check box at the top of the pane. If you deselect the Sync check box at the top of the Music pane, for example, when you sync, all the music on your iPhone will be deleted, although it remains on iTunes.

Disconnecting iPhone mid-sync

Sometimes you get a call while you're syncing your iPhone, but your iPhone is so smart that it pauses the syncing session when the phone rings. You can disconnect your iPhone and answer the phone and have your conversation. When you finish, reconnect your iPhone to your computer, and iTunes and iPhone take up syncing where they left off.

Responding to a dialog to copy your photos and/or videos

If you've taken any photos with your iPhone since the last sync, your photo management software may automatically open and ask if you want to import the photos from your iPhone. To turn this function on, or off, do the following:

On a Mac:

1. Choose Finder⇨Applications or click Launchpad on the Dock.

2. Double-click Image Capture.

3. Click your iPhone in the Devices list.

4. In the pop-up menu entitled Connecting this iPhone Opens, choose No Application if you want no application to open when you connect your iPhone to your computer. Alternatively, you can choose from one of the applications shown to open that application when you connect your iPhone.

5. Choose Image Capture⇨Quit Image Capture to exit Image Capture. The new setting is saved and occurs the next time your connect your iPhone.

On Windows Vista or 7:

1. Choose Start⇨Control Panel.

2. Choose hardware and Sound.

3. Choose AutoPlay.

4. Open the Apple iPhone list in the Devices section.

5. Choose Take No Action if you want no application to open when you connect your iPhone to your computer. Alternatively, you can choose from one of the applications shown to open that application when you connect your iPhone.

We talk more about photo management in Book V, Chapter 1.

Sometimes, the sync takes longer than you thought, and you have to go out and take your iPhone with you. While your iPhone is syncing, a slider bar appears on iPhone's screen that says Slide to Cancel. Drag your finger across the slider bar and the sync is interrupted. At that point, you can safely disconnect the USB connector cable from your computer and iPhone and put your iPhone in your pocket or purse and be on your way. When you reconnect, the sync resumes.

Syncing with iCloud

iCloud is Apple's over-the-air syncing and storage service, which replaced MobileMe. You use your e-mail address, or create one as explained at the beginning of this chapter, to sign in to the iCloud service, and then choose which types of data you want to store on iCloud. iCloud offers an e-mail account and 5GB of free storage for your mail, contacts, calendars, documents, and backup. Purchased apps and media including music, iTunes Match content, TV shows, and books, and photos stored in Photo Stream don't count toward the 5 GB. If you need more storage space, you can purchase an additional amount on a yearly basis directly from the iCloud settings on your iPhone.

When data, such as your contacts, calendars, or notes, is stored on iCloud, that data is pushed to all your iOS 5 devices — your iPhone, iPad, and iPod touch — and your computer.

You can choose which types of data you want to store and sync with iCloud and which you want to sync with iTunes. However, iTunes stores and syncs all your media, whereas iCloud stores and syncs only media purchased on iTunes or through iTunes Match. And, you have to use iTunes to move photos from your computer to your iPhone, although Photo Stream will move up to 1,000 new photos taken on other devices to your iPhone.

iCloud comes with Mac OS X 10.7.2 Lion and the iCloud Control Panel for Windows (Vista SP2 or later or Windows 7) is available to download at `support.apple.com/kb/DL1455`.

Follow these steps to use iCloud:

1. **Tap Settings⇨iCloud.**

   If you see the e-mail you used to set up your Apple ID, go to step 5.

2. **Type in your Apple ID and password, as shown in Figure 1-14, and then tap Sign In.**

   iCloud only works with e-mail style Apple IDs. If your Apple ID is something like "johnsmith," you must create a new one as explained at the beginning of this chapter.

3. **iCloud asks if you want to merge calendars, contacts, reminders, and bookmarks on your iPhone with iCloud. Tap Merge.**

4. **iCloud asks to use the location of your iPhone, which enables the Find My iPhone feature. Click OK.**

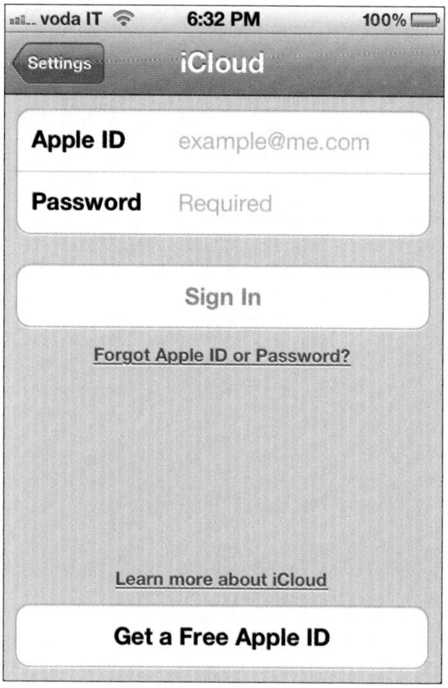

Figure 1-14: Use your Apple ID to sign in to iCloud.

5. **The iCloud screen appears, as shown in Figure 1-15.**

The switches you tap On indicate which data you want stored on iCloud. Any changes you make on your iPhone are pulled into iCloud and pushed to the other devices, and vice versa when your devices are signed in to iCloud and connected to Wi-Fi. iCloud keeps all your devices in sync.

The exception is Photo Stream, which automatically uploads up to 1,000 photos taken in the last 30 days from your iOS devices — your iPhone, iPad, or iPod Touch — or imported into iPhoto or Aperture on your computer and pushes them to the other devices and your computer.

Figure 1-15: Choose the type of data you want to share with other devices using iCloud.

6. **If you want to use iCloud to backup your iPhone (instead of iTunes), scroll towards the bottom of the screen and tap Storage and Backup.**

   The Storage & Backup screen opens.

7. **Tap iCloud Backup On.**

8. **Tap Manage Storage.**

   The Manage Storage screen opens.

9. **Tap your iPhone.**

   The Info screen opens, as shown in Figure 1-16.

voda IT 6:55 PM 98% ▭

Manage Storage   **Info**

Barbara's iPhone
This iPhone

Latest Backup   Incomplete

Backup Size   295 MB

Backup Options
Choose the data you want to back up.

Next Backup Size   0 bytes

Camera Roll   [ON   ]
86.0 MB

Stanza   [ON   ]
17.0 MB

24.6 GB available of 25.0 GB on iCloud

Figure 1-16: Choose the data you want to back up to iCloud.

10. **A list of iCloud-enabled apps appears in the Backup Options section. Tap the switches On or Off to select which kind of data you want to back up. For example, tap a drawing app On to back up sketches you make.**

11. **Tap Manage Storage in the upper left corner, and then tap Storage & Backup in the upper left corner of the next screen to reach the Storage & Backup screen.**

12. **Scroll to the bottom of the screen and tap the Back Up Now button.**

    The first backup may take a few minutes, depending on how much data you have on your iPhone. Your iPhone is backed up to iCloud. Subsequent backups take place once a day when your iPhone is attached to a power source, connected to Wi-Fi, and locked.

Gauging your iPhone's storage capacity and limits

When you're ready to sync, make sure you have enough room on your iPhone before actually hitting the Sync button. Your iPhone's storage capacity depends on which version of iPhone you have.

Considering that the operating system itself takes up about one gigabyte of memory, that leaves you with 15 gigabytes on an 16GB phone, 31 on a 32GB phone, or 63 on a 64GB phone. That sounds like a warehouse of storage, until you start loading movies, TV shows, podcasts, and games on your iPhone, when you find out it fills up fast. There are two ways to know how much space you have on your iPhone:

- **On iPhone:** From the Home screen, tap Settings ⇨General⇨About. The list tells you how much memory is occupied by Songs, Videos, Photos, and Apps and tells you how much memory is Available.

- **On iTunes:** When your iPhone is connected to iTunes and selected in the source list, you see a colored bar near the bottom of the iTunes window (as you see in the preceding figures) that illustrates how much space each type of data will occupy

on your iPhone when you perform the sync you've set up. If you are in the Music pane and you deselect the Sync Music box, the blue section of the bar that represents audio files shrinks. If your iPhone is nearly full, you can play with your syncing options and see how they affect the storage capacity. Click once on one of the titles under the chart and the number of items in each category is displayed. Click a second time and it displays how long it will take to listen to all the audio and video in your library. Click a third time to return to the gigabyte numbers.

If you have more media than memory, you have a couple of choices for managing and choosing which data to sync:

- Manually select which music, videos, and podcasts you want on your iPhone and sync only those.

- Select Automatically Fill Free Space with Songs, and iTunes fills any free space with music. iTunes chooses songs it thinks you'll like based on your most played and most recent music.

REMEMBER

Choose one syncing option for your Info pane data. So, if you use iTunes to sync your contacts, calendars, bookmarks, and notes, don't use iCloud for that same data or vice versa.

Syncing with More Than One iPhone or iTunes Computer

Used to be that you had one computer every two and a half households and the only music you heard through the phone was your father singing "Happy Birthday" to you. Today, you probably have a computer at home and one at work, and maybe a notebook computer, too. Perhaps you share your home computer with your significant other or children and each of them has an iPhone. Apple has lightened up on its one iPhone— one computer monogamy policy by adding in iTunes. We give you a way to use multiple iPhones with one computer, too.

One iPhone, multiple computers

The fact is different pieces of our lives often overlap. You want the contacts on your notebook and desktop computers and your iPhone to be the same and you want the option of making changes in either of those places and syncing with the other two. The simplest solution is an over-the-air, or OTA, syncing and storage service, like iCloud as explained previously.

However, iTunes lets you merge contacts, calendars, e-mail accounts, bookmarks, and notes from two or more computers on your iPhone. It works like this:

1. Follow the instructions outlined previously in this chapter, sync your iPhone and one of your computers, for example, a notebook.

2. Connect and sync your iPhone with the other computer, say, a desktop. Set the same preferences in the Info pane as you did on your notebook. iTunes give you two options:

   • **Merge Info:** iPhone keeps the information from your notebook and merges it with the information on your desktop.

   • **Replace Info:** the information that was synced from the first computer is replaced by the information on the second computer.

One computer, multiple iPhones

Your family members share one computer and each of you has an iPhone. You can sync more than one iPhone with the same computer. Each device is recognized by its unique name.

On a Mac, each iPhone can use different sync settings; on Windows, each phone has to use the same settings. Each person has a separate Apple account because each iPhone has an Apple account associated with it. You probably each have different media that you'd like to sync with your respective iPhones.

The ideal solution is to set up separate user accounts on the Mac or Windows computer for each user, who in turn would have his own iTunes library to sync to his iPhone.

If for some reason the idea of separate user accounts doesn't work for you, you can sync different sets of media by setting up a different iTunes library for each family member:

**Book II
Chapter 1**

**Syncing, Backing
Up, and Updating
Your iPhone**

1. **Hold down the option key (Mac) or the shift key (Windows) and open iTunes.**

   A dialog gives you the options of creating a new library or choosing which you want to open.

2. **Select Create Library.**

   Type in a name and location for the library.

3. **Whenever you start up iTunes, hold down the Option (Mac) or Shift (Windows) key and to open your personal library.**

4. **Sync your iPhone with your library.**

Make sure you uncheck Copy Files to iTunes Media Folder When Adding to Library. On Mac, this is found under iTunes⟳Preferences⟳Advanced; on Windows, Edit⟳Preferences⟳Advanced.

Banking on Backups in Case Things Go Kerflooey

Murphy's Law: Whatever can go wrong, will go wrong. There may come a time when you need to restore your iPhone from a backup. If you regularly sync your phone with iTunes, you have a backup on your computer as recent as your last sync because iTunes creates an backup of all the data and apps contained on your iPhone each time you sync. iTunes also asks if you want to back up before it installs any new iPhone firmware from Apple and before you use the Restore option.

If you use iCloud's backup feature, you have an online backup. iCloud backs up your iPhone once a day when your iPhone is connected to a power source, has a Wi-Fi connection, and is locked.

What gets backed up? Here's the breakdown:

- ✔ **iTunes:** Calendars, contacts, mail, network, and sound settings, call history, text messages, and notes. Camera roll and Saved Photos albums are backed up. Media files and apps aren't backed up, but you can restore them by syncing with iTunes on your computer or accessing your purchase history. After you purchase something in the iTunes or App Stores, it can be downloaded again.

- ✔ **iCloud:** iPhone settings and app data, Home screen and app organization, iMessage, SMS, and MMS messages, ringtones, and purchased music, TV shows, apps, and books. Anything else you store on iCloud, such as contacts, calendars, notes, reminders, as well as documents and data, is used if you have to reload data to your iPhone. Music purchased in iTunes is also stored in iCloud.

In the terrifying event that you lose everything on your iPhone or you have to send it in for repairs, you can reload the data and apps using the backup that iPhone keeps for you. To load the backup file onto your iPhone or onto a new iPhone if you've upgraded:

1. **Connect your iPhone to the computer you usually use to sync.**

2. **Open iTunes, if it didn't automatically open (depends on how you set it up).**

3. **Click iPhone in the Source list.**

4. **Click the Summary tab.**

5. **Click Restore.**

   iTunes gives you a chance to back out of your choice or go ahead.

6. **If you see multiple backup files, choose the most recent one associated with your iPhone.**

7. **Sync your music, videos, podcasts, and books as we explained earlier in this chapter.**

If you like to keep things minimalistic, you can delete older backups. Go to iTunes⇨Preferences (Edit⇨Preferences on Windows), and click Devices. You see a list of your backups. Just clock the one or ones you want to delete then click Delete Backup. Poof! Gone.

To load the backup file from iCloud:

1. **Choose Settings⇨General⇨Reset.**

2. **Tap Erase All Content and Settings.**

3. **When the Setup Assistant opens, tap Restore from iCloud Backup.**

4. **Sign in to iCloud with your Apple ID and password.**

   iCloud pushes the most recent backup to your iPhone.

Updating Apps

You're probably familiar with software updates on your computer. You may have set your computer to scan the Internet for updates for the applications and operating system you use on a regular basis, once a week or once a month. Apps for iPhone have frequent updates too. Apps are often developed and released quickly and then improvements are made based on the feedback users give to the developers. You must be connected to the Internet to search for app updates; larger apps, such as games, are more easily updated with a Wi-Fi connection. To find updates for the apps on your iPhone, follow these steps:

1. **Tap the App Store button on the Home screen**.

2. **Tap the Updates button in the bottom right corner.**

   A badge shows the number of updates available and a list of the updates appears in the Updates screen, as shown in Figure 1-17.

Figure 1-17: The Updates screen displays which apps have updates available.

3. **Choose to update all the apps by tapping the Update All button at the top.**

   Or

   Select the individual apps you want to upgrade by clicking on the app in the list.

   An Info screen, which outlines the improvements the update makes, opens. Tap the Update button to proceed.

   On the Home screen, the buttons of the apps you are updating are dimmed. The action taking place is written underneath: waiting and then loading. When the app is downloaded, the progress bar disappears.

4. **The next time you sync your iPhone with iTunes, the backup will include a copy of the updated apps, and you see the apps on the Apps pane.**

Upgrading iPhone Features and Functions with Software Updates

Apple and third-party apps developers are constantly working to improve iPhone's operating system (iOS) and apps software. You download those improvements by way of updates, which iTunes automatically seeks. During the next sync, those updates are installed on your iPhone.

**Book II
Chapter 1**

Syncing, Backing
Up, and Updating
Your iPhone

If you heard a rumor that Apple has released an iPhone operating system software update, you can manually check in one of the following ways (your computer must be connected to the Internet):

1. **Tap Settings⇨General⇨Software Update.**

   Your iPhone searches for software updates and either downloads any available updates or displays a message that reads Your Software Is Up to Date.

2. **Press the Home button to return to the Home screen.**

   Or

3. **Connect your iPhone to your computer and open iTunes.**

4. **Click your iPhone in the Devices section of the Source list.**

   The Summary tab opens.

5. **Click Check for Update in the Version section.**

   iTunes automatically checks for updates. If your iOS is up to date, a message appears that reads "This version of iPhone software (version number) is the current version."

   If an update is available, the message tells you it's available and gives you the option of updating your iPhone.

6. **Click iTunes⇨Check for Updates to Make Sure You Are Running the Most Recent Version of iTunes.**

   iTunes automatically checks for updates. If iTunes is up to date, a message appears which reads "This version of iTunes (version number) is the current version."

   If an update is available, the message tells you it's available and gives you the option of downloading and installing the update.

It's always a good idea to install updates when they are available — after all, like iTunes, iOS updates for your iPhone are free. And as far as we're concerned, free is good.

Chapter 2: Apps 411: Browsing, Installing, and Managing Apps

In This Chapter

✔ Searching for and installing apps

✔ Reading publications in Newsstand

✔ Syncing with Automatic Downloads

✔ Updating apps

✔ Deleting apps

✔ Reviewing apps

*Y*our iPhone, out of the box, is a great phone, Internet browser, compass, alarm clock, stock watcher, music player, personal assistant weather channel, and video camera, but it can be so much more. "How?" you ask?

"Apps!" we answer. In this chapter, we tell you all about apps — not so much specific apps, but apps as a subject. We cover how the App Store works, some tips for using reviews to choose apps, how to install and delete apps, and obtain app updates and upgrades. At the end of the chapter, we talk a bit about organizing your apps.

ᵣe ▸ Education ▸ Sunset Lake Software

Molecules

Description

Molecules is an appl
rotate the molecules
by moving two finge

Sunset Lake Softwa

Free App ▼

app is designed for both
ᵢPad

What's New in

- Reenabled two fing
screen at all time
- Fixed a r

Discovering the Joy of Apps: "There's an App for That!"

With more than half a million apps (and counting!) available at the time of publication and more being released every day, there is truly an app for virtually every task, interest, or necessity. We make some recommendations in the online bonus content, but to give you an idea, you can find apps for recipes, games, electronic readers, home banking, photo enhancement, conversion tools, flashlights, and music identification.

A handful of apps are developed by Apple, and the rest are developed by third-party developers. You download apps from Apple's App Store, which you access either via your iPhone or via iTunes on your computer. The nice thing about the App Store is that it offers one-stop shopping. You don't have to shop from website to website for the best price or the latest version; everything is in one place. And Apple reviews the app before it goes up on the App Store, so it's been tested to work with your iPhone.

What's more, if you lose your iPhone or your iPhone or computer crashes before you've had a chance to back up the apps you've downloaded, the App Store has a record of everything you've downloaded and you can download your apps again (if they're still available) — without paying for them a second time. That's why you need an Apple ID to sign in to the App Store or iTunes, even to download free apps.

Free or for a price?

There are two kinds of apps: free and paid. Some of the coolest apps are free. Apps developers continue to sprout like mushrooms, and the relative ease with which an app can be written and distributed makes app programming, for some developers, a relaxing pastime. We like to divide the free apps into four types:

- **Stand-Alone Apps:** Found in all categories, these apps work on their own and can be games, financial management, recipes, or just about whatever you can think of.

- **Support Apps:** Vendors who provide an app that either is an iPhone version of their website or gives specific information. Home banking apps and real-time public transit information apps are two examples. Often, you find a link to the App Store on the website of the vendor or service provider.

- **Teaser or Intro Apps:** Pared-down versions of fee-based apps. One of Barbara's favorites, the iHandy Level, is the free app of a fee-based carpentry app suite that includes a protractor, plumb bob, ruler, and surface level for 99 cents each.

- **Revenue-Generating Apps:** These apps provide frameworks for the real meat of the app, such as magazine subscription apps or gambling apps. The app is free, but you pay for the content.

We think of paid apps in two categories:

- **Low-priced:** Most are just 99 cents and the highest runs $5. They run the gamut of categories. Some developers have become rich overnight with the idea that selling a lot for a low price is more effective than selling two at a high price. We're happy for their success and for the accessibility low prices provide.

- **Higher-priced:** More than $5. For the most part, these apps, such as scientific journals or GPS navigation tools, give access to costly, copyrighted information.

Universal apps that run on iPad and iPhone

If you're one of the lucky owners of both an iPhone and an iPad, you'll be pleased to know that some apps run on both devices. These apps are known as *universal apps.* A plus sign to the left side of the price of an app (on lists of apps and on the app information screen) indicates that it works on both iPhone and iPad.

Searching for and Installing Apps

Now that you know a bit about what you're looking for, we tell you how to get your hands on some apps. You can enter the App Store through iPhone or iTunes doors.

Searching the iPhone App Store

With the hundreds of thousands of apps available, it's hard to know where to begin, let alone actually choose an app. Apple helps you by making some recommendations for apps, showing you bestsellers, best earners, and some Apple favorites. To begin navigating through the sea of apps on your iPhone, tap the App Store button on the Home screen, a screen like Figure 2-1 appears. Across the bottom, you see five buttons:

- **Featured:** Shows 30 Apple-recommended apps divided into

  - **New:** Tap here to view the week's newest arrivals.

  - **What's Hot:** Here you find the most popular — that is, the most downloaded — apps, regardless of whether they are free or paid.

  - **Genius:** Gives you recommendations based on your downloading and purchasing history.

- **Categories:** The first screen shows a list of categories. Tap on one of the categories to see a list of apps in that category. Some apps fall into more than one category, in which case it shows up on two different lists. Some categories are divided into subcategories. Games is divided into 19 subcategories, which include action, board, casino, card, and educational. When you get to the list of apps in the category or subcategory, you also get three options for finding apps within that category:

  - **Top Paid:** The first 25 most-downloaded paid games are shown. Scroll to the bottom and you can see 25 more.

  - **Top Free:** The same deal as top paid, only these apps are free.

- **Release Date:** Shows a mix of paid and free apps. The list begins with the most recently released app in that category.

✏ **Top 25:** The top of the charts of apps. These are divided between Top Paid, Top Free, and Top Grossing, which is the app that's earned the most.

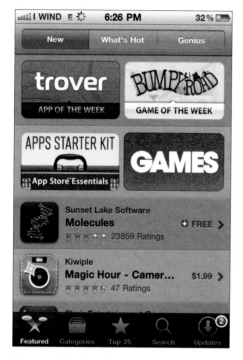

Figure 2-1: The App Store gives you many ways to find apps.

You see apps under Top Grossing that are free, and you may wonder how can a free app be top-grossing. Two ways:

- There's an app called Free App a Day that lets you make a wish that an app is free. If a single app gets enough wishes, it can be downloaded free for a limited time, but word gets out about how great the app is and people pay for it anyway after the free period is over.

- In-App Purchases: The app is free, but you then buy things within the app. For example, a poker game is free, but you buy 25 gold chips for $1.99.

✓ **Search:** You can search by the name of the app, if you know it, or by key words. The more words you search by, the narrower your search.

✓ **Updates:** Because the App Store knows which apps you've purchased and downloaded, it automatically sends you a notification when an update is available. The number you see in the badge on the Updates button is the number of apps that have updates. We talk about updates a little farther along in this chapter.

However you arrive at a list of apps, each list displays the same kinds of information. You see the icon and name of the app, the name of the developer, the number of ratings stars and the total number of ratings, and the price (if you're looking at the Top Free list, the word FREE is written where the price would be on the Top Paid list).

Tap the app that interests you and an Info screen opens, as seen in Figure 2-2. At the very top, you see the name of the app, the developer's name, the star ratings, the category, and a button that displays either the price or "free." A description of the app follows, which may include a list of features and some blips from reviews, followed by a few screenshots of the app. Just below the screenshots is a Ratings button.

You see the number of ratings and the average stars the app's been given. Tap the Ratings button to read the written reviews. The number in parentheses at the top of the reviews screen is the number of reviews written.

When you're choosing apps, read the description, which is written by the developer, to understand exactly what you should expect from the app. Then read the reviews with a discerning eye as to whether the app does what the description says it does, whether it's buggy, whether it's lame. Some reviewers write a bad review because they expected the app to do something that it never claimed to do. Look for a positive or negative consensus in reviews to help you make a downloading decision.

The lower portion of the Info screen lists the company name and website, the post date, which is the date the app was put on the App Store, the version number, the size, and the age rating, which indicates the minimum age considered appropriate for this app: 4+, 7+, 12+, and 17+. There are three more buttons:

✓ **Tell a Friend:** Send a link to this app via e-mail. A new message opens in Mail. You need only enter the address of the person you want to send the link to.

Book II
Chapter 2

Apps 411: Browsing, Installing, and Managing Apps

✔ **Gift This App:** Appears only if this is a paid app and lets you purchase the app and send it to a friend as a gift.

✔ **Report a Problem:** Opens a form that you complete, describing the problem you had. The problem is sent directly to the developer.

Figure 2-2: The app's Info screen gives detailed information about the app, including a description, screenshots, and reviews.

Installing from the iPhone App Store

If you decide to download the app, tap the button at the top of the screen where you see the price or Free. The button changes to Install. Tap the Install button. You may be asked to enter your Apple ID and password, as shown in Figure 2-3. (See Book II, Chapter 1 for setting up an Apple account if you haven't done so already.)

Figure 2-3: Type in your Apple ID and password when asked.

If you chose a paid app, you have to enter your credit card information, have your on-file charge card charged, redeem an iTunes or Apple Store card, or have a credit balance in your iTunes account. After the App Store has the information it needs from you, the Home screen opens. The button of the new app appears across the bottom. A Waiting or Loading progress bar appears beneath the app, as seen in Figure 2-4.

If you frequently download items from the iTunes store, you can associate a credit card with your iTunes account or purchase iTunes or Apple store cards. Open the iTunes site on your computer and click on the iTunes Store. Sign in with your Apple ID and password and then click Redeem under your name or in the Quick Links section. Type in the code found on the back of the iTunes or Apple store card.

Figure 2-4: After you tap Install and enter your Apple ID and Password, the download begins.

You can't use store credits to give an app to someone as a gift. If you have both a store credit and a credit card on file and gift an app to someone, it will automatically be charged to your credit card.

If you lose your Internet connection or for some reason the download is interrupted, the next time you have an Internet connection, the download starts again. If, instead, you open iTunes on your computer and sign in to your account with the same Apple ID you used to begin the download that was interrupted, iTunes completes the download.

Searching with iTunes

While you can window shop the App Store from your iPhone to your heart's content, you can only download apps up to 20MB in size from your cellular network. To download apps larger than 20MB, you have to have a Wi-Fi connection on your iPhone or go through iTunes on your computer. To reach the App Store on your computer, follow these directions:

1. **Open iTunes on your computer.**

2. **Click iTunes Store under Store in the Source list.**

3. **Click the App Store tab at the top of the window.**

4. **Click the iPhone button at the top if it isn't highlighted.**

    iPhone's apps section of the iTunes Store opens, as seen in Figure 2-5.

Figure 2-5: The iPhone apps section of the iTunes Store.

The App Store tab is also a drop-down menu, which has links to various departments of the App Store such as books, music, or finance.

The window you see is divided into sections that give you suggestions for apps to download or purchase, similar to what you see when you open the App Store on your iPhone.

At the top, you see rotating banner ads. Below the ads, there are four sections, each of which contains square app icons that you click to open information about that app. Between each section, you find larger, rectangular icons, which represent a group of related apps. All the ads and icons are clickable and link to information about the app or group of apps.

As you scroll down the window, you find the following sections. Each section is horizontally scrollable and contains more clickable icons:

  ✔ **New and Noteworthy:** These are selected by Apple for the week.

  ✔ **What's Hot:** These are the most popular, that is, the most downloaded apps.

✔ **Season-Specific:** Apps that are associated with events or holidays that week.

✔ **Staff Favorites:** Apple editors recommend their favorite apps.

Click See All to see the entire selection from a section. The See All view shows a grid format, rather than a list. Apps in the See All view can be sorted by clicking the pop-up menu in the upper right corner.

Down the right side, you see two sections:

✔ **App Store Quick Links:** Click the links here to see the prior week's selection or find an app that you saw on an iPhone ad on television.

✔ **Top Charts:** These are the same categories you see on your iPhone: Paid Apps, Free Apps, and Top Grossing. You see the first ten but clicking See All takes you to a more extensive list.

When you click on an app's icon or name, from anywhere in the iTunes store, the App information window opens. Figure 2-6 shows an example. These are the parts:

✔ **Name**

✔ **Release date and version**

✔ **Price or free button**, which you click on to download the app.

✔ **Pop-up menu:** Click the triangle next to the price for a pop-up menu that has options to gift the app to a friend, add it to your own wish list, tell a friend about it, copy the link, or share the app info via Facebook or Twitter.

✔ **Ratings:** To determine age appropriateness. The rating number corresponds to the minimum age this app is appropriate for based on language, violence, and sexual content. Apps with a 17+ rating must be purchased by someone 17 or older.

✔ **Developer**

✔ **Developer's website link**

✔ **App support website link**

✔ **Description:** The first few lines of the description are visible. If the description is longer, click More on the right side to expose the complete description.

✔ **Screen shots**

✔ **Reviews:** Users can give a simple star rating, from zero to five, or write a review.

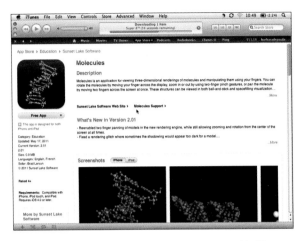

Figure 2-6: Information about the app is displayed in iTunes.

When you know what you're looking for

If you have a specific type of app in mind or know the name of the app you want, you can skip the banner ads and lists of recommendations, and search for the app you seek.

Type the name or a couple of key words in the Search field at the top right of the window, and then press return. A list of matching results appears. The results are culled from the entire iTunes Store but are divided by category. If you click Apps in the Filter by Media Type section, you'll only see iPhone and iPad apps.

Click See All next to the iPhone Apps title to see all the iPhone apps found that meet your search criteria. If you want to narrow your search, click the Power Search button.

The Power Search lets you narrow your search by providing more detailed criteria like the developer's name or a specific category or device you want to find apps for. Adjust the criteria and click the Search button to come up with more precise search results.

Downloading apps from iTunes

When you've found an app you like, click the Buy App button and it's downloaded to iTunes. Click Apps in the Library section of the Source list to see the apps you have, as in Figure 2-7. When you download apps via iTunes, you then have to sync the app to your iPhone, which we cover under the next section.

Figure 2-7: The Apps section of the Library shows which apps you have in iTunes. The Cover Flow view is seen here.

The number next to Apps in the Library list indicates how many updates are available. You can view your apps in the following iTunes views by clicking the view buttons at the top of the screen:

 List: Shows the app's name and age rating, seller, genre, and size. Click the heading of any part of the list and the list is sorted by that heading; for example, Name sorts alphabetically. Click the triangle to the right of the name to sort in the opposite direction, such as largest to smallest, or vice versa.

 Album List: Shows the app's icon and name with age rating, seller, and genre.

Grid: Click the apps button at the top and you see the apps' icons in two sections. Those that work on iPhone, iPod Touch, and iPad and those that work on iPhone and iPod touch. The category is shown under the name of the app. Click Genres and you see an icon for each genre with the category name and the number of apps you have in that category. Click on the genre icon and a list of apps in that genre opens.

 Cover Flow: Displays the app's icon in the top half of the screen and a list of the apps in the bottom half. Move from one app to another by clicking the app on the list or using the scroll bar or the directional arrows at either end of the scroll bar. Tap the full-screen button to see the cover flow display on your entire screen.

In any of the lists — List, Album List, or the list in Cover Flow — click once on an app and a triangle appears next to the age rating. Click this triangle to open a menu that takes you to the iTunes store and shows three choices, which you can click on to go to a destination in the iTunes store. The first takes you to the app itself, the second, to apps by the same developer, the third, to apps in the same category.

Apps that find you

Sometimes an app finds you. A lot of information providers, like newspapers or radio broadcasts, service providers, such as banks and FedEx, and social networks, like Facebook or Twitter, caught on to the power of apps right from the beginning and developed slimmed-down versions of their Internet offerings.

If you visit the FedEx website via Safari on your iPhone, you'll be prompted to download the FedEx app so you can track deliveries or request pickups. Barbara's bank sent her an e-mail invitation to download its online banking app. These apps give you direct access to the iPhone versions of their web-sites, which allow you to access the essentials without the extemporaneous fluff that takes a long time to load across a cellular data network.

Another way you can find apps for products and services you use frequently is to scan 2D barcodes, which are those one-by-one inch square graphic images that look like a labyrinth. You have to download a 2D barcode scanning reader such as QR Reader for iPhone or i-nigma QR. (QR stands for Quick Response.) After you have the reader app, you open the app and hold it over one of those barcodes. You are automatically sent to a mobile web page for the product or service associated with that barcode.

Reading the News with Newsstand

You may have noticed the Newsstand button on the Home screen — it looks like a wooden bookshelf. You download a publication's app (usually for free) by tapping the Newsstand button and then tapping Store. You subscribe to magazines or newpapers through an in-app purchase. New issues are delivered automatically to your iPhone and a badge on the Newsstand icon indicates how many have arrived. All your publications are neatly stored in Newsstand, as shown in Figure 2-8. Just click on the publication on the Newsstand shelf to read the issue.

Figure 2-8: Newsstand stores your newspaper and magazine subscriptions in one place.

Syncing Apps

We talk about syncing in depth in Book II, Chapter 1, but here we want to mention Automatic Downloads. If you set up Automatic Downloads in iTunes, any purchase you make on one device, such as your computer or iPhone, is automatically downloaded to other devices linked to the same Apple ID. Automatic Downloads have made syncing practically obsolete. Here's how to set up Automatic Downloads:

1. **Open iTunes on your computer.**

2. **Choose iTunes⇨Preferences and click the Store tab.**

    The window shown in Figure 2-9 appears.

3. **Check the type of media you want downloaded simultaneously to all devices.**

    You see in the figure we checked only Music and Apps.

4. **Click OK.**

5. **On your iPhone, tap Settings⊏⊐Store and then tap On next to the items you want activated for Automatic Downloads (such as Music, Apps, Books, or Newsstand).**

Store Preferences

General Playback Sharing Store Parental Devices Advanced

Automatic Downloads

iTunes can automatically download new purchases made on other devices using "barbaradepaula". To change to a different account, sign in to the iTunes Store.

☑ Music ☑ Apps ☐ Books

You can enable automatic downloads on your iOS device by tapping Settings > Store.

☑ Always check for available downloads
☐ Automatically download pre-orders when available

iTunes Pass and other pre-orders will download to this computer as they become available.

Cancel   OK

Figure 2-9: Set up Automatic Downloads to send syncing to obsolescence.

Deleting Apps

You may tire of an app or find you downloaded an app that's a dud and you want to delete it. We explained this in Book I, Chapter 3, but here's a quick review. To delete apps from your iPhone, do the following:

1. **Press and hold any app on the Home screen until all the apps start wiggling.**

2. **Tap the X in the corner of the apps you want to delete.**

3. **Press the Home button when you're finished and the apps stand still.**

After you download an app, it remains associated with your Apple ID on iTunes. If you accidentally delete an app from your iPhone, you can download again from the AppStore, as explained in the next section, or re-sync with iTunes on your computer, as explained in Book II, Chapter 1.

Identifying and Reinstalling Apps You Already Own

Mistakes happen. Computers crash. iPhones fall out of windows of moving cars. The result may be that you accidentally lose an app, could be a favorite game that you purchased or your online banking app. In any case, if you lose one app or all of them, the App Store knows what apps you already bought and lets you download them again (if they're still available from the App Store), free of charge. Here's how to do it on your iPhone:

1. **Locate the app in the App Store.**

   The Free/Buy button on apps you already purchased or downloaded for free reads Install.

2. **Tap Install.**

   Type in your Apple ID and password, if requested.

3. **Click OK.**

   The app downloads to your iPhone.

On iTunes, the procedure is similar:

1. **Locate the app on iTunes.**

   The Free/Buy button on apps you purchased and/or downloaded in the past reads Download.

2. **Click the Download button.**

   Type in your Apple ID and password, if requested.

3. **Click OK.**

   The app is downloaded to iTunes and automatically downloaded to your iPhone too, if you have actived Automatic Downloads in iTunes preferences.

If you don't remember the exact names of your apps and you've lost all of them, you can access your purchase history on your computer or iPhone:

- ✐ **iTunes on your computer:** Choose Account from the pop-up menu in the upper right corner where your account name is, or click Store➪View My Account. When your account information opens, click Purchase History. A list appears of all the items you have purchased on iTunes with the Apple ID you used to sign in.

- ✐ **App Store on your iPhone:** Tap App Store on the Home screen and then tap the Updates button. Tap Purchased at the top of the list.

Updating and Upgrading Apps

An update is — almost always — an improvement to an app, usually to fix bugs. The App Store automatically checks for apps once a week, and also looks for updates whenever you sign in. Updates are free. You know you have updates when you see a numbered badge on the App Store button on your Home screen or on the Updates button at the bottom of the App screen. The number tells you how many apps have updates. Here we tell you the different ways you can find and install updates.

Using iPhone's App Store to update

You can update one app at a time or update all the apps at once. Follow this procedure:

1. **Tap App Store on the Home screen.**

2. **Tap the Updates button on the bottom right corner of the App Store.**

   A list of apps which have updates appears, as shown in Figure 2-10. The version number and date are shown under the name of the app.

3. **Tap the app in the list to see what changes or fixes the update made.**

   An Info screen opens with a description of the changes.

4. **Tap the Update button on the Info screen.**

Figure 2-10: The Updates screen shows you a list of which apps have updates available.

OR

5. Tap Update All on the Updates screen.

With Automatic Downloads, the apps in iTunes will be updated as well.

Using iTunes to update

A badge next to Apps in the Source list of the iTunes window indicates how many app updates are available. Click Apps to open the Apps section of iTunes and then click the Updates Available button at the bottom of the window. The My App Updates window opens, where you can tap the Get Update buttons next to each individual app or click Download All Free Updates to get all the updates at once. The apps on your iPhone are updated as well if Automatic Downloads is activated.

Upgrading from within the app

When a new version of an app is released, you are notified by the App Store on your iPhone and iTunes. Some apps let you know within the app that a new version is available. You might be playing a game and a notification appears telling you that a new version is available. Simply click the link that appears to get the new version. The link usually takes you to the App Store, and there may be a fee involved if it's an upgrade, say from a barebones free version to a paid-for full version.

Buying more content

Earlier in this chapter, we mentioned add-ins like the chips you can buy so you can play the poker game. To keep things simple, add-ins are managed by the App Store. With our poker game example, after you've downloaded the app, you can purchase chips directly from within the app.

App Info and Settings

In iTunes on your computer, click on an app in a list, and then select File⇨Get Info. The app Info window opens, which has several tabs across the top. You're probably most interested in the Summary screen where you can see the version number of the app, its size and age rating, and when it was downloaded. You can also see what kind it is to determine if it works on both iPhone and iPad.

Some app settings are managed on your iPhone under Settings. Tap Settings on the Home screen and scroll down to the bottom. The last section you see is the list of apps that have settings you can change. Each app has different settings so click through and play around with the settings for the apps that you have.

Other app settings are managed from within the app. There's no cut-and-dried rule to follow. You can visit the support page for an app to learn where the settings are and what they do. Again, we recommend playing a bit with the apps you have and trying different settings to make the app useful and enjoyable for you.

Reviewing Apps and Reporting Problems

New apps come out on a daily basis and, while some are terrific and praise-worthy, others have problems or just don't do what the developer's description says the app does. You can contribute to the improvement of the app world by writing reviews and reporting problems. Your fellow app users will thank you and, our experience is that developers thank you too and quickly fix the problem. When you have a good, or bad, experience, write a quick review or at least give the app a few stars. If you encounter a repeating problem, let the developer know. Here's how to submit reviews and problems on your iPhone and through iTunes.

On your iPhone

Open the App Store from the Home screen and locate the app you want to write a review or report a problem on. For either one, go to the bottom of the Info screen that opens when you click on an app that you found.

To write a review:

1. **Tap the Ratings button.**

2. **Tap Write a Review at the top of the page.**

    You may be asked to sign in to your Apple account.

3. **Tap the number of stars you want to give the app, and then fill in the form and write your review.**

4. **Tap Send to submit your review.**

To report a problem:

1. **Tap the Report a Problem button.**

    The Report a Problem screen opens.

2. **Click one of the options and add a comment if you want.**

3. **Tap the Report button.**

On iTunes

To write a review from iTunes, locate the app in the App Store and click the Write a Review button just under Customer Reviews, about halfway down the page. You also have the option of Reporting a Concern about a review that someone else wrote, which isn't an option from the App Store on your iPhone.

Unlike the App Store, which gives you the option to report a problem directly, from iTunes, you go to the app support site. Click the link at the top of the page and follow the instructions for contacting the developer.

If you are having a problem downloading or launching an app you recently downloaded, go into your Purchase History from Store⇨View My Account. Tap Report a Problem next to the app you are experiencing download problems with. You'll be connected to Apple's App Store support page.

Chapter 3: Enhancing and Protecting iPhone with Add-ons

In This Chapter

✏ **Considering neat-o iPhone add-ons and accessories**

✏ **Protecting iPhone with screen protectors and cases**

✏ **Tuning in to headphone and headset options**

✏ **Plugging in to cable and dock choices**

✏ **Touring in-car helper gizmos**

✏ **Pumping up the volume with external speaker add-ons**

*E*ver since Apple introduced the first iPod, the so-called "iAccessories" market continues to come up with all kinds of add-ons and accessories for all things i — including, of course, your iPhone.

Just how big is the add-ons and accessories business? With so many categories and products to cover, we could literally fill an entire book. And with every new iPhone Apple releases, those new (and usually improved) add-ons and accessories hit the market, too. So instead of trying to cover every possible accessory category and type, we've selected just a few of our favorites to illustrate some of the most popular types of add-ons and accessories for your iPhone.

Let's go shopping!

Although many iPhone (and iPod touch) cases, cables, docks, and other accessories may *look* similar or just seem like they'd work with some or all of the i-device products, they rarely do. This explains why Apple created the "Made for iPhone" label, which is what you want to look for when you're shopping for iPhone accessories. What's more, you want to note *which* iPhone model (or models) a particular product is designed to work with, so you can be sure the product works with *your* iPhone.

Taking Protective Measures

iPhones are rugged little gizmos. Even so, the two most popular iPhone add-ons that most people buy for their beloved gadget are screen protectors and protective cases (which are not to be confused with iPhone cases that are all about glitz or fashion but offer zero or minimal actual protection).

Screen protectors

The iPhone screen is made of hardened glass that's so strong you can drag your car key back and forth across it and you still won't be able to scratch the glass.

Still, some iPhone owners swear by those sticky-backed screen protectors you can stick to your iPhone's screen to protect it from scratches. And while neither of us uses a screen protector on our iPhones, we both agree with two potential byproduct benefits of using a screen protector, which are

- **Minimizing smudges:** Certain screen protectors minimize how much of the finger oil smudges you see.

- **Preventing bits of glass from falling free if you shatter your iPhone's screen:** Joe can attest to the fact that although his iPhone 3G's screen shattered to bits when he knocked it off his desk and it landed face down on the floor, the screen was still able to function and respond to his finger taps. Luckily, he could continue using the smashed-screen iPhone until he was able to replace it with a new iPhone. (Of course, had Joe enclosed the befallen iPhone in a protective case that offered cushioning around the front edges, the screen probably would have survived the short fall intact, screen protector be damned — more on protective cases in a moment.)

You can buy two main kinds of screen protectors:

- **Easy On/Off:** Semi-rigid, easy-to-apply or remove plastic screen protectors in either glossy or matte (anti-glare) finishes that don't always look so great because it's next to impossible to apply them without dust or air bubbles getting trapped beneath the surface when you first apply the screen protector.

- **Semi-Permanent:** Pliable, adhesive-backed plastic film protectors that require special handling and spraying your iPhone's screen with a special liquid to apply them to your iPhone's screen — but which benefit from a durable, fingerprint-hiding, permanent-feeling fit and finish that feels like they're part of iPhone's design, while minimizing or even completely eliminating any unsightly (read: distracting) dust particles or air bubbles from appearing beneath the surface.

Our favorite screen protector picks for the two categories described previously are

✔ **Belkin MatteScreen Overlay** (www.belkin.com)**:** An anti-glare finish makes this one great for reducing unwanted glare, especially in harsh light sources.

Because some iPhone cases include a plastic screen protector, consider buying one of those two-for-one options if you're planning on buying a case as well, rather than laying out cash to buy both add-ons separately.

✔ **Zagg invisibleSHIELD** (www.zagg.com)**:** Joe has applied the invisibleSHIELD — based on a clear, thin, and very durable military film originally made to protect U.S. military helicopter blades from high-speed damage — to numerous iPhones and iPads and has always been happy with the results. Choose from full-body or screen-only options (as shown in Figure 3-1), all of which come with a spray bottle of fluid used to help position the film, and a squeegee to squeeze out fluid and air bubbles.

Zagg recommends you don't touch your iPhone for 24 hours after you apply the invisibleSHIELD; however, in Joe's experience, applying the screen protector before bed allows sufficient time for the shield to dry and set overnight. That said, you should still be gentle with your iPhone the next morning and wait until later in the day or evening to really manhandle your gadget or outfit it with a protective case (which may pinch the edges) to ensure best possible results.

**Book II
Chapter 3**

Enhancing and
Protecting iPhone
with Add-ons

Figure 3-1: Zagg offers screen-only or full-body invisibleSHIELD options.

Cases

Of course, a screen protector won't protect your iPhone's screen from breaking if it's struck with considerable force — or even just on a corner or edge. To protect your iPhone's screen from breaking, your best bet is to buy a protective case or at the very least (for minimalist types), a bumper.

Protective cases generally come in three styles:

- ✔ **Bumper case**, which is sort of like a semi-rigid rubber-band that wraps the frame of your iPhone. The edges are well protected, and the case has holes for the volume buttons and connector ports. The bumper extends slightly beyond the front and back so that if your iPhone falls flat on its face, the bumper hits the ground first.

- ✔ **Minimal case**, which covers the back and sides of your iPhone, and usually the four corners, but not always the front face, which may leave your iPhone's screen vulnerable to breakage if it endures a forceful fall or impact.

- ✔ **Surrounded case**, which covers the back, sides, corners and front edges of your iPhone, and provides a scant but potentially screen-saving lip and layer if your iPhone falls or is impacted facedown or on any edge or corner. Surround-type cases generally come in two styles:

  - One-piece construction that you squeeze your iPhone into

  - Two-piece, or "slider" construction that you slide onto either end of your iPhone until the inner edges meet in the middle (or in nearly in the middle in some cases); or two-piece "snap" case construction that's typically a larger, fuller back and sides half, and a second front "frame" that snaps to the front of the back half to seal the full-case protection deal . . . er, design.

Because new and recent model iPhones feature pretty darn scratch-resistant screens (and backs), choosing a bumper case like the ones sold by Apple (www.apple.com), as shown in Figure 3-2, can provide you with reasonable peace of mind in the event you drop your iPhone and it lands on one of its vulnerable front edges — or even facedown. At the same time, the Bumper's lack of a back cover makes this case feel close to going naked — from your iPhone's point of view, of course.

Figure 3-2: Apple's iPhone Bumper Case offers the "bare" minimum protection.

TIP

Some minimal protection cases — which are so thin, they're sometimes referred to as *skins* — don't provide corner or front screen edge protection for your iPhone. As such, choosing one of those types of cases is more of a fashion over function purchase. To each his or her own!

Surround-type cases offer the best protection for your iPhone, with choices ranging from lightweight (yet still offering full protection) to thicker, heavier weight models designed to endure the most rugged conditions or environments — including falling from the sky, or landing in a puddle of water, as some of the choices below illustrate.

A few of our favorite surround type cases include the following:

✔ **Incase Perforated Slider** (www.goincase.com)**:** This interesting looking case, shown in Figure 3-3, offers two, two, two great features in one: the all-round protection of Incase's standard Slider Case, with a lightweight, minimalist look.

Figure 3-3: Full protection, minus the bulk and weight.

✔ **Grove Bamboo Case** (www.grovemade.com)**:** Beautiful and better for the environment — that's what you get when you go with one of these handmade cases. Choices include plain or engraved, as shown in Figure 3-4. You can also send your own custom design, but be warned: The engraved or custom styles can take six or more weeks to arrive at your doorstep.

✔ **Griffin Survivor Extreme-Duty Case** (www.griffintechnology.com)**:** Steer your web browser to a special video clip on Griffin's website (www.griffintechnology.com/armored) and watch in horror as an iPhone inside a Survivor case gets thrown down a paved street, flung across an icy creek, hurled down a hillside, bowled with on a concrete floor, and slammed into an office wall — all of which iPhone survives, intact. (It doesn't survive a car peeling out over it, however.) In other words, if you're the rough outdoors type (or just clumsy), consider the Griffin Survivor case, as shown in Figure 3-5.

Figure 3-4: The eco-friendlier Grove Bamboo Case for iPhone.

Figure 3-5: Give your iPhone a reason to sing "I'm a Survivor!"

✓ **Mophie juice pack** (www.mophie.com)**:** Although recent and new model iPhones feature rechargeable batteries that are mighty enough to see you through at least a full day of typical usage, some heavy-usage iPhone owners may have to carry their chargers so they can plug in and juice up their iPhone when the battery is running low. Or you can leave the charger home and opt for the Mophie juice pack, shown in Figure 3-6, which pulls double-duty as both a protective case and an extra power source that can greatly extend your iPhone's uptime.

Figure 3-6: A protective case and battery booster in a single package.

Discovering Headphones and Headsets

iPhone's bundled stereo earphones with mic offer pretty good sound quality and the added bonus of letting you control a bunch of your iPhone's features, like answering and controlling phone calls and playing and pausing music and video. For most people, that's good enough.

But for some folks, spending extra to replace the bundled earphones is a must: for instance, audiophiles who want higher quality sound output (or make that input into the gray space between your ears), or frequent phone-callers who would like the hands-free convenience of making and receiving phone calls without wires getting in the way of their conversations. And ditto for anyone who enjoys (or depends on) listening to their favorite musical performers to help push them harder when they're working out or running without those dangling wires to get in the way of their own performance.

Some of our favorite headphone and headset choices include the following:

✓ **Sennheiser QXM 680i (**www.sennheiserusa.com**):** For outdoorsy types or runners (like Joe), these sweat and water resistant headphones feature Kevlar reinforced cables that can stand up to the elements, and ear clips that keep them in place without wobbling or bouncing no matter what terrain you're traversing. The built-in remote and mic makes it easy to answer that important call you're waiting for, or control music playback and volume. Work it!

✔ **Bose QuietComfort 3** (www.bose.com): Although they're technically lightweight as far as full-size headphones go, Bose's not-so-cheap noise-canceling headphones, shown in Figure 3-7, produce incredibly high-quality sound while cancelling out background noise. They're a perfect choice for the most discriminating audio types, but be prepared to shell out more than $300 for these babies.

Figure 3-7: Keep the good sound in and the distracting sound out.

✔ **JayBird Sportsband Bluetooth Headphones** (www.jaybirdgear.com): Less pricey than Bose's headphones and minus the wires, the Sportsband connects to your iPhone using iPhone's Bluetooth feature; a built-in mic and five easy-to-reach and -press buttons make for smooth music and call control. An optional "apt-X" adapter that plugs into your iPhone's connector port kicks up audio fidelity for even higher-quality listening pleasure.

✔ **Jabra STONE2** (www.jabra.com): Not your ordinary-looking hands-free headset, the STONE2, shown in Figure 3-8, doesn't operate like ordinary Bluetooth headsets, either. Thanks to complete voice control features, you don't even need to touch the headset to answer or reject calls — just say the word, and the STONE2 obliges. Now that's what I'm tawkin' about!

Figure 3-8: The Jabra STONE2 offers truly hands-free operation.

Hooking Up with Cables and Docks

You can never have too many connections. Especially iPhone-friendly ones that enhance your iPhone's features by letting you do things like connect your iPhone to your TV to watch photo slideshows or videos you shoot with iPhone — or movies you buy or rent from the iTunes Store — just to name a few scenarios.

Some of our favorite cable and dock options you can buy for your iPhone include the following:

✐ **Apogee JAM Guitar Input** (www.apogeedigital.com)**:** Connect the Apogee JAM Guitar Input into your iPhone (or iPad, as shown in Figure 3-9) and your guitar and record your jam sessions to GarageBand running on your iPhone; an input gain control knob makes it easy to pump up the volume — and green and red indicator lights make it easy to keep an eye on whether you're rocking within an agreeable range, or too hard to the point of un-harmonic distortion. Sweet!

Figure 3-9: A full-on guitar jam in the palm of your hand.

✔ **Apple Universal Dock** (www.apple.com): Set your iPhone into this dock for fumble-free desktop syncing and charging, and when the work day is done and it's time to play, press Play on the included remote to watch movies or listen to music thanks to ports that connect the dock to your TV and external speakers or stereo sound system.

✔ **Apple AV Adapter and Cables** (www.apple.com): Plug the Apple Digital AV Adapter into your iPhone (shown in Figure 3-10), and then connect the adapter to your HDTV with an HDMI cable (sold separately) and va-va-voom: Your iPhone can now entertain the entire room on the big-screen. Show off what you see on your iPhone screen (be it a game of Angry Birds, or the latest blockbuster you rent or buy from the iTunes Store), while keeping your iPhone juiced to last through the entire per-formance, thanks to a second port on the adapter that accommodates your iPhone's charger cable. The Composite and Component AV cable options let you connect your iPhone to a non-HDTV or HDTV. Although they don't let you mirror games or other apps, they do let you view photo and video content like movies and Camera Roll slideshows.

Another awesome (and totally wireless) option for streaming your iPhone's video and music to your TV and sound system is Apple's AppleTV product, which we write about in Book I, Chapter 2.

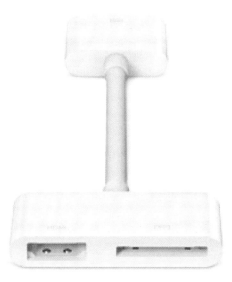

Figure 3-10: The Apple Digital AV Adapter.

Taking It on the Road with Car Accessories

It goes without saying (but we'll say it anyway) that neither of us advocates using your iPhone to carry on phone or text (!) conversations while driving — and we mean never, ever. If you need to send or reply to a text message, or make or answer a call, do yourself — and everyone in your car or on the road — a favor and pull over. (This public service announcement brought to you by "Common Sense.")

That unsaid rule said and out of the way, here are a few of our favorite iPhone accessories for the car (that don't have anything to do with using your iPhone while driving to participate in phone or text conversations):

- **Belkin TuneBase FM with Hands-Free** (www.belkin.com)**:** Connect your iPhone to the TuneBase FM receiver, shown in Figure 3-11, and you can listen to your music through your car stereo system by connecting through your FM radio receiver, with no special installation or wiring.

- **Griffin PowerJolt** (www.griffintechnology.com)**:** Charge your iPhone while you're on the road with this low-profile cigarette-lighter adapter that features a two-amp charging circuit for fast battery boosting charges. Be sure to purchase the model that works with your model of iPhone.

Figure 3-11: Listen to your iPhone's music tracks through your car's speakers.

✓ **Magellan Premium Car Kit** (www.magellangps.com)**:** Pair with the Magellan RoadMate App, and your iPhone becomes a full-on GPS navigation system — it also charges your iPhone while it's plugged in to the cradle, as shown in Figure 3-12.

Figure 3-12: Turn your iPhone into a full-on navigation system.

Checking Out Speakers

Listening to music using your iPhone's bundled earphones is fine when you want to tune out the world, but sometimes you want to share your sounds with others — which means tapping into external speakers that can play your tunes to a room full of friends, or even a small crowd.

Below are some of our favorite iPhone speaker add-ons:

- **iHome iP88 Dual Dock Stereo Triple Alarm Clock Radio for** (www.ihome audio.com)**:** Set your iPhones in the iP88 stereo alarm clock, as shown in Figure 3-13, and you and your bedmate can both charge your iPhones while you're snoozing, and then wake up to your preferred music alarm all charged up to start the day. A built-in AM/FM radio and included remote control round out this multi-faceted add-on's timely, tuned-in features.

- **Logitech Pure-Fi Anywhere 2** (www.logitech.com)**:** These are portable iPhone speakers that produce clear sound and maximum bass on the go. A rechargeable battery provides up to ten hours of music-listening while also charging your iPhone at the same time, and an included remote control makes switching and shuffling tracks a cinch from across the room — or the volleyball court.

Figure 3-13: Recharge iPhone's battery while you recharge yours two — er, too!

✔ **Philips Fidelio SoundAvia Wireless Speaker with AirPlay** (www. philips.com)**:** Stream music, podcasts, and audiobooks from your iPhone to these desktop speakers with AirPlay on your local Wi-Fi network, no wires or connector cables needed. The free Fidelio App (downloadable from the App Store) adds features and functions so you can listen to Internet radio stations, control the sound settings, and set up alarms and a sleep timer. At just around $200, we think it offers a good quality-price ratio.

✔ **Bang and Olufsen BeoSound 8** (www.bang-olufsen.com)**:** Okay, we admit the $1,000 price tag goes above and beyond what most of us want to (or can!) pay for external speakers, but if money is no object and great sound is, the BeoSound 8, shown in Figure 3-14, will feel right at home in your mansion . . . or studio apartment.

Figure 3-14: Beauty and brilliant sound — at a beastly price.

Book III

Communications Central: Calls, Messages, and the Web

The 5th Wave   By Rich Tennant

"Other than this little glitch with the landscape view, I really love my iPhone."

1 mpatient readers will probably open this minibook first — caught you, didn't we? Each of the next four chapters focuses on an aspect of communications. Chapter 1 shows you how to make phone calls with your iPhone. You might be thinking, "How hard can that be?" It's not difficult, but there's a difference between making simple phone calls and using all of your iPhone's phone-calling features, such as FaceTime video calls and voice-controlled dialing. Chapter 2 is all about messaging. We explain how to send both SMS and MMS messages and manage them, and we tell you how they differ too. Wax your (key) board because the third chapter is an invitation to a web surfin' Safari. We present an in-depth study of navigating the web on your iPhone. Chapter 4 explains Mail: how to set up an e-mail account and how to write, send, receive, respond to, and manage messages. At the end of this minibook, you'll wonder how you ever communicated without your iPhone.

Chapter 1: Managing Phone and FaceTime Video Calls

In This Chapter

✔ Taking note of Phone notifications

✔ Perusing and adjusting phone-related settings

✔ Listening to and managing voicemail messages

✔ Creating and organizing favorites and contacts

✔ Making and receiving calls

✔ Juggling call options and conference calls

✔ Face-to-face video chatting with FaceTime

We're guessing you've already made and received phone calls with your iPhone before you arrived at this chapter. You probably also listened to voicemail messages for calls you were unable to answer, and maybe you even changed the ringtone that plays when calls come in.

Even if you've already done some or all of those things, this chapter is all about maximizing your up-close-and-personal relationship with iPhone's phone-related features.

In this chapter, we introduce you to the Phone app you use to make or manage calls, and we tell you about the different ways iPhone notifies you when you miss a call. Next, we point out often-overlooked phone-related settings you may want to familiarize yourself with before you start making calls — especially if you're traveling overseas. We then show you how to listen to and manage your voicemails, step you through all of the ways you can make, receive and manage calls, and tell you how to conduct face-to-face video chat calls using FaceTime.

Homing in on Phone

 Tapping the Phone icon on the Home screen brings up the image in Figure 1-1 and is indisputably the most obvious way to use your iPhone as, well, a phone.

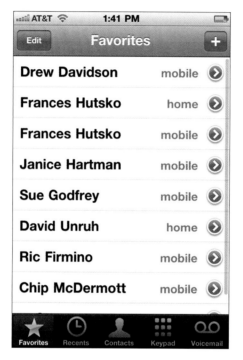

Figure 1-1: The Phone app: More ways to make calls than meets the eye.

Some not-so-obvious ways that can also land you on Phone screen include answering an incoming call, tapping a phone number in an e-mail or text message you receive to call that number back, or by speaking the name or number you want Siri (iPhone 4S) or iPhone's Voice Control feature to dial on your behalf.

 We assume that your iPhone currently enjoys an active connection with your provider's cellular network, as indicated by the cell signal strength icon in the top left corner of iPhone's status bar. The more bars you see, the better the signal. If instead of any bars you see No Signal, you won't be able to make or receive calls until you're once again in range of your provider's cellular network signal. To familiarize yourself with other icons you see in the status bar, check out Book I, Chapter 2.

Whichever way you reach the Phone screen, you always see the following icons at the bottom of the screen that activate Phone app's main features:

✔ **Favorites:** iPhone's version of speed dial, offering quick, one-tap dialing access to the fifty people you call the most.

✔ **Recents:** A roll-call list displays up to 75 of the most recent calls you placed, answered, missed, or hung up on. With one tap, you can dial anyone on the list or get more information about any of those callers.

✔ **Contacts:** Phone-book central for finding, calling, creating, or editing contact "cards" stored in the Contacts app; also displays your own phone number when you scroll up or tap the status bar to reach the top of the list. See Book IV, Chapter 1 to learn about the Contacts app.

✔ **Keypad:** An on-screen keypad that works like the physical, old-fashioned keypads of yore, for dialing phone numbers; a quick-add button lets you create a new contact card with the displayed phone number.

✔ **Voicemail:** Your inbox for listening to, replying to, managing, deleting, and getting more information about voicemail messages you receive; also the screen you visit to change your voicemail greeting message.

We write about all five of those Phone features listed above in more detail (as well as using Voice Control) in the sections "Visiting Voicemail" and "Making Calls."

Whenever a call is underway — whether you placed or answered the call — the active call screen is displayed, as shown in Figure 1-2.

When you're engaged in an active call, you can switch to another app to do other things, like looking up recipe ingredients you jotted in Notes, or reading an e-book while you're stuck on hold. When you switch to another app while engaged in a call, the pulsing active call banner shown in Figure 1-3 appears at the top of the screen. Tapping the active call banner returns you to the active call display.

**Book III
Chapter 1**

**Managing Phone
and FaceTime Video
Calls**

Figure 1-2: The active call screen.

Answering Calls

Because you never know when you might get a call, mastering the art of answering calls (or rejecting ones you're unable or not in the mood to answer) is a useful iPhone talent to acquire sooner than later.

When you receive a call, your iPhone displays one of the incoming call screens shown in Figure 1-4, depending on whether your iPhone is locked (left) or awake (right). You'll hear your chosen ringtone and, if your iPhone is on your person — depending on how sensitive you are — you may feel it vibrating. If the information of the person calling you is saved in Contacts, you'll see the person's name (and photo, if you assigned a photo to that person's contact card). If the caller isn't one of your contacts, you either see the caller's phone number and name, or "Unknown" if the caller has chosen to block their Caller ID from appearing when they place calls.

Tap the active call banner to return to your call.

Figure 1-3: The active call banner.

Figure 1-4: Two incoming call screens: One locked (left), the other not (right).

To instantly quiet your iPhone's ringtone when you receive an incoming call, tap either volume button once, or press the Sleep/Wake button once. See Book I, Chapter 2 to identify the physical buttons on your iPhone.

To decline an incoming call, do one of the following:

- ✔ Press the Sleep/Wake button twice.

- ✔ Tap the Decline button (if your iPhone is awake).

- ✔ Simply ignore iPhone's pleas to get your attention. After a few moments, the call is automatically declined.

When a call is declined, the caller hears your voicemail greeting, followed by the option to leave you a voicemail message. Ditto if someone tries calling you when your iPhone is turned off.

To answer an incoming call,

- ✔ Drag the Slide to Answer button to the right (if your iPhone is locked)

- ✔ Tap Answer

When you answer an incoming call, the active call screen appears (refer to Figure 1-2). You're welcome to tap the options you see to find out what they do, or you can get the full 411 on those options in the section "Managing Calls" a little farther along in this chapter. It's your call, so to speak.

To adjust the volume level during an active call, press iPhone's volume buttons up or down.

Answering or declining calls while using your iPhone's stereo headphones is merely a matter of working the remote button as follows:

- ✔ Click the center button once to answer a call, or twice to decline a call.

- ✔ Click the volume + or - buttons to adjust the volume level.

Taking Note of Phone Notifications

Using the Phone app puts you in control placing and answering calls and voicemail messages when you want. iPhone works behind the scenes as your personal answering service, alerting you to missed calls or voicemail messages by displaying notifications and badges, as shown in Figure 1-5. Read more about notifications in Book I, Chapter 4.

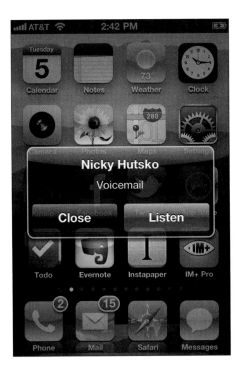

Figure 1-5: iPhone answers for you when you're unable to pick up for yourself.

You can set how your iPhone alerts you to incoming calls by going to Settings⟳Sounds, as explained in the "Perusing Phone Settings" section later in this chapter.

The different notification messages iPhone displays when you miss (or decline) calls or receive new voicemail messages include the following:

- **Missed Call:** Displays the phone number, or name of one of your contacts, whose call went unanswered.

- **Voicemail:** Displays the phone number or name of one of your contacts who has left you a voicemail message (refer to Figure 1-5).

- **Missed Call and Voicemail:** Combines both of the notifications we told you about in the two previous bullet points.

The different notification badges iPhone displays when you miss (or decline) calls or receive new voicemail messages are as follows:

- **Phone App Icon:** A red badge indicates the combined number of missed calls and/or new voicemail messages.

✔ **Phone screen:** Two numbered badges — Recents and Voicemail — as shown in Figure 1-6, indicating the number of missed calls and/or new voicemail messages in your voicemail inbox.

Numbered badges

Figure 1-6: The Phone screen notification badges.

 If your iPhone is unable to receive calls because it's in Airplane Mode, is out of your cellular network range, or is powered off, notifications messages, badges, and sounds for any missed calls or voicemail messages won't appear until your iPhone is able to receive calls again.

Perusing Phone Settings

 From the moment your iPhone is activated, you can use the Phone app to make, receive, and manage calls, and to listen to voicemail messages — all without ever needing to adjust (or even know about) any of your iPhone's many phone-related settings options.

We show you how to change a few phone-related settings throughout this chapter on a "need to know" basis, however, we encourage you to take a moment to get acquainted with the full spectrum of those settings now.

Why? Because by touring iPhone's phone-related settings options, you can maximize your awareness of every call-related feature, and potentially minimize the risk of incurring unexpected charges on your monthly phone bill by acquainting yourself with certain options that can cost you an arm and a leg if you happen to turn them on without realizing the implications.

iPhone's various phone-related settings populate four different Settings screens. Tap Settings to view the following options:

✔ **Airplane Mode:** Instantly toggles your iPhone's every wireless connection on or off; when off, calls you receive go straight to voicemail.

✔ **Wi-Fi:** Handy for toggling Wi-Fi on after activating Airplane Mode so you can connect to a Wi-Fi network to use Internet apps like Safari and Mail; any calls you receive go straight to voicemail.

Options you can review and adjust include the following:

✔ **Set Up Personal Hotspot:** Requires an optional personal hotspot data plan that you pay for separately. Such a plan uses your carrier's network to turn your iPhone into a Wi-Fi hotspot you (and a number of others determined by your carrier) can tap into with other Wi-Fi or Bluetooth-enabled devices; a USB "tethering" option lets you connect your notebook to your iPhone with a USB cable to tap into the Personal Hotspot feature.

✔ **Notifications:** Tap Phone in the list on the screen that opens to choose whether you want Phone notifications listed in the Notification Center. Choose the alert style you prefer: None, Banners (which appear at the top of the screen then disappear automatically), or Alerts (which block your phone until you do one of the actions). Choose whether you want the badge to appear on the Phone icon and whether you want to see notifications when the screen is locked.

✔ **Location Services:** When turned on, location-aware apps use your current location. For example, searching for Pizza in Maps gives you nearby pizzerias instead of worldwide pizzerias; search results that show phone numbers can be dialed directly from Maps.

✔ **Sounds:** For choosing options shown in Figure 1-7, like the ringtone that plays, whether you want iPhone to vibrate when you receive calls, and whether you want to hear an alert sound when you receive a new voicemail message. Scroll to the bottom of the screen to choose a different vibration pattern or create one of your own.

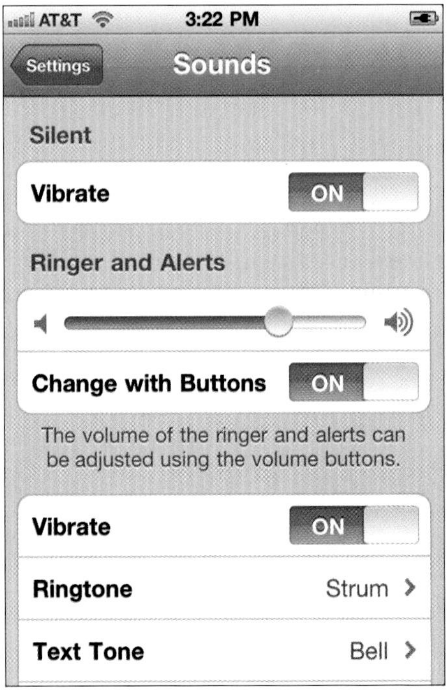

Figure 1-7: Sounds settings for choosing ringtones — and unsound options too.

Tap Settings⇨General to view the second set of phone-related settings:

✔ **Usage:** For viewing call and data related usage information.

✔ **Network:**

- **Enable 3G:** For turning on or off data-related options for accessing the Internet using your carrier's basic data network and/or faster 3G data network (only AT&T or unlocked iPhones have this feature).

- **Cellular Data:** When turned off, you can use apps that access the Internet like Safari, Maps, or Mail only via Wi-Fi. Turned off, it also prohibits data roaming.

- **Data Roaming:** For accessing Internet and voicemail using another carrier's cellular data network when you're outside your own carrier's network, either locally or out of the country.

Turning on the Data Roaming feature can wind up costing you an arm and a leg on your phone bill, so be sure you read and fully understand your carrier's roaming coverage rules, rates, regulations and any other specifics before you even *think* about turning on this option.

- **Personal Hotspot:** Opens the same screen as from Settings.

- **VPN:** For configuring access to a Virtual Private Network used by your employer and other organizations you have dealings with. You can also use it to run apps that allow remote access to your computer.

✔ **Bluetooth:** For turning on or off and managing wireless Bluetooth hands-free phone accessories like hands-free headsets and headphones, and hands-on input devices such as Bluetooth keyboards.

✔ **Auto-Lock and Passcode Lock:** For setting the length of time iPhone waits before automatically locking the screen, and for creating a secret passcode, as shown in Figure 1-8, that must be typed to unlock iPhone when the screen is locked. You can turn off Simple Passcode if you want to use a more complicated and secure code. See Book I, Chapter 4.

✔ **International:** Used to adjust location-related settings like preferred language, keyboard type, and regional formats.

✔ **Accessibility:** For turning on and customizing features that can make using iPhone easier for people with vision, hearing, and physical (hand and fingertip) control-related challenges (also see TTY, a few bullet points on). See Book I, Chapter 2 for more information.

Figure 1-8: Your passcode is a secret best kept to yourself.

Tap Settings⇨Phone to view the third set of phone-related settings:

- ✔ **My Number:** Displays your personal phone number.

- ✔ **Call Forwarding, Call Waiting, Show My Caller ID (GSM models):** For turning those features on or off. See the section "Making Calls" to learn how to activate these features.

- ✔ **TTY:** To turn on iPhone's ability to connect to a Teletype machine to enable deaf or hearing-impaired users to communicate by reading and typing text (requires the iPhone TTY Adapter cable, sold separately; we write about all of iPhone's Accessibility features in Book I, Chapter 2).

- ✔ **Change Voicemail Password:** To change your numeric voicemail password.

- ✔ **International Assist:** To have iPhone automatically add proper prefix number when calling the U.S. from abroad.

- ✔ **SIM Pin (GSM models):** To turn on, choose, and change the secret code you can use to lock your iPhone's SIM card; when activated, you must type in the PIN code whenever you turn iPhone off then on again.

After three failed attempts to unlock the SIM code, you may need to type in a Personal Unlocking Key (PUK) code in order to unlock your iPhone; if so, contact your cellular carrier's customer service number to find out your iPhone's PUK code.

✓ **Carrier Services (depends on iPhone model and carrier):** One-touch speed-dial access for dialing up various phone account-related information like your current bill balance, data and minutes usage, and directory assistance, as shown in Figure 1-9.

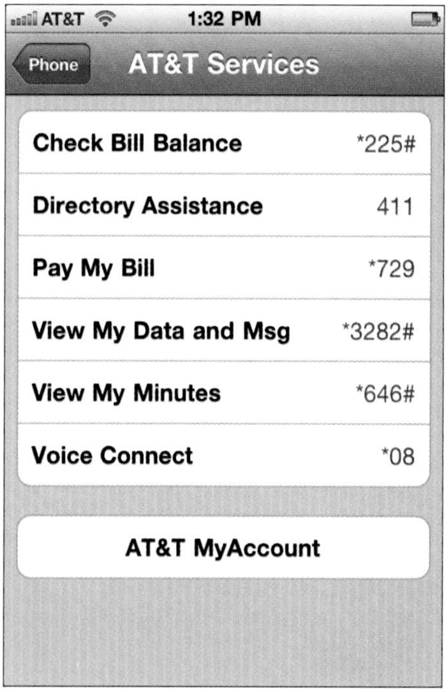

ᵃᵢᵢᵢᵢ AT&T 📶	**1:32 PM**	▭
◁ Phone	**AT&T Services**	

Check Bill Balance	*225#
Directory Assistance	411
Pay My Bill	*729
View My Data and Msg	*3282#
View My Minutes	*646#
Voice Connect	*08

AT&T MyAccount

Figure 1-9: An easy way to get in touch with your cellular provider.

Tap Settings⟳FaceTime to view the fourth set of phone-related settings:

✓ **FaceTime:** iPhone 4 or 4S, enables or disables FaceTime video chat calling feature. You can log in to your Apple account, specify which e-mail accounts you wish to associate with FaceTime, and which Caller ID you want to appear. We explain how to use FaceTime in the specific FaceTime section of this chapter.

We revisit the previous phone-related settings as needed throughout the rest of this chapter.

Visiting Voicemail

Setting up your voicemail greeting, and listening to and managing voicemail messages, are two things you may want to do before diving into the rest of this chapter.

To familiarize yourself with the different ways your iPhone notifies you when you receive voicemail messages, check out "Taking Note of Phone Notifications" in the section prior to this one.

Tap Phone⇨Voicemail to display the Voicemail screen, as shown in Figure 1-10.

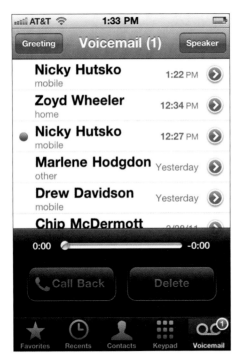

Figure 1-10: The Voicemail screen lists your voicemail messages.

**Book III
Chapter 1**

**Managing Phone
and FaceTime Video
Calls**

When we refer to doing things with voicemail on your iPhone in this chapter (and throughout the book), we're referring to the visual kind — also known as "visual voicemail," which we define in the nearby sidebar, "Visual voicemail: Seen *and* heard." But visual voicemail isn't a feature you always find on every iPhone. In some cases, you may have to pay an extra monthly fee for the feature. In other cases, the visual voicemail feature may not be available at all in certain countries or regions.

Visual voicemail: Seen and heard

Visual voicemail is called that because you actually see your voice messages listed in a nice and neat stack just like your e-mail messages, whereas typical "non-visual" voicemail only appears . . . well, nowhere, because only visual voicemail messages can be seen and heard. If you've never had voicemail, you may be unfamiliar with what it's like to retrieve your voicemail messages the "old-fashioned way" by dialing into your voicemail mailbox. Then pressing buttons on the keypad to skip, fast forward, rewind, and delete those messages as they rattle off one after the other — all of which visual voicemail lets you do with your fingertips. You can select the messages you want to hear and listen to them in the order you want. Better yet — ask Siri to read your list of visual voicemail messages to you.

Recording and changing your greeting

If this is the first time you're visiting the Voicemail screen, iPhone prompts you to record your voicemail greeting. Repeating the same steps is how you change your voicemail greeting message whenever you want.

Tap Greeting to display the Voicemail Greeting screen shown in Figure 1-11, and then choose one of the following options:

- Tap Default if you want callers to hear your cellular provider's generic voicemail message (which says something like "the person you are trying to reach at" — your phone number — "is not available," followed by instructions on how to leave a message, yada yada yada).

- Tap Custom if you want to record (or change) a personal greeting message in your own words, and then tap Record to record your greeting; tap Play to listen to your greeting.

- Tap Save when you're happy with your choice, or tap Cancel if you've changed your mind and you want to keep the existing greeting.

Listening to and managing voicemail messages

When you tap a voicemail message in the voicemail list to select that voicemail message, your selection is highlighted, the Call Back and Delete buttons become active, a tiny Play/Pause button appears on the left side of your selection, and the message's length is displayed to the right side of the playback scrubber bar beneath the voicemail message list, as shown in Figure 1-12.

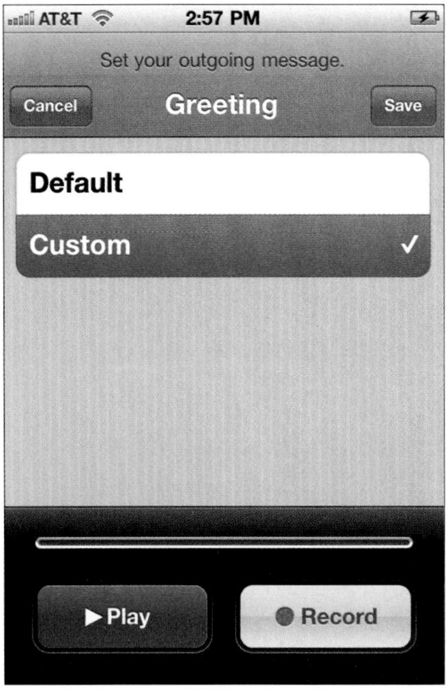

Figure 1-11: The Voicemail Greeting screen.

To listen to and control playback of a voicemail message,

- ✔ Tap the Play button to listen to the message. A Pause button replaces the Play button. You can juggle between the two to play and pause playback.

- ✔ Drag the playhead in the scrubber bar to move to any location in the voicemail message.

- ✔ Tap the Speaker button (refer to Figure 1-12) at any time to hear messages out loud through iPhone's speaker (rather than holding iPhone to your ear or listening through headphones).

Messages you've listened to remain in your voicemail inbox until your cellular carrier deletes those messages. This means that even if you delete a message, it may pop back into the Inbox at a later date. The length of time messages you've listened to remain in your voicemail box varies; check with your carrier.

Book III
Chapter 1

Managing Phone
and FaceTime Video
Calls

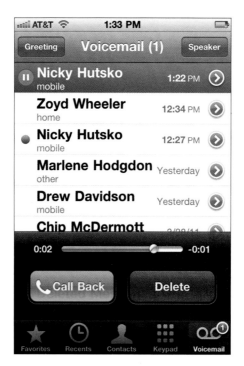

Figure 1-12: Listening to a voicemail message with the speakerphone turned on.

To display more information about the caller, tap the > button on the right side of your selected voicemail message to display the Info screen, as shown in Figure 1-13.

See "Using Contacts" later in this chapter to find out how to do things with the caller contact Info screen.

Tap Call Back to call the person who left you the selected message.

Tap Delete to delete the selected voicemail message. When you delete a voicemail message, the message is removed from the Voicemail list screen, and is saved in the Deleted Messages folder, which is automatically created if it isn't already displayed.

Tap the Deleted Messages folder to display the Deleted screen, as shown in Figure 1-14.

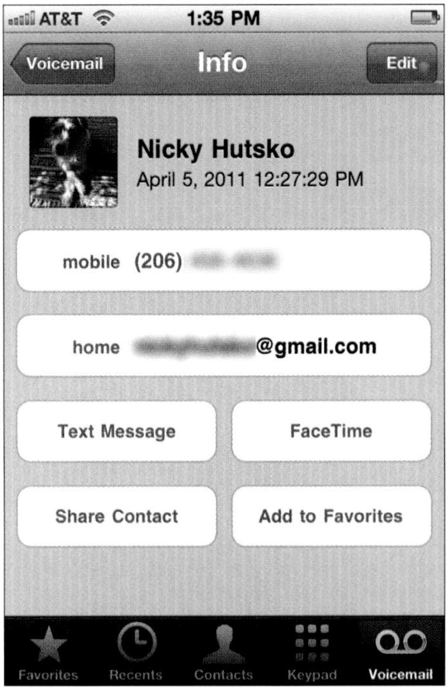

Figure 1-13: Seeing information about a person who left you a voicemail message.

Book III
Chapter 1

Managing Phone
and FaceTime Video
Calls

When viewing the Deleted screen, you can

✔ Tap a voicemail message to select it, and then

- Tap Play to listen to the message
- Tap Undelete to move the message out of the Deleted Messages folder and back to the Voicemail messages screen

✔ Tap Clear All to remove all deleted messages from the Deleted Messages folder and back to the Voicemail messages screen.

With Visual Voicemail at your service, the idea of ever going back to the old way of dialing in to your voicemail box and tapping buttons to skip through your messages seems like torture. That said, you can relive the past by pressing and holding the 1 button on the keypad to automatically dial into and begin listening to your voicemail messages, or by typing your own phone number and pressing Call, and then pressing * and entering your password to listen to your voicemail messages. Like we said, torture!

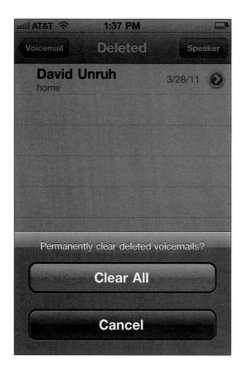

Figure 1-14: The Delete screen lists items in the Deleted Messages folder.

Making Calls

iPhone lets you make calls a number of ways — from tapping out numbers the old-fashioned way using the on-screen keypad, to saying the number or name of the person you want to call out loud without having to bother touching the screen at all.

But wait, there's more: In addition to these Phone-app ways of making calls, the nearby sidebar "Even more ways to make calls" describes even more ways you can initiate calls with your iPhone.

To simply make a phone call, tap the Phone app on the Home screen, and then tap one of the five buttons at the bottom of the Phone screen (which we show you at the very beginning of this chapter back in Figure 1-1).

Here's a quick rundown of the ways to use the Phone app, Voice Control, or Siri to make calls (all of which we cover in depth in the following sections):

 ✔ Tap Favorites, and then tap the contact you want to call.

 ✔ Tap Recents, and then tap the name or number you want to call.

✔ Tap Contacts, find and tap the contact you want to call to display his contact card, then tap the phone number you want to dial.

✔ Tap Keypad, type the number you want to call, and then tap Call.

✔ Tap Voicemail, tap the name or number you want to call, and then tap Call Back.

✔ Press and hold the Home button to activate Siri (iPhone 4S only) or Voice Control, and then say the name or number you want to call.

Using Favorites

Tapping Favorites displays the names of up to 50 people and organizations you deem important enough to score a spot on what is essentially iPhone's version of your speed-dial list, as shown in Figure 1-15. You add people and organizations to your favorites list from Contacts; locate the contact in Contacts, then tap the Add to Favorites button. Tap a favorite to call the phone number associated with that favorite.

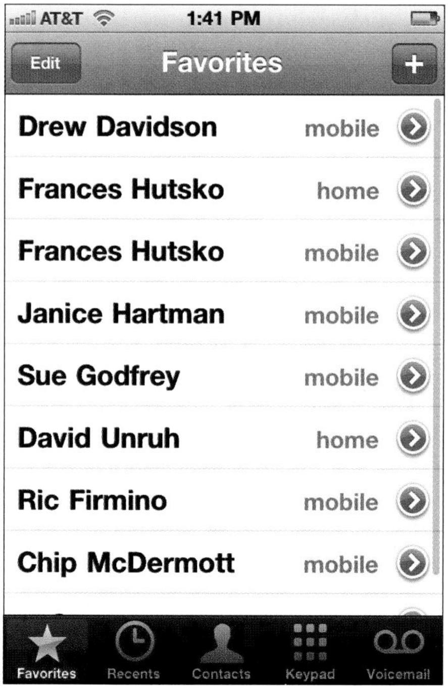

Figure 1-15: A single tap is all it takes to call a Favorite phone number.

Even more ways to make calls

Besides using the Phone app, Voice Control, or Siri to make calls, you can also initiate calls by tapping phone numbers that appear on web pages you're browsing, in e-mail, notes, or text messages you receive, and in other near and possibly faraway places like the search results you turn up when you use Maps to locate a restaurant, business, or other organization. To make a call from Maps, tap the arrow next to the name on the map to open up an information screen, and then tap the phone number to make the call. (See the calling sequence for Maps in the two figures.) Tapping a phone number in any app displays a dialog, which gives you the option to call the number, whereas pressing and holding on a number serves up even more options for doing things besides just calling the number, including sending a text message to the number, creating a new contact card for the number, or adding the number to an existing card already saved in Contacts.

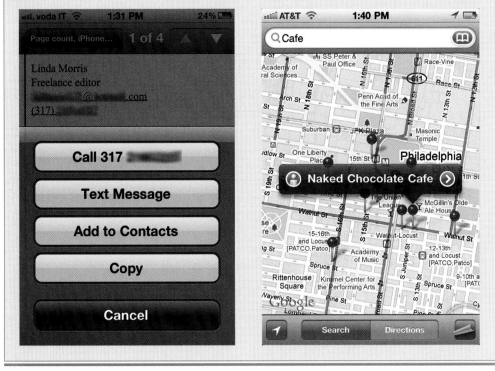

A description of the phone number associated with each favorite appears to the right of the contact's name, to indicate "mobile," "home," or another label you selected when you created the person's contact card. A camera icon appears alongside any names you add as FaceTime favorites (as we explain in the "Doing FaceTime Video Chat Calls" section at the end of this chapter).

You can add, edit, rearrange, remove, and do other things with Favorites as follows:

✓ **Add a favorite:** Tap the + (plus sign) button to display your contacts, and then search or scroll through your contacts to find the one you want to add; tap the contact you want to add to your favorites list, and then choose the phone number you want to associate with that contact's favorite place on your list. A dialog asks if you want to add the number as a favorite for Voice Call or FaceTime, as shown in Figure 1-16. Tap the one you want.

Groups: The Groups button only appears in the All Contacts list if you've created groups in your computer's address book program for organizing your contacts, or if you have contacts for more than one e-mail account configured on your iPhone in Settings⇨Mail, Contacts, Calendars, or both. Tap Groups and choose the particular e-mail account's contacts list, or tap all contacts to list every available contact.

TIP

The + button doesn't appear after you've reached the Favorites list limit of 50 favorites. You'll need to delete an existing favorite from your list to make the + appear again so you can tap it to add a new favorite.

A few things to be aware of when viewing and choosing contacts in your favorites list include

- A blue star appears next to a contacts phone number if that number is already saved in your Favorites list. Tap another number for that contact to add a second favorite number for that contact (for instance, one for Mom's mobile number, a second for her home number).

- Contacts already added to your favorites list with no second or remaining phone numbers to add won't appear in your contacts list when adding new contacts to Favorites (because you've already added them).

Figure 1-16: A number can be assigned as a FaceTime or Voice Call favorite.

Although you can designate a phone number as a FaceTime favorite, the FaceTime Failed message appears if a person you try to call isn't using a FaceTime-capable device such as an iPhone 4 or a Mac running the FaceTime app.

You can also add contacts to your Favorites list using the Phone app's Recents, Contacts, Keypad, and Voice Mail features, as we explain in the sections for each of those features, following this section.

↙ **Delete or rearrange Favorites:** Tap Edit to display the Favorites list edit screen shown in Figure 1-17, and then do one or both of the following:

- Delete a favorite from the list by tapping the red button to the left of the name, then tapping the delete button that appears to the right (your no-longer-favored contact's name only vanishes from your Favorites list, but her card is not deleted from your saved Contacts).

- Move a favorite up or down the list by tapping the grip handle button and dragging up or down your list (refer to Figure 1-17), and then let go to save your favorite in its new location.

- Tap the Done button when you finish.

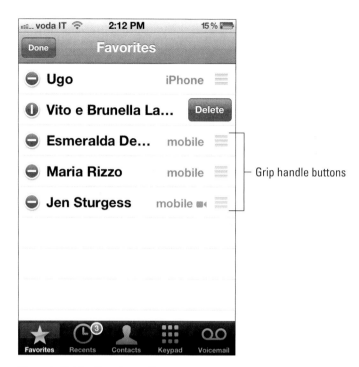

Figure 1-17: The Favorites edit screen.

Book III
Chapter 1

Managing Phone
and FaceTime Video
Calls

🖊 **Get More Info/Edit a Favorite:** Tap the blue arrow to display a favorite's contact Info screen. The person's contact card displays any information you filled in for that contact, including phone numbers and e-mail addresses. A blue star appears next to the phone number associated with that favorite. We explain Contacts more in Book IV, Chapter 1, but the things you can do while viewing a contact Info screen include

- Tap a phone number to call the contact.

- Tap an e-mail address to open and automatically address a new e-mail message to the contact.

- Tap Edit and then add, edit, or delete any information in the contact card's details fields.

- Tap the Send Message, FaceTime, Share Contact, or Add to Favorites buttons to do any of those things with your currently selected contact card.

We write about those other things you can do in the "Managing Calls" section of this chapter.

Using Recents

Tapping Recents displays a chronological list — also referred to as your phone's call log — of up to 75 of the most recent numbers your iPhone has called, received or missed calls from, or hung up on (more than one call from the same number counts as one of the 75), as shown in Figure 1-18. A label next to the recent caller/callee's number — such as home, mobile, or other — is displayed if you assigned that label to the number in Contacts or the contact management app you use.

Tap a name or number in the Recents list to call that person or phone number.

Calls you place are marked with the outgoing phone call icon, whereas missed calls are hard to miss on your list because they're the items displayed in red type.

Recents items with names indicate calls to or from people whose numbers are saved in your Contacts, while recent items that appear as phone numbers aren't associated with a person's contact card. (That doesn't mean you can't save a phone number in Contacts without a name — you can. But why you'd want to is anyone's guess.)

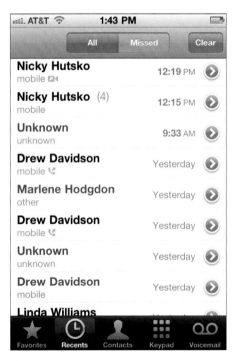

Figure 1-18: Recents displays a list of all incoming and outgoing phone activity.

Recents thoughtfully combines incoming and outgoing calls from or to the same person or phone number and displays a number in parentheses next to the name or number (refer to Figure 1-18). Tap the blue arrow button to see more information about the call activity, as shown in Figure 1-19.

Other things you can do with the Recent items screen include the following:

✔ Tap the Missed button to view only those incoming calls you didn't answer (as shown in Figure 1-20); tap All to switch back to the full list of every recent call, missed, made, and otherwise.

✔ Tap the Clear button clears *all* items from the Recents list even if you tap Clear while viewing only Missed calls.

✔ Swipe across an individual call then tap the Delete button that appears to delete only that recent call from the list.

✔ Tap the blue arrow button to display the Info screen, to see detailed information (refer to Figure 1-19) about the day and time (or consecutive times) a contact or phone number reached out to you (or you reached out to them).

▪▪▪▪▪ voda IT 📶	**2:32 PM**	14% 🔋
Recents	**Info**	**Edit**

Ugo
ICE - In Case Of Emergency

Incoming Calls		**October 20, 2011**
10:43 AM	34 seconds	
7:22 PM	32 seconds	Oct 19, 2011
7:37 PM	16 seconds	Oct 18, 2011

Outgoing Calls		**October 20, 2011**
10:38 AM	cancelled	
10:36 AM	cancelled	

work	**06 77054303**
work	**06 77054215**

★	🕐	👤	⚏	◖◗
Favorites	**Recents**	Contacts	Keypad	Voicemail

Figure 1-19: Tap the blue arrow to see the time and duration of calls from the same number.

Any information you have saved in the contact's Contacts card is also displayed, including any additional phone numbers, e-mail or street addresses, and other details. A blue star appears next to any of that contact's phone numbers you designated as favorite.

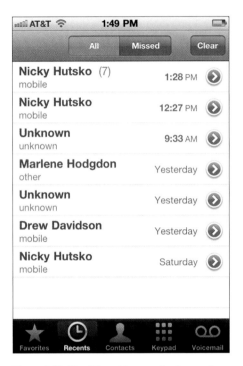

Figure 1-20: The Missed button displays only those calls you missed.

Using Contacts

Tapping Contacts displays your iPhone's central directory for storing and managing contact "cards" containing the names, phone numbers, e-mail and street addresses, and other information, as shown in Figure 1-21. The Contacts you see in the Phone app are the same as those in the Contacts app.

Tap a contact card to display the contact's Info screen, as shown in Figure 1-22, and then tap the phone number you want to call to dial that number.

You can search your contacts from the Contacts list three ways:

- ✒ Drag or flick up or down the list until you see the contact you want.

- ✒ Tap a letter in the A to Z index on the right edge to jump to contact names beginning with that letter, and then drag to scroll through the list until you see the contact you want.

✔ Tap the Search field and begin typing the name (or company name) of the person you're searching for to display any contacts that match what you type, and then tap the contact that matches the one you're looking for, as shown in Figure 1-23.

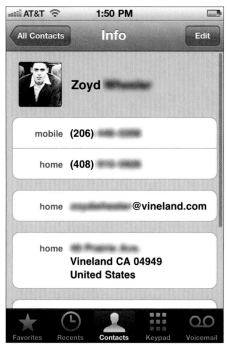

Figure 1-21: Contacts lists every contact "card" saved on your iPhone.

If you don't see the search field, tap the teeny tiny magnifying glass icon at the top of the alphabet index list on the right edge, or tap the clock in the Status bar at the top of iPhone's screen to jump to the top of your contacts list and reveal the Search field.

You can also search for your contacts (and oodles of other things like e-mail and text messages, notes, and songs stored on your iPhone) using Spotlight search, which you access by flicking the main Home screen to the right; we tell you everything you need to know about using the Spotlight feature in Book I, Chapter 3.

 Tap the + button to open a New Contact card that you can fill in to create a new contact you want to save in Contacts. We write about creating, using, and managing Contacts in Book IV, Chapter 1.

Figure 1-22: Tap a contact's phone number to call that number.

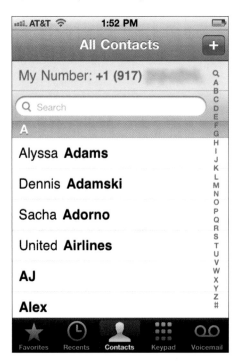

Figure 1-23: Honing in on contacts with the Search feature.

Instead of adding contacts to your iPhone by hand, it's easier to fill up your Contacts list (if you haven't already done so) by syncing your iPhone with iTunes or iCloud. Learn about syncing in Book II, Chapter 1.

If your iPhone is the type that requires a SIM card to operate, you may be able to copy contacts from your prior mobile phone's SIM card to your iPhone by tapping Settings➪Mail, Contacts, Calendars➪Import SIM Contacts.

Using the Keypad

Tapping the Keypad display's the onscreen keypad shown in Figure 1-24.

Figure 1-24: Dialing phone numbers the "old-fashioned" way.

Tap the numbers of the phone number you want to call and then press Call to dial your number.

Tap the delete button to backspace over a number (or numbers) you mistyped.

Some nifty things you can do (and see!) when you're using Keypad include the following:

✔ Enter a "soft" pause by pressing and holding the * key until a comma appears in the phone number display. A soft pause is two seconds. You could use this feature if you call in for your voicemail at work and have to call the phone number, and then enter an access code, and then perhaps a passcode. Putting a soft pause between the phone number and each code gives the system time to receive the information and go to the next step.

✔ Enter a "hard" pause by pressing and holding the # key until a semicolon appears in the phone number display. A hard pause waits for your confirmation (tap the Dial button) before transmitting the next series of numbers. For example, when calling a company, you have to wait for the line to be answered before entering an extension.

✔ Paste a phone number you copied to the clipboard from another app into Keypad by tapping the display zone above the numbers keys, and then tapping Paste in the pop-up that appears.

✔ See the contact name magically appear beneath a number you tap in if that number is on any contact's card.

 ✔ Tap the Add Contact button (to the left of the Call button) to either create a new contact card with the phone number you're typing, or to add the phone number to an existing contact, as shown in Figure 1-25.

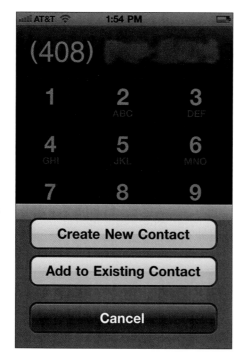

Figure 1-25: Putting a new phone number to good use.

Using Voicemail

One of our favorite things about the Phone app's Voicemail feature is how *seeing* those messages in the voicemail inbox helps to remind us to call back any of those people we want to chat with.

Tap a name or number in the Voicemail list screen and then tap Call Back to call that person or phone number.

To learn about the other things you can do on the Voicemail screen besides returning phone calls, check out the section "Visiting Voicemail," earlier in this chapter.

Using Voice Control and Siri

Both iPhone's Voice Control and Siri (only on iPhone 4S) features are all ears when it comes to using your voice to make your iPhone do things for you — including making phone calls. In Book I, Chapter 3, we explain all the other things Voice Control and Siri can do for you. Here, we explain phone calls.

REMEMBER

You can use Voice Control or Siri but not both at the same time, and you need either a cellular data or Wi-Fi connection to the Internet to use Siri.

Voice Control

Press and hold the Home button to activate Voice Control, the screen as shown in Figure 1-26 opens, (you'll also hear a double-tone sound), and then say "Call" or "Dial," followed by the name of the person or phone number you want to call. A slightly robotic voice repeats your request aloud and then places your call for you.

 No Match Found: That's what the Voice Control robot says (followed by three tone sounds) if it can't find a phone number in Contacts that matches the name you said; or if it can't understand the phone number you gave it to dial for you. Either way, you can try again by immediately repeating the name or number (perhaps more slowly this time).

Voice Control may have trouble understanding you in a crowded place with a lot of ambient noise such as a party or street corner. If you are calling someone with a foreign name, say it with an English pronunciation. For example, Barbara's husband's name is Ugo (pronounced oo-go), but for Voice Control to understand, Barbara must say "call *hew-go*".

 Multiple Numbers: If a contact you're calling has more than one phone number, the Voice Calling robot says the contact's name aloud, and then rattles off the different phone numbers it finds for that contact, such as "home, mobile, or work?". Say the one you want and Voice Control completes the call request.

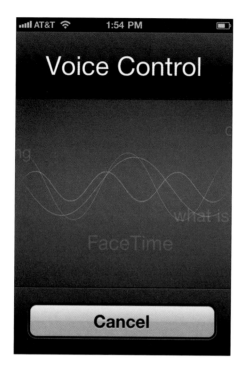

Figure 1-26: The Voice Control screen.

Ways Voice Control may respond to your request include the following:

✔ **Multiple Matches Found:** That's what Voice Control tells you if it finds multiple numbers for a name you say, such as "Call Joe;" Voice Control lists the names of contacts with the same name so you can pick one, or it asks you to be more specific.

When saying a person's name, you can differentiate between people who have the same first name by adding their last name, as well as say the specific phone number you want to call if you have more than one phone number for the person:

✔ Say "Call" or "Dial," and then say

- "Joe Smith"
- "Joe Smith at work"
- "Joe Hutsko, mobile"

Tips to keep in mind when saying phone numbers you want to call include

✔ Speak each number clearly and separately; for instance, if you want to call 555-6666, you would say "Call five five five, six six six six."

✔ If you're calling an 800 number, you can say "eight hundred," followed by the rest of the number you are calling.

Siri

Siri is a bit more intelligent than Voice Control, or perhaps she has better ears. Press and hold the Home button until the Siri screen opens, as shown in Figure 1-27, and Siri asks, "How may I help you?"

Figure 1-27: The Siri calling screen.

Speak your command, more or less as if you were talking with a person. You can give complex instructions, like "Call Joe on his cell phone." Siri looks first in your Favorites for people named Joe and then for Joe's mobile phone number. Siri responds along the lines of "Calling Joe Hutsko on mobile phone." If there is no Joe in your Favorites, Siri asks for more information. Speak the requested information and Siri makes the phone call when she finds the number. If the person you want to call isn't in your Contacts or somewhere else on your iPhone, Siri can search the Internet for the number, and then connect you. You get the picture. If the person isn't available, you can ask Siri to send the person an e-mail.

The Voice Control and Siri features work even if your iPhone is locked, which is a handy feature — unless you misplace or lose your iPhone and someone picks it up and starts making international calls. To turn off the ability to make Voice Control calls when your iPhone is locked, go to Settings⇨General⇨Passcode Lock, and turn off the Voice Dialing option, as shown in Figure 1-28. When the Voice Dialing feature is off, you can still use Voice Control or Siri when your iPhone is locked to do things like play or pause music or say "What time is it?" to hear the local time. If you say "Call Joe Hutsko," however, the ever-watchful genie that lives inside your iPhone politely responds, "Voice dialing is disabled."

![Passcode Lock screen showing Turn Passcode Off, Change Passcode, Require Passcode After 15 min., Simple Passcode ON, Voice Dial ON, Erase Data ON]

Figure 1-28: Disable or enable the Voice Dialing or Siri feature when iPhone is locked.

Call Forwarding, Call Waiting, and Caller ID Blocking

Some phone-related settings you may want to take advantage of include call forwarding, call waiting, and caller ID blocking. To turn those features on or off for GSM model iPhone's like the ones that work with AT&T or the unlocked model you can buy at the Apple Store, tap Settings⇨Phone, and then tap the setting you want to turn on or off, as shown in Figure 1-29.

Figure 1-29: Setting Call Forwarding, Call Waiting, and Caller ID Blocking options.

Book III
Chapter 1

Managing Phone
and FaceTime Video
Calls

If you turn on Call Forwarding, a prompt appears so you can type in the phone number you want your calls forwarded to.

The call forwarding icon appears in the Status Bar when you turn on the Call Forwarding feature on GSM model iPhones.

To turn those features on or off for CMDA model iPhone's like the ones that work with Verizon, use the Phone app's Keypad to type in the appropriate special code below for the particular feature you want to manage:

- ✔ **Call Forwarding on:** Type *72 followed by the phone number you want your calls forwarded to, and then tap Call.

- ✔ **Call Forwarding off:** Type *73, and then tap Call.

- ✔ **Call Waiting off for a call you are about to make:** Type *70, and then type the number you want to call and tap Call.

- ✔ **Block Caller ID for a call you are about to make:** Type *67, and then dial the number you want to call and tap Call.

On CMDA model iPhones, you can only turn off call waiting and caller ID blocking on a per-call basis, but you can't turn either feature off for all calls the way you can with GSM model iPhones.

Managing Calls

In the previous sections, we tell you about (almost) every which way you can answer and make calls with iPhone. In this section, we tell you about the things you can do while you're engaged in an active call: Things like adjusting the volume for your call, as shown in Figure 1-30, or using the active call screen to do other things while you're actively engaged in a call.

Figure 1-30: The volume level indicator and the active call screen.

What kinds of other things? Neat stuff like switching on iPhone's speakerphone and making or accepting a second call while you're on your current call, then merging those two calls together so everyone can join the conversation.

The Active Call screen displays information about the person or business you're speaking with such as the phone number or name (if saved in

Contacts), and the length of time you're engaged in your call from the moment you connected. You'll also see a photo of the person if you saved a photo with his contact card in Contacts.

- ✔ Press iPhone's volume up and down buttons to increase or decrease the volume level of your call. (If you're using headphones or a Bluetooth headset, you can also press the volume + and - buttons on those listening devices to adjust the call volume.)

- ✔ Tap Ignore or Hold Call + Answer if a second call comes in while you're engaged in your current call, as shown in Figure 1-31. (We give you more details on juggling more than one call at a time in the section "Making and Managing Dual and Conference Calls.")

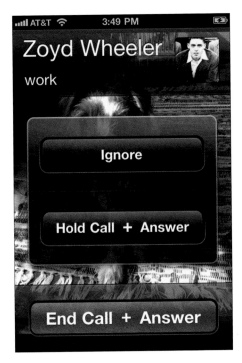

Figure 1-31: Options for responding to a second incoming phone call.

When you make a call while you're connected to a Bluetooth headset you paired with your iPhone (or other Bluetooth audio device), the Audio Sources screen shown in Figure 1-32 appears while your call is being connected. Tap iPhone or Speaker if you want to switch to either of those audio sources instead of your Bluetooth device; or tap Hide Sources to display the active call screen (refer to Figure 1-30), which automatically appears after your call is connected. (We tell you how to set up and manage Bluetooth devices in Book I, Chapter 2.)

Figure 1-32: Choosing your preferred audio source while making or managing a call.

Ways you can use the active call screen while you're engaged in a call include the following:

✓ **Mute:** Tap Mute to prevent your caller from hearing sound on your end of the conversation, even though you can still hear your caller; tap again to turn off Mute.

✓ **Keypad:** Tap Keypad to display the keypad, and then tap any numbers or the * and # buttons to do things like respond to options when calling automated customer service phone numbers, or check your work voice-mail inbox.

✓ **Speaker:** Tap the Speaker icon to hear your caller's voice through iPhone's built-in loudspeaker.

✓ **Add Call:** Tap Add Call to display your Contacts, choose the contact you want to call, and then tap the number that you want to dial; you can also tap Favorites, Recents, Keypad, or Voicemail to add your second call; while engaged in two calls, the active multiple calls screen appears, as shown in Figure 1-33.

✔ **Hold:** Press and hold the Mute button; the mute button changes into the Hold button; tap Hold again to turn off Hold. When you place a call on hold, neither you or the person on the other end can hear the other.

✔ **Contacts:** Tap Contacts to browse your contact cards to do things like find and share a phone number with the person you're currently speaking with, or choose another contact's phone number that you want to call while engaged in your current call.

✔ **Switch Audio Device:** Tap Audio Source to display the Audio Sources options (refer to Figure 1-32), and then tap the audio source choice you want to switch to; tap Hide Sources to return to the active call screen.

Figure 1-33: The active multiple calls screen.

Book III
Chapter 1

Managing Phone
and FaceTime Video
Calls

We show you how to juggle more than one call at a time in the section "Making Dual and Conference Calls."

✔ **Use FaceTime:** Tap FaceTime to switch your current voice-only call to a FaceTime video chat call, which we write about in the section "Making a FaceTime Call," later in this chapter.

Using FaceTime requires you to be connected to a Wi-Fi network, and the person on the other end of your conversation must be using either an iPhone capable of making FaceTime calls, or the FaceTime program on a Mac equipped with an iSight or external webcam, an iPad2, or a fourth generation iPod touch.

Making Dual and Conference Calls

While you're engaged in an active call, you can make a second call, or you can answer an incoming call (unless you've turned off your iPhone's call waiting feature, which we explain in the "Call Forwarding, Call Waiting, and Caller ID Blocking" section of this chapter). If you have a GSM-model iPhone, you can also initiate a conference call that lets you speak with up to five people at once.

Making a second call

While on an active call, you can make a second call by doing the following:

🢗 **Tap Add Call to display your iPhone Contacts, and then find and choose the contact you want to call, as shown in Figure 1-34.**

You can tap the Favorites, Recents, Keypad, and Voicemail buttons at the bottom of the screen to use any of those options to add your second call.

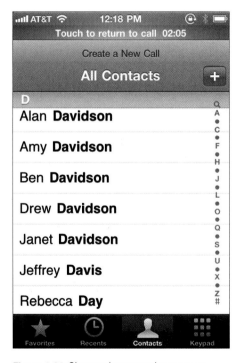

Figure 1-34: Choose the second person or number you want to call.

When your second call is established, the active multiple calls screen appears (refer to Figure 1-33).

✔ **Switch between your callers to speak privately with one or the other by tapping the caller's name at the top of the screen.**

✔ **Tap End Call to hang up on the caller you're currently speaking with.** Your other caller becomes your active call and you can press End Call when you're finished conversing with that caller.

Answering a second incoming call

When you receive a second call, you can respond to the incoming call screen (refer to Figure 1-31) by doing one of the following:

✔ **Tap Ignore to continue your current conversation without interruption.** The second incoming call is sent to your voicemail.

✔ **End Call + Answer to disconnect with your current call and answer your second incoming call.**

✔ **Tap Hold Call + Answer to put your current call on hold and answer your second incoming call.** When you choose this option, the active multiple calls screen appears (refer to Figure 1-33).

Making a conference call

You initiate a conference call by making or answering a second call as described previously. After your second call is established, the multiple active calls screen appears (refer to Figure 1-33).

To turn your two calls into a conference call, or to add more callers to your two calls and turn those calls into a conference call, do the following:

✔ Tap Add Call if you want to add a third caller to your current call, and then repeat for any additional callers you want to add to your current group call.

✔ Tap Merge Calls to combine your two or more calls into a single Conference Call in which everyone can speak and hear everyone else.

The conference call screen shown in Figure 1-35 appears, grouping all of your active callers as a single item at the top of the screen.

Figure 1-35: The Conference call screen.

Managing a conference call

When a conference call is underway, you can use the conference call screen to manage your conference call (refer to Figure 1-35) by doing the following:

- ✒ Tap the combined callers group at the top of the screen to display the active callers screen, as shown in Figure 1-36.

- ✒ Tap the End Call button to the left of a caller's name or number to disconnect that caller from the conference call.

- ✒ To speak privately with one caller in your conference call, tap the Private button to the right of the caller's name to speak that caller; your other callers are put on hold while you speak privately with a single caller.

Click to disconnect a caller from the call.

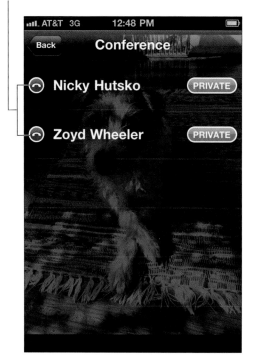

Figure 1-36: Juggle individual callers during a conference call.

Doing FaceTime Video Chat Calls

iPhone 4 and 4S models offer the FaceTime feature, which lets you speak with and see a person who is also using the FaceTime-capable device that can make and receive FaceTime calls, as shown in Figure 1-37. FaceTime calls other iPhones with the phone number or e-mail address, but uses an e-mail address to call FaceTime-enabled Macs, iPod touches, or iPads.

Figure 1-37: The active FaceTime call screen, live and in-person (virtually speaking).

To use FaceTime, either one of the first, and the second, requirements must be met:

1a. You and the person you want to FaceTime with are both using iPhone models that offer the FaceTime feature, and that feature is turned on in Settings⇨Phone⇨FaceTime. (The FaceTime feature is turned on by default; additionally, the FaceTime feature can also be turned off in Settings⇨General⇨Restrictions.)

1b. Your iPhone meets the preceding requirement, and the person you want to connect with is using another FaceTime-capable device, such as an iPad 2, a fourth generation iPod touch, or a Mac with FaceTime.

2. You're both connected to a Wi-Fi network.

Although FaceTime requires a Wi-Fi connection on both ends, you can download other video chat apps that let you chat using either Wi-Fi or a cellular data connection. We write about these apps in the online bonus content, Bonus Chapter 3.

Making a FaceTime call

As we mention in the "Managing Calls" section, you can switch an existing voice call to a FaceTime call, or you can initiate a FaceTime call by first making a call using any of the methods we show you in the "Making Calls" section.

Some things to consider when making FaceTime calls:

- **During a Call:** Tap the FaceTime button in the active call screen to switch your voice call to a video chat call.

- **Using Favorites, Recents:** The FaceTime camera icon indicates phone numbers and names that you can tap to call using FaceTime. Alternatively, tap the More Info button, tap the FaceTime button, and then tap the e-mail address or phone number you want to call.

- **Using Keypad:** Type the phone number you want to call using FaceTime, and then tap Call; tap the FaceTime button once the call is in progress.

- **Using Voicemail:** Tap the More Information button on an item in your Voicemail list, tap the FaceTime button, and then tap the e-mail address or phone number you want to call.

- **Using Contacts:** Tap the contact you want to call, tap the FaceTime button, and then tap the e-mail address or phone number you want to call.

- **Using Voice Control**: Press and hold the Home button and then say "FaceTime" followed by the name or number of the person to call.

- **Caller ID Block:** Your phone number appears when you make a FaceTime call even if you have activated your iPhone's Caller ID Block feature (which we write about in the section "Call Forwarding, Call Waiting, and Caller ID Blocking," earlier in this chapter.)

The FaceTime Failed message appears if a person you try to call isn't using a FaceTime-capable device or FaceTime is turned off on that device.

When your FaceTime call is established, the active FaceTime call screen appears (refer to 1-37).

Accepting a FaceTime call

The FaceTime incoming call screen appears when you receive an incoming FaceTime call invitation, as shown in Figure 1-38.

Tap Accept or Decline to answer or decline the FaceTime invitation.

**Book III
Chapter 1**

Managing Phone
and FaceTime Video
Calls

Figure 1-38: An incoming FaceTime call invitation.

Managing a FaceTime Call

When you're engaged in a FaceTime video chat call (or when someone accepts your invitation), the active FaceTime call screen appears. The person you're connected with fills up most of iPhone's screen, while your own mug appears in a tiny window that you can drag to whichever corner you want.

During an active FaceTime call, you can do a bunch of neat things, including the following:

✓ **Changing to Landscape View:** Rotate your iPhone sideways to view your caller in Landscape mode.

✓ **Switch Cameras:** Tap the Switch Cameras button to switch your live video feed from iPhone's front-facing camera to the higher-resolution rear-facing camera. You can use this feature to show off things around you, like the snoozing kitty in your lap, or the snowstorm coming down outside your office window. Tap the Switch Cameras button again to switch back to iPhone's front-facing camera and its focus on you.

✏ **Mute Your Sound:** Tap the Mute icon to squelch the mic on your end of the video chat conversation. When you mute your mic, you can still hear sound from the person on the other end of your chat, and they can still see your video. Tap Mute again to allow yourself to be heard again.

✏ **Pause Your Video:** Tapping Home and switching to another app puts your FaceTime video on hold; the person on the other end will still hear you, but you won't see each other while you're away from the FaceTime screen; tap the banner that appears at the top of iPhone's screen (as you would in a regular phone call) to return to your FaceTime call, where you'll be both seen and heard once more.

✏ **Capture a Screenshot:** Press Home and Sleep/Wake at the same time to capture a screenshot of your FaceTime chat; iPhone saves your screen-shot in the Photo app's Camera Roll album. (You can capture a screen-shot this way in other apps too, not just in FaceTime.)

International Calling Options

You can use your iPhone to make calls to other countries, but doing so gen-erally costs you extra fees beyond your cellular provider's plan for making calls within your own country. Before making calls overseas, you may want to check with your cellular provider to find exactly what those calls may cost you.

Depending on which iPhone model you own, you may be able to use your iPhone while you're traveling overseas. Again, using this feature is typically a very costly proposition, and again, your best plan is to contact your pro-vider before you take off. If it turns out you can use your iPhone while travel-ing overseas, you can then turn on the data roaming feature in Settings↪ General↪Network↪Data Roaming, to enable that feature.

Check out the online bonus content, Bonus Chapter 3 for free apps that use a Wi-Fi connection to make calls to and from overseas.

Go to Settings↪Phone↪International Assist to facilitate dialing from over-seas, and Settings↪Carrier to choose which of your provider's network part-ners you want to use when using data roaming overseas.

Chapter 2: Sending and Receiving Text and Multimedia Messages

In This Chapter

✏ **Setting up for SMS and MMS messages**

✏ **Sending and receiving messages**

✏ **Managing messages**

*B*efore iPhone revolutionized the way we think about cell phones, sending text messages, or texting, was a somewhat laborious task that involved lots of tapping on the numbers of the dial pad to form the words we wanted to send. For example, to type the word *open*, you had to tap **666 7 33 66**. Then came smart texting, where you began typing a word using the numbered keypad, and suggested words popped up based on the initial letters you typed. Finally iPhone came on the scene to make texting as easy as, and similar to, sending an e-mail.

As with other apps, you have more than one way to perform the task at hand. In this chapter, we show you the different ways you can send messages with and without photos and video, how you'll know when you've received a message, and how to manage all those messages you've been sending and receiving. We also tell you how to send and receive free messages with your other i-device–toting friends with iMessage.

Before all that, however, we're going to give you a quick run-through of the settings for the Messages app.

Reviewing Messages Features and Adjusting Settings

To understand the Messages features and settings, you should familiarize yourself with the parts of a message as shown in Figure 2-1.

✔ **To field:** Enter names or phone numbers of people you want to send messages to.

✔ **Text and Subject fields:** Type your message here; the Subject field within the Text field is a feature you can turn on or off in Settings➪Messages.

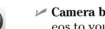 ✔ **Camera button:** Tapping the Camera button lets you add photos or videos to your messages.

✔ **Character count:** This keeps track of how many characters your message contains. Again, this is a feature you can switch on or off in Settings.

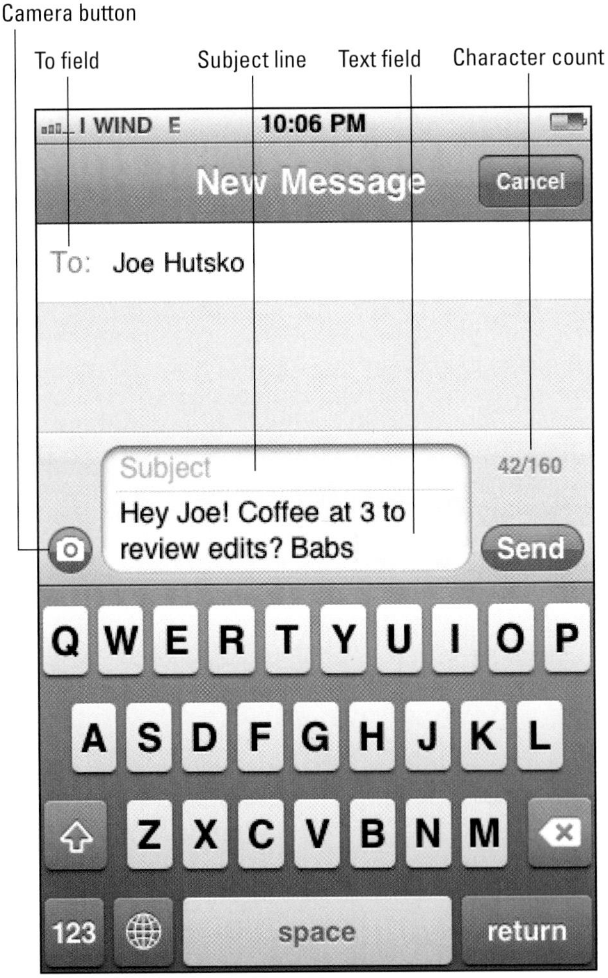

Camera button

To field   Subject line   Text field   Character count

.ıll I WIND E	**10:06 PM**

New Message   Cancel

To: Joe Hutsko

Subject   42/160

Hey Joe! Coffee at 3 to review edits? Babs   Send

Q W E R T Y U I O P

A S D F G H J K L

⇧ Z X C V B N M ⌫

123 ⊕ space return

Figure 2-1: The features of a new message.

Setting up Messages settings

By now, you're probably familiar with the Settings app. It's where you turn the features for the other iPhone apps on or off. The settings for Messages let you personalize the way iPhone alerts you that you have messages and offers some options for composing messages.

To open Settings for messages, tap Settings⬚Messages. You'll have to scroll down because Messages is a little way down the list after General. You see what's shown in Figure 2-2.

Figure 2-2: The Messages Settings screen.

Book III
Chapter 2

Sending and
Receiving Text and
Multimedia
Messages

- ✔ **iMessage:** Tap this toggle switch on to activate the iMessage service, which lets you exchange messages with other iOS 5 devices, such as iPhone, iPad, and iPod touch, for free (over Wi-Fi). We explain this service in the "Addressing, Writing, and Sending Text Messages" section of this chapter.

- ✔ **Send Read Receipts:** When turned on, people who send you messages will be notified when you read their sent message.

- ✔ **Send As SMS:** If iMessage is unavailable, your message is sent as an SMS text message. Your cellular service plan may charge an extra fee for SMS.

✔ **Receive At:** Add additional e-mail addresses where you want to receive iMessages (in addition to your mobile phone number). Tap Receive At. The iMessage screen opens. Tap Add Another Email. The keyboard appears where you can type in the e-mail address you wish to add. Tap Messages at the top when you finish.

Scroll down to see the last three choices:

✔ **MMS Messaging:** With this feature on, you can send and receive photos, video, and voice memos and insert a subject line in the text field. You may have to enter information from your cellular service provider in the MMS section of Settings➪General➪Network➪Cellular Data Network, and there may be an additional charge to send MMS.

✔ **Show Subject Field:** With this switch on, a subject line appears before any text messages that you write — just like e-mail. However, this turns an SMS (Short Message Service) into an MMS (Multimedia Message Service). If you're sending to someone who doesn't have MMS capabilities, they may not receive your message. If you leave the subject field blank, it remains an SMS, or you can just keep this setting off.

✔ **Character Count:** iPhone conveniently splits messages longer than 160 characters into multiple messages so people without an iPhone (poor souls) who have limited text capabilities can still receive messages from you. The kicker is that each section of the message counts as one message, meaning one three-part message is billed as three messages. Turn this switch on and a character counter appears to the right of the text-entry field in the New Message screen so you can keep an eye on the length of your message. If you are sending an SMS to another iPhone, you can write a whole novel and the message still counts as just one message, but your thumbs might be tired.

✔ **Group Messaging:** If you turn this on, you can send one MMS message to several people, although responses come back only to you. This option isn't available in all areas.

Change switches from on to off, or vice versa, with a simple tap. No swiping needed.

New message alert

You can choose the audible alert you want to hear when someone sends you a message, or choose none if you prefer only a visual alert:

✔ To change the alert sound for Messages, tap Settings➪Sounds➪Text Tone. A list of potential alert tones appears.

✔ To preview the sounds, tap the names on the list. Tap the name of the sound that you want to hear when a new message arrives or tap None. A checkmark indicates the sound you've chosen.

✔ Tap Sounds⬄Settings to return to the Settings screen or press the Home button to return to the Home screen.

Addressing, Writing, and Sending Text Messages

Sending text messages, or texting, is a quick, efficient way to, well, send a message to a person or a group of people. You can ask your spouse to pick up milk and bread on the way home or send a phone number to a colleague, and neither of them have to write anything down because they have your messages to refer to. You can let your book club members know the meeting is cancelled because the host has the flu, contacting 15 people with one message instead of making 15 phone calls.

To send a message:

1. **Tap the Messages icon on the Home screen.**

2. **Tap the Compose button in the upper right corner. It's the one that looks like a pencil and piece of paper.**

   A New Message screen opens.

3. **Address and write your message as explained in the following section.**

4. **Tap the Send button.**

**Book III
Chapter 2**

**Sending and
Receiving Text and
Multimedia
Messages**

Addressing and writing your message

When you open a New Message screen by tapping the Compose button, the keyboard is active and the cursor is in the To field, where you fill in the name or number of the person you want to send your message to. You can address your message in one of three ways:

✔ Tap the 123 button in the lower left corner of the keyboard to change the top row of letters to numbers. Type the phone number.

✔ If the person you want to send the message to is in Contacts, begin typing the recipient's name in the To field. Names of people in Contacts that begin with the same letters show up as a list from which you can choose. Your choices narrow as you type more letters. (See Figure 2-3.)

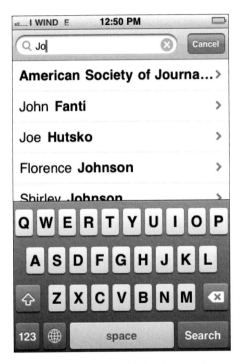

Figure 2-3: Begin typing the first letters of your recipient's name and the Contacts list opens.

Make sure you choose a cell phone number. Text messages can't be sent to a land line.

✔ Alternatively, tap the plus sign (+) button in the upper right corner, which opens Contacts. Find the name you want by doing one of the following:

• Scroll through the list until you find the name of the person you want to send a message to.

• Tap the first letter of the name in the alphabet that runs down the right side of the screen to jump to names beginning with that letter. Scroll through that section to find the person you're searching for.

• Tap the magnifying glass icon at the top of the alphabet list. The cursor blinks in the Search field. Type the name of the person you're looking for. As with any Search field, matches pop up when you type the first letter and diminish as you narrow your search by typing more letters.

✔ After you've found it, tap the name of the person you want to send a message to. If the contact has just one phone number, when you tap the name, you automatically return to the New Message screen and the name of the recipient will be in the To field. If the contact has more than one phone number, the contact information opens. Tap the number you want to send the SMS to and you'll bounce back to the New Message screen.

✔ If you want to send your message to more than one person, just tap the plus sign (+) button and repeat the preceding steps to add a person from the contact list or type in a phone number.

From Contacts, you can tap the Text Message button on the Info screen of the contact to open a New Message screen with your chosen contact in the To field. From your Favorites list, tap the blue arrow button on the right, and then scroll down and tap the Text Message button, which takes you to a New Message screen.

Writing your message

After you've entered the names of the message recipients, tap return. The cursor moves to the text field:

1. **Type your message.**

   Any features you've activated for the keyboard in Settings, such as Auto-Correction or Enable Caps Lock, are active in Messages. (See Book I, Chapter 3 for details on keyboard settings.)

2. **When you've finished typing your message, tap the Send button and it's on its way.**

   You'll see a progress bar at the top of the screen, as shown in Figure 2-4, and hear a whooping sound when the message has been sent.

To avoid accidentally hitting Send when you're aiming for the letter *o* or *p*, write your message before filling in the To field. The Send button is activated only after a recipient's name or a phone number has been entered. This tip only works when you are initiating a thread, not when responding to a message.

If you use an iPhone 4S and have activated Siri, tap the Dictation button to the left of the space bar if you prefer to dictate your message instead of typing it. (Refer to Book I, Chapter 3.)

If you make a mistake and need to edit your message, the Text field has the same functions for typing as other apps, as explained in Book I, Chapter 3.

Book III
Chapter 2

Sending and
Receiving Text and
Multimedia
Messages

Figure 2-4: The Sending progress bar shows your message is on its way.

iMessage

Address and write your Messages text message to one person or a group, as explained previously. Messages recognizes phone numbers or contact names associated with iOS 5 devices, such as an iPhone, iPad 2, or iPod touch. When you tap the contact name of someone who uses an iPad or iPod touch, Messages uses the associated e-mail address to send the iMessage. When sending to an iPad or iPod touch, which don't have phone numbers, choose the e-mail address. Like magic, Messages sends your outgoing text message as an iMessage. iMessages travel over the cellular data network or a Wi-Fi Internet connection so you don't pay an SMS fee, although you do use your data allotment if there's no Wi-Fi. If an Internet connection isn't available, your message is sent as a normal SMS or MMS.

You know you're sending an iMessage because you see New iMessage written across the top of the message (as shown in Figure 2-5) instead of New Message. The bubble around the name in the To field and incoming text bubbles are blue. You see an ellipsis while the other person is typing a response to your sent message.

To use iMessage, you must activate iMessage (Settings⇨Messages⇨iMessage On) and have an active Internet connection.

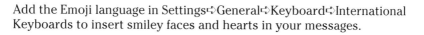

Figure 2-5: Send unlimited iMessages to other iOS5 devices — for free!

Add the Emoji language in Settings⇨General⇨Keyboard⇨International Keyboards to insert smiley faces and hearts in your messages.

Receiving and Replying to Text Messages

Ding-ding! You've got a message. If you're doing other things, a notification shows the name or phone number of the sender along with a line of the message. Or maybe not. You set your preferred way of being notified of new messages in Settings. Go to Settings⇨Notifications and click Messages. Select your notification choices as explained in Book I, Chapter 4. You may be notified of new messages in one or more of the following ways:

- A notification banner appears at the top of the screen and discreetly fades after a few seconds, to be found later in the Notifications Center.

- An alert calls for your undivided attention and you must choose to close it or reply before it leaves you alone.

Book III
Chapter 2

Sending and
Receiving Text and
Multimedia
Messages

✒ A numbered red badge appears on the shoulder of the Message icon on the Home screen, letting you know how many unread messages you have, as you can see in Figure 2-6.

✒ In the Message list, unread messages have a blue dot next to them.

After you read a message, the badge on the Messages icon on the Home screen disappears, or displays a lower number, the blue dot in the Message list goes away, and the Notification in the Notification Center disappears.

Figure 2-6: A badge on the Messages icon tells you how many unread messages you have.

After you've received a message, you'll want to read it and maybe respond. Here's how to read your messages:

1. **If you didn't read the message as soon as it arrived, tap Messages on the Home screen. An unread message has a blue dot next to it.**

   In the Messages list (refer to Figure 2-7), you'll see the name or number of the person or entity who sent the message, the time or date it was received, and the first two lines of the message.

2. **Tap the message and a message screen opens, displaying the whole message. The text of incoming iMessages is in a blue bubble; that of an SMS is in a green bubble.**

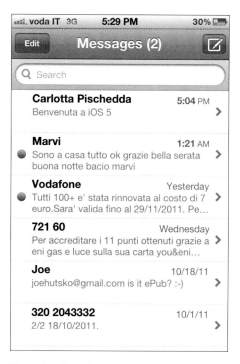

Figure 2-7: The Messages list shows read and unread messages you've sent and received.

Book III
Chapter 2

Sending and
Receiving Text and
Multimedia
Messages

You can choose to reply with a message or call the person back.

✏ To call, just tap the Call button at the top of the screen. If you don't see the Call button, tap the status bar to automatically scroll back to the top.

✏ To communicate via FaceTime, just tap the FaceTime button. We explain FaceTime in Book III, Chapter 1.

✏ To reply, tap once in the Text field. The keyboard opens. When you've finished writing your message, tap Send. As with a message you initiated, you see a Sending progress bar and, if you chose a sound in Sound settings for Sent Mail, you hear a tone indicating that the message has been sent.

If your iPhone is unable to receive incoming calls, it's also unable to send or receive messages. Whether it's in Airplane mode, is out of range of your carrier's cellular network, or is powered off, notifications, badges, and sounds for any new SMS or MMS messages won't appear until your iPhone is able to receive calls — and messages — again. If you try to send a message and it doesn't reach its destination, an alert badge that looks like an exclamation point appears on the Messages icon on the Home screen. (iMessages still work if you have Wi-Fi service.)

A received message has information about a person or company that you can store in Contacts. To add a new name and phone number or new information to an existing contact, do the following:

1. **From within the message, tap the Contact button at the top left of the screen.**

   A message rectangle opens, giving you the option to Create New Contact or Add to Existing Contact, as shown in Figure 2-8.

2. **To add a person or entity, choose Create New Contact.**

   You are bounced to a New Contact screen that is partially filled out with the name and number. You can fill in the other information if you like. Save by tapping Done. You are then returned to the message where you began.

3. **To add a new number to an existing contact, tap Add to Existing Contact.**

   This brings up the All Contacts screen, where you select the name of the Contact you wish to add this information to. Tap on the name of the desired Contact and type in the new information.

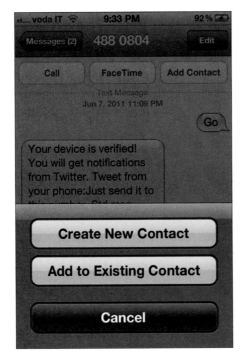

Figure 2-8: Add new information to Contacts directly from Messages.

If the person the message is from already exists in Contacts, the button on the upper right of the screen is Contact Info. Tapping that button takes you to the Contact Info screen of the person.

SMS and MMS are acronyms for Short Message Service and Multimedia Messaging Service, respectively. These are the protocols used for transferring text and multimedia with cellular phone technology.

Sending and Receiving MMS Multimedia Messages

Now things get fun. You probably want a way to share the photos and videos that you take with your iPhone and to send multimedia messages. MMS is a quick way to do that when e-mail isn't an option.

Capturing and sending a video or photo

Say you're taking a walk and find a stray puppy along your way. You want to take a picture and send it to your spouse with a clever message about the new addition to the family. Here's how:

1. **Tap Messages on the Home screen, and then tap the Compose button.**

2. **Fill in the To field as described in the previous section.**

   If your recipient uses iOS 5, your MMS may be sent with iMessage if the iMessage requirements are met.

3. **Tap the Camera button.**

   Three buttons appear — Take Photo or Video, Choose Existing, and Cancel (if you changed your mind about the pup). See Figure 2-9.

4. **Tap Take Photo or Video to open the camera and then tap the Camera button at the bottom of the screen.**

   The photo, or video, is taken and a Preview screen opens. You have the option of retaking the photo, by tapping Retake in the lower left corner, or using the photo, by tapping Use in the lower right corner.

5. **If you don't like the photo, tap Retake and try again, and again, and again until you have a photo or video you like.**

6. **If you're the next Ansel Adams and got a great shot on the first take, tap Use. Either way, when you take a photo you like, tap Use.**

   Messages opens and, instead of New Message, the screen now reads New MMS at the top. You see your photo or video in the Text field and the cursor blinking under the image, as shown in Figure 2-10.

**Book III
Chapter 2**

Sending and
Receiving Text and
Multimedia
Messages

Figure 2-9: Tap Take Photo or Video to insert a new image.

7. Type your message and tap Send.

You see a Sending progress bar and, if you chose a sound in Sound settings for Sent Mail, you hear whatever sound you chose when the message has been sent.

If you don't see the Camera button, make sure MMS Messaging is On in Messages Settings.

You can also open Camera, take your photo or video, and send an MMS from Camera. Full details are in Book V, Chapter 2.

Copying and sending existing videos, photos, and voice memos

Sometimes you already have a multimedia file — that is a photo, video, or voice memo — on your iPhone. There are two ways to send that file via MMS. Your first option is from within Messages, the second option is from the Photos or Voice Memos apps. The procedure is virtually the same, only your point of departure changes.

Figure 2-10: A new message becomes a new MMS when multimedia files are inserted.

Book III
Chapter 2

Sending and
Receiving Text and
Multimedia
Messages

✔ Tap Messages on the Home screen, and then tap the Compose button. Address your message as explained previously. Tap the Camera button to the left of the Text field. A screen appears asking if you want to Take Photo or Video or Choose Existing. Tap Choose Existing and the Albums screen opens showing a list of your Albums. Tap the Album where the photo or video you wish to send resides, and then tap the photo or video you want to send. A Preview screen opens, allowing you to choose that image or cancel. Tap Choose and you return to the New Message screen. Add a written message. When the message is ready, tap Send.

✔ To send directly from the Photos app, tap Photos on the Home screen. The Album list opens. Tap the Album that contains the video or photo you want to send. Three icons appear at the bottom of the screen, as shown in Figure 2-11. Tap the Action button, which is the first one on the left, and tap Message from the list of choices. A New Message screen opens. Address, write, and send your message as previously explained.

Figure 2-11: Tap the first button on the left to place a photo or video into your message.

 ✔ To send a recording from Voice Memos, tap Voice Memos on the Home screen. Tap the List button on the lower right corner to open the Voice Memos list. Tap the memo you want to send. Tap Share, as shown in Figure 2-12, and then tap the Message button. The New Message screen opens. Address the message and type in an accompanying message in the Text field, and then tap Send.

WARNING! As with most things, you have to pay a price for messaging. Depending on the phone plan you have, you may pay a per-message fee for sending and receiving SMS or MMS, usually around 20 cents, or you can opt for a bundled flat fee for a number of messages per month. One message to 25 recipients doesn't count as one message but 25 messages, so keep your plan in mind when doing group sends to avoid unpleasant end-of-the-month invoice surprises. And remember iMessages are free — that is, part of your cellular data plan, not your SMS/MMS plan.

Figure 2-12: Tap the blue Share button to send a Voice Memo in a message.

Book III
Chapter 2

Sending and
Receiving Text and
Multimedia
Messages

TIP

If someone sends you an image or video, you might want to save it outside Messages. When you receive an MMS, tap the image in the speech bubble. It opens on the full screen. Tap the Action button and choose Save Image (or Video) The image or video is saved to the Camera Roll on your iPhone.

Saving, Deleting, and Forwarding Messages

Like a packet of love letters tied in a pink ribbon, some messages are worth saving. You may want to delete others even before they've been read. And some, you'll want to share with your best friend.

As you send and receive messages, they stack up in reverse chronological order within the Messages app — what we've been referring to as the Message list (refer to Figure 2-7).

Ongoing conversations

Incoming and outgoing messages exchanged with the same person are called conversations — notice that the icon for Messages is a conversation bubble. You see the name of the person you have exchanged messages with in the Messages list. Tap on that name and you see all the messages you've exchanged with that person that you haven't deleted. Received messages are shown in grayed conversation bubbles on the left. Sent messages are on the right in green or blue conversation bubbles, as shown in Figure 2-13. Only the most recent message is shown in the Messages list, whereas the most recent 50 messages are shown in the conversation. You can download older messages by tapping the button. The newest message is displayed at the bottom — Messages opens to show this message — so if you scroll to the top of the screen, you can read from top to bottom and follow the conversation as it occurred.

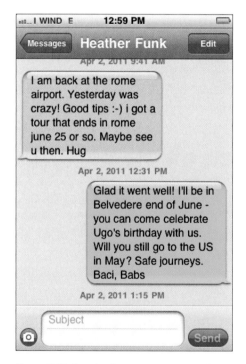

Figure 2-13: Received message conversation bubbles are on the left; sent messages are on the right.

Deleting messages

Text messages often contain information of fleeting importance, so you probably don't want to keep them and clutter up your Messages list. You can choose to delete some or all of the messages in a conversation. In this section, we show you several ways to delete messages.

If you want to delete some of the messages, tap the Edit button in the upper right corner. Circles appear to the left of each portion of the conversation. Tap the circle next to the part you wish to delete and it becomes a white checkmark in a red circle, as shown in Figure 2-14. Two options are highlighted at the bottom of the screen: Delete or Forward. To delete the portion of the conversation that you checked, just tap Delete. If you want to clear the whole conversation, tap Clear All at the top of the screen on the left. This only clears the conversation; the name or phone number remains in your Message list and new messages from that contact show up in the Message list under that person's name.

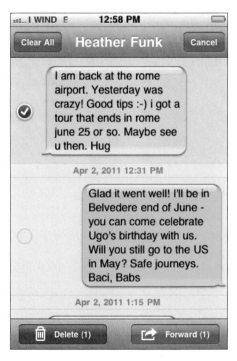

Figure 2-14: You can delete portions of a conversation.

Book III
Chapter 2

Sending and
Receiving Text and
Multimedia
Messages

If you want to clear a single message, do this from the Messages list. You can use either a two-step method or a three-step method. After a message is deleted, it's gone, so if you want an extra step to think about what you're about to delete, use the three-step method:

✔ Tap Edit and red circles with hyphens appear next to each message. Tap the circle next to the message you want to delete. The circle rotates 90 degrees and a Delete button appears to the right of the message, like you see in Figure 2-15. Tap the Delete button and poof! The message is gone. When you've finished deleting messages, tap Done to return to the Messages list.

✔ If, on the other hand, you don't worry about deleting something by mistake, use the two-step method. Swipe across the entry for the message you want to delete. A Delete button appears next to that message, as in Figure 2-16. Tap the button and the message is deleted.

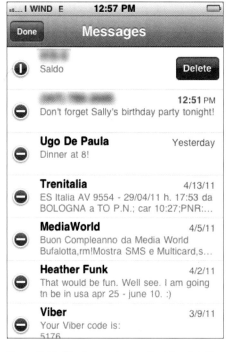

Figure 2-15: The three-step method for deleting messages.

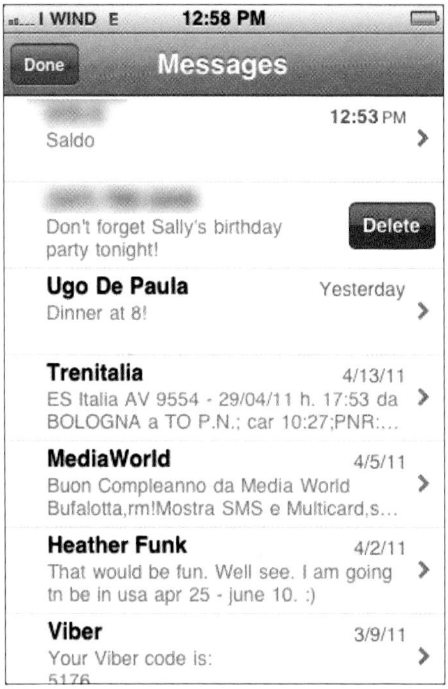

Figure 2-16: The message-deleting two-step.

To forward a message, do these steps:

1. **Choose the message you want to forward from the Messages list.**

   If the message is part of a conversation, open the conversation by tapping the message from the list.

2. **Tap the Edit button and transparent circles appear next to the message or messages that make up the conversation.**

3. **Tap the circle next to the message(s) you want to forward.**

   The red circle with the white checkmark appears.

4. **Tap the Forward button in the bottom right corner.**

   A New Message screen opens with the message you wish to forward in the text box.

5. **Insert a phone number or a name from Contacts in the To field and tap the plus sign (+) button if you want to add additional recipients.**

6. **Tap Send when you're ready to send the message.**

Book III
Chapter 2

Sending and
Receiving Text and
Multimedia
Messages

The Sending progress bar opens at the top of the page, if you chose a sound in Sound settings for Sent Mail, you hear whatever sound you chose when the message has been sent.

You can search for text within messages in the Messages list by using the Search box at the very top of the list. Just type the specific word or phrase you're searching for and tap the magnifying glass.

Sending and Receiving Map Locations and Web Page Links

Say you've made dinner plans with friends, but they need directions to the restaurant. Combining Maps and Messages, you can send the address and directions directly and avoid the hassle of explaining how to get there:

1. **Tap Maps on the Home screen and search for a location by typing the address or name of the business or restaurant in the Search field.**

2. **When you find the address, tap the blue and white arrow to see the information about the location you're searching for.**

3. **Scroll to the bottom of the Info screen and tap the Share Location button.**

4. **Tap the Message button that appears as shown in Figure 2-17.**

   The New Message screen opens with a link to the map location you were browsing.

5. **Address, write, and send the message as detailed earlier in this chapter.**

Say you're browsing the web on your iPhone and you find a review of that great restaurant you're headed to tonight. You want your friends to read it before the dinner hour. (We assume you're already in Safari — read all about that in Chapter 3 of this minibook.) Here's how to send the link:

1. **At the top of the screen is the web page's full web address or URL. Press and hold on a web page link to display the link's information and options screen of Cut, Copy, Paste, as shown in Figure 2-18.**

Figure 2-17: Map location links are sent via MMS.

Book III
Chapter 2

Sending and
Receiving Text and
Multimedia
Messages

2. Tap Copy and then press the Home button.

3. Tap Messages. When the Messages list opens, tap the Compose button.

4. Press and hold in the Text field until an options screen opens, as shown in Figure 2-19.

5. Tap Paste.

6. The link you copied is pasted into your text message, as shown in Figure 2-20. Address your message and tap Send.

Figure 2-18: Tap Copy in the options screen to grab the web link.

Figure 2-19: Tap Paste to insert the web link in your text message.

Figure 2-20: The link inserted in your message.

Now your friends have the link for the restaurant review. *Bon appétit!*

Receiving links to locations or websites is even easier than sending them. If you receive messages that have URLs embedded in them, the links are active, which means you can just tap them, right in the message, and Safari opens to the linked page.

Chapter 3: Surfing the Web with Safari

In This Chapter

- Touring Safari's features
- Opening and viewing web pages
- E-mailing and printing web pages
- Viewing and listening to video and audio content
- Searching the web Safari-style
- Adjusting general and security settings

*R*eady to surf the web with Safari? If your answer is yes, you've come to the right place. We begin this chapter with a guided tour of iPhone's Safari web browser, pointing out basic features and ways you use Safari to browse web pages. We then walk you through actually opening and viewing pages, showing you neat things along the way, like zooming in and out of web pages, or turning your iPhone sideways for a wider view of a web page — and for easier typing when you need to fill in web forms.

After getting your feet wet with a little basic web surfing, we show you how to juggle multiple web pages you want to view, how to control video and audio content, how to save images to your iPhone's camera roll, how to view documents, and how to create bookmarks for web pages you often visit so you can view those web pages with a few taps of your finger.

Near the end of our surfin' safari, we show you the ins and outs of using Safari's Search feature to find web pages you're looking for — and to find things on those web pages you've found. And finally, we conclude this chapter by giving you a rundown of Safari settings you may want to adjust to make your web surfing experience smoother — and safer.

Surfin' Safari Tour

Touring Safari's main screen is akin to getting acquainted with the dashboard of a new car (or spaceship) you're about to commandeer. There's no time like the present to take a quick tour of the Safari screen so that we'll be on the proverbial "same page" as we navigate our web excursion in the pages that follow.

Your iPhone needs to be connected to a Wi-Fi network or your cellular provider's data network in order to follow along with all of the Safari goodness contained within these pages.

To launch Safari, tap Home, and then tap the Safari.

The Safari screen appears, as shown in Figure 3-1, and displays the last website you viewed the last time you used Safari. Of course, the web page you viewed will very likely be different from the one pictured here.

Or you may not see a web page at all, but rather the Bookmarks screen shown in Figure 3-2. If you see the Bookmarks screen, that means you either launched Safari for the very first time, or you closed any open web page (or web pages) the last time you used Safari.

If you're greeted with the Bookmarks screen instead of the last web page you viewed, no worries: Just tap one of the bookmarks you see to open that bookmark's associated web page. Or you can tap Done and type a web address into the Web Address field, and then tap Go to open that web page (which we cover in fuller detail in a few moments).

For our brief introductory tour, we focus on the three main zones of the Safari screen (refer to Figure 3-1), and what you find in those zones:

> ✔ **Title bar:** Shows the name of the web page you're viewing at the very top, the Web Address field and Stop/Reload button, and the Search field.
>
> If you don't see the title bar, tap the Status bar at the top of iPhone's screen to make the title bar appear.
>
> Besides the name of the web page you're viewing, the title bar's three other points of interest include the
>
> - **Address field:** Displays the web address's URL (which stands for Uniform Resource Locator); the Address field is also what you tap to make the keyboard appear, so you can type in a web page address you want to open and view.
>
> - **Stop/Reload button:** A dual-purpose button you can tap to stop a web page from loading, or to reload a web page to see any new information that may have been updated on that web page, such as breaking news stories on a news web page.

- **Search field:** What you tap to make the keyboard appear, so you can type in a name of a person, place, or anything you're searching for, such as a restaurant, a weather report, or the name of your favorite *For Dummies* author.

✔ **Tool bar:** Contains five buttons you can tap to do the following things:

- **Previous/Next:** Previous goes back to the previous web page you viewed; Next moves you Forward to the web page you just left when you pressed Previous. (One or both buttons may be dim until you navigate away from the current web page you're viewing.)

Web page

Title bar   Address field   Stop/Reload   Search

Previous   Next   Send   Bookmarks

Toolbar

Figure 3-1: The Safari web browser screen displaying a web page.

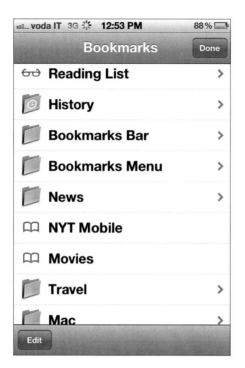

Figure 3-2: The Bookmarks screen.

- **Action:** Displays options for sharing or doing something with the current web page you're viewing, including saving the web page as a bookmark, adding the page to your Reading List, creating a Home Screen icon for the web page, creating an e-mail message containing a link to the web page that you want to send to someone, tweeting the link with Twitter, or printing the web page.

You can also print other types of content you can open and view in Safari, such as PDF (Portable Document Format) or Microsoft Word docs, Excel spreadsheets and, photos — in other words, anything iPhone's QuickLook feature can open and display on the screen, you can print to an AirPrint-enabled printer.

- **Bookmarks:** Displays Bookmarks screen, which holds a list of links to your Reading List and to bookmarks and bookmarks folders that give you quick access to web pages you frequent or those you want to remember even if you don't go to them all that often. Your Reading List is where links to articles you want to read or refer to later are stored.

Your iPhone comes preloaded with a handful of bookmarks Apple thinks you may find useful; you may also see bookmarks you have saved on your computer's web browser that iTunes or iCloud automatically copies to your iPhone when you sync your iPhone with iTunes or iCloud.

- **Web pages:** And last but not least, there's the most interesting zone of all: the actual web page you're looking at. The beauty of web pages is that no two are exactly alike — which can also be the frustrating thing about web pages. From the desktop versions of my own web page and the *New York Times* web page, to the mobile versions of both of those web pages, what you see on any given website varies from site to site, as Figure 3-3 illustrates.

Figure 3-3: Two ways of looking at the same web pages.

A tale of two web pages

The notion behind "mobile" web pages is that they minimize graphics and much of the other extraneous "stuff" that normally appears on the desktop version of the web page, so as to make it easier for you to use the mobile version of those web pages. Some web pages gauge whether the web browser you're using is a desktop browser or a mobile browser, and automatically present the one or the other, based on your browser. Other times, you type in a specific mobile web page address like `mobile.nytimes.com` to access the mobile version of that web page. Sometimes typing the mobile address for a web page using your computer's browser has no effect and the desktop version of the web page opens anyway and vice versa: Sometimes typing the full desktop version of a web page on your iPhone ignores your wish and forces you to view the mobile version of the web page.

And still other times, you get the best of both worlds: A web page that automatically opens the mobile version when it detects you're using an iPhone, with the option to switch to the desktop version of that web page if you so desire.

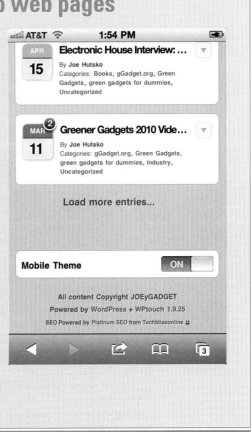

The first and third web pages shown in Figure 3-3 are miniature versions of the same "desktop" versions of what the web pages look like if you view them using your computer's web browser, whereas the second and fourth web pages are the "mobile" versions of those same web pages, respectively. In the nearby sidebar, "A tale of two web pages," we give you a brief explanation of the ins and outs of desktop versus mobile web pages.

Sometimes Safari launches automatically when other things you're doing depend on Safari to take you to a particular web page. Some of those other ways Safari automatically launches itself via other programs include tapping

- A link in an e-mail or text message
- A link on a Facebook page or in a tweet update on Twitter on either of those social networking services' web pages, or in the app versions of either of those services

✔ A link in the Info screen for a business or other location you find using Maps

✔ A link listed along with several links that appear when you use iPhone's Search feature on the Home screen and choose the Search web option

✔ A Send or Share button that offers an Open in Safari option

✔ A link that's disguised as a button

When viewing a web page, you can control and change your view of the web page by

✔ Turning your iPhone sideways to view the web page in widescreen landscape mode

✔ Scrolling up and down web pages

✔ Zooming in and out of web pages

On many web pages, you can interact with the web page by doing things like

✔ Tapping links, buttons, or other elements that take you to another spot on the web page, to a web page on the website you're accessing, or to another web page on another website; sometimes a link you tap causes whatever page you're viewing to be replaced with the new web page the link takes you to; other times, a link you tap may open a new window to display the new web page

✔ Tapping fields to type in information; for instance, your user name and password so you can check your bank balance, or the shipping address where you want to receive a sleek new iPhone case you order from an online store, or a tracking number so you can find out when the heck that new iPhone case you ordered is expected to show up (at the address you typed in, after you checked your bank balance to make sure you could afford that diamond-encrusted case you wanted to order in the first place)

✔ Saving images or graphics on a web page to your iPhone's Camera Roll in the Photos app, where photos you capture with your iPhone are stored

✔ Tapping a link to upload an image, such as a photo of your new puppy that you want to post to your Facebook page

✔ Tapping a phone number that appears on a web page to dial or send a text message to that phone number, or to create a new contact card using the number, or add the number to an existing contact card

✔ Tapping a street address on a web page to view that address in Maps

✔ Searching for specific text on a web page so you can find exactly what you're looking for

In the following pages, we show you how to do those things and more.

Book III
Chapter 3

Surfing the Web with Safari

Opening Web Pages

To begin using Safari to open and view web pages, tap the Safari icon on the Home screen to launch Safari. The Safari screen appears, displaying either the last web page you viewed, or the Bookmarks screen.

The most common ways you go about opening web pages are as follows:

- **Using Bookmarks:** Tap the Bookmarks button in the tool bar (if the Bookmarks screen isn't already displayed), and then tap a web page bookmark you want to open (refer to Figure 3-2).

  Safari loads then displays the web page for your chosen bookmark.

- **Using Search:** Tap the Search field to display the keyboard, and then type a word, name, phrase, ZIP code, or whatever you're searching for. See the section "Searching Tips and Tricks" for details.

- **Using Address Field:** Tap the Address field to display the keyboard, type in the web address of a web page you want to view, and then tap Go.

Safari then displays the web page for the address you typed in.

A few things worth noting when opening web pages using the Address field:

- If you don't see the Address field at the top of the Safari screen, tap the Status bar at the top of iPhone's screen to instantly scroll to the top of the web page and reveal the Address field.

- You don't need to tap the erase button to clear the Address field before you type the web page address you want to open — the Address field is instantly erased as soon as you begin typing the web address you want to open.

- Notice anything *strange* about the keyboard when you were typing in the web address you want to open? Strange how, you ask? Oh, you know, just little things — like that fact that there's no spacebar key!? Before you begin worrying your iPhone's keyboard may be hexed, we can assure you there *is* a method to this seemingly keyboard-oversight madness. In fact, we write about tapping into Safari-friendlier keyboard features and shortcuts in the section "Safari Keyboard Tips and Tricks" later in this chapter. (For a complete hands-on rundown of iPhone's multiple-personality keyboard features, check out Book 1, Chapter 3.)

Stopping and Reloading Web Pages

Whichever way you choose to open a web page, after Safari actually begins loading the web page, a trio of visual cues appears to let you know Safari is processing your request. Those cues include a blue progress bar in the Address field, the Reload button changing to the Stop button, and the twirling network activity icon in the upper left corner of the status bar.

You can stop or reload a web page by doing one of the following:

✔ Tap the stop button if you want to instantly stop loading a web page that seems to be taking forever.

✔ Tap the reload button to reload the web page and display any new information that may have been added to the web page since you began viewing it (such as the latest-breaking news on a news web page).

Safari Keyboard Tips and Tricks

The following tips and tricks can help you maximize your Safari keyboard experience, while minimizing how much typing you actually have to type:

✔ **Skip the www:** You don't have to type "www" when you're typing a website address into the Address field; Safari fills that in for you.

✔ **Type www sometimes:** You may *want* to type www when you're typing in certain website addresses in order to open the full-size versions of those web pages instead of the mobile version. Case in point: Typing www.nytimes.com opens the full-size web page, but typing nytimes.com opens the mobile version of the web page (refer to Figure 3-3 near the beginning of this chapter to see what we're talking about).

✔ **Press to complete:** Tap and hold the .com button to display a list of alternate completion options, and then drag your finger to the one you want and let go to fill in that choice (.net, .edu, .org, .us, and .com).

✔ **Landscape keyboard:** Rotate your iPhone sideways to display the wider-reaching landscape keyboard for easier, more accurate typing.

✔ **Use AutoFill:** Use Safari's AutoFill feature to automatically fill in common fields such as name, address, and phone number fields, e-mail address fields, and user name and password fields. We tell you about AutoFill later in this chapter.

Viewing Web Pages

When the web page appears, you're free to move about the cabin — er, we mean view the web page — in any number of free-ranging ways.

Using widescreen and portrait views

When it comes to viewing web pages, Safari lets you have it both ways: portrait orientation view (taller than it is wide) and landscape orientation view (wider than it is tall), as shown in Figure 3-4. Switching between these views is merely a matter of turning your iPhone sideways or upright, depending on whether you want to view your web page in landscape or portrait view, respectively.

Figure 3-4: Rotating iPhone sideways displays the landscape view.

If you see the Portrait Orientation Lock icon in the top right corner of the status bar (refer to Figure 3-4), turning your iPhone on its side won't switch your web page to the wide-screen landscape view. To turn the Portrait Orientation Lock feature off or on, double-click the Home button, and then slide the recent apps icon list at the bottom of the screen to the right. Tap the Portrait Orientation Lock icon to toggle that feature on or off.

Switching to Landscape orientation when you use the keyboard displays the wider, bigger-keys version of the keyboard — a definite plus-size advantage that makes for quicker, more accurate typing!

Using Reader

If you see a Reader button in the Address Field, you can view the article in Reader. Reader displays the text of the article on a plain white page without any of the ambient noise that surrounds it on the web page itself, as shown in Figure 3-5.

Tap the Font button in the upper left corner to change the size of the text. Tap the Action button to reveal the same tasks that appear when you tap the Action button from a web page view, such as printing the article or saving the link to your Reading List. Tap Done when you finish reading.

**Book III
Chapter 3**

**Surfing the Web
with Safari**

Figure 3-5: Reader makes reading web articles easier.

Scrolling web pages

One thing you do a lot of when you're viewing a web page is scrolling — up, down, and sometimes all around — to see all of the information on the web page. In rare instances, you may also come across a web page that contains a scrollable frame of text *within* the web page — which is referred to as a *text frame*.

Ways you can scroll a web page you're viewing include

✔ **Scrolling carefully:** Drag a web page up or down, or sideways; don't worry about accidentally tapping something on the web page — as long as you drag your fingertip as soon as you touch the screen, Safari interprets your gesture as a scroll (or flick) rather than a tap.

✔ **Scrolling quickly:** Flick up or down to scroll in those directions more quickly.

✔ **Scrolling instantly to the top:** Tap the status bar at the top of iPhone's screen to instantly scroll to the top of a web page.

✔ **Scrolling inside a text frame:** Drag two fingers up or down in a text frame within a web page to scroll just the text in that frame up or down.

Zooming web pages

Using Safari's zoom view features can make scrolling web pages (and text frames within web pages) easier on your eyes — and fingertips.

Fortunately, many web pages automatically display an easier to read mobile version of themselves when they detect you've opened the web pages using a smartphone like the iPhone, which means you typically won't need to (or won't even be able to) zoom in or out of the contents of those web pages.

Other times, a web page may not offer a mobile viewing option, which means you're faced with viewing the full-size version of the web page that is designed to be viewed with your computer web browser program.

Thankfully, Safari's zoom in and out features make it easy to narrow your focus on just the section of a full-size web page that you want to view.

Ways you can zoom in and out of web pages include the following:

✔ **Double-tap zooming:** Double-tap a column on a web page to zoom in to or out of that column, as shown in Figure 3-6.

✔ **Spread and pinch zooming:** Spread two fingers apart or pinch together to zoom out or in to a web page

To quickly reset a web page to the full-screen view, double-tap anywhere on the screen to home in on a column, and then double-tap again to zoom all the way out to the full-screen view.

Although you can always zoom in and out of any full-size web page on iPhone's screen, not all mobile versions of certain websites allow zooming.

Figure 3-6: Zooming in on a web page with a double-tap — or a pinch.

Navigating Web Pages

Browsing the web can be like wandering through a maze with lots of doors that lead to other sections of the maze or to other mazes altogether. But instead of turning door knobs to open new doors, you tap web links on a web page, which in turn shuttles you to another web page (or another location on the same web page), and so on.

Safari's navigation features can help you stay the course as you wind your way from web page to web page, as we explain in the following subtopics.

Going back, forward

Before we tell you about the many ways you can tap links to joyfully (or frustratingly) lose yourself in the web maze, it can help to know up front how to use Safari's Previous and Next navigation buttons to move backward or forward through web pages.

Using Safari's Previous button, you can always backtrack one or two or ten or more steps to return to whatever web page you started on before you wound up getting inadvertently lost (or (un)intentionally sidetracked). And using Safari's Next button, you can repeat your steps forward to the farthest web page you visited before you backtracked *away* from that farthest point by tapping the Previous button.

‣ Tap Previous to go back to the previous web page you viewed

‣ Tap Next to go forward to a page you were viewing before you tapped the Previous button

Using Safari's History feature, which we explain a little farther along in our mutual journey through this section, is another (often more direct) way you can go back to a web page you previously visited.

Juggling multiple websites

In Settings⇨Safari⇨Open Links, you have two choices for how Safari juggles multiple websites:

‣ **In New Page:** A web link you tap for a different website, shifts the Safari page you're viewing to one side, and opens a new Safari page window to display the different website you tapped the link for. Links that are for web pages within the same website do not open a new Safari page. The Previous/Next buttons work only within the same website. To access different Safari pages, you have to tap the Web Pages button and flick between them.

‣ **In Background:** A web link you tap replaces whatever web page you're viewing with the web page the link you tapped leads to. The Previous/ Next buttons take you back and forth between all the web pages you visited.

With either choice, you can always open a new Safari page window on your own to open another web page you want to view, and then switch between the web page you were viewing and the new web page you opened.

To help you juggle, open, and close those multiple web page windows, you use Safari's Web Pages button.

The Web Pages button displays the number of web pages you have open in Safari. You won't see a number on the Web Pages button when you have only one web page open.

Tap the Web Pages button to display the Web Pages screen, as shown in Figure 3-7.

Figure 3-7: The Web Pages screen.

You can open and work with up to eight Safari pages at a time.

A thumbnail image of the web page you were viewing appears in the center of the Web Pages screen with that page's title above the thumbnail. Dots beneath the thumbnail indicate how many web pages you have open.

Things you can do when viewing the Web Pages screen include the following:

- **Open a new web page:** Tap New Page to create and open a new, blank Safari web page, and then use one of the methods described in "Opening Web Pages" earlier in this chapter to open a web page you want to see.

- **Switch between web pages:** Flick left or right to see thumbnails and titles of other open web pages, and then tap the web page you want to view to open that web page.

- **Close a web page:** Tap the red X button in the upper left corner of a web page thumbnail to close that web page.

- **Close the Web Pages screen:** Tap Done to close the Web Pages screen.

Book III
Chapter 3

Surfing the Web
with Safari

Revisiting History with History

Sometimes you want to go back to a web page you viewed a few minutes ago, or a few hours ago, or even a few days or weeks ago. Thanks to Safari's History feature, you can do just that. Think of the History feature as a kind of virtual bag of popcorn, which drops a kernel of popcorn for every web page you visit, so you can instantly teleport your way back to any given kernel of popcorn (er, web page) without having to actually tap the Previous button a zillion times to retrace your steps.

Opening previously viewed web pages

To view your Safari web history, tap Bookmarks, and then tap the History folder to view your web history activity, as shown in Figure 3-8. Tap any item in the list to reopen that web page you previously visited.

To help keep the History screen neat and manageable, Safari creates folders for web pages you visited earlier in the day, and for web pages you visited before today. Tap any of those folders to view web pages you previously visited, and then tap any of the items listed to revisit that web page.

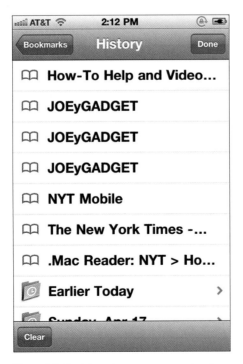

Figure 3-8: Revisit web pages you previously viewed in the History folder.

If you don't see the History folder shown in Figure 3-9, that means you previously navigated to another Bookmarks folder; tap the Bookmarks button in the upper left corner to back your way out of whatever folder you're in until you see the History folder, and then tap the History folder to view your Safari web history.

Although the History folder is stored inside Safari's Bookmarks folder, you can't save a Bookmark in the History folder the way you can save a Bookmark in the main Bookmarks folder, or another folder you have saved in the Bookmarks folder. We tell you how to save bookmarks and manage the Bookmarks folder in the section "Playing Favorites with Bookmarks," a little later in this chapter.

Erasing your web history

On the History screen (refer to Figure 3-8), you may have noticed the Clear button in the lower left corner. By tapping that button, you can wipe out your entire Safari web browsing history in one fell swoop if you're the sort of person who'd rather not keep a record of your web browsing around.

(One hypothetical example: maybe you share your iPhone with another person who might find it disconcerting that you spent half the morning tapping your way through the Hot or Not website when you were supposed to be writing a chapter for a book your publisher is waiting oh-so-patiently for you to complete. We repeat, this is only a *hypothetical* example.)

To clear your Safari web history, tap Bookmarks⟿History, and then tap the Clear button in the lower left corner. The Red Clear History button appears, giving you a moment to reconsider whether you really want to wipe out your web history. Tap Clear History if you really do, or tap Cancel if you change your mind and you want to keep your web history on hand.

Another way you can clear Safari's web history — and other data gathering bits of information Safari stores as you browse web pages — is to press the Home button, and then tap Settings⟿Safari⟿Clear History. We write more about Safari's settings in the section "Adjusting General and Security Settings" near the end of this chapter.

Tapping into Web Page Links

When you open and view a web page, more often than not, you wind up tapping a link on that web page, which takes you to another web page. For instance, when you view the *New York Times* web page, you scroll up and down the list of news stories, and then you tap the web page link for the news story you want to read, and then *that* web page replaces the one you were viewing with the news story.

**Book III
Chapter 3**

**Surfing the Web
with Safari**

Web page links are typically highlighted in blue text so they're easy to spot, and they may be underlined too, so they're even easier to recognize.

Tap a web page link to view the web page that link is connected to. The web page replaces the one you were viewing. Or Safari may open a new web page screen to display the web page, if that's the way the web page's designer configured the web page link to behave when it's tapped.

Other types of web links you can click are ones that may

- ✒ Display a graphic or photo or a photo slideshow you can tap through to view a series of photos

- ✒ Display a form with fields you can fill in with information, such as your shipping address on a shopping site, or your e-mail address, so you can receive a weekly newsletter from a museum you're fond of

- ✒ Play an audio file, such as a news story, a podcast, or a song

- ✒ Play a video file, say a movie trailer or a friend's dog catching a Frisbee

- ✒ Display the text of an e-book or a list of Twitter postings, or your sister's Facebook Wall updates

Sometimes tapping a link opens another app or special content screen, so you can view or listen to the content the link is connected to, such as a video or PDF document file, or an audio file. For instance, tapping a video link on your friend's Facebook wall opens the Video app so you can watch the video. The Video app closes after the video is done playing.

Other times, a link you tap may open another app that you then must exit in order to return to Safari. For example, you tap a link to download a free e-book, and then Safari opens that e-book in iBooks so you can begin reading the e-book. But maybe you don't want to read the e-book right now, in which case you can double-tap the Home button and then tap Safari in the recent apps bar to return to the web page you were viewing so you can look for other e-books to download.

In the remainder of this section, we tell you about opening a new, separate web page screen to view web pages. We also tell you about doing other things with phone numbers, e-mail and location addresses, and web page address links. And we tell you how to view and do things with content-rich web links, such as saving photos or graphics to your iPhone's Photos app, or opening other apps to view the contents of a link, like Word or PDF documents, or a PowerPoint presentation.

Working with basic links and forms

As we mentioned previously at the beginning of "Tapping into Web Page Links," all you need to do to open a web page link is tap it, and that linked web page will replace the one you're viewing, or it will open a new Safari page screen to display the linked web page.

Pressing and holding on a web page link displays the link's information and options dialog, as shown in Figure 3-9.

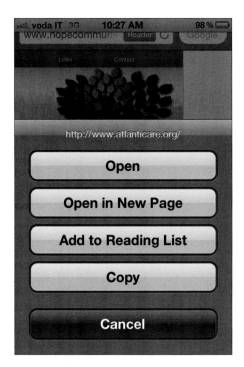

Figure 3-9: The web page link info and options dialog.

The web page link's full web address (URL) appears at the top of the dialog, and below the web address are buttons you can tap to do the following things:

- **Open:** Opens the web page link.

- **Open in New Page:** Forces Safari to open the web page link in a new Safari page screen instead of replacing the web page screen you are viewing when you tap the link (see "Juggling multiple web pages" earlier in this chapter).

- **Add to Reading List:** Places the link in your Reading List so you can come back later and read whatever it is that interests you on this web page. This is a type of temporary bookmark; in fact, Reading List is found in the Bookmarks list.

☛ **Copy:** Copies the web page address to the clipboard so you can paste the web address elsewhere, like in a note in the Note app, or in a text message in the Messages app, as shown in Figure 3-10.

☛ **Cancel:** Closes the web page information and options screen.

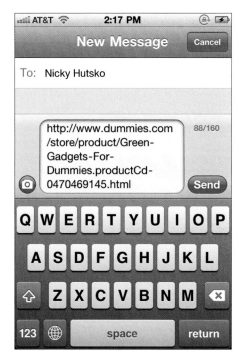

Figure 3-10: Paste a web page address into a text message to send it to others.

Filling in forms and fields

When it comes to filling in forms, Safari serves up some useful helpers to make tapping out type and numbers using the keyboard as easy as possible.

Tap a field and begin typing. If you're having trouble seeing the field you're typing in, you can zoom in and out of the web page even while the keyboard is displayed.

Tap Next to move the cursor to the next field in the form. Tap Previous if you need to go back to a prior field you filled in. Tapping either of those two buttons repeatedly quickly moves you from field to field. You can also scroll down to tap into any other fields you need to complete.

Tap Done when you finish filling in the form fields.

Using AutoFill to do the typing for you

Safari's AutoFill feature automatically fills in common fields with your personal information with a single tap instead of requiring you to fill in those fields individually. Another common type of information Safari can automatically fill in for you is user names and passwords.

To turn on Safari's AutoFill feature and options, tap Home, and then tap Settings⇨Safari⇨AutoFill to display the AutoFill settings screen, as shown in Figure 3-11.

▪▪▪ voda IT 3G	1:07 PM	87% ▭

◁ Safari **AutoFill**

Use Contact Info   ON ⬤

My Info   Barbara Boyd ❯

Names & Passwords   ⬤ OFF

Clear All

Automatically fill out web forms using your contact info or previous names and passwords.

Book III
Chapter 3

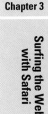

Surfing the Web
with Safari

Figure 3-11: Safari's AutoFill settings screen.

Tap Use Contact Info to tell Safari you want it to do exactly that whenever a web page presents a form you need to fill in with your personal information. Where that personal information comes from in the first place is answered by the My Info option, just below the Use Contact Info switch. You should see your own name in the My Info option field. That means Safari copies the information you have saved in the name, address, phone number, and e-mail address fields of your own Contacts card and pastes those bits of information into the appropriate fields when you tap AutoFill on a web page form.

If you don't see your name in the My Info option field, tap that field to display your Contacts, and then locate and tap your own Contacts card name to select it as the card you want to use for the My Info option.

Tap the Names & Passwords option if you want Safari to remember any user names and passwords you type in to access certain web pages. To wipe out any saved user names and passwords Safari has saved so far, tap Clear All, and those saved user names and passwords are history.

Saving user names and passwords

The first time you type in your name and password on a web page that requires that information, Safari displays a pop-up message, asking if you'd like to save the password, as shown in Figure 3-12. Tap Yes if you would, Never for This Website if you never-ever-ever want to save the password for the web page, or Not Now, if you don't want to save the password right now, but you want to keep your option of saving the password open the next time you visit the web page.

Figure 3-12: Safari offers to save passwords so you don't have to.

Pop-ups, pick-lists, check boxes, and radio buttons

Sometimes you encounter on-screen controls and gizmos on certain web pages, such as pop-up menus and pick-lists you tap and scroll through to select predetermined information such as the state you live in or a quantity of something you may be ordering.

Using these digital doodads, like the pop-up and pick-list shown in Figure 3-13, is usually pretty self-explanatory: Tap to display the pop-up menu, and then scroll up or down the list and tap your choice.

Figure 3-13: Tap a pop-up menu and then flick to scroll up and down lists.

Book III
Chapter 3

Surfing the Web with Safari

You may also come across check boxes and radio buttons on certain websites. Tap these boxes or buttons to mark or unmark your selection.

Opening Map and app web links

Sometimes a web link you tap closes the Safari screen and opens another app to display the contents of the link you tapped. For instance, you might be viewing the location and contact information web page for a new restaurant you want to try, and when you tap a web link labeled Map or Get Directions, your iPhone closes the Safari screen and opens the Maps app to display the restaurant's location.

Whenever you leave Safari and a web page you were viewing to use another app, you can always go back to that web page by pressing Home, and then tapping Safari or pressing the Home button twice to open the recent apps bar, and then tapping Safari.

Using phone and e-mail address links

When you encounter phone number and e-mail address web links, you can use those links to call the number you see, or create an e-mail message using the e-mail address you see. You can also send a text message or add the phone number or e-mail address to a contact card you have saved on your iPhone, or create a new contact card using either or both of those links.

Tapping into Phone links

Tap a phone number link you want to dial, and then tap Call in the pop-up screen that appears, as shown in Figure 3-14. The Safari screen closes and the active call screen appears as your iPhone places your call.

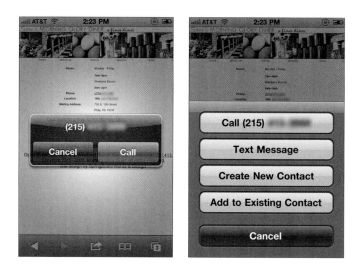

Figure 3-14: Tap a phone number link to dial, or press and hold to see more options.

To do other things with a phone number link, press and hold on the phone number to display phone number link options screen, and then choose one of the following options:

✔ **Call:** Dials the phone number

✔ **Text Message:** Opens a new text message and pastes the phone number into the To field

✔ **Add to Contact:** Opens an Info screen in Contacts where you can choose to Create a New Contact or Add to (the number) an Existing Contact. After you choose one, either a New Contact screen opens or your Contacts list opens and you scroll through to find the contact to which you want to add the number.

✔ **Copy:** Puts the phone number in the clipboard so you can then open another app, and then tap and hold where you want to insert the number. Tap Paste when the option is offered.

Employing e-mail links

Tap an e-mail address you want to use to send an e-mail message, and a new message appears with the address already filled in the To field. Complete your new e-mail message and then tap Send. The e-mail message screen closes and your Mail inbox appears. Tap the Home button, and then tap Safari to return to Safari.

To do other things with an e-mail address link, press and hold on the e-mail address to display the e-mail link options screen, and then choose one of the following options:

✔ **New Message:** Creates a new e-mail message with the e-mail address you tapped already filled in the To field.

✔ **Add to Contact:** Opens an Info screen in Contacts where you can choose to Create a New Contact or Add to (the number) an Existing Contact. After you choose one, either a New Contact screen opens or your Contacts list opens. Scroll through to find the contact to which you want to add the number.

✔ **Copy:** Copies the e-mail address to the clipboard so you can paste the e-mail address into another app such as Notes or Messages.

**Book III
Chapter 3**

**Surfing the Web
with Safari**

E-mailing and Copying Web Page Links

Say you want to send someone an e-mail with a link to a web page you want them to look at. Or maybe you want to copy a web page link so you can paste it in another program such as Notes, for instance, where you might be creating a list of favorite recipe web pages. You can do both of those things.

To e-mail a link to a web page, tap the Action button, and then tap Mail Link to This Page. A new e-mail message appears with the web page address pasted into the body of the message; address and type a Subject and any additional text you may want to add to the e-mail message, and then tap Send to send your e-mail message. Your message disappears into the ether and the web page you were viewing appears front and center once more.

To copy a website address, tap the address field once to activate the keyboard, and then tap the address field again and choose Select All from the pop-up options. Tap Copy, and the web address is copied to the clipboard so you can paste the web address into a note in Notes or in a text message in Messages.

Printing Web Pages

It's kinder to the environment to print things only if you really need to. After all, your iPhone's display is so sharp and clear that it's often easier to read than any ol' printed page. But if you absolutely must print a web page you're viewing, by all means, be our guest.

To print a web page:

1. **Tap the Action button, and then tap Print to display the Printer Options screen.**

2. **(Optional.) Tap Select Printer if your printer isn't already selected, and then tap the printer you want to print to.**

3. **(Optional.) Tap the + (plus) sign repeatedly to print multiple copies of the web page.**

4. **Tap Print, and Safari does its thing to print your web page to your chosen printer.**

We tell you about ways you can print using your iPhone in Book I, Chapter 2, and in the online bonus content, Bonus Chapter 2.

Opening Photo, Video, Audio, and Document Links

Sometimes links you tap on a web page open photos, or play music or audio, or a video. Typically Safari figures out how to handle these other kinds of content all by itself, by playing an audio or video you tap, or by opening a comment type of document file using iPhone's built-in Quick Look feature.

You can usually save photos and graphics files to the Camera Roll album in the Photos app, and sometimes you may want to choose to open a file you're viewing with another app you have installed on your iPhone.

For instance, you may want to open a Word document using QuickOffice or Documents to Go if you have either of those apps installed on your iPhone. That way, you can save and edit the file, rather than just viewing the file using iPhone's built-in Quick Look feature, which lets you view common file types like Word docs, Excel spreadsheets, and PDF files.

Some of the other kinds of content, like streaming video or audio files, let you watch or listen to those kinds of files using Safari's built-in video and audio player features, but you can't save the files on your iPhone.

You can use iTunes to sync podcasts and other kinds of audio and video content you subscribe to your iPhone, to watch or listen to whenever you want. We tell you how to do those things in Book II, Chapter 1, and Book V, Chapters 3 and 4.)

Opening streaming video and audio links

Tapping a streaming video or audio link on a web page is all you need to do to start watching or listening to that link's video or audio content, like the links to those types of content shown in Figure 3-15.

When you tap one of those content links, Safari opens and begins playing the link with its built-in video or audio player feature, also shown in Figure 3-15.

Figure 3-15: Safari's built in video (left) and audio (right) player features.

Book III
Chapter 3

Surfing the Web
with Safari

When you begin watching or listening to a video or audio web link content, the appropriate player displays all of the controls you need for starting, pausing, stopping, rewinding, fast forwarding, and adjusting the volume of the content you're watching or listening to (refer to Figure 3-16).

When you're watching video content, those controls typically disappear after a few moments, so you can enjoy the video without having those distracting controls blocking your view.

A few things you can do when you're watching video content include

✔ Tap the screen to make the video controls reappear after they disappear

✔ Double-tap the screen when you're watching a video in portrait mode to zoom in or out

✔ Rotate your iPhone sideways to watch a video in landscape mode to enjoy the fullest possible view

Sometimes instead of seeing a thumbnail of a video on a web page, you may see a message informing you that your web browser requires Adobe Flash to view the video. Unfortunately, viewing Flash videos with Safari isn't possible because of Apple's choice to not support Flash on iPhone.

Your iPhone supports the video playing features of the web programming language known as HTML5, or Apple's own QuickTime video feature. The good news is that more and more websites are using HTML5 to create or revise their web pages. And, Adobe has released a software tool that developers can apply to their Flash videos, which makes them viewable on an iPhone, although this tool doesn't enable Flash-based games.

Saving photo and graphic files

Most of the time, you can save a photo or other graphic image file you encounter on a web page to the Camera Roll album in the Photos app, your iPhone's resident photo management app that we discuss in Book V, Chapter 1. Press and hold on a photo or other kind of image file to display the Safari options screen, and then tap Save Image to save that image file to the camera roll in the Photos app, as shown in Figure 3-16.

A bit of copyright "fine print" you ought to keep in mind: Although it's generally acceptable to save any photo or other kind of image file for your own viewing pleasure, you're generally not permitted to use those photos or other image files to share with others — on your own website, or in a magazine you write for, for instance — without the express consent/permission of the person or organization who owns the rights to those image files you may have saved to your iPhone.

Viewing and opening document files

Often you can view certain documents files you may encounter on your web adventures. Tapping on a document link on a web page you're viewing prompts Safari to try to open the document file using its built in Quick Look feature, as shown in Figure 3-17.

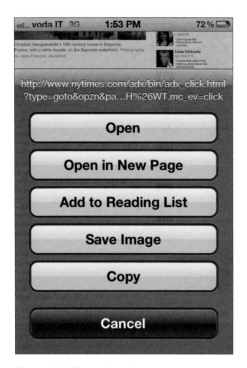

Figure 3-16: Choose Save Image to copy a photo from a web page.

The Quick Look feature can display a number of popular document file types, including Microsoft Word, Excel, and PowerPoint documents, and PDF documents.

Sometimes you may want to open a document you're viewing using another app you have installed on your iPhone.

To open a document using another app, tap the Open In <appname> button on the right to use the default app displayed on that button, or tap the Open In button on the left (refer to Figure 3-18) to display other apps on your iPhone that you can use to open the app. Tap the button that corresponds to the app you want to use to open the document. Safari closes and the app launches and loads the document.

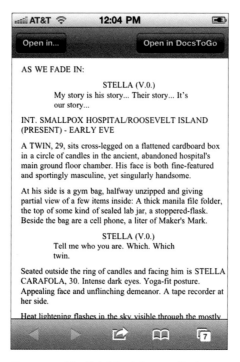

Figure 3-17: The Quick Look feature displays documents quickly, or you can open them in another app.

Playing Favorites with Bookmarks

As we mention earlier in this chapter, Safari on your iPhone syncs any bookmarks you have saved in Safari on your Mac or Windows PC (or Internet Explorer on your Windows PC if that's your preferred web browser) with your iPhone, and the other way around.

Any bookmarks you create using your iPhone get synced back with your Mac or PC web browser. This back and forth magic happens whenever you sync your iPhone, either with iTunes or iCloud. It can also happen almost instantly if you have an iCloud account set up on your iPhone, and if you've turned on the sync bookmarks setting for that account. (Turn this setting on by tapping Home➪Settings➪iCloud, and then tap the switch to turn the Bookmarks setting on or off, as you like.)

We tell you how to sync bookmarks and all kinds of other stuff between your iPhone and your computer in Book II, Chapter 1.

Viewing, opening, and creating bookmarks

To view a bookmarked web page, tap Bookmarks to display the Bookmarks screen (refer to Figure 3-2), and then tap the bookmark you want to open that web page. You may need to scroll down your list or tap a folder stored in the Bookmarks list to find the bookmark you want to open.

To create a new bookmark for a web page you're viewing, do the following:

1. **Tap the Action button to display the Action option screen, and then tap Add Bookmark to display the Add Bookmark screen.**

   The keyboard appears, and the blinking cursor is positioned at the end of the web page name.

2. **(Optional.) Edit the name of the website if you don't like the name that's automatically created for the bookmark.**

3. **(Optional.) Tap the bookmarks folder in the bottom half of the screen to choose a different folder than the one that's already chosen.**

4. **Tap Done to save your new Bookmark.**

We tell you how to use the Add to Home Screen bookmark option in the section "Creating Home screen bookmark icons."

Organizing bookmarks

You can create a new folder in the Bookmarks list or delete or rearrange folders and bookmarks using the Bookmarks edit feature.

Tap Bookmarks, and then tap Edit to display the Bookmarks edit screen, shown in Figure 3-18.

- ✔ To rearrange your bookmarks, tap the Rearrange button to the right of a bookmark, and then drag the bookmark up or down the list and release your finger to drop the bookmark in its new location.

- ✔ To delete a bookmark or bookmark folder, tap the red – (minus) sign to the left of a bookmark or folder you want to say goodbye to, and then tap the Delete button. The bookmark or folder disappears.

- ✔ To create a new bookmark folder:

  1. Tap New Folder, and then type a name for your new bookmark folder, as shown in Figure 3-19.

     Optionally, you can tap the folder name beneath the bookmark name to choose the folder you want to store your new folder in.

  2. Tap the folder button in the upper left corner to save your new folder and return to the Bookmarks screen.

✏ Tap Done when you're finished playing around with the Bookmarks edit screen (refer to Figure 3-18), and Safari returns you to the web page you were viewing before you started tweaking your bookmarks.

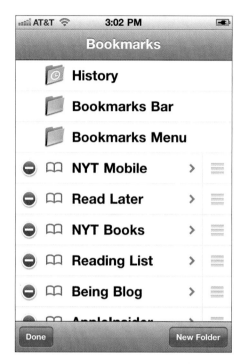

Figure 3-18: The Bookmarks edit screen.

Creating Home screen icons

If you visit a particular web page very often, you can create a Home screen icon, called a Web Clip, for that web page. The Web Clip appears on the Home screen, just like your iPhone's app icons. Tapping the Web Clip automatically opens the web page.

To create a Web Clip:

1. Open the web page you want to create a Web Clip for.

You can zoom in to a particular column on the web page you want to add to your Home screen, and when you tap the icon on the Home screen, Safari opens the web page to that same section — very handy for tracking just a column of information, like the daily menu special at your favorite diner.

Figure 3-19: Naming a new bookmarks folder.

2. **Tap the Action button to display the Action options screen, and then tap Add to Home Screen.**

   The Add to Home screen appears, displaying a name and icon for the Web Clip you want to add to the Home screen.

3. **Edit or type a new name for the web page if you don't like the one that's automatically filled in for you, and then tap Add.**

   Safari closes and ushers you to the Home screen where your new Web Clip has been added.

If you don't see the Add to Home Screen button in Step 1, that's because your iPhone's Home screen is filled to capacity, in which case you'll need to delete an app or Web Clip you have saved on your Home screen. Alternatively, you can make more space by moving one or more Home screen icons into folders that occupy only one icon space themselves and can hold up to 12 icons inside them. We show you how to add, remove, and organize Home screen icons and folders in Book 1, Chapter 3.

Searching Tips and Tricks

Safari's Search field is the place to go to whenever you want to find something on the web. When you first begin using your iPhone, Google is the search engine that Safari counts on to find things you search for using the Search field.

If you'd rather depend on Bing or Yahoo! to carry out your web searches, you can change your search engine choice by tapping Settings on the Home screen, and then tap Safari⟳Search Engine and pick your preferred search engine. We tell you about the rest of Safari's settings you can change at the end of this chapter.

Searching the web

To Search the web using Safari's search feature:

1. **Tap the Search field to display the keyboard, and then begin typing the word, name, phrase, ZIP code, or whatever you're searching for.**

   As you type, a list of suggested matches appear, as shown in Figure 3-20, based on web pages you may have already visited, or bookmarked, or one which your chosen Search engine provider thinks may match what you're looking for.

   At this point, you can do one of the following:

2a. **Tap one of those suggested matches if it matches your criteria.**

2b. **Ignore those suggested matches that appear and finish typing what you're looking for in the Search field, and then tap the Search button.**

   Either way, Safari displays a list of search result links (refer to Figure 3-20) that you can then tap to explore any of those possibilities.

Searching from the Home screen

Besides using Safari's Search field to search the web, you can also search the web from iPhone's Home Search screen.

To search the web using iPhone's Home Search screen:

1. **Press the Home button to display the Home screen, and then navigate to the first screen of icons if you're not already there. (You can press Home again, or flick to the right until you reach the first Home screen.)**

2. **Press the Home button on the first Home screen (or flick to the right or tap to the left of the row of dots showing how many home screens you have) to display the Home Search screen and the keyboard.**

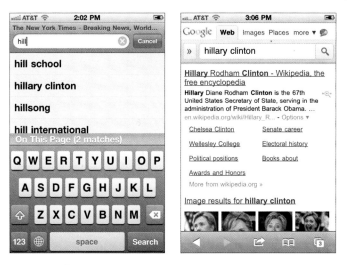

Figure 3-20: Suggested matches and results for what you're in search of.

3. **Begin typing the word, name, phrase, ZIP code, or whatever you're searching for.**

   As you type, a list of any suggested matches stored on your iPhone appear (based on your contacts, calendar items, notes, and other sources), followed by two options: Search web and Search Wikipedia, as shown in Figure 3-21.

4. **Tap Search Web (or Search Wikipedia if you want to search** www.wikipedia.org **instead of the web at large).**

   The Home Search screen closes and Safari displays a list of web (or Wikipedia) links that match the word or phrase you typed.

5. **Tap a web link to open and view that link's associated web page.**

You can ask Siri to search for you if you have an iPhone 4S. Press and hold the Home button until you hear Siri ask how she can help you, and then speak your request or question.

Searching on a web page you're viewing

Sometimes you want to find something on a web page you're currently viewing (that you maybe even found by searching for that web page in the first place). Instead of scrolling up and down a web page to hunt down a word or phrase, you can use Safari's search feature to locate and highlight the word or phrase on the web page for you.

Book III
Chapter 3

Surfing the Web with Safari

Figure 3-21: Search the web from the Home
Screen Search feature.

To find a word or phrase on a web page you're viewing:

1. **Tap the Search field, and then type some or all of the word or phrase you're looking for.**

   As you type, a list of suggested web page matches appear, but you can ignore those because you're already on the web page you want to be on.

2. **Flick the list of suggestions up toward the top of the screen.**

   The keyboard closes, and at the bottom of the suggestions is another list under the heading On This Page, followed by the number of matches found on the web page you're viewing.

3. **Tap the item beneath On This Page to display those matches on the web page.**

   A yellow highlight appears around the word or phrase that matches what you're looking for, as shown in Figure 3-22.

4. **(Optional) Tap Next to display the next highlighted match (if more than one match was found), and continue to tap Next if necessary until you find what you're looking for on the web page.**

5. **Tap Done to close the On This Page search screen buttons and view the web page.**

Figure 3-22: Finding what you're looking for on a web page you're viewing.

Viewing RSS and Web-Apps Web Pages

Two types of web pages you may not know about — and you may be happy to know more about — that can make your Safari web browsing experience faster and smoother are

✔ **RSS (*Really Simple Syndication*):** If you've ever wondered what that little doohicky symbol (see the following figure) you see on many web pages is all about, the answer is really simple, as in Really Simple Syndication, which are also referred to as *feeds*. RSS feed web pages are accessed by typing `feed://` followed by a web address. For instance, typing `feed://feeds.nytimes.com/nyt/rss/HomePage` into Safari's Address field and then tapping Go opens the RSS version of the *New York Times* Home page, as shown in Figure 3-23.

✎ **Web-apps:** Web applications are teeny tiny web pages designed to fit on your iPhone screen that look and work pretty much as though they're standalone apps. You can find a bookmark named iPhone Web Applications that Apple loads in the Bookmarks folder on every iPhone. Tap it to view a directory of web apps you can view, including the one shown in Figure 3-23. In truth, web apps were neat when original iPhone buyers had nothing better to do than wait an entire year until Apple unveiled the App Store. But web apps aren't very interesting anymore because many websites already offer mobile web pages that mimic or best those web apps the bookmark takes you to. And better still, many *real apps* that tap into the web — like the NPR app, for instance — go above and beyond the features and experience found in the mobile or web app versions of those apps.

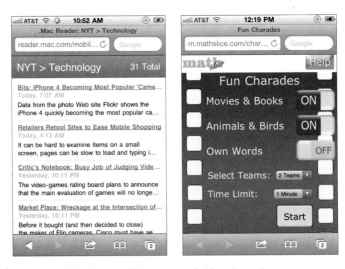

Figure 3-23: Viewing an RSS web page (left) and a web-app.

Adjusting General and Security Settings

In the sections before this one, we occasionally ask you to check out or adjust a particular Safari setting, like turning on the AutoFill feature, for instance. In this section, we give you a complete rundown of Safari's settings and feature options.

Press the Home button, and then tap Settings➪Safari to display the Safari Settings screen, as shown in Figure 3-24.

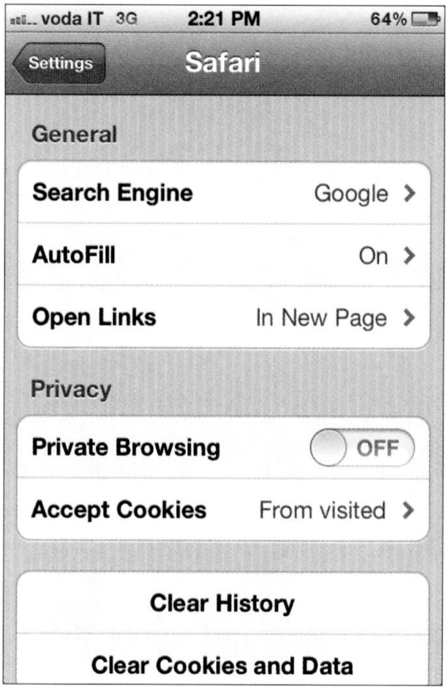

Book III
Chapter 3

Surfing the Web
with Safari

Figure 3-24: Safari's settings screen.

The 411 on Safari's settings is as follows:

- **Search Engine:** Tap and choose your preferred Search provider.

- **AutoFill:** Tap to activate and adjust the AutoFill features described in the earlier section, "Using AutoFill to Do the Typing for You."

- **Open Links:** Tap this button to choose what you want Safari to do when you tap a link in a web page. See the section "Juggling multiple websites" for a full explanation.

✔ **Private Browsing:** With Private Browsing On, Safari doesn't keep a history of websites you visit. This is convenient if you share your iPhone with others and don't want your secret web habits revealed.

✔ **Accept Cookies:** Cookies are bits of information certain websites store, so those websites can know and remember certain things about you. Tap and choose whether you want to receive cookies Never, From Visited, or Always. From Visited is the choice we recommend so that websites you go to can remember things like your ZIP code for giving you the weather forecast and so on. Choosing Never may result in some websites not functioning properly, and choosing Always allows websites to gather information about you every time you visit those sites.

✔ **Clear History, Clear Cookies and Data:** Tapping any of these three erases their respective saved files from your iPhone. Clear History wipes out Safari's memory of any websites you visited. Clear Cookies and Data erases any crumbs of cookie information you may have typed in to certain websites, like your ZIP code.

✔ **Fraud Warning:** Turn this on if you want Safari to warn you if what seems like a legitimate website you want to open may in fact be a potentially harmful site.

✔ **JavaScript:** Turned on, this feature allows certain websites to present information and options in fancy ways, with things like pop-up buttons, swirling graphics, and interactive features that won't appear or work if you turn this feature off.

✔ **Block Pop-ups:** This feature does its best to prevent any annoying pop-up advertisements from getting in the way of your web browsing experience.

✔ **Advanced:** Opens the following two choices:

- **Website Data:** Tap to view any databases that are automatically created by certain websites so those websites can speed up your web browsing experience when you use them. You may see databases for `mail.google.com`, for instance, if you use Safari to read your email. Tapping a database item listed in the Databases screen displays more information about how much, and the maximum amount of, space that database is taking up on your iPhone.

- **Debug Console:** Website developers turn on this feature to help them troubleshoot problems the web pages they create may run into. Average Joes like you and me can keep this option turned off.

Chapter 4: E-mailing Every Which Way You Can

In This Chapter

⊿ **Configuring your e-mail account**

⊿ **Using Mail**

⊿ **E-mailing from other apps**

⊿ **Adjusting your e-mail account settings**

⊿ **Playing Fetch with your e-mail**

⊿ **Using different e-mail apps**

*J*ust about everyone has an e-mail address these days. E-mail is a quick and easy way to send and request information, make reservations, keep in touch with family and friends who live far away or, sometimes, are just down the hall in another room. With a little web research, you can find the name of the CEO of your favorite company and send her a message about how much you like the latest model of the doohickey they've released. You can also complain directly to the head of research, development, and manufacturing when your beloved doohickey breaks a week after you bought it.

With your iPhone, you have e-mail at your fingertips. In this chapter, we're assuming (always dangerous, we know) you already have an e-mail account. We show you how to configure your e-mail account on the Mail app so you can access your e-mail from your iPhone. Then, we explain the ins and outs of Mail — writing and sending a new message, receiving and replying to a message, and saving and deleting messages. We also go over initiating an e-mail from other apps such as Notes, Maps, and Photos. Then we take a look at the account settings you can change. Your iPhone comes with preset choices for these features that probably are fine for 90 percent of users, but for the remaining 10 percent and the purely curious, we explain all the settings one by one. At the end of this chapter, we review some of the other e-mail apps that reside in the ether world of the Internet and App Store.

Configuring Your E-Mail Account

Before you can actually send and receive e-mail messages, you have to configure your account. You can set up your e-mail by yourself on your iPhone or connect your iPhone to your computer and use iTunes to sync the e-mail account information from your computer to your iPhone. We explain that method first. Then, we go on to explain how to configure an e-mail account directly on your iPhone.

Configuring your e-mail account with iTunes

You may have done this already if you connected your iPhone to iTunes, (see Book II, Chapter 1) but we go through the steps here anyway:

1. **Connect your iPhone to your computer with the USB cable or turn on iTunesWi-Fi sync in Settings⇨General and connect both your iPhone and your computer to the same Wi-Fi network.**

2. **Open iTunes.**

3. **Click the name of your iPhone under Devices in the source list on the left side of the window.**

4. **Click the Info tab at the top of the window.**

5. **Scroll down to Sync Mail Accounts, as shown in Figure 4-1.**

6. **Select the mail accounts you wish to sync to your iPhone.**

   Only the account information, not the messages that are present in that account, are synced.

7. **Click the Sync button on the bottom right of the window.**

That's it. You can disconnect your iPhone and begin using Mail right away.

Configuring your e-mail account on iPhone

You can configure your e-mail account directly on your iPhone with a series of taps. Apple has been kind enough to insert the technical stuff needed to access some of the most used e-mail services. For the following e-mail services, you need to have just your e-mail address and password handy:

- iCloud
- Microsoft Exchange
- Google Mail
- Yahoo!
- AOL

✔ Windows Live Hotmail

✔ MobileMe

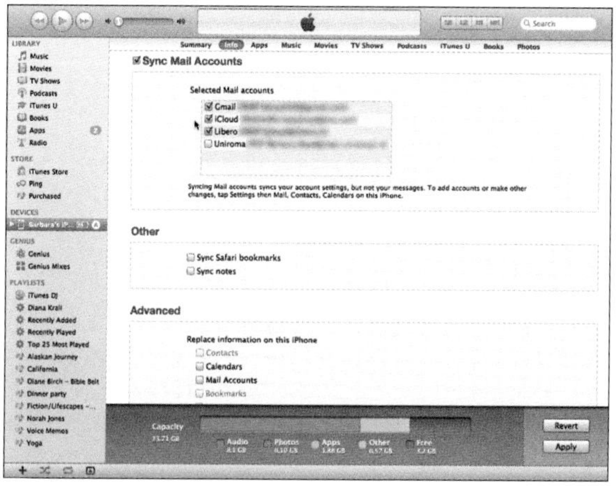

Figure 4-1: Use iTunes to sync e-mail accounts from your computer to your iPhone.

Setting up iCloud, MobileMe, Google Mail, Yahoo, AOL, and Windows Live Hotmail accounts

Apple has already put the incoming and outgoing server information for the most popular e-mail providers on iPhone. If you have a MobileMe account or have set up an account through iCloud, you have an @me.com or an @mac.com e-mail account. Follow these steps to set up e-mail on your iPhone:

1. **Tap Settings on the Home screen, and then tap Mail, Contacts, Calendars. You have to scroll down — it's right below General.**

2. **The Add Account screen opens, as shown in Figure 4-2.**

3. **Tap iCloud, even if you have a MobileMe account.**

   iCloud can use your @me.com or @mac.me e-mail address and MobileMe is valid only until June 2012.

4. **Type in the e-mail address and password associated with your Apple ID and then tap the Next button.**

   If you don't have an Apple ID, click Get a Free Apple ID and follow the on-screen instructions to set one up.

   Your account is verified.

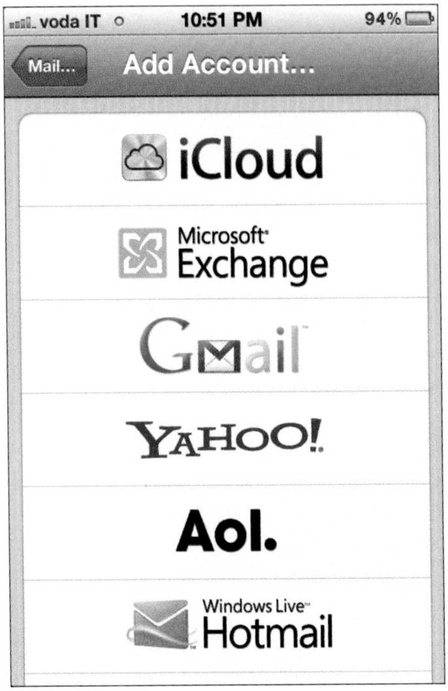

Figure 4-2: The Add Account screen.

5. **The iCloud screen opens.**

A message asks if you want iCloud to use the Location of Your iPhone. We suggest you tap OK. Find My iPhone is explained in Book I, Chapter 4.

On the screen shown in Figure 4-3, you have a series of options and toggle switches that turn those options on. Turning an option on means that the information in that app is shared between your iPhone and iCloud and any other devices you access iCloud with. Any time you make changes to one of them on one device, the changes go up to the iCloud and rain down on the other device.

- **Mail:** Turn this on and you receive your iCloud mail on your iPhone.

- **Contacts, Calendars, Reminders, and Bookmarks:** Turn these switches on and information in these apps, previously synced with your Mac or Windows PC, is merged with iCloud. The information is consequently updated on all devices when changes are made on one device.

- **Notes:** New notes or changes to existing notes are sent to all devices.

- **Photo Stream:** When on, sends up to 1,000 of the most recent photos taken in the past 30 days in Photos on your iPhone to iCloud. (See Book V, Chapter 1 for details.)

- **Documents & Data:** Allows apps to store documents and data in iCloud, as explained in Book II, Chapter 1.

- **Find My iPhone:** This app allows you to find your phone if it's lost or stolen (Gasp!). It also allows you to use iCloud to erase the data in iPhone remotely and lock it in the tragic event that your iPhone is stolen or lost. All this is explained in detail in Book I, Chapter 4.

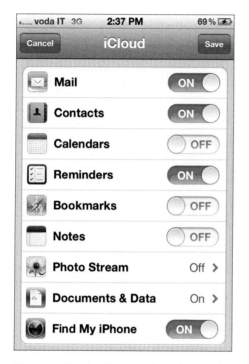

Figure 4-3: Tapping Contacts, Calendars, and Bookmarks On automatically merges their contents with iCloud.

Book III
Chapter 4

E-mailing Every
Which Way You Can

If you use Gmail, Yahoo!, AOL, or Windows Live Hotmail, do the following:

1. **Tap Settings on the Home screen, and then tap Mail, Contacts, Calendars. You have to scroll down — it's right below General.**

2. **Tap Add Account.**

3. **The Add Account screen opens. (Refer to Figure 4-2.)**

4. **Tap the name of the account you use; for example, Google Mail, also known as Gmail.**

5. **The Google Mail (or Yahoo! or AOL or Windows Live Hotmail) screen opens, as shown in Figure 4-4.**

Filling in the Name field is optional (Windows Live Hotmail doesn't even have one). Type your e-mail address in the Address field and your password in the Password field.

Figure 4-4: Type your name, e-mail address, and password in the designated fields.

6. **Tap the Next button in the upper right corner.**

   The Google Mail screen opens. You have three options to consider turning on or off, depending on the services you use:

   - **Mail:** This connects you to your Gmail account so that messages download to your iPhone in the Mail app and you can send messages from your Gmail account in Mail.

   - **Calendars:** When you turn this on, you have the option of keeping or deleting existing calendars on your iPhone. The Keep On My iPhone option may cause duplicates. After you turn this feature on, changes you make to your calendar on your computer are synced to your iPhone, and vice versa.

   - **Notes:** If you turn this on, you see notes you write in Notes within your Gmail account on Mail. This is handy if you frequently e-mail notes from Notes.

After you're happy with the settings, tap Save.

The Description field is automatically filled in with Google Mail, Yahoo!, AOL, or Windows Live Hotmail but if you tap there, you can change it. For example, we set up two Gmail accounts: one for personal e-mail exchanges and another for newsletter subscriptions. This way, we don't have to weed through a dozen or more daily newsletters to find more important messages. In the Description field, we named one Friends and the other Subscriptions. More about that in the Viewing E-Mail Messages section later in this chapter.

Setting up other IMAP and POP accounts

If you use another e-mail provider or you want to add your work e-mail, you'll need some other information from that e-mail provider. You can find this information on the website of the provider on the page that references iPhone or smart phone setup, or ask the tech support person or network administrator at your office. Jot down the following information:

- Whether you're using an IMAP — Internet Message Access Protocol or POP — Post Office Protocol account.

- The Incoming Mail Server information, which lets iPhone receive your mail. Jot down the Host Name, which is usually something like *mail. providername.com*, the User Name, which is the name you gave when you signed up for this e-mail service, and the password you established for this account when you signed up. Your User Name is often the part of your e-mail address before the @ (at) symbol.

- Lastly, note the Outgoing Mail Server Host Name. This enables your iPhone to send e-mail messages.

IMAP services keep your messages on the e-mail or Internet service provider server, even after you've read them, whereas POP services only store your messages temporarily. After you've downloaded them, they're no longer on the server, unless you change the settings in your Mail program that you want to leave them on the server after being downloaded.

Most web-based e-mail service providers, such as Google Mail, Yahoo!, or AOL, use IMAP. IMAP is convenient if you want to read e-mail messages on both your iPhone and from a computer in a different location, although you do need to delete messages now and then so your mailbox doesn't fill up and reject new incoming messages.

Other e-mail service providers use POP, which is convenient because the messages are literally on your iPhone or on your computer if you've downloaded them there first. After you download the messages, they reside where you first read them. You can configure both your computer and iPhone to leave the messages on the server after you've downloaded them so you can access them from the other device at a later time. We explain that just a bit further on in this chapter under "Incoming Settings" later in this chapter.

Armed with this data, you're ready to set up your e-mail. Here's how:

1. **Tap Settings on the Home screen, and then tap Mail, Contacts, Calendars. You have to scroll down — it's right below General.**

2. **The Add Account screen opens (refer to Figure 4-2).**

3. **Tap Other at the bottom of the list.**

4. **Tap Add Mail Account, the first button on the screen.**

   A New Account screen opens.

5. **Fill in your name, address (your e-mail address), your password, and a description if you want something different than what is automatically entered. See Figure 4-5.**

Figure 4-5: Fill in the requested information in the New Account screen.

6. **Tap Next and iPhone searches the Internet for your account.**

   If you account is found, a second New Account screen opens, as shown in Figure 4-6. This is where you need the information you gathered before beginning this sequence of steps.

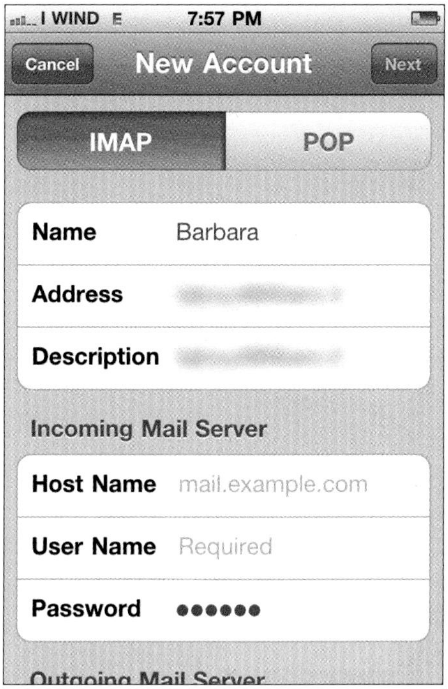

Figure 4-6: Fill in the information about incoming and outgoing mail servers.

7. **Choose the type of account — IMAP or POP.**

8. **Your name, address, and description are filled in the appropriate fields automatically.**

    You need to fill in the Incoming Mail Server and Outgoing Mail Server information.

9. **For Incoming Mail Server, fill in the following:**

    • **Host Name:** This will be something like *mail.providername.com.*

    • **User Name:** This is the name you used to sign up for the service, usually the first part of your e-mail address (the part before the @ (at) symbol).

    • **Password:** This is the password you assigned, usually the same as your e-mail password.

10. **Under Outgoing Mail Server, fill in**

    • **Host Name:** This may have *smtp* or *mail* in it.

    • **User Name:** This may be optional, depending on your service provider.

    • **Password:** This may be optional, depending on your service provider.

11. **Tap Save.**

The information you entered is verified by the service you use.

After the account is verified, you'll see it added to your list of accounts in the Mail, Contacts, Calendars screen in Settings.

SMTP stands for *Simple Mail Transport Protocol*. This is the transmission protocol used by Internet Service Providers (ISPs).

Setting up Microsoft Exchange

If you use Microsoft Exchange, follow these steps to set up a Microsoft Exchange account on your iPhone:

1. **Tap Settings⇨Mail, Contacts, Calendars⇨Add Account⇨Microsoft Exchange.**

The Exchange screen opens, as shown in Figure 4-7.

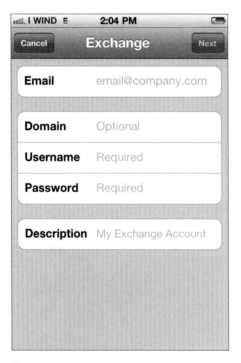

Figure 4-7: Fill in the Microsoft Exchange screen to add Exchange to your e-mail accounts.

2. **Fill in the information requested.**

   You may have to ask your network administrator for some of the details.

3. **Tap Next.**

   If the Microsoft Autodiscovery service didn't fill in the server address, type it in. It will be something like *exchange.company.com*.

Using Mail

iPhone's Mail app works like most e-mail programs. Terms we've come to know and love for printed material that is delivered to our homes and offices — mail, inbox, carbon copy — are used to describe electronic material that is delivered to our homes and offices via our computers and iPhones. We're going to start by explaining how to create and send a message, and then tell you about replying to, forwarding, filing, and deleting messages. Next, we go through the ways you can view and organize messages. Lastly, we show you how to search messages.

Creating and sending e-mail messages

To create and send an e-mail message, just follow these steps:

1. **Tap the Mail button on the Home screen.**

   The Mailboxes screen opens, as seen in Figure 4-8.

2. **Tap the inbox for the account you want to send the message from.**

3. **Tap the Compose button.**

   A New Message screen opens. The cursor is blinking in the To field.

4. **In the To field, type the e-mail address of the person you want to send the message to.**

   If the person you want to send the message to is in Contacts, begin typing the recipient's name in the To field. Names of people in your Contacts database that begin with the same letters show up as a list from which you can choose. The more letters you type, the narrower your choices become. See Figure 4-9.

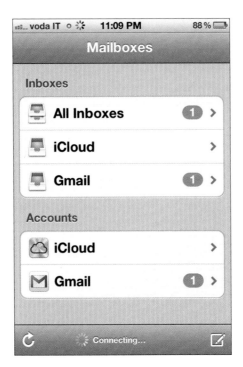

Figure 4-8: The Mailboxes screen lists the inboxes and accounts on your iPhone.

When you find the name you want, tap it. If you want to add another recipient, repeat the previous step.

To open Contacts and choose the recipients from there, tap the plus sign button on the right of the To field. Contacts opens. Scroll through the list and tap the names of the desired recipients.

5. **If you want to send a Cc — Carbon Copy, or Bcc — Blind Carbon Copy, to other recipients, tap the Cc/Bcc field.**

   The field expands into three fields: Cc, Bcc, and From. Fill in the Cc and/ or Bcc fields the same way you fill in the To field.

   If you want to change the address from which the message is sent, tap the From field and choose the address you wish the message to be sent from, as seen in Figure 4-10.

Figure 4-9: Type the first letters of the name of the person you want to send a message to find the e-mail address in Contacts.

6. **When you finish addressing the message, tap Return.**

   The cursor moves to the Subject field.

   You can move names from one address field to another, such as from To to Bcc, by clicking and dragging them where you want.

7. **Type the subject of the message, and then tap Return or tap directly in the message field.**

   The cursor moves to the message field.

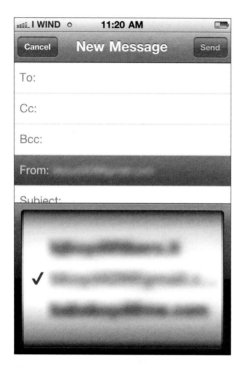

Figure 4-10: Tap Cc/Bcc to expand the field and type in an additional address or change the From address.

8. **Type your message or, if you have an iPhone 4S with Siri turned on, tap the Dictation button and dictate it.**

   You can select text and make it bold, italic, or underlined and also indent sentences or paragraphs. Double-tap a word to highlight it and activate grabbers. Drag the blue grabbers to highlight the word or words you want to format. Tap the Cut, Copy, or Paste buttons if you want to perform those editing actions on your test. If you select just one word, you also have a Suggest option that gives you a list of synonyms for the selected word. Tap the arrow on the right end of the bar where you see the Cut, Copy, Paste, and Suggest editing buttons. Tap B/U to open a button bar with bold, italic, and underline options, which you tap to format the selected text. Tap Quote Level to open a button bar that offers an increase (indent) or decrease (outdent) option. Tap the one you want to use. Repeat the process to apply more than one formatting option to the same text or to remove the format. (Refer to Figure 4-11.)

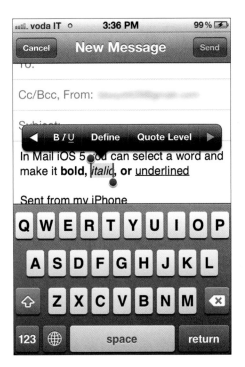

Figure 4-11: Format text with in-message editing buttons.

9. Tap the Send button.

The word *Sending* and a turning gear appear at the bottom of the screen, and then a sending progress bar opens. Faster than you can put a stamp on an envelope, your message is on its way. If you've turned on the Sent Mail alert under Settings⇨Sounds, a rushing sound confirms your message has been sent.

If you're composing a message and have to stop midway, perhaps to find information you want to include in the message, you can save it as a draft. Tap Cancel in the upper left corner. Three buttons appear, as in Figure 4-12. You can choose to Delete Draft, and the message disappears forever. Choose Save Draft, and the message goes into your Drafts inbox to be opened later and modified. Choose Cancel to return to the message and continue writing.

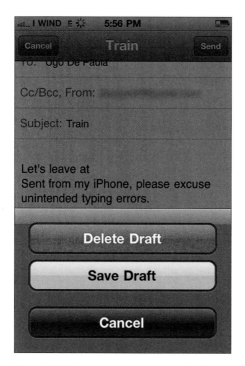

Figure 4-12: You can save a message in the Drafts file to finish writing it later.

Replying to, forwarding, filing, printing, and deleting messages

iPhone has several ways of letting you know you've received a message. If Badge App Icon is turned on in Settings⇨Notifications⇨Mail, the Mail icon on the Home screen wears a badge showing the number of unread messages you have. If the Notification Center and Alert Styles are selected in Settings⇨Notifications⇨Mail, you are alerted that way. Also, an audible alert plays if you turned on New Mail alerts under Settings⇨Sounds. See Book I, Chapter 4 to learn more about notifications settings.

To read your messages, tap Mail on the Home screen. The Mailboxes screen opens as shown in Figure 4-8.

✔ To access all your incoming messages, tap All Inboxes. If you have only one e-mail account on your iPhone, this is the only inbox you'll see.

✔ To access the messages in one specific inbox, tap the name of that inbox. A list of the messages opens, as shown in Figure 4-13. Unread messages have a blue dot next to them. The gray To label indicates that Barbara was a direct recipient of the message. The gray Cc means Barbara was receiving a copy of the message. We explain how to activate this feature in the section "Adjusting E-Mail Account Settings."

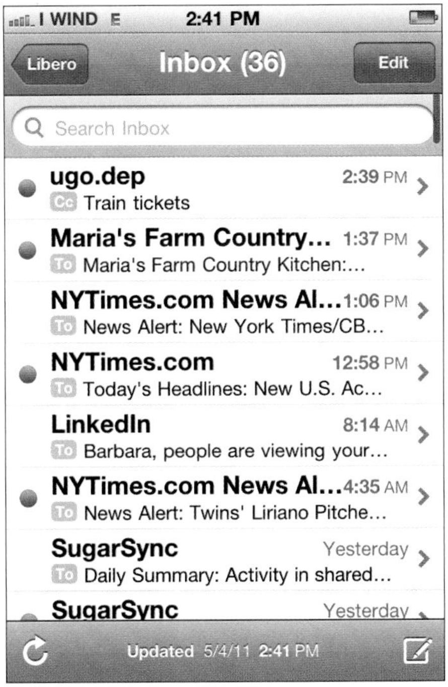

Figure 4-13: Messages are listed in reverse chronological order within a mailbox.

Book III
Chapter 4

E-mailing Every
Which Way You Can

✔ Tap on the message you want to read, and it opens as in Figure 4-14.

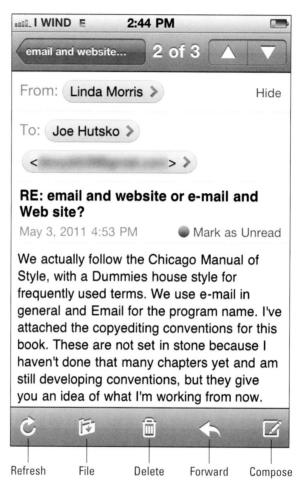

Figure 4-14: A received message.

You have several options from the message screen:

- ✔ Tap the up and down triangles in the upper right corner to read the next or previous message.
- ✔ Tap the Refresh button and Mail checks for new incoming messages.

 ✔ Tap the File button, and a screen opens as shown in Figure 4-15. Tap the folder where you want the message to reside. To file the message in a different mailbox, tap Accounts, and then tap the folder to which you want to move the message. If you change your mind, tap Cancel.

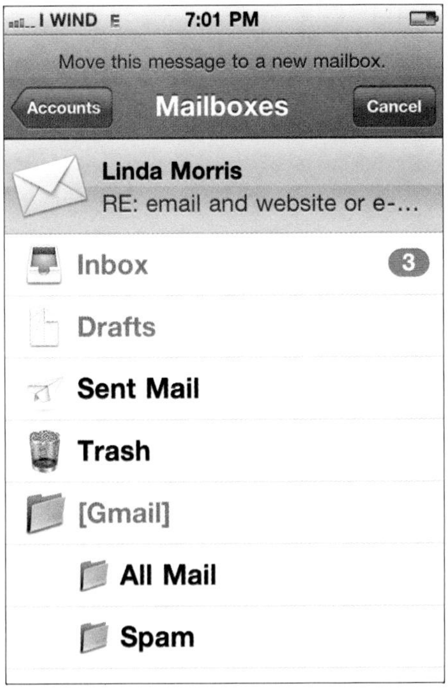

┌─────────────────────────────────────┐
│ ▂▃▃ I WIND E   7:01 PM   ▭▌│
│   Move this message to a new mailbox. │
│ ⟨Accounts⟩   **Mailboxes**   ⟨Cancel⟩ │
│ ┌─────────────────────────────────┐ │
│ │ ✉ **Linda Morris**   │ │
│ │   RE: email and website or e-... │ │
│ ├─────────────────────────────────┤ │
│ │ 💻 Inbox   ❸   │ │
│ ├─────────────────────────────────┤ │
│ │ 📄 Drafts   │ │
│ ├─────────────────────────────────┤ │
│ │ ✈ **Sent Mail**   │ │
│ ├─────────────────────────────────┤ │
│ │ 🗑 **Trash**   │ │
│ ├─────────────────────────────────┤ │
│ │ 📁 [Gmail]   │ │
│ ├─────────────────────────────────┤ │
│ │   📁 **All Mail**   │ │
│ ├─────────────────────────────────┤ │
│ │   📁 **Spam**   │ │
│ └─────────────────────────────────┘ │
└─────────────────────────────────────┘

Figure 4-15: Choose the folder where you'd like to file the message.

✔ Tap the trashcan button to delete your message. Tap one of the two buttons that appear: a Delete Message button and a black Cancel button.

✔ If Archive Messages is on, you won't see a trashcan button. Activate or deactivate the Archive Messages feature in Settings⇨Mail, Contacts, Calendar⇨*Account Name*.

✔ Tap the Forward button, and the options as shown in Figure 4-16 appear.

✔ **Reply:** Tap to reply to the sender of the message. When you finish writing your message, tap Send.

✔ **Reply All (if there are other recipients besides you):** To send a reply to the sender and to all addresses in the To or Cc list, tap this button. When you finish writing your message, tap Send. The entire message is placed in the body of your reply. If you want to include only a portion, highlight that portion before tapping the Reply button.

Figure 4-16: Tapping the Forward button gives you four options.

✔ **Forward:** To forward a copy of the message to someone else, tap the Forward button. If there are attachments, Mail asks you if you want to include the attachments. After you make this choice, the message window opens with the cursor blinking in the To field. Address the message as explained previously. Write something in the message field, and then tap Send. The Re in the subject field changes to Fwd so the recipient knows this is a forwarded message.

You can receive e-mail attachments and view many of them. Attachments you can read include PDF files, images files such as JPEG, TIFF, and GIF, and iWork and Microsoft Office files. You can forward any kind of attachment, even those you can't open with iPhone.

Tap and hold an image attachment, and then tap Save Image to save it to your Camera Roll.

✔ **Print:** To print the message, you must have access to an AirPrint-enabled printer. Do the following:

1. **Tap Print.**

   The Printer Options screen opens, as shown in Figure 4-17.

2. **Tap Select Printer.**

   iPhone looks for available printers. When one is found, you return to the Printer Options screen.

3. **Increase the number of copies you want printed by tapping the plus sign to the right, or leave it at the default of one copy.**

4. **Tap Print.**

   Your message is printed.

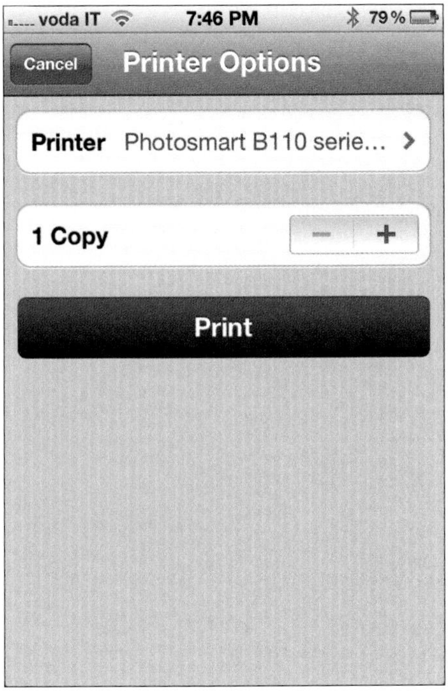

Figure 4-17: Choose the printer and the number of copies to print from the Printer Options screen.

✔ **Compose:** The last button on the right is the compose button, which takes you to a New Message screen to write a new message.

You may want to delete multiple messages, move several from the inbox to another folder, or flag a selection of messages or mark them as unread, all at once. Here's the way to do that:

1. **Tap Mail⇨All Inboxes or one of the account-specific inboxes.**

2. **Tap the Edit button in the upper right corner.**

   Empty circles appear to the left of each message.

3. **Tap the circle next to the messages you want to delete, move, or mark.**

   A white checkmark in a red circle appears.

4. **After you've selected all the messages you want, tap the appropriate button: Delete, Move, or Mark, as shown in Figure 4-18.**

   Move opens the filing options (refer to Figure 4-15). Mark lets you flag the messages, in which case a little flag waves next to the message in the message list, or mark as *unread*, which replaces the blue dot next to the message that indicates unread messages. Repeat the steps to Unflag or Mark as Read messages that are flagged or marked as unread.

5. **You can also swipe on the message in the list to make a red Delete button appear.**

   Tap the Delete button and the message is deleted.

Figure 4-18: Tap Delete, Move, or Mark when managing messages.

The thing is, just because you clicked Delete, your messages still aren't really deleted. They've been moved to the trash. To truly take out the trash or delete your messages from you iPhone, follow these steps:

1. **Tap Mail then the name of the account in the Accounts list.**

2. **Tap the Trash button, which looks like a trashcan.**

   If Archiving is on, instead of the trashcan, you see an archival box icon.

3. **Tap Edit.**

   The red Delete All button is activated.

4. **Tap Delete All.**

   Your messages are truly deleted.

But wait! What about that Move and Mark buttons?

1. **Follow steps 1 through 3 above.**

2. **Tap in the empty circles to the left of the messages you want to remove from the trash, flag, or mark as unread.**

   The Move and Mark buttons are then activated.

3. **Tap the Move button to put the selected messages in the folder you want or the Mark button to flag or mark the messages as unread.**

Viewing e-mail messages

An incoming message contains much more than just the written message. Take a look at these features:

- Tap the blue bubble with the name of the sender or one of the other recipients of the message. A screen opens that gives you an option of creating a new contact or adding this e-mail address to an existing contact (refer to Figure 4-19).

- Tap Mark to flag or mark the message as unread. (Tap *Details* next to the sender's name if you don't see the Mark option.) A flag waves or the blue dot remains next to the message in the message list.

- Phone numbers, e-mail addresses, and website addresses that appear blue and underlined are active links. Tap the phone number, and an option of calling that number appears. Tap the e-mail address, and a New Message screen opens. Tap a website address to open the page in Safari.

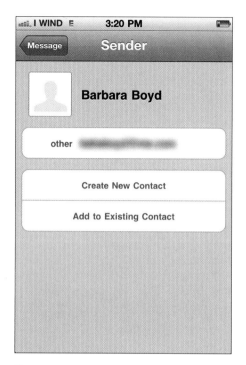

Figure 4-19: The sender's address can be added to Contacts from Mail.

✏ Tap Hide/Details, next to the sender's name, to hide or show the recipients of the message. When there are a lot of recipients, it's helpful to tap Hide so you can see more of the message in the opening screen.

✏ If you receive an invitation from a calendar app that uses the iCalendar format, tap on the file and the Event Details open. Tap the Add to Calendar button at the bottom of the screen and then choose the calendar where the event should be inserted. For more details about sending and receiving event invitations, see Book IV, Chapter 2.

✏ Zoom in on the message by flicking on the screen.

If you follow a link and move from Mail to Safari, you can return to Mail by tapping the Home button twice to open the recent apps bar. Tap the Mail button to return to the open message you were most recently reading.

If you return to the Home screen or flip to another app with multitasking, Mail (or any app for that matter) remains where it was. Say you're reading a message and then remember a phone call you have to make. You finish the call and then tap the Mail button. Mail opens on the message you were reading, not the first Mailboxes screen. To return to the Mailboxes screen, tap the back button in the top left corner of the screen.

Multiple inboxes

You can skip this section if you have one e-mail account. If you do have just one e-mail account, you may be wondering why you would have more. Sometimes it's as simple as having a work e-mail address and a personal e-mail address. Beyond that, say you manage the tennis league. A separate e-mail address is useful to represent the team when corresponding with sponsors and opposing team representatives. We mentioned earlier that we have one e-mail address for newsletters we subscribe to and another for personal e-mail exchanges. If you already have more than one e-mail account or are thinking of adding another, read on.

When you tap Mail on the Home screen, the first screen that opens shows a list of inboxes and a list of accounts. You can choose All Inboxes to see a chronological list of all the messages you've received. Tap an account-specific inbox and you see a list of messages from that e-mail account only. For example, tap Google Mail to see only messages that have been sent to your Google Mail address.

You can turn an account off by going to Settings➪Mail, Contacts, Calendars. Tap the name of the account you want to turn off. Tap the Mail button off. This is handy if you're going out of town and want to limit the messages that arrive on your iPhone.

E-mail account folders

If you want to see the other folders for a specific account, tap on the name of the e-mail provider in the Accounts list. You may have to scroll down if you have more than six e-mail accounts. Here you find the folders where you filed your message in the previous section.

Threaded messages

A thread is created when you receive a message and respond, then the sender responds to you, and one of the copied recipients chimes in. Turning this feature on puts related messages, the so-called thread, together. In the main message list, as shown on the left of Figure 4-20, you'll see the most recent message of the thread. Tap that message and you see the thread of messages, as shown on the right of Figure 4-20. The number to the right of the sender's name indicates how many messages are in the thread.

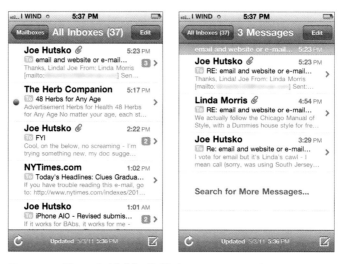

Figure 4-20: The main Mail list (left) shows messages. Organize by Thread (right) groups related messages together in a sublist.

Searching messages

There are times when you know who sent you an e-mail, you know it arrived sometime between last Thursday and Friday, you know the subject was something about a train, but you cannot find the message. Thankfully there's Spotlight, iPhone's searching tool that works with Mail, as well as many other apps such as Contacts, Reminders, and Messages. To use Spotlight:

1. **From within a mailbox — it can be All Inboxes, a specific mailbox, or even the Trash box — tap the status bar at the top of the iPhone screen or scroll up until you see the Search field with the magnifying icon on the left.**

2. **Tap in the Search field.**

   The keyboard opens as seen in Figure 4-21. Note that the gray text in the Search field reads *Search Trash*. This tells you where the search will take place. It would say *Search Inbox* if we were searching in the inbox.

3. **Type in the word or phrase you are searching for.**

4. **Choose the field you want to search: From, To, Subject, or All.**

   The search looks in the field you selected or, in the case of All, searches the From, To, and Subject fields as well as the body text of your messages (but not the attachments). Some IMAP mail accounts let you search messages on the server, although you must have an Internet connection to perform this type of search.

   A list begins to appear with the first letters you type. The choices narrow as your type more letters.

5. **Tap the message or messages you want to read from the list that appears.**

Figure 4-21: Spotlight searches for messages within Mail.

E-mailing Notes, Web Page Links, Map Locations, Pictures, and Videos

One of the great things about the Mail app is its flexibility and bandwidth. It's the backbone for sending so much more than just e-mail messages. The process for each type of object is the same: open the app, open the thing you want to send, tap the action button, and then tap the E-mail button. We'll take you through each one anyway, to clear up any little tweaks that might differ from app to app.

E-mailing notes

We love Notes. Barbara got her first iPhone just about the time that she moved into a smaller home and began working from her dining table instead of a fairly large desk with filing drawers in a home office. (It's not as bad as it sounds — she traded a home office in a high rise for a lovely garden.) Her dislike of clutter forced her to develop a literally paperless office. iPhone was a huge help in that effort, and Notes is a big part of it. We keep lists of everything: books we want to read, ideas for books we want to write, grocery lists, even things we have to remember to tell our moms the next time we talk to them. This isn't the chapter about Notes; that's Book IV, Chapter 4. But here's how to e-mail notes:

1. **Open Notes from the Home screen.**

2. **Tap the note you want to e-mail.**

3. **Tap the Action button at the bottom of the page.**

4. **Tap E-mail.**

   An e-mail message opens with the title of your note in the Subject field. The cursor is blinking in the To field.

5. **Address the message as explained at the beginning of this chapter.**

   You can also change the Subject field and write something in the message field in addition to your note text, if you want.

6. **Tap Send.**

Sending web page links

How many times have you swirled down into the Internet vortex and found something that you absolutely had to tell your best friend about? If you surf the Internet from your computer, you probably know about the Mail Link to this Page option. It exists on iPhone too. You just need to take three steps:

1. **From Safari, tap the action button at the bottom of the screen while you're looking at the page you want to send.**

   A list of buttons pops up.

2. **Tap the Mail Link to this Page button.**

   A new e-mail message opens.

3. **Fill it out as explained previously and tap Send.**

You can learn more about Safari in Book III, Chapter 3.

Sending map locations

We explain the Maps app in detail in Book IV, Chapter 3. Follow this procedure to send a map location from Maps with Mail:

1. **Open Maps from the Home screen.**

2. **Tap the arrowhead icon in the lower left corner to pinpoint your current location.**

   or

   Type the address you want in the Search field at the top of the screen.

3. **Tap the blue and white arrow to the right of the location banner.**

   An Info screen opens with several options, as seen in Figure 4-22.

4. **Tap the Share Location button.**

   A list with three buttons pops up.

5. **Tap the Email button.**

   A new e-mail message opens with the address as the subject. In the Message field, the address is blue and underlined, which means it's an active link in the e-mail you send. Recipients with HTML-enabled e-mail just need to tap or click on that link to be taken to the indicated location in Google Maps.

6. **Fill in the address of the recipient in the To field, type in any message you want to accompany the location link, and then tap Send.**

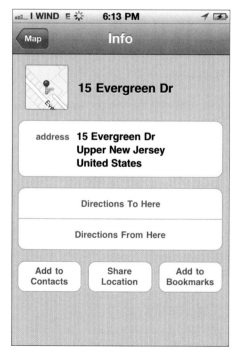

Figure 4-22: Tapping the blue and white arrow takes you to the Info screen.

Sending photos and videos

You can send photos and videos from your iPhone using Mail. It's a great way to quickly send an image without having to sync to your computer to send.

1. **Open Photos from the Home screen.**

2. **Choose the photo or video you want to send from one of the albums.**

3. **Tap the Action button and choose E-mail Photo from the buttons displayed.**

4. **A new message opens with your image inserted.**

5. **Fill in the To and Subject fields.**

   Write a message to accompany the image if you'd like.

6. **Tap Send.**

To send multiple photos in one e-mail, tap Camera Roll and then tap the Action button in the upper right corner. Tap the photos you want to send (a red and white check mark appears on the selected thumbnails). Tap share, and then tap the E-mail button and proceed with filling out the message.

Your cellular service provider may have a limit on the file size that you can send across the cellular data network. Sending files, particularly video or multiple photos, while your iPhone is connected to a Wi-Fi network is faster and lets you send larger files.

Some social network sites, such as Facebook, have an app for e-mailing images directly to your profile. You sign up for the app and are assigned a personal e-mail address to which you send your image. It's automatically uploaded from your iPhone to your page.

Adjusting E-Mail Account Settings

When you set up your e-mail account on iPhone, you've pretty much set up everything you need with regard to the technical information about the account. However, if you have more than one e-mail account on your iPhone or you absolutely have to know every detail about your iPhone, knowing your way around the settings might be helpful. When you open Settings⇨ Mail, Contacts, Calendars, you see the portion of the screen in Figure 4-23. We're going to take you through the e-mail settings options, one by one, so you get your mail how and when you want. The setting for Contacts and Calendars are covered in Book IV, Chapters 1 and 2.

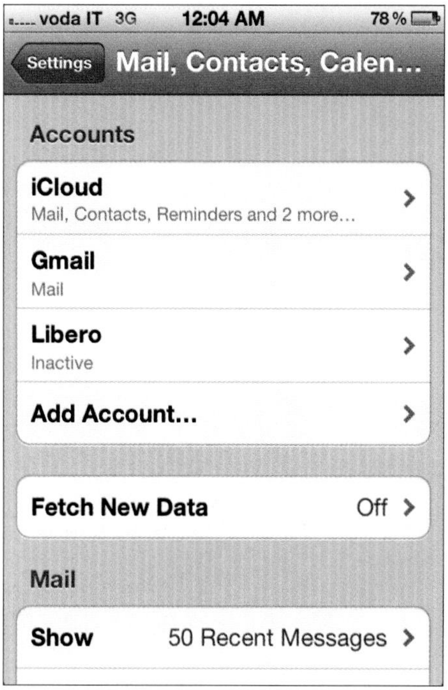

Figure 4-23: The Settings screen for Mail, Contacts, Calendars.

Some settings are specific to each account and some settings are associated with the Mail app. Account-specific settings are represented in a slightly different order for each account, but the titles and functions are the same. You may have to tap through several screens to reach your final destination:

✔ **Outgoing Mail Server:** This feature controls which server your mail is sent from. If you have only one e-mail account on your iPhone, leave this alone. You can skip down to the next subheading.

If you have more than one e-mail account on your phone, each one has an assigned outgoing mail server. This is called the Primary Server for that account. You have the option of turning on the outgoing server associated with another e-mail account so that if the primary outgoing mail server of one e-mail doesn't work, iPhone tries one of the other servers. If you look at Figure 4-24, Gmail uses the `smtp.gmail.com` server to send mail. If that server is down and Barbara's trying to send a message, iPhone uses `smtp.libero.it` to send it because that server is turned on in the list of Other SMTP servers.

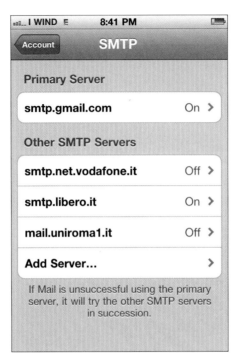

Figure 4-24: If your primary server is down, iPhone attempts to send messages with a secondary server.

The From address on your e-mail is the one associated with the server that sends the message. For example, if your work server is down and you've set your personal Gmail account as the secondary server, the e-mail is sent from your Gmail account. Your colleagues, clients, or CEO see the e-mail as coming from `hotdiggitydog@gmail.com` rather than `johnsmith@ab12.org`.

- **Mailbox Behaviors:** This setting controls where your draft messages and deleted messages are stored, either on iPhone or on the mail server. Depending on your e-mail service provider, you may also have the option of when the deleted items are ultimately deleted; for example, immediately, a week after they've been removed, or once a month.

- **Incoming Settings:** These advanced settings control the path and port your messages follow to get to you. If you are using a POP account, this is also where you establish how you want the server to handle messages after you've downloaded them on your iPhone. As you can see in Figure 4-25, you have three options for deleting messages from the server:

  Never: Messages remain on the server after you've downloaded them to your iPhone. This means you may access them on another device.

Seven Days: Messages are deleted from the server after seven days, whether you've read them or not.

When Removed from Inbox: Messages are deleted from the server when you delete them from the inbox on your iPhone.

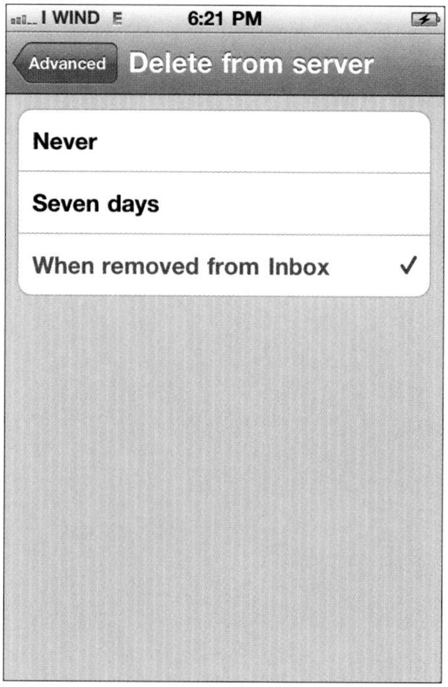

---

ooo. I WIND E   **6:21 PM**

‹ Advanced   **Delete from server**

Never

Seven days

When removed from Inbox   ✓

Figure 4-25: You can choose when messages are deleted from the server of a POP account.

Book III
Chapter 4

E-mailing Every Which Way You Can

Configure your computer e-mail program to leave messages on the server as well. Go to the Preferences or Tools menu and follow the instructions for your particular e-mail program.

When you tap on one of the preset accounts, like iCloud or Google Mail, you see the toggle switches that you turned on or off when you set up the account — Mail, Calendars, Notes, and so on.

At the bottom of the specific account's opening screen, you see a Delete Account button, as shown in Figure 4-26. Tap this and you completely eliminate that e-mail account and all the messages in it. That doesn't mean the account itself is eliminated from the Internet, only that it has been eliminated from your iPhone.

Figure 4-26: Tapping the Delete button deletes the specific account from your iPhone, but does not eliminate it from the Internet or close your e-mail account.

Setting up outgoing mail servers

These are the steps for managing your outgoing mail servers. If you have just one e-mail account, you'll probably never need to fuss with these settings. If you have more than one account, take a look to see how it works:

1. **Tap Settings➪Mail, Contacts, Calendars.**

   The Mail, Contacts, Calendars screen opens.

2. **Tap the name of the account you want to work on under the Accounts list. We use Gmail as the example.**

   The Google Mail screen opens.

3. **Tap the Account button.**

   The Account screen opens, as shown in Figure 4-27. This shows you the name and address as you typed it.

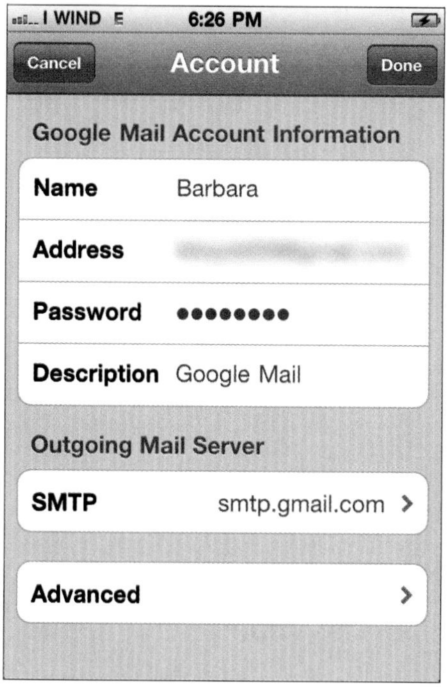

Figure 4-27: The Account screen for a Google Mail account.

4. **Tap the SMTP button.**

   The SMTP screen opens. As in Figure 4-24, you see which outgoing servers are used for sending your mail.

5. **For curiosity's sake, tap the button under Primary Server.**

   A screen opens with details of that server. The details of the Outgoing Mail Server are gray. This information is automatically entered for the preset e-mail providers that come with iPhone.

6. **Again, out of curiosity, open one of the servers from the Other SMTP Servers list.**

   You can edit the information or you can delete this server entirely by tapping the red Delete Server button at the bottom of the page. If this outgoing mail server is the primary server for another account, you have to make changes on the account settings for that e-mail account.

7. **To add a server, tap Add Server at the bottom of the list of servers.**

   An Add Server screen opens.

8. **Type in the Host Name, for example,** `smpt.verizon.com`. **Then type in your user name and password.**

9. **Tap Save.**

Working with advanced settings

You can manage two advanced settings, as we mentioned previously: Mailbox Behaviors and Incoming Settings. In the next couple of sections, we tell you how they work.

Mailbox Behaviors

Mailbox Behaviors has to do with how Mail handles your messages. Different e-mail service provides have slightly different options. Even if your provider lets you manage different mailboxes, the process is the same:

1. **Tap Settings⟲Mail, Contacts, Calendars.**

   The Mail, Contacts, Calendars screen opens.

2. **Tap the name of the account you want to work on. We use Gmail as the example.**

   The Google Mail screen opens.

3. **Tap the Account button.**

4. **Tap the Advanced button.**

   The Advanced screen opens. On the left side of Figure 4-28, note the sections: Mailbox Behaviors and Incoming Settings. With other e-mail services, such as iCloud, there may be additional buttons, as you can see on the right side of Figure 4-28.

5. **Tap Drafts Mailbox.**

   This setting controls where your draft messages are kept.

6. **Tap Drafts under On My iPhone if you want to keep your draft messages on your iPhone.**

   A checkmark shows up next to Drafts, as shown in Figure 4-29.

7. **Tap Drafts (or another folder if you want) in the list under On the Server if you want your draft messages to be stored on the server.**

   If you have large draft files, perhaps with multimedia attachments, it may be more convenient to store them on the server so as not deplete the memory on your iPhone.

The S/MIME option lets you add certificates for signing and encrypting outgoing messages. To install certificates, you need a profie from your network administrator or from a certificate issuer's website on Safari or sent to you in an e-mail.

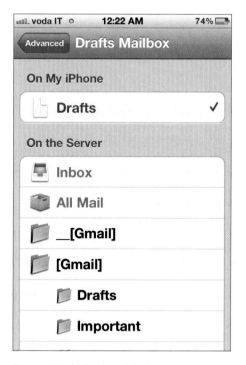

Figure 4-28: The Advanced features allow you to manage where your draft and deleted messages are stored and adjust the pathway for incoming mail.

Figure 4-29: A checkmark indicates where you've chosen to store your draft messages.

Incoming Settings

The Incoming Settings section gives you limited options for encrypting incoming e-mail and changing the path it comes in on. You probably shouldn't change these settings unless instructed to do so by a technical support person from your cellular provider or a network administrator at your place of employment. Here, we go through the settings briefly, but remember: You probably don't want to change them.

1. **Tap Settings⇨Mail, Contacts, Calendars.**

   The Mail, Contacts, Calendars screen opens.

2. **Tap the name of the account you want to work on. We use Gmail as an example.**

   The Google Mail screen opens.

3. **Tap the Account button.**

4. **Tap the Advanced button.**

5. **Turn Use SSL (Secure Sockets Layer) on or off.**

   Ideally, this setting is on as it encrypts incoming messages, making them unreadable to shady types who want to "eavesdrop" on your e-mail conversations.

6. **Tap Authentication to establish the mode in which your account needs to be verified.**

   Password is the most common type of authentication used for iPhone-supported e-mail accounts. If your server provider uses one of the other types — MD5 Challenge-Response, NTLM, or HTTP MD5 Digest, you'll be given the necessary information when you sign up.

7. **The last two, IMAP Path Prefix and Server Port, should really be left alone unless you are instructed to change them by a technician.**

If you're using iCloud, the sequence to reach the Outgoing Mail Server is Settings⇨Mail, Contacts, Calendars⇨iCloud⇨Account⇨Mail. Tap the SMTP or Advanced buttons.

If you're using a POP or IMAP account, the sequence is Settings⇨Mail, Contacts, Calendars⇨Account Name. Then scroll down to the Outgoing Mail Server section of the screen to access the SMTP and Advanced buttons.

Using Push and Fetch

Going back to the Mail, Contacts, Calendars screen, you see a button called Fetch New Data. Think of the Mail app as the dog and your incoming e-mail messages as the ball. The mail server throws — the terminology is *pushes* — your messages and iPhone catches — or downloads — them. Alternatively, the messages are on the server and Mail goes and fetches them when told.

Once again, you have the option of turning Fetch and Push on or off. Here's how to activate or deactivate Fetch:

1. **Tap Settings➪Mail, Contacts, Calendars➪Fetch New Data.**

   The Fetch New Data screen opens, as seen in Figure 4-30.

Figure 4-30: Fetch New Data lets your iPhone play catch with incoming e-mail messages.

2. **Turn Push on and new data is pushed to your iPhone from the server.**

   Whether Mail is open or not, messages arrive in real-time in your mailbox and you hear an audible alert as they arrive, if you've established one.

3. **Choose a frequency for Fetch.**

   Tap one of the four time choices.

   If you turn Push off or use an application that doesn't support Push, your iPhone automatically downloads messages at the frequency you chose.

4. **Scroll down the screen and tap the Advanced button.**

   A screen opens that lists the e-mail accounts you have set up on your iPhone (refer to Figure 4-31).

Figure 4-31: You can choose to retrieve incoming messages using Push, Manual, or Fetch settings.

5. **Tap the name of the account you want to manage.**

   A screen opens with the schedule options available. Buttons for Push, Fetch, and Manual or, if Push isn't supported, for Fetch and Manual appear in list.

6. **Tap the option you want:**

   Push: To automatically retrieve new messages as they arrive in your inbox on the server.

   Fetch: To check for messages at the interval you previously established.

   Manual: To check for messages only when you open the Mail app.

7. **Tap the back buttons in the top left corner to return to the Settings screen you want or press the Home button to go to the Home screen.**

Settings for message presentation

There's one last group of settings options to go through and then you'll know all there is to know — or at least all *we* know — about Mail settings. This group of settings manages how your messages appear and are organized in the inbox list, and how the message itself appears when opened.

Tap Settings⇨Mail, Contacts, Calendars and scroll down to the Mail section. Refer to Figure 4-32 for this section.

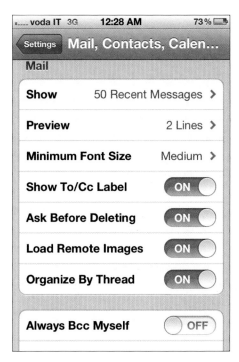

Figure 4-32: The Mail settings section of Mail, Contacts, Calendars screen.

These options have to do with the local management of your messages. We explain each one in the following list:

- **Show:** Tap this button and choose how many messages you want to see in your inbox and outbox on Mail. If you have 100 messages to download but have chosen 50 to see, you'll see the first 50 to start. As you file or delete the messages, others from the 100 are added to the box. If you receive or send a lot of messages, you may want to choose one of the higher limits.

✔ **Preview:** Tap this button to choose how many lines of a message you want to see in the list of e-mail messages. You may choose from zero (None) to five lines.

✔ **Minimum Font Size:** Tapping this button opens a list of options for the size of font used for text within the messages you receive and send. For incoming messages, the chosen size is the minimum displayed, so if someone sends you a message written in a miniscule type, it is enlarged if you've chosen Giant. If, however, the message is sent in Times 24 point, you'll see it as large as it was sent. The name, address, and subject lines remain the standard size.

✔ **Show To/Cc Label:** This puts a small label next to the subject line in the list of messages in your inbox. *To* means that the message was sent directly to you; *Cc* means you were sent a copy of the message whose primary recipient was someone else.

✔ **Ask Before Deleting:** If you're prone to accidentally tapping the trashcan button when you don't want to, turn this on so that iPhone asks if you want to delete a message before it's actually deleted.

✔ **Load Remote Images:** Remote images reference an image on a web page that Mail would have to access, which gives the hosting site an opportunity to log your activity. You can save cellular time, and increase your privacy, by turning this off, which leaves you the option to manually open the images.

✔ **Organize by Thread:** This turns threading on or off.

✔ **Always Bcc Myself:** A Bcc is a blind carbon copy, meaning the recipients of your message don't see this name on the list of recipients, but the person who receives the Bcc sees all the (non-Bcc) recipients. If you turn this switch on, you receive a Bcc of every message you write.

✔ **Signature:** This is the line that appears at the end of e-mail messages you write. The default is *Sent from my iPhone*. Tap the button, and a screen opens where you can type a new signature line, as shown in Figure 4-33.

✔ **Default Account:** The default account is used to send messages from other apps, like Maps or Safari. If you have multiple e-mail accounts, tap this button and choose the account you want to be the default account.

Figure 4-33: Write a custom signature line for your outgoing e-mail messages using the Signature feature.

Book IV
Making iPhone Your Personal Assistant

The 5th Wave — By Rich Tennant

"Okay, the view's just up ahead. Everyone switch to 'America the Beautiful' on your iPhone playlist."

As much as we believe they make the office or small business run more smoothly and efficiently, secretaries and administrative assistants seem to be rare outside of a large corporate setting. (If you are a secretary or admin, we tip our hats to you.) If you don't have a secretary, your iPhone can be a fair substitute. And, if you are one of the sacred secretaries out there, your iPhone can help make your job easier too.

Chapter 1 of this minibook is about keeping in touch. We show you how to import your contacts to your iPhone and then how to keep all your devices in-sync and up-to-date. Chapter 2 reviews the Calendar and Clock apps that came with your iPhone and gives you tips for managing your time and being on time. Chapter 3 helps you get where you need to go with the Maps and Compass apps. We also introduce you to the Weather app so you know if you need an umbrella where you're going. The Calculator and Stocks apps are covered in Chapter 3 so you can add up your investments. We present the Notes app in the last chapter. This minibook could be your gateway to the paperless office!

Chapter 1: Perfecting Your People Skills with Contacts

In This Chapter

✓ **Adding existing Contacts**

✓ **Creating new Contacts**

✓ **Viewing and grouping Contacts**

✓ **Adjusting iPhone's Contacts Settings**

✓ **Searching Contacts**

✓ **Sending things to a Contact**

*W*e humans used to live in small groups — families, tribes, villages — call them what you will. Everyone knew everyone or at least knew "of" everyone. Chances are there were fewer than 100 people, maybe even fewer than 50 in a one- or two-mile radius. If you needed to talk to someone, you just moseyed on over to his front porch and knocked on the door. Needless to say, times have changed. Most people go away to college and begin making new friends, and then go to work and add colleagues to an ever-expanding social circle. Volunteer activity or joining a sports team leads to more acquaintances. Re-writing all those names, addresses, and phone numbers in a crisp, new address book has become virtually impossible, not to mention time-consuming.

The Contacts app on your iPhone replaces the address book and more. Contacts is malleable and, unlike its paper predecessor, has unlimited lines so you can add birthdays, anniversaries, and even notes about the person or entity. And when information changes? No need for correction fluid or an eraser: With a few taps, you can change as much and as often as you wish. If you already have an iPhone-compatible electronic address book, you can transfer the data to your iPhone by syncing your iPhone and your computer. This also means if you have a lot of data to enter or change, you can type it in on your computer then sync with your iPhone.

In this chapter, we begin by explaining how to sync your existing electronic address book with Contacts on your iPhone. If you read Book II, Chapter 1, you learned about syncing, but we go through the specifics for Contacts here. We explain the editing procedures for a single contact: adding a new contact, making changes, even deleting a contact. If you have more than one screen full of contacts (and you probably do), you'll need to know how to search for a contact. We show you how. We conclude this chapter with the interactive aspects of Contacts, sharing your contacts with someone else and contacting your contacts via phone, Facetime, e-mail, and text messages.

Adding Existing Contacts

You probably have some form of electronic address book on your computer. If you don't, skip over this section and go ahead to the section "Importing Contacts from a SIM Card" (if you're switching from a cell phone that stored phone numbers on its SIM card to a GSM iPhone) or go directly to creating new contacts, in which case you create your address book in the Contacts app on your iPhone.

Your existing contacts could be in many places: on your computer — in a program such as Address Book, Entourage, or Outlook on the Macintosh or Microsoft Outlook, Windows Address Book, or Windows Contacts on Windows — on Microsoft Exchange or Google, on the SIM card of a previous cell phone, in or in a combination of places. In this section, we go through importing your contacts from these different programs onto Contacts on your iPhone. We also show you how to sync them in the future so your data is the same in all the places you access it. We begin with the simple sync with iTunes and iCloud then go to more specific imports from Microsoft Exchange, Google, Yahoo!, LDAP or CardDAV formatted data, and a SIM card. We end the chapter with the procedure for adding contact information from incoming phone calls, voicemail, SMS, MMS, and vCards attached to e-mail. See Figure 1-1 for the syncing options we talk about here.

If you use IBM Lotus, you need a third-party contact management app such as DejaOffice (www.dejaoffice.com) to sync your contacts to your iPhone.

If you use Windows, you can sync with just one application. On a Macintosh, you can sync with multiple applications.

The overall set of all your contacts is called All Contacts. Within All Contacts, you can have subsets, which are called Groups. You can't set up groups on your iPhone, although you can assign a new contact created on your iPhone to an existing group. Even though a Contact is in a group when you select All Contacts, you see all your contacts, regardless of what group they're in. Address Book on the Macintosh uses the same name, All Contacts and Groups. What Entourage calls Categories become Groups on your iPhone. Now you know what we mean when we talk about Groups throughout this chapter.

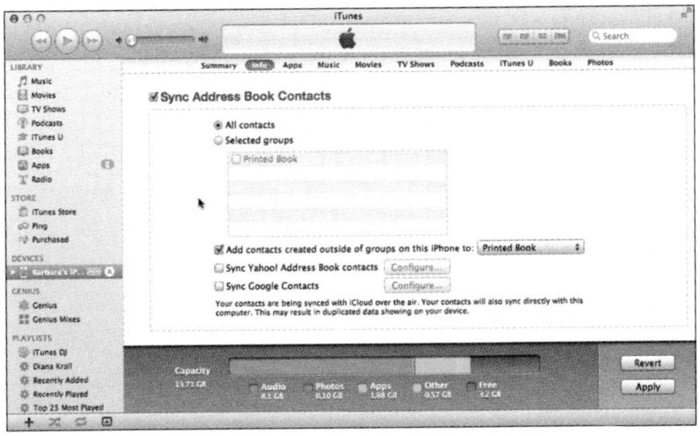

Figure 1-1: Select your sync settings from the Info tab in iTunes.

Importing Contacts from iTunes

Follow these steps to import a copy of your electronic address book from your computer to your iPhone:

1. **Connect your iPhone to your computer with the USB connector cable or connect both your iPhone and computer to the same Wi-Fi network.**

2. **Open iTunes, if it didn't open automatically.**

3. **Click on your iPhone in the Devices section of the Source list.**

4. **Click the Info tab at the top of the content pane.**

5. **Click Sync Address Book Contacts (Mac) or Sync Contacts (Windows).**

   If you use Outlook, you must first change the preferences from within Outlook. Click Outlook⇨Preferences. Select Sync Services from the list on the left. Click Synchronize Contacts with Address Books. Click OK. A dialog box appears asking how you want to synchronize your data; choose accordingly.

6. **Click All contacts, if you want to sync all the contact groups that appear in the list below.**

   Or

   Click Selected Groups and choose which of the groups of contacts in the list you want to sync. (Groups correlate to Categories in Outlook and other Windows address book applications.)

7. **If you have added contacts to your iPhone but haven't assigned them to a group, select the check box next to Add Contacts Created Outside of Groups on This iPhone To and choose which group you want those contacts to go into.**

   Leave it unchecked if you just want those contacts to remain part of All Contacts and not part of a group.

8. **Click Sync in the lower right corner.**

   If you made changes to your syncing criteria, the Sync button reads Apply. Click Apply.

The next time you connect your iPhone to your computer to perform a sync, the settings you chose will be used.

If you set up iTunes Wi-Fi Syncing (see Book II, Chapter 1), your Contacts are synced when your iPhone is connected to a power source, up to once a day.

Accessing your Contacts from iCloud

We explain how to set up an iCloud account in Book II, Chapter 1. Essentially, iCloud stores your data, such as contacts, calendar information, your iTunes media library, photos, and documents on a remote server — called a *cloud* — which pushes data updates to your iPhone and any other computers or iOS 5 devices you have associated with your iCloud account. To sync Contacts on your iPhone with your computer and other iOS 5 devices via iCloud, do the following:

1. **Tap Settings⇨iCloud.**

2. **Tap Contacts ON, as shown in Figure 1-2.**

   If your screen doesn't look like Figure 1-2, go to Book II, Chapter 1 to set up an iCloud account.

3. **If you previously synced the contacts on your iPhone with your computer, perhaps with iTunes, a message appears letting you know that the contacts you previously synced with your computer will be merged with iCloud. Tap Merge.**

   Any changes you make in Contacts on your iPhone or on other devices associated with iCloud, such as your computer, iPad, or iPod touch, are automatically pushed to all devices. You will never have conflicting information again!

If you do turn on Contacts in iCloud, a message at the bottom of the Contacts portion of the Info screen lets you know that you are syncing your contacts with iCloud. You can still sync with iTunes, but you may create duplicate records.

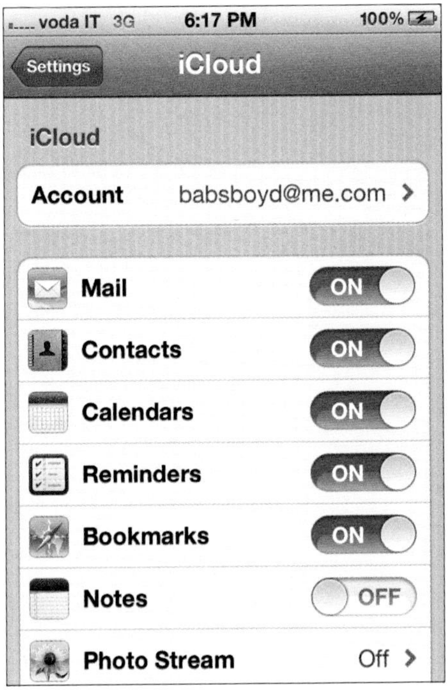

voda IT 3G   6:17 PM   100% 🔋

Settings   **iCloud**

iCloud

Account   babsboyd@me.com >

✉ **Mail**   ON

👤 **Contacts**   ON

📅 **Calendars**   ON

📋 **Reminders**   ON

Bookmarks   ON

Notes   OFF

Photo Stream   Off >

Figure 1-2: Turn Contacts On in iCloud to automatically sync Contacts on your iPhone with other devices using iCloud.

TIP

If you want to use iCloud with your Windows PC, download the iCloud Control Panel for Windows app from Apple (www.apple.com/icloud/setup/pc.html).

Adding and syncing Microsoft Exchange contacts

Particularly in a corporate setting, some of your contacts, such as the company directory, may be in Microsoft Exchange. As long as the technical support folks in your office will give you the access information, you can sync the contacts from Microsoft Exchange with your iPhone. Microsoft Exchange uses over the air or OTA syncing to import and exchange information between the Contacts app on your iPhone and the contact data stored in the Microsoft Exchange cloud.

You can still sync with iTunes if you have different contact data on your computer, like your friends and family, whose information obviously isn't stored on your company server. That makes your iPhone a one-stop source for all your contact information.

Follow these steps to set up the account on your iPhone:

1. **Tap Settings⇨Mail, Contacts, Calendars.**

   The Mail, Contacts, Calendars screen opens.

2. **Do one of the following:**

   1. **If you set up a Microsoft Exchange account when you first set up your iPhone or when you set up e-mail as explained in Book III, Chapter 4, tap the name of that account in the list that appears.**

   2. **Turn Contacts On with the toggle switch in the account screen.**

   Or

   1. **Tap Add Account to set up a new account.**

   2. **Tap Microsoft Exchange.**

   3. **Fill in the requested information.**

   4. **Tap Next.**

      After the information you entered is verified, you'll be asked to turn on a series of switches to establish which types of things you want to sync. Turn on Contacts. (Turn on the others such as Mail, Calendars, Bookmarks, or Notes if you want to sync those with Exchange.)

   You now see Microsoft Exchange in the list of accounts on the Mail, Contacts, Calendars settings screen.

3. **Tap the Save button in the upper right corner and you return to the Mail, Contacts, Calendars settings screen.**

4. **Tap Fetch New Data.**

5. **Tap Push On.**

   Anytime changes are made to the contacts on the server now associated with your Microsoft Exchange account, those changes are pushed to your iPhone.

6. **If your server doesn't support push, or you want to conserve battery power, select a default fetch interval — every 15 or 30 minutes, or hourly.**

   Your iPhone contacts the server for new data at the interval you select.

Importing Yahoo! contacts

Apple has made importing your contacts from Yahoo! simple. Referring to Figure 1-1, notice the last two options in the Contacts section: Sync Yahoo! Address Book contacts and Sync Google Contacts.

If you already set up an e-mail account for Yahoo!, as explained in Book III, Chapter 4, you need only select the box next to Sync Yahoo! Address Book contacts and then click Configure. Agree to let iTunes access your information from Yahoo!. Type in your Yahoo! ID and password, and then click OK. When you click Apply, your Yahoo! contacts and your iPhone contacts sync.

If you need to set up a Yahoo! account on your iPhone, follow these steps:

1. **Tap Settings on the Home screen, and then tap Mail, Contacts, Calendars.**

2. **Tap Add Account.**

3. **Tap Yahoo! on the Add Account screen.**

4. **The Add Account screen opens.**

   Filling in the Name field is optional. Type in your e-mail address in the Address field and your password in the Password field.

5. **Tap the Next button in the upper right corner.**

   The Yahoo! screen opens.

6. **Tap the Contacts switch On.**

Yahoo! Address Book is stored on a remote server, so you have to have an Internet connection to access it.

Importing and syncing with Google Contacts

Importing Google Contacts to your iPhone is a two-part process to be done in this order; otherwise, you risk losing your contacts.

1. **Sync your contacts between your iPhone and iTunes so that iTunes has a backup of your contacts.**

2. **On the Info screen, click Sync Address Book Contacts and the box next to Sync Google Contacts.**

3. **Enter your Google ID (your e-mail address) and password, and then click OK.**

4. **Click Apply in the lower right corner.**

   iTunes copies your contacts to Google Contacts, under the My Contacts group.

5. **Go to Settings⇨Mail, Contacts, Calendars.**

6. **Tap Add Account.**

7. **Tap Microsoft Exchange. (Yes, Microsoft Exchange.)**

   The Exchange screen opens.

8. **Type your Google e-mail address in the Email field.**

9. **In the Username field, type in your Google Mail address again.**

10. **Type in your password.**

11. **Tap Next in the upper right corner.**

12. **Type** m.google.com **in the Server field.**

13. **Tap Next.**

Your account is verified, as seen in Figure 1-3.

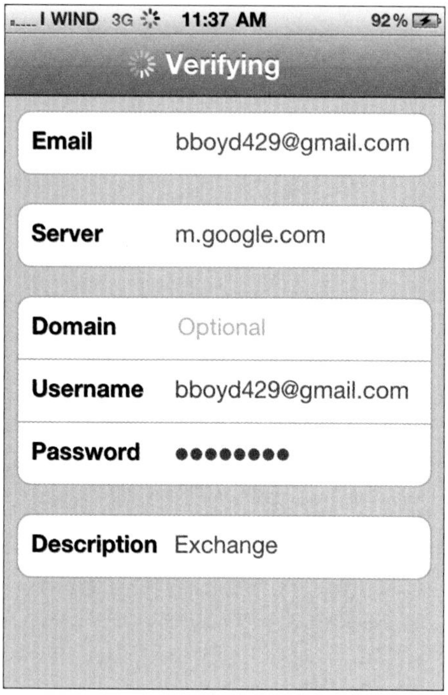

Figure 1-3: Use Microsoft Exchange to sync
Google Contacts with your iPhone.

14. **Tap Contacts On in the Microsoft Exchange Account screen.**

15. **Tap Save.**

16. **Sync again with iTunes.**

Microsoft Exchange replaces everything on your iPhone with the contacts that are on Google Contacts, which is okay since they were just synced there in the first place.

17. **Subsequent syncs go both ways, between your iPhone and Google Contacts.**

Configuring LDAP or CardDAV contacts accounts

LDAP (Lightweight Directory Access Protocol) and CardDAV (Card Distributing Authoring and Versioning) are Internet protocols that allow access to data on a remote server. Multiple users can access the same information so it is often used in business and organization settings. The difference between the two is that LDAP data remains on the server — you access it from your iPhone via an Internet connection, but it isn't synced to your iPhone. CardDAV data is synced over the air to your iPhone, and depending on the way the server is set up, you may be able to search the server for contact information.

If your employer uses an LDAP or CardDAV supported contacts program that you want to access or sync with your iPhone, you can add an LDAP or CardDAV account. You'll need some account information from your IT department or network support person:

- **Server:** This has your company or organization information.
- **User Name:** This is your identification.
- **Password:** A password is required.
- **Description:** This name shows up on the list of accounts on the Mail, Contacts, Calendars settings screen.

After you've gathered the necessary information, set up the account on your iPhone by following these steps:

1. **Tap Settings⇨Mail, Contacts, Calendars.**

2. **Tap Add Account.**

3. **Tap Other.**

4. **In the Contacts section, tap Add LDAP or Add CardDAV Account, whichever is indicated.**

5. **Type in the information requested.**

6. **Tap the Next button in the upper right corner.**

   After your account information is verified, the contacts data are added to your iPhone.

7. **Tap the Save button in the upper right corner and you return to the Mail, Contacts, Calendars settings screen.**

8. **Tap Fetch New Data.**

   The Fetch New Data screen opens.

9. **If your server supports push notifications, Tap Push On.**

   Anytime changes are made on the server where the contacts reside, that change is pushed to your iPhone, and vice versa.

10. **If your server doesn't support push, select a default fetch interval —
    every 15 minutes, every 30 minutes, or hourly.**

    Your iPhone contacts the server for new data at the interval you select.

If your contacts are in another program, you can try exporting them as
vCards (the file will have a .vcf suffix) and then importing them into Address
Book or Entourage on the Mac or Outlook or Windows Address Book on a
Windows PC. Follow the previously outlined procedure for syncing.

Importing contacts from a SIM card

Although your iPhone doesn't store information on the SIM card, if you are
transferring to iPhone from another cellular phone, you may have contact
information on the old SIM card that you want to transfer. Follow these steps:

1. **Insert the SIM card that contains the information into your iPhone
   (unless it's the SIM card you use with your iPhone).**

2. **Tap Settings⟿Mail, Contacts, Calendars.**

3. **Scroll down to the Contacts section of Mail, Contacts, Calendars settings, as seen in Figure 1-4.**

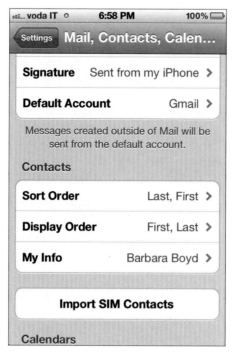

Figure 1-4: Import contacts from a SIM card
from Contacts settings.

4. **Tap Import SIM Contacts.**

   A dialog box opens, telling you that the SIM contacts are being imported.

5. **Return to Contacts.**

   The information that was on the SIM is now in Contacts.

The four major carriers each offer backup apps on their respective websites. If you're moving from a smartphone to an iPhone, you can transfer your contacts by running Google Sync on the old phone and the new iPhone. If you have a feature phone, you have to export your contacts to a .csv file, usually by going through your computer, and then import the .csv file to your Google account and sync your iPhone with Google.

Creating New Contacts

You meet new people all the time and you're usually not at your computer when you meet them. Unless you develop the mnemonic skills of the ancient Greeks, you probably want to add new friends, colleagues, and acquaintances to Contacts on your iPhone, and the new information will be transferred to your computer automatically if you use iCloud or the next time you perform a sync with iTunes. Contacts stores so much more than a name, address, and phone number. You can add a photo of the person, a birthday or anniversary — which nicely links to Calendar — e-mail addresses, websites, and whatever kind of field you want to invent, like favorite color or namesake holiday date. In this section, we show you how to create new contacts, fill in the contact info with everything you know about the person, make changes, and well, delete them if things go bad in the relationship, for whatever reason.

Filling in name, address, phone number, and more

Follow these steps to fill in basic information about your contacts:

1. **Tap Contacts on the Home screen or in the Dock within the Phone app.**

   If you have Groups set up, tap the Group you want the new contact to be associated with or tap All Contacts if you want it on its own.

   At the top of the screen, you see either All Contacts or the name of the group, which tells you where the new contact will be inserted.

2. **Tap the plus sign in the upper right corner.**

   A New Contact screen opens.

3. **Tap in the field that reads First.**

   The cursor appears in that field and the keyboard opens.

4. **Type in the first name of your new contact.**

   Not all contacts have first and last names and you are not obligated to fill in any field that you don't have information for. If you just have the name and phone number of a company, you can fill in only those fields.

5. **Tap Return to move from one field to the next.**

   Continue typing in the information you have for your contact.

The following sections describe fields that have specific functions.

Phone, E-mail, and URL fields

The Phone, E-mail, and URL fields behave the same way, but their behavior may seem a bit peculiar at first. Here we give you a few tips to help you understand them:

- As soon as you begin typing in the first field, say, phone number, a minus sign appears to the left and a new field is added beneath it. You can type a second phone number in this field. As soon as you begin typing in the second phone number field, a third one appears. This happens with the Phone, E-mail, and URL fields. Don't worry: Those empty fields won't clutter up the final view of your contact's info screen. You only see the blank field in Create or Edit mode.

- Notice that there's a line between the field name and the empty field for Phone, E-mail, and URL. You can change the field name of these fields by tapping on the field name to the left of the line. A Label list opens. Click the label you want to associate with the phone number, e-mail, or URL that you type in the adjacent field.

- Scroll down to the bottom of the Label list and you see Add Custom Label. Tap this and you can enter a label of your own for the field.

Ringtone, Vibration, and Text Tone fields

You can assign a special sound or vibration so that when a contact calls or sends a text message, you know by the sound who is calling or who the message is from:

- Tap Ringtone. A list opens from which you choose the ringtone you want to hear when that contact calls.

- Tap Vibration. A list gives you options for the vibration you want associated with that contact. Click Create New Vibration to record your own custom vibration.

- Tap Text Tone. A list opens to choose the sound you hear when that contact sends you a text message. Tap Buy More Tones to access the ringtone section of the iTunes Store and download tones that can be used for ringtones or text tones.

You can only have one ringtone, one vibration, and one text tone per contact. You can't assign a different ringtone for each number associated with a contact.

Add New Address

You can tell how little importance is given to our physical addresses anymore. This field is at the bottom of the list like a rarely used option. To add an address, tap the plus sign to the left of the field or in the blank field. The field expands as shown in Figure 1-5. Type in the address.

Figure 1-5: The Add New Address field expands so you can type in the street address, city, state, ZIP, and country.

Here, too, as soon as you begin typing a second field opens, so you can add a second address. And, tapping on the field name to the left, you can change the field name so it reflects which address it's associated with, like work or home or even a custom field, like cabin or boat slip.

Add Field

The last field has options that can be added to the previous fields. Tap on the plus sign or in the empty field and the list of Add Field options opens, as in Figure 1-6. After one of the options is used, it no longer appears in the Add Field options list.

✔ The first six field options are related to the name of the contact:

  • **Prefix:** Adds a field before first name where you can type in a title such as Mr. or Princess.

  • **Phonetic First Name and Phonetic Last Name:** Are inserted immediately after the First or Last Name fields so you can type in a phonetic spelling of the names that are pronounced differently than they are spelled.

  • **Middle:** Adds a field between the First and Last Name for a middle name.

  • **Suffix:** To add common suffixes like M.D. or Jr.

  • **Nickname:** Comes right before company.

✔ **Job Title and Department:** Are inserted before Company.

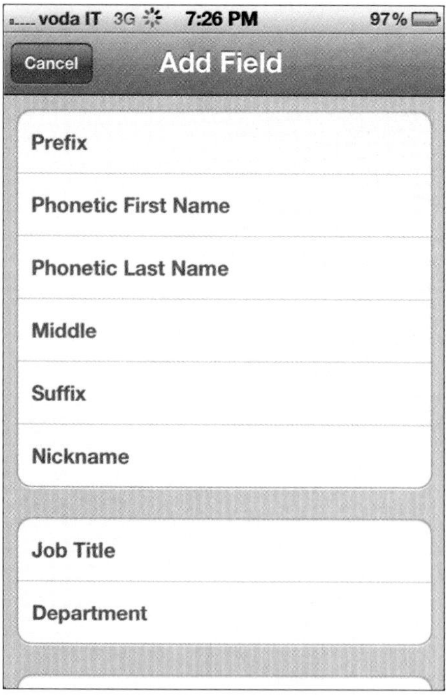

Figure 1-6: The Add Field options add details like phonetic spellings and job titles to your contact's info.

✔ **Twitter/Profile:** You can add one social network profile user name to each contact. Tap Twitter to add a Twitter user name. Tap Profile to add a user name for Facebook, Flickr, LinkedIn, or Myspace. After tapping the Profile option, the Info screen re-opens. Tap the field label to the left of user name to choose which social network you want.

Twitter can add Twitter user names and profile photos to your contacts. Tap Settings⤳Twitter, sign in to your Twitter account, and then tap Update Contacts.

✔ **Instant messenger:** After tapping this option, you return to the Info screen. Enter the User Name and then tap the field below it to reveal a list of ten IM services plus an option to add a custom service. Tap the service you use to instant message with this contact. You can also edit the name of this field by tapping on the field name on the left. The options are Home, Work, Other, or Add Custom Label.

✔ **Birthday:** Tap birthday and a rotor opens, as shown in Figure 1-7, so you can choose the month, day, and year of the contact's birth date. A birthday that is added to a contact appears in Calendar if you activate the Birthday calendar. Read more about Calendar in Book IV, Chapter 2.

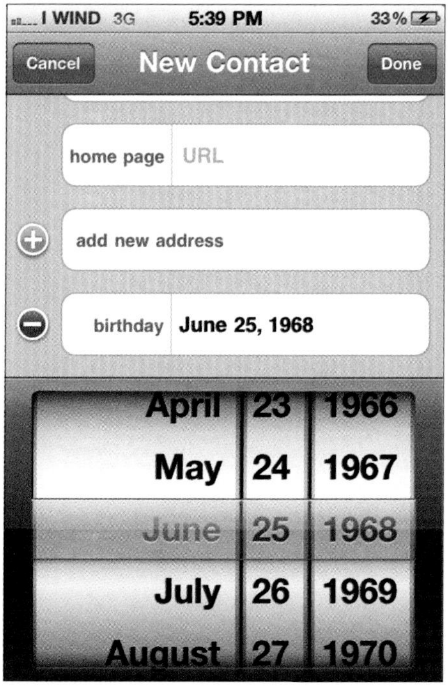

Figure 1-7: Use the rotor to set your contact's birthday.

✔ **Date:** The first field name that comes up is Anniversary for this field, after which you can add as many other important dates related to this contact as you want. Use the rotor to put in the date you want. Like the Phone, E-mail, URL, and Address fields, as soon as you add this field, a blank one appears beneath it. You can also edit the name of the field by tapping on it and choosing other or adding a custom label.

✔ **Related People:** Add people who are related to the Contact, such as parent, spouse, sibling, partner, assistant, or manager. After tapping the option, you return to the Info screen. Tap the field label to reveal a list of choices for the type of relation, and then type in the name or the relation or tap the blue and white arrow to choose someone else from your Contacts list.

Create a New Contact for yourself including your own related people and then specify which is your card by going to Settings➪Mail, Contacts, Calendars➪My Info, which opens Contacts. Choose the contact you created for yourself. The My Info card is used by Siri, Reminders, and other apps to understand commands like "Remind me upon arriving Home" or "Call my sister." Specify the My Info card for Siri by going to Settings➪General➪Siri➪My Info.

Each time you add a custom label, that label is added to the list beneath whatever options Contacts gives you for that field. If you add a lot of custom labels, the Add Custom Label button is all the way at the bottom — just scroll down to find it. You can delete custom labels from the list by tapping the Edit button. Tap the minus sign that appears next to the label you want to delete, and then tap the Delete button. If the custom label was being used on a contact, it will be replaced by a generic label.

Adding photos

The first thing you see on the New Contact screen is a field in the upper left corner called Add Photo. This lets you add a photo of the contact and when a call comes in from any of the phone numbers of that contact, the photo appears on your Home screen. You have two ways to add photos:

1. **Tap Add Photo.**

   A dialog appears as shown in Figure 1-8, which gives you the option to take a photo or choose an existing photo.

2. **Tap Take Photo.**

   The Camera app opens. Book V, Chapter 1 talks all about the Camera, but here's a quick rundown.

   1. **Aim the camera at the subject you want to photograph, and tap the Switch Camera button if you see yourself instead of your subject. When you're satisfied, tap the green camera button or the volume up button.**

2. **If you like the shot, you can re-size it by pinching or spreading your fingers on the image and drag to move it to a pleasing position.**

3. **If it's just not right, tap Retake, and try again.**

4. **When you like the result, tap Use Photo.**

   You see the photo you took in the photo field on the Contact Info screen.

Or

Tap Choose Photo.

The Photos app opens.

1. **Tap the album where the photo you want to use is stored.**

2. **Tap the photo you want to use.**

3. **Move and scale as explained in step 2 previously.**

4. **When you like the photo, tap Choose.**

   The photo is saved to the New Contact screen.

Book IV
Chapter 1

Perfecting Your
People Skills with
Contacts

Figure 1-8: You can take a photo or use an existing photo to add to your contact.

The data in Contacts in the Phone app is the same data as in the Contacts app — just two ways to reach the same information.

Adding contacts from Phone calls and voice mail

If you receive a phone call from a number that isn't in Contacts, or make a call to a number that isn't in Contacts, you may want to add that number to an existing contact or create a new contact. Here's how:

1. **After you finish a conversation, tap Phone⇨Recents.**

   A list of recent incoming and outgoing calls appears.

2. **Tap the blue and white arrow to the right of the number you want to add, it can be from a call you received or one you initiated.**

   An Info screen opens, as shown in Figure 1-9.

3. **Tap Create New Contact.**

   A New Contact screen opens. Type in the information you have and select a special ringtone if you want.

Figure 1-9: Add the phone number of an incoming call to an existing contact or create a new one.

Or

4. **Tap Add to Existing Contact.**

   The Contacts screen opens.

5. **Search for the contact you want to add the number to and add the number in the appropriate field.**

6. **Tap Done.**

To create a new contact or add a number to an existing contact from the keypad, when you call a new number:

1. **Tap Phone⟳Keypad.**

2. **Enter the number you want to call, but don't tap Call.**

3. **Tap the plus sign to the left of the Call button.**

   A dialog gives you three choices:

   - Create New Contact

   - Add to Existing Contact

   - Cancel

4. **Tap the button for the action you want to take.**

5. **Follow the procedure for creating a new contact or adding a number to an existing contact.**

6. **Tap Done.**

Editing and Deleting Contacts

People move, change jobs, phone numbers, and names, and you want to keep Contacts current with the state of affairs. The point of departure for editing and deleting contacts is the same:

1. **Tap Contacts on the Home screen or in the dock of the Phone app.**

2. **Tap the name of the contact you want to edit or delete.**

3. **Tap the Edit button in the upper right corner.**

4. **Tap in the field you want to edit.**

   The keyboard opens so you can make your change.

   Scroll to the next field you want to edit and make any other changes.

5. **To delete a field, tap the red and white minus sign to the left of the field, as shown in Figure 1-10.**

If you want to delete a field that you added from the Add Field selections, tap that field, tap the X that appears to the right, and then tap Done. When the field is empty, it will no longer appear on the Contact Info screen.

6. **To add an additional phone, e-mail, website, or address, tap in the blank field below the last filled-in field.**

7. **To add a field, tap the Add Field field at the bottom of the screen and proceed as explained previously in the "Creating New Contacts" section.**

8. **Tap Done in the upper right corner.**

   The corrected contact info screen appears.

To delete a contact, tap the name of the contact, tap edit, and then tap the Delete Contact button at the bottom of the edit screen.

Changes and deletions you make will be automatically pushed to your computer if you use over the air syncing or will be synced with iTunes the next time you perform a Wi-Fi sync or connect your iPhone to your computer.

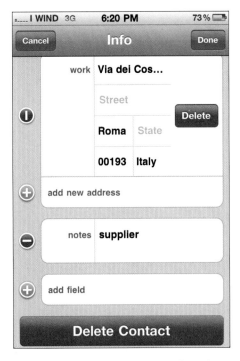

Figure 1-10: Tap the red and white minus sign to delete a field; tap Delete Contact at the bottom to delete a contact.

Viewing and Grouping Contacts

As we mentioned at the beginning of the chapter, you can view contacts by group on your iPhone, but you can't create the groups themselves. You have to set up your groups, or categories, in the contact management application you use on your computer. On your iPhone, to view a group:

1. **Open Contacts from the Home Screen or the dock of the Phone app.**

2. **Tap the Groups button in the upper left corner.**

   The Groups list opens.

3. **Tap the name of the group you want to view.**

   All Contacts is always the first name on the list.

4. **Tap All Contacts to see everyone.**

You can adjust the sort order and the display order in Settings⟳Mail, Contacts, Calendars and scroll down to the Contacts section (refer to Figure 1-4). The settings apply to groups and All Contacts.

- ✒ **Sort Order:** Tap to open options for choosing to sort your contacts by first name and then last name, or vice versa.

- ✒ **Display Order:** Tap to open options for viewing your contacts by first name followed by last name, or vice versa.

You can mix and match the options in four different ways, for example, you can sort by last name and then display by first name, whatever makes the most sense to you.

Searching Contacts

If you have fewer than eight contacts, you can see them all at once on the Contacts screen and can skip this section. If you have more, you'll need to know how to search for Contacts, so read on. You can search Contacts in three ways. Each time you open Contacts from another app, which we talk about in the next section, the search and find process is the same. Tap Contacts on the Home screen and choose either All Contacts or the group you want to search in:

- ✒ Scroll through the list until you see the name you want. If you scroll very fast, tap to stop the scrolling, and then tap on the name you want.

- ✒ In the index that runs down the right side of the screen, tap the letter that corresponds to the initial letter of the name of the person you're looking for. Then scroll through that section of the alphabet to find the person.

✔ Open Spotlight Search by tapping the status bar at the top of the screen or by tapping the magnifying glass icon above the A in the index. Tap in the Search field to open the keyboard. Begin typing the name of the person you want to find. A list of possible matches appears. The more you type, the fewer the choices. Contacts looks at the first letters of first names, last names, and words that are part of a company name. If you type "Jo," first names like **Jo**e or **Jo**anne come up, last names, like **Jo**hnson and **Jo**nes appear, and companies or organizations such as **Jo**lly Ice Cream and Association of Writers and **Jo**urnalists show up as well. (Refer to Figure 1-11.)

Whichever way you choose to search, when you find the name you are looking for, tap on the name to either open the Contacts info screen or to add that name to the To field in the program you're sending from.

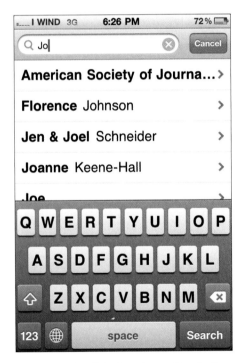

Figure 1-11: Spotlight Search matches the first letters of first and last names and words in a company name.

If you are searching for a contact that you know is in Contacts but can't find it, make sure you are looking in the right group or switch to the All Contacts view to search your entire address book.

When you search in Spotlight Search from the Home screen, Contacts is included in your search. Read more about Spotlight Search in Book I, Chapter 3.

Calling Your Contacts

We delved into the Phone app and FaceTime in Book III, Chapter 1. You can make calls directly from Contacts or open Contacts directly from Phone, as you wish.

- **To call from Contacts:** open Contacts, find the person or business you want to call, tap the phone number you want to dial.
- **To call from Phone:** open Phone, tap the Contacts button at the bottom of the screen, proceed as above.

If you have numbers that you call frequently, you can add them to the Favorites list on the Phone app. Open the Contact you call frequently and tap the Add to Favorites button at the bottom of the Info screen. If there's just one phone number, the contact is added automatically. If there are multiple numbers, a dialog shows all the numbers and you tap on the number you want to add to the Favorites list in Phone.

Sending One Contact to Another

Say a friend compliments you on your new haircut and asks for your stylist's name and phone number. You can dictate the name and number or write it down on a scrap of paper or you can send the information directly from Contacts:

1. **Open the contact you want to share.**

2. **Tap the Share Contact button at the bottom of the screen.**

3. **Choose to send the information by e-mail or MMS.**

   A new message screen opens.

4. **Fill in the address and tap Send.**

   The information is sent in vcf or vCard (Versit Consortium Format), which is a file format for electronic business cards.

A Share Contact button on the Info screen also opens when you tap the blue and white arrow on the Recent Calls list.

Using Contacts to Send Messages, Photos, and More to Your Contacts

Although you use Contacts to manage information, you can also generate communications directly from contacts, as we explained previously when we discussed how to make phone and FaceTime calls directly from a Contact Info screen. You can send messages from Contacts too:

✔ Tap the e-mail address on the Contact Info screen and a New Message in Mail opens, addressed to the contact. Type in a subject and message and tap Send.

✔ To send an SMS or MMS, tap Send Message at the bottom of the Contact Info Screen, as shown in Figure 1-12, and then choose the correct phone number from the choices that appear. A New Message in Messages opens, addressed to the contact. Type your message and tap Send.

Figure 1-12: Send e-mail and text messages directly from the Contact Info screen in Contacts.

You can also access Contacts from communication apps that use the information in Contacts — Phone, Mail, and Messages. Contacts also appears when you want to send things from non-communication apps like Photos and Safari. We take you through the process for each one in their respective chapters, but after you learn to send things to a contact from one app, you pretty much know how to send them in any app. Ah, the beauty of iPhone!

Read about each of apps that use Contacts in the following chapters:

- **Mail:** Book III, Chapter 4.

- **Messages:** Book III, Chapter 2.

- **Notes and Voice Memos:** Book IV, Chapter 4.

- **Photos:** To send still images and video, see Book V, Chapter 1.

- **Safari:** To send links to web pages, see Book III, Chapter 3.

- **Maps:** To send links to a specific map or directions, see Book IV, Chapter 3.

Chapter 2: Managing Your Time with Calendar, Clock, and Reminders

In This Chapter

✒ Adding and syncing existing Calendars

✒ Viewing and hiding Calendars

✒ Creating, changing, and deleting Calendar events

✒ Searching Calendars

✒ Using Clock to help pass the time

✒ Considering other calendar and clock apps and options

✒ Remembering with Reminders

*T*he modern world is a busy place, and everyone has appointments to keep, phone calls to make, bills to pay, birthdays to remember, and vacations every now and then. With all those tasks to remember, a calendar that puts them in one place would be handy.

The Calendar app on your iPhone can do just that, and it syncs with calendars you have on your computer and remote calendars you subscribe to. Calendar inserts events you receive invitations to and alerts you to upcoming deadlines. We begin this chapter by explaining how to add and sync your existing electronic calendars to your iPhone. Then, we show you Calendar's different views and settings. Next, we look at creating and editing events on your iPhone and how to respond and add event invitations.

The last Calendar item we present is how to search for an event in Calendar. While we're on the subject of time, we explain the Clock app too. You learn that it's not just your ordinary clock but a world clock, alarm, stopwatch, and timer. We round off the chapter by explaining Reminders, the new to-do list and automatic reminding app that comes with iOS 5.

Adding and Syncing Existing Calendars

If you don't have a calendar program on your computer or on a remote server, you can skip this section and go on ahead to Calendar's views and settings. For those of you who do have an existing electronic calendar, we explain how to add that calendar to your iPhone and keep all your calendars synced in the future.

We cover the basics of syncing in Book II, Chapter 1; here, we focus only on syncing calendars. iPhone's Calendar app supports the following electronic calendars:

- ✔ **Macintosh:** iCal, Entourage, and Outlook sync with iTunes. You can sync more than one calendar application on your iPhone with a Macintosh.

- ✔ **Windows:** Outlook 2003, 2007, and 2010 sync with iTunes. Windows limits syncing to one calendar application.

- ✔ **Both platforms:** iCloud, Microsoft Exchange, Google, Yahoo!, and CalDAV accounts with over-the-air syncing.

Calendar information can reside in one of three places: on your iPhone, on your computer, and on a remote server (or several remote servers). If you only use your iPhone and your computer to record appointments and events, you simply sync between the two devices.

If you access calendar information from a remote server, like Microsoft Exchange, iCloud, a CalDAV server, Google Calendar, or an iCalendar subscription (we explain each of those in just a little bit), you have to set up an account on both your iPhone and your computer.

On a Macintosh, set up an account in iCal:

1. **Click iCal⇨Preferences and then click Accounts.**

2. **Click the plus sign at the bottom left of the window to add an account.**

3. **Fill in the information requested, and then click Create.**

If you're using Microsoft Exchange, you're probably in a corporate setting with your computer already set up. Go to the section "Adding and Syncing Microsoft Exchange Calendars" for instructions to set up your iPhone.

Importing calendars from iTunes

If you set up iTunes Wi-Fi Syncing (see Book II, Chapter 1), your Contacts are synced once a day when you connect your iPhone to a power source and to the same Wi-Fi network your computer uses, so you can skip this section. If you don't use Wi-Fi syncing, follow these steps to import a copy of your electronic calendar from your computer to iTunes:

1. **Connect your iPhone to your computer with the USB connector cable or to the same Wi-Fi network as your computer.**

2. **Open iTunes, if it didn't open automatically.**

3. **Click on your iPhone in the Devices section of the Source list.**

4. **Click the Info tab at the top of the window (see Figure 2-1).**

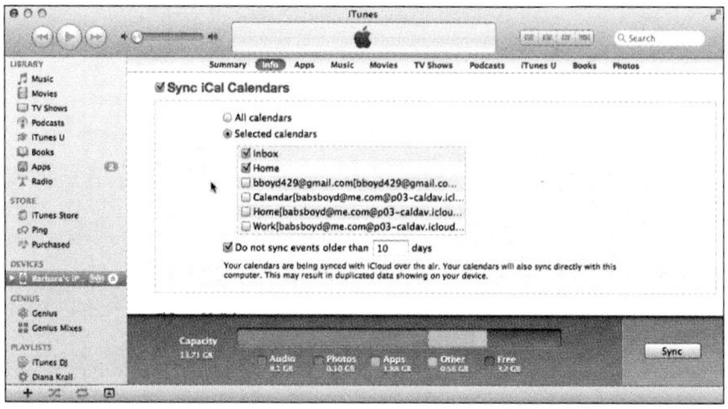

Figure 2-1: Select your sync settings from the Info tab in iTunes.

5. **Click Sync iCal Calendars.**

   If you use Entourage or Outlook, you must first change the preferences on your computer. Click Entourage↪General Preferences. Select Sync Services from the list on the left. Click Synchronize Events and Tasks with iCal. Click OK. A dialog appears, asking how you want to synchronize your data; choose accordingly. An Entourage option appears on the Info tab by the iCal Calendars tab. In Outlook, click Outlook↪Preferences. Click the Sync Services icon and then check the box next to Calendars.

6. **Click All calendars if you want to sync all the calendars that appear in the list below.**

   Or

   Click Selected Calendars and choose which of the calendars in the list you want to sync.

7. **Select the check box next to Do Not Sync Events Older Than 30 Days.**

   You can change the time period (30 days is the default). If you want to have an historic record of your calendar on your iPhone, type in the number of days history you want. A shorter period of time takes less time to sync.

8. **Click Sync in the lower right corner.**

   If you made changes to your syncing criteria, instead of Sync you see Apply. Click Apply.

The next time you connect your iPhone to your computer to perform a sync, the settings you chose are used.

Accessing your Contacts from iCloud

We explain how to set up an iCloud account in Book II, Chapter 1. Essentially, iCloud stores your data, such as contacts, calendar information, your iTunes media library, photos, and documents on a remote server, — called a *cloud* — which pushes data updates to your iPhone and any other computers or iOS 5 devices you have associated with your iCloud account. To sync Contacts on your iPhone with your computer and other iOS 5 devices via iCloud, do the following:

1. **Tap Settings⇨iCloud.**

2. **Tap Calendars On, as shown in Figure 2-2.**

   If your screen doesn't look like Figure 2-2, go to Book II, Chapter 1 to set up an iCloud account.

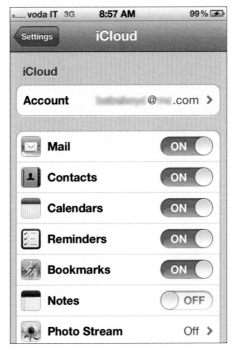

Figure 2-2: Turn Calendars On in iCloud to automatically sync Calendars on your iPhone with other devices using iCloud.

3. **If you previously synced the calendars on your iPhone with your computer, perhaps with iTunes, a message appears letting you know that the calendars you previously synced with your computer will be merged with iCloud. Tap Merge.**

   Any changes you make in Calendar on your iPhone or on other devices associated with iCloud, such as your computer, iPad, or iPod touch, are automatically pushed to all devices. You will never have conflicting information again!

If you do turn on Calendar in iCloud, a message at the bottom of the Calendars portion of the Info screen lets you know that you are syncing your contacts with iCloud. You can still sync with iTunes, but you may create duplicate records.

If you want to use iCloud with your Windows PC, download the iCloud Control Panel for Windows app from Apple (`www.apple.com/icloud/setup/pc.html`).

Adding and syncing Microsoft Exchange calendars

If you use Microsoft Exchange, you use over-the-air or OTA syncing to import and exchange information between the Calendar app on your iPhone and the Microsoft Exchange calendar. When you use this option, you no longer need to sync with iTunes; in fact, doing so may cause duplicate calendar entries. However, you do need to set up an account on your computer, as explained previously. Follow these steps to set up the account on your iPhone:

1. **Tap Settings⇨Mail, Contacts, Calendars.**

   The Mail, Contacts, Calendars screen opens.

2. **Do one of the following:**

   1. **If you set up a Microsoft Exchange account when you first set up your iPhone or when you set up e-mail as explained in Book III, Chapter 4, tap the name of that account in the list that appears.**

   2. **Turn Calendars On with the toggle switch in the account screen, as shown in Figure 2-3.**

   Or

   1. **Tap Add Account to set up new account.**

   2. **Tap Microsoft Exchange.**

   3. **Fill in the requested information.**

Figure 2-3: Turn Calendars on in the account screen if you want to use the calendar feature of Microsoft Exchange.

4. **Tap Next.**

   After the information you entered is verified, you'll be asked to turn on a series of switches to establish which types of things you want to sync. Turn on Calendars. (Turn on the others such as Mail, Contacts, Bookmarks, or Notes if you want to sync those with Exchange.)

   You now see Microsoft Exchange in the list of accounts on the Mail, Contacts, Calendars settings screen.

3. **Tap the Save button in the upper right corner and you return to the Mail, Contacts, Calendars settings screen.**

4. **Tap Fetch New Data.**

5. **Tap Push On.**

   Anytime you make a change to the calendar on your computer that's associated with your Microsoft Exchange account, that change is pushed to your iPhone, and vice versa.

If you use over-the-air syncing, such as iCloud or Microsoft Exchange, the Sync Calendars in iTunes option is disabled. You can choose to sync both with OTA and iTunes, but doing so means you run the risk of having duplicate entries. Our advice: Stick with OTA-only to ensure you're truly in sync across all of your devices.

Configuring CalDAV calendar accounts

CalDAV is an Internet protocol that allows access to data in the iCalendar format on a remote server. Multiple users can access the same information so it is often used in business and organization settings. If your employer uses a CalDAV supported calendar program, and you want to access that calendar from your iPhone, you can add a CalDAV account. You'll need some account information from your IT department or network support person:

- ✔ **Server:** This has your company or organization information.
- ✔ **User Name:** This is your identification.
- ✔ **Password:** A password is required.
- ✔ **Description:** This name shows up on the list of accounts on the Mail, Contacts, Calendars settings screen.

Armed with this information, set up an account on your computer as explained at the beginning of this section. Next, set up the account on your iPhone by following these steps:

1. **Tap Settings⇨Mail, Contacts, Calendars.**

2. **Tap Add Account.**

3. **Tap Other.**

4. **Tap Add CalDAV Account in the Calendars section.**

5. **Type in the information requested.**

6. **Tap the Next button in the upper right corner.**

    After your account information is verified, the calendar data is added to your iPhone.

7. **Tap the Save button in the upper right corner and you return to the Mail, Contacts, Calendars settings screen.**

8. **Tap Fetch New Data.**

    The Fetch New Data screen opens, as shown in Figure 2-4.

9. **If your server supports push notifications, Tap Push On.**

    Anytime you make a change to the calendar on your computer that's associated with your MobileMe or Microsoft Exchange account, that change is pushed to your iPhone, and vice versa.

10. **If your server doesn't support push (or you want to conserve battery power — Push is power hungry), select a default fetch interval — every 15 minutes, every 30 minutes, or hourly.**

Your iPhone contacts the server for new data at the interval you select.

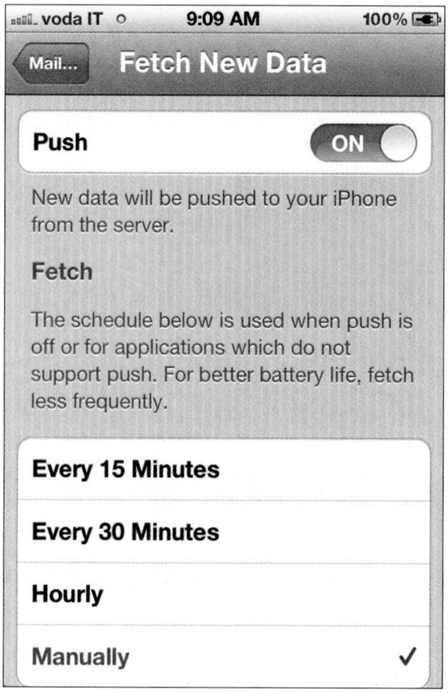

Figure 2-4: The Push feature sends calendar updates to your iPhone as they happen on the remote server.

Importing Google and other calendars

The Google suite of programs, such as Google Mail, Google Calendar, or Blogger, is so popular that Apple has made it very easy to sync your iPhone and Google. Same goes for Yahoo!. If you use Google or Yahoo! calendars, all you need is your e-mail address and password. To set up an account on your iPhone, follow these steps:

1. **Tap Settings on the Home screen, and then tap Mail, Contacts, Calendars.**

2. **Tap Add Account.**

3. **Tap Google Mail or Yahoo! on the Add Account screen.**

4. **The Add Account screen opens.**

   Filling in the Name field is optional. Type in your e-mail address in the Address field and your password in the Password field.

5. **Tap the Next button in the upper right corner.**

   The Google Mail or Yahoo! screen opens.

6. **Tap the Calendars switch On.**

   The calendar you added shows up as one of your calendars in the Calendar app.

By default, only the primary Google calendar is synced to your iPhone, so if you don't see the calendar you're looking for, log into the Google account (you can do this on your computer if you want) where the calendar resides, and then go to www.google.com/calendar/iphoneselect. Select the calendar from the list that you want to sync to your iPhone and click Save. Tap the Calendar button on the Home screen and you find the additional Google calendar in the calendar list.

If you create a remote calendar account on iCal or Microsoft Exchange Active Sync, the calendar data syncs between iCal or Exchange and the remote server. The data, but not the account information, syncs to your iPhone and shows up in the calendar list From My Mac/PC.

Subscribing to iCalendar (.ics) calendars

Electronic invitations — invitations that are sent via e-mail — have gone far beyond the corporate world. Now you can send electronic invitations for bridal showers and cocktail parties as well as gallery openings and yard sales. Sports teams can post the season's game dates on a public calendar site and you can subscribe to that calendar so you don't miss a game.

An iCalendar or .ics file is the standard file type for exchanging calendar information. iCal, Outlook, Google Calendar, and Calendar on your iPhone support the .ics standard. If you receive an e-mail with an invitation attached, the invitation probably has the .ics suffix. You simply click that attachment, either from the e-mail message on your computer or on your iPhone — the event is automatically added to your calendar. The next time you sync, the event is copied to the other device. (If you use OTA syncing, the event syncs automatically.)

If you receive a list of events in Mail, tap the calendar file within the message. When the list of events appears, tap Add All. Choose the calendar where you want to add the events, and then tap Done.

But what about those sporting events? You can search on a site like http://icalshare.com/ or on Google Calendars and subscribe to the calendars that interest you. Some organizations post a subscription link on their website so you can automatically receive notifications of their events. To add a calendar subscription on your iPhone:

1. **Tap Settings⊃Mail, Contacts, Calendar.**

2. **Tap Add Account.**

3. **Tap Other.**

4. **Tap Add Subscribed Calendar (at the bottom of the screen).**

5. **Type in the server address for the calendar on the Subscription screen, as seen in Figure 2-5.**

6. **Tap Next.**

   The server address is verified and a Subscription screen appears. You may have to enter a username and password to have access to the calendar. Some calendar providers ask you to use SSL (secure socket layer) for security reasons. See Book III, Chapter 4 to learn how to turn SSL on in Mail.

7. **The calendar appears on the calendar list in the Calendar app.**

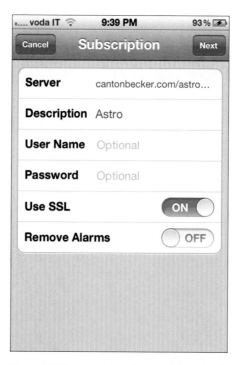

Figure 2-5: You can subscribe to public calendars that use the iCalendar standard.

8. **During the next sync, choose to sync that calendar in the Sync settings on the Info window of iTunes.**

You can make changes to the event in Calendar, but the changes are not reflected on the source calendar (such as GoogleCalendars), which is stored on a remote server and accessed on the Internet.

Viewing and Hiding Calendars

You now have one or multiple calendars on your iPhone. Calendar neatly puts the data in four formats: in portrait (vertical) view Calendar displays a month-at-a-glance, a day-at-a-glance, and List, which is a scrollable list of your events and appointments. Turn your iPhone to the landscape (horizontal) position to see a week-at-a-glance. To choose which calendars you want to see:

1. **Tap Calendars on the Home Screen.**

2. **Tap the Calendar button in the upper left corner.**

   A list of your calendars opens, as shown in Figure 2-6.

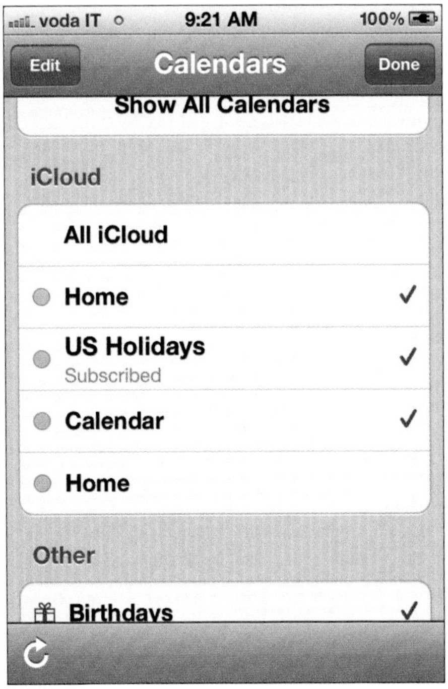

Figure 2-6: The Calendar list shows you the calendars you sync with and those you subscribe to.

Book IV
Chapter 2

Managing Your
Time with Calendar,
Clock, and Reminders

3. **Tap the name of the calendar you want to see or hide.**

   If there's a checkmark next to the name of the calendar, events in that calendar show up in the four views. Note that the Calendars are color-coded. Events shown in List and Day views are color-coded to respond to the calendar they come from.

4. **Tap Show All Calendars if you want to see all events.**

5. **Tap Done.**

   Calendars opens to the view you most recently used.

List, Day, Week, and Month views

When you open Calendar from the Home screen, you see one of the screens as shown in the upcoming figures. The buttons on the screen, from top to bottom, work as follows:

- **Calendars:** Takes you to the list of your calendars.

- **Plus Sign:** Tap this button to add an event to your calendar. We explain that in detail in the next section.

- Between the Calendar and Plus Sign buttons, you see the number of calendars shown. In Figure 2-9, you see "2 Calendars," which means the events you see come from five different calendars, as selected on the Calendars screen in the previous procedure. You see All Calendars if you choose Show All Calendars or just the name of the calendar if you selected only one from the Calendars screen.

- **Left and right arrows (day and month views only):** In Day view, these arrows move a day before (left) or a day ahead (right). If you tap and hold the arrow, the day changes quickly. The arrows on Month view work the same but take you from one month to the previous or next; tap and hold moves quickly through the months.

- **Today:** Tap on the Today button at the bottom of the page in any of the views, and today is highlighted. If you make an appointment on a day two weeks in the future, tapping Today quickly takes you back to today rather than scrolling through with the arrows at the top.

- **List:** Opens the List view as shown in Figure 2-7. You see five or six events. If you have a busy day, you may see only one day. If you have just one or two things each day, you see more days. The colored dot to the left of the event corresponds to the calendar it comes from. You can scroll up and down this list to see what you did or what's coming up.

✔ **Day:** All-day events are shown at the top, and then you see a list of the days appointments, much like a paper agenda or planner that you may be used to using, as shown in Figure 2-8. Scroll up and down the day's appointments to see different hours of the day. The background color of the event corresponds to the calendar it comes from.

✔ **Month:** Days with appointments have a dot under the number. The active day, for which you see two events in the list at the bottom, is highlighted in blue. If you click on a day other than today, the day you click is blue and today is gray (flip ahead to Figure 2-9 to see this).

✔ **Invitations Inbox:** A red numbered badge appears on this button when you receive invitations; the number indicates how many invitations. Click on the button and the invitation opens. We talk about responding to invitations in the "Responding to meeting invitations" section later in this chapter.

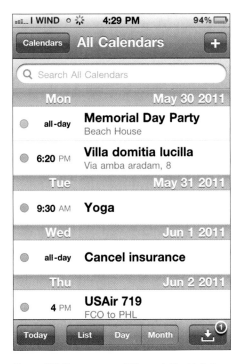

Figure 2-7: You can scroll through the List view to see your appointments and events.

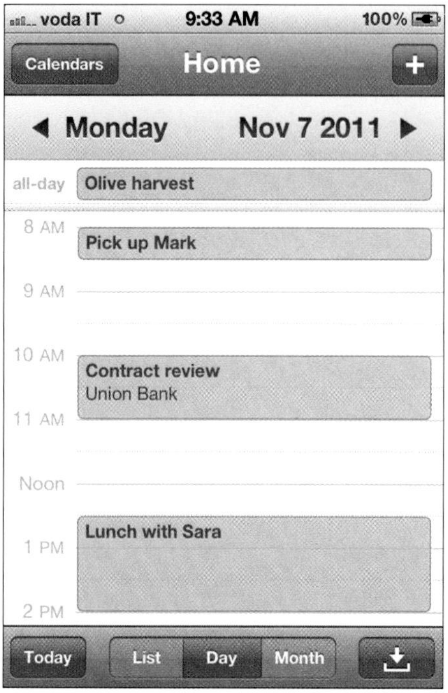

Figure 2-8: Day view shows your appointments for the selected day.

To view your calendar week by week, as shown in Figure 2-10, rotate your iPhone to landscape view and you see a weekly calendar. Swipe left and right to scroll to previous and upcoming days. Swipe up and down to scroll from morning to evening. All-day events are posted at the top of the day. Multi-day events are highlighted across all the days of the event.

Showing birthdays

If you use Contacts, you probably know that you can put a birthday as part of the contact information. (We explain Contacts in Book IV, Chapter 1.) Calendar links to Contacts and can display the birthdays on your calendar.

Scroll to the bottom of the Calendars List screen. You find the Other section and Birthdays. A checkmark indicates that Birthdays is selected; tap Birthdays if it isn't selected. Tap Done. Birthdays are automatically inserted as all-day events.

You now see birthdays in the List and Day views and a dot on the date in Month view. The gift icon is next to the event so you know it's a birthday.

Figure 2-9: A dot under the number indicates an appointment on that day in Month view.

Figure 2-10: Turn your iPhone to landscape view to see a week-at-a-glance calendar.

You can set a default alert for birthdays by tapping Settings➪Mail, Contacts, Calendars➪Default Alert Times➪Birthdays and choosing when you want to receive an alert that someone's birthday is near (from a week before to the day of).

Book IV
Chapter 2

Managing Your
Time with Calendar,
Clock, and Reminders

If you use birthdays from Contacts and add the birthday as an event, it shows up twice on your calendar.

Creating, Changing, and Deleting Calendar Events

We explained how to sync calendars to your iPhone, but there are times when you want to add, change, or even delete an event and you aren't near your computer. In this section, we show you how to create new events and change or delete existing ones. We explain setting up repeating events and alerts so you don't miss any important scheduled encounters, and we discuss how to respond to invitations.

Filling in who, what, where, and when

If you're familiar with iCal, creating events in Calendar will be a breeze. Even if you use Entourage or another calendar program, Calendar is pretty straightforward. Here's how to add an appointment or event:

1. **Tap Calendar on the Home screen.**

2. **From List, Day, or Month Calendar view, tap the plus sign button in the upper right corner to open the Add Event screen.**

   In Day or Month view, press and hold the time or day where you want to add an event until an Add Event screen appears.

3. **Tap the first field, where you see Title and Location.**

   The keyboard appears.

4. **Type in the name of the event or appointment in the Title field.**

5. **Tap Return, and then type in a Location or something else pertinent to the appointment. This field is optional.**

6. **Tap Done in the upper right corner.**

7. **Tap the Starts Ends field.**

   The screen as in Figure 2-11 opens, with the Start field highlighted.

8. **Using the rotor, set the date and time the appointment begins.**

9. **Tap the Ends field. Set the date and time the appointment ends.**

10. **If it's an all-day event such as a meeting or anniversary, tap the All-Day switch to On.**

    The rotors change and show only the month, day, and year. If the event is more than one day, say a conference or vacation, choose the beginning and ending dates.

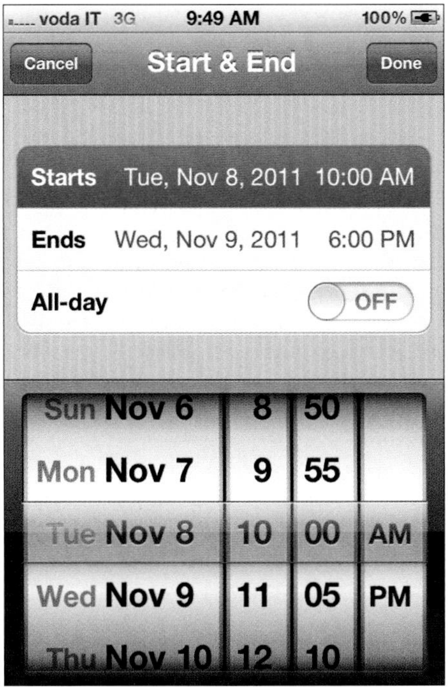

voda IT 3G 9:49 AM 100%

Cancel **Start & End** Done

Starts Tue, Nov 8, 2011 10:00 AM

Ends Wed, Nov 9, 2011 6:00 PM

All-day OFF

Sun **Nov 6** 8 50
Mon **Nov 7** 9 55
Tue **Nov 8** 10 00 AM
Wed **Nov 9** 11 05 PM
Thu **Nov 10** 12 10

Figure 2-11: Use the rotor to set the starting and ending date and times for your event.

The advantage to using the all-day feature instead of setting the beginning time to 8 a.m. and the ending time to 8 p.m. is that in Day view, the event shows up at the beginning of the day rather than as a highlighted event over the course of the whole day. This way, you can add specific appointments during the course of the all-day event. In List view, All-Day appears next to the event title.

11. **Tap Done.**

    You return to the Add Event screen.

12. **Tap the Calendar field.**

    The Calendar screen opens.

13. **Tap the calendar you want to put this event on if it's different than what is shown in the field. You choose the default calendar under Settings, which we explain a few sections ahead.**

    This is the only thing you can't edit at a later date. If you want to move this event to another calendar, you have to create a new event and choose a different calendar.

14. **Tap Done.**

You can stop here or you can add some more details to your event with the remaining fields: Repeat, Alert, and Notes. You can even add attachments or links to websites in Notes. If you use an over-the-air calendar like iCloud or Microsoft Exchange, you also have the options of indicating if you're busy or free during the event and of inviting people to your event.

Setting up a repeating event

The default of a new event is Never. If your event is a one-time only, skip this. For yearly events like an anniversary or weekly events, such as a tennis lesson, the repeat function is handy.

You only have to enter the information once and Calendar takes care of the rest, saving you the hassle of both remembering to re-enter the event the next time it's coming around and of re-typing the information. Here's how:

1. **Tap Repeat on the event you created.**

   If it's an event that you created previously, open that event and tap Edit in the upper right corner.

2. **Choose the frequency with which you want the event to repeat.**

3. **Tap Done.**

   You return to the Add Event screen but another field is added under Repeat: the End Repeat field.

4. **Never is the default, which you probably want to leave for events such as anniversaries. Your tennis lesson may be seasonal, so tap the End Repeat field.**

5. **Use the rotor to choose the date the event ends.**

6. **Tap Done.**

Adding Alerts

If you have a lot on your plate — and who doesn't? — alerts can be a big help. Your iPhone beeps (or vibrates if the Ring/Silent switch is set to Silent) and sends a notification message at the interval you select, from five minutes to two days before your event.

Even if your iPhone is sleeping and/or locked, Calendar wakes your iPhone. You hear the beep and the notification appears, as shown in Figure 2-12. Slide the slider bar to view the event. When you sync your calendars, alerts sync to the corresponding calendar on your computer, and vice versa.

You can even receive two alerts, so you can be reminded of your dear Aunt Sybil's retirement dinner two days before the event, giving you time to get a gift, and then again, the day of the dinner. Follow these steps:

1. **Tap Alert on the Add Event screen or the Edit screen, if you want to add an alert to an event you already created.**

2. **Tap how long before the event you want to receive an alert.**

3. **Tap Done.**

   You return to the Add Event screen, but another field is added under Alert, the Second Alert field.

4. **Tap Second Alert if you want to receive two alerts for the same event.**

5. **Tap how long before the event you want to receive a second alert.**

6. **Tap Done.**

If you don't want an audible alert but just a written notification, turn Calendar Alerts off. Tap Settings⇨Sounds. Scroll down to Calendar Alerts and tap the switch to Off.

Figure 2-12: Alerts are received even if your iPhone is locked or sleeping.

You can set default alerts for events or all-day events by tapping Settings⟹ Mail, Contacts, Calendars⟹Default Alert Times. Then tap Events or All-Day Events and choose when you want to receive an alert. This gives you an alert for all of those kinds of happenings, so if you have a lot of events, setting up default alerts may be more a cause of confusion than a reminder. In that case, you may want to only assign individual alerts to your most important events.

Adding Notes

Adding a note to an event is a great way to remember things associated with that event: for example, if you need certain files for a meeting, or want to save the phone number of the person you're going to meet or the confirmation number for a flight.

You can also copy and paste to the Notes field from a contact, website, note, or an e-mail. To add a note:

1. **Tap Notes on the Add Event screen, or Edit screen if you want to add an alert to an event you already created.**

2. **Type in the information you want.**

   Or

   Switch to the app that contains information you want to copy.

   Copy that information. Double-click the Home button to open the process bar and tap Calendar. You return to the Notes screen where you left off. Press and hold in the field until the magnifying loupe appears. Lift your finger, and then tap Paste. Voila! The information you copied is now in the note of your event.

3. **Tap Done.**

Indicating your availability

You may put an event on your calendar, like a holiday or a visit from an overseas co-worker, that doesn't really occupy your time. You can indicate that you are free, or busy, during events that you post by tapping Availability on the Add Event screen, and then tapping Busy or Free, as appropriate. Tap Done.

Inviting people to your event

If you use an over-the-air calendar, like iCloud or Microsoft Exchange, or use Mail on a Mac, you can invite people to your event directly from Calendar. Make sure you accurately complete the details of your event before sending it to the invitees. Then follow these steps:

1. **Tap Invitees.**

   The Add Invitees screen opens.

2. **Type in the e-mail addresses of the people you want to invite or tap the plus sign on the right.**

   Contacts opens. Scroll the list or tap the letters down the right side or use the Search function to find the name you're looking for.

3. **Tap the name of the person you want to invite.**

   You return to the Add Invitees screen and the name appears in the space at the top.

4. **Repeat steps 2 and 3 to add more people.**

5. **Tap Done in the upper right corner.**

   An event invitation is automatically sent to your invitees.

Figure 2-13 shows a completed Add Event screen.

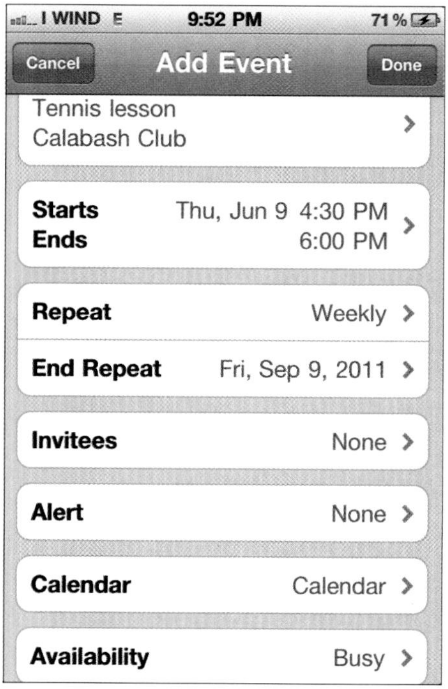

Figure 2-13: A completely filled-in Add Event screen.

Editing and deleting events

Meetings get cancelled, appointment times and dates get changed, and in the old pen and paper calendar world, we used a lot of correction fluid. You can swiftly edit or delete appointments and events on your iPhone without inhaling those nasty fumes.

1. **Tap Calendar from the Home screen.**

2. **Locate the event you want to change or delete from one of the views. We find List or Day easiest.**

3. **Tap the event you want to work on.**

   An Event Details screen opens, as you see in Figure 2-14.

4. **Tap Edit in the upper right corner.**

   The Edit screen opens, which looks like the Add Event screen except it's filled in.

5. **Tap in the field you want to change.**

6. **Make changes using the same techniques you use to enter data in a new event.**

7. **Tap Done.**

If you want to delete the event, instead of editing as in step 5, tap the red Delete Event button at the bottom of the screen. Two buttons pop up, Delete Event and Cancel. Tap the appropriate one.

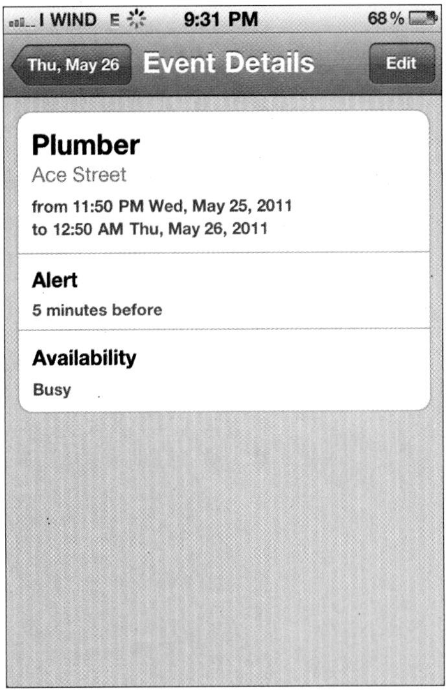

Figure 2-14: The Event Details screen shows information about events you created.

Responding to meeting invitations

Meetings are a fact of life in large and small business. Once upon a time, we used the phone to invite people to meetings, but e-mail and electronic calendars have changed that. You can receive and respond to meeting invitations on your iPhone if you have enabled calendars on Microsoft Exchange or iCloud.

You receive four types of notifications when someone sends you an invitation:

- ✔ **Notification box:** An alert beep sounds and a notification box gives you minimal details about the event and the choice to close the box or view the complete details of the event. You can turn New Invitation Alerts off in Mail, Contacts, Calendar Settings.

- ✔ **On your calendar:** The meeting appears on a gray background with a dotted line around it.

- ✔ **On the Calendars screen:** A numbered alert badge appears in the inbox on the lower right corner.

- ✔ **On the Home screen:** A numbered back appears on the Calendar button.

Tap the inbox on the Calendars screen to view invitations received. Tap on the invitation to open the details, see Figure 2-15. You have three response choices:

- ✔ **Accept:** This puts the meeting on your calendar at the indicated date and time. Your name is added to the list of attendees.

- ✔ **Maybe:** On both your calendar and the sender's calendar, the meeting appears tentative if you select Maybe.

- ✔ **Decline:** This sends a response to let the person know you won't be attending. Nothing is added to your calendar and the invitation is deleted from your iPhone.

Tapping Add Comments in any of the three responses and typing a response sends an e-mail to the sender; otherwise, your response is sent with an empty e-mail.

If you receive an invitation in an e-mail, it shows up as an attachment with an .ics suffix, which indicates the iCalendar standard. Tap on the attachment and the Event Info screen opens. You can then add the event to your calendar and respond.

**Book IV
Chapter 2**

**Managing Your
Time with Calendar,
Clock, and Reminders**

Figure 2-15: You can Accept or Decline an invitation, or choose Maybe while you think about it.

Searching Calendars

You can click on a date to see what events and appointments you have scheduled, but what if you know you have a dentist appointment but can't remember the exact day? You can search in Calendar to find the missing event. Calendar searches in the title, location, notes, and invitees fields of calendars that are active — those you have selected in the Calendars list. Follow these steps:

1. **Tap Calendar on the Home screen.**

2. **Tap the List button at the bottom of the screen.**

3. **Tap the Spotlight Search field at the top.**

   The cursor appears in the field and the keyboard opens.

4. **Begin typing a keyword from your appointment.**

   Matches come up as soon as you type the first letter. The results narrow as you type more.

5. **Tap the Search button in the bottom right corner to close the keyboard.**

6. **Tap the event you were searching for when you see it on the list.**

   The Event Details screen opens.

7. **If that isn't the event you were looking for, tap the Search button on the top left to return to the search screen and try again.**

8. **Tap Cancel when you've finished.**

Adjusting iPhone's Calendar Settings

You can change five Calendar settings from the main Settings app on your iPhone. To access them, tap Settings ⇨Mail, Contacts, Calendars. Scroll down to the bottom of the screen. The Calendars settings are in the last section, as shown in Figure 2-16. You can adjust five items:

✔ **New Invitation Alerts:** When this is set to On, you receive an alert when a new invitation arrives from a remote calendar, such as Outlook. If you're feeling overwhelmed by the number of meeting invitations you receive, tap this setting Off.

✔ **Sync:** Appears if you use an OTA calendar. Choose how much event history you want to include when you sync your events. Tap to open the Sync screen and choose 2 Weeks Back; 1, 3, or 6 Months Back; or All Events. If you sync using iTunes, you set up the historical syncing timeframe on the Info window.

✔ **Time Zone Support:** Time Zone Support is turned On when you first use your iPhone. The time zone that your iPhone is set to appears next to the Time Zone Support button. Events and alerts you enter in Calendar maintain the time you enter, regardless of what time zone you're actually in. We recommend that you leave it that way because switching between On and Off changes the times on events you already created.

To change your time zone, tap Time Zone Support on the Mail, Contacts, Calendar Settings screen. The Time Zone Support screen opens. Tap the switch On and then tap Time Zone. The Time Zone screen opens with a keyboard. Begin typing the initial letters of the city or country of the time zone you want to use. A list of potential cities appears and the results narrow as you type more letters. Tap a city that's in the time zone you want. You return to the Time Zone Support screen. Tap the Mail button in the upper left corner to return to the Settings screen.

Turn Time Zone Support off and your events reflect the local time of your current location. The times for events you already created change. For example, an event at 9:30 a.m. in London changes to 2:30 a.m. when you land in Atlanta.

**Book IV
Chapter 2**

**Managing Your
Time with Calendar,
Clock, and Reminders**

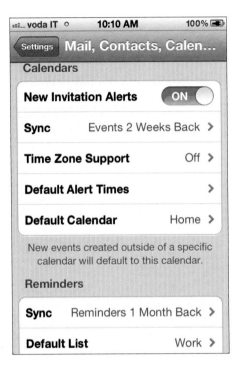

Figure 2-16: Calendar settings galore.

✔ **Default Alert Times:** Set alerts for all birthdays, all events, or all all-day events. See the section "Adding Alerts" earlier in this chapter for the steps to use this feature.

✔ **Default Calendar:** Choose which calendar you want as the default. Any new events you create automatically are placed on the default calendar, unless you change it on the Add Event screen. Tap Default Calendar. The Default Calendar screen opens, which displays the calendars that are available. Click the calendar you want. A checkmark appears to the right of the selected default calendar.

Using Clock to Help Pass the Time

Your iPhone has not one but four time tools: a world clock, an alarm, a stopwatch, and a timer. If you keep your iPhone by your side, you can pretty much eliminate every other clock-like gadget in your home. With the Clock app, you can do things like use the world clock to make sure you don't call your cousin in Mongolia at 2 a.m. Or, set an alarm to wake you up in the morning and separate alarms to wake your children in time for school. Help your friend track trial times for the 100 meter dash. Set a timer for the cake you've put in the oven and to turn off your iPod when you fall asleep. We take you through each of these marvelous clocks features, one by one.

Adding clocks from around the world

When you tap the Home button to wake your iPhone, you see the time on the screen. You set that time on the World Clock function of your iPhone's Clock app. You can also set up clocks from other time zones to keep you informed of what time it is in your overseas office or in the country where your sister is studying.

You only see four clocks at a time, but you can scroll down the list and have as many clocks as there are time zones.

Follow these steps:

1. **Tap Clock on the Home screen.**

2. **Tap the World Clock button in the bottom left corner.**

3. **Tap the plus sign in the upper right corner.**

   The search field opens with a keyboard below.

4. **Begin typing the city or country that you want to add a clock for.**

   If I type **S**, both Scotland and San Rafael come up, as does Detroit, U.S.A. The more letters you type, the narrower your search results.

5. **Tap the city you want to add.**

   If you don't see the exact city you were searching for, tap one that's in the same time zone.

6. **The World Clock screen returns, as shown in Figure 2-17.**

   You see the city you chose added to the list. The clock has a white face if it's daytime in that city and a black face if it's night.

7. **To rearrange the order of the clocks, tap the Edit button in the upper left corner.**

8. **Tap and hold the reorder button on the right, and then drag the clock to the position you want.**

9. **When the clocks are in the order you want, tap Done.**

10. **To delete a clock, tap the Edit button in the upper left corner.**

11. **Tap the red button on the left.**

    A delete button appears on the right.

12. **Tap Delete.**

13. **Tap Done after you finish.**

Book IV
Chapter 2

Managing Your
Time with Calendar,
Clock, and Reminders

Figure 2-17: World Clock shows clocks from multiple time zones.

Setting Alarms

Some of the things we like about the Alarm function are that you can have multiple alarms, choose the days an alarm should repeat, select the sound you want it to have, and add a snooze function. If you want the alarm to vibrate only, leave your iPhone in Ring mode but turn the volume completely down.

Keep in mind that the alarm sounds even when your iPhone is in Silent mode.

Here's how to set alarms:

1. **Tap Clock on the Home screen.**

2. **Tap the Alarm button at the bottom of the screen.**

3. **Tap the plus sign in the upper right corner.**

   The Add Alarm screen opens, as seen in Figure 2-18.

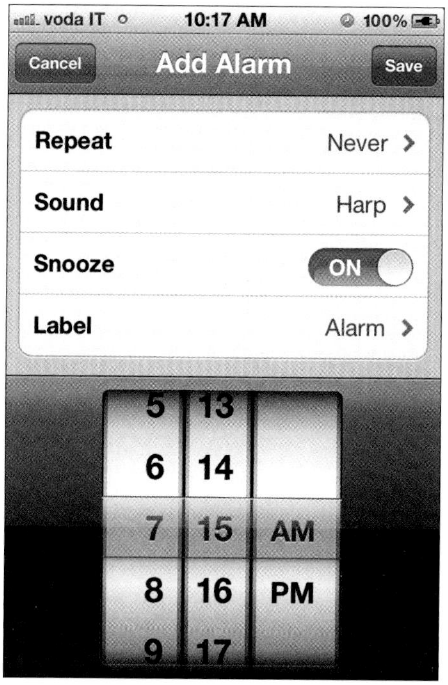

Figure 2-18: Set the time, sound, and repeating options on the Add Alarm screen.

4. **Use the rotor to set the time you want the alarm to sound.**

5. **Tap Repeat if you want to create a repeating alarm.**

   You can choose any day of the week or a combination of days, which means you can have a Monday through Friday alarm, which is labeled Weekdays on the alarm list, whereas a Saturday/Sunday alarm is labeled Weekends.

6. **Tap Back after you choose the days you want the alarm to repeat.**

7. **Tap Sound to choose the sound you want for your alarm.**

   Choose a sound from the list — scroll down to see all the options. You can buy more tones by tapping the button at the top of the list, which takes you to the iTunes store.

8. **Tap Snooze On or Off.**

   Snooze lets you tap the alarm off when it sounds. After ten minutes, it sounds again.

9. **Tap Label to name your alarm.**

The Label screen opens with a field and keyboard. Click the X on the right end of the field to delete the default Alarm label, type the name you want, and then tap Done.

10. **Tap Save.**

The alarm is added to the list of alarms on the Alarm screen.

To make changes to an existing alarm, tap the Edit button on the top left of the screen, and then tap the name of the alarm you want to change. The Edit Alarm screen opens, which is the same as the Add Alarm screen but has the information of the selected alarm.

To delete an existing alarm, tap the Edit button. Tap the red button to the left of the alarm time, and then tap the Delete button that appears on the right. Tap Done after you finish.

When you set an alarm, the alarm icon, which looks like a clock, appears in the status bar at the top of your iPhone's screen.

Timing events with Stopwatch

You can use the Stopwatch to time single events such as a speech or laps. Tap Start to start counting.

To time one thing, let it run until the action stops, and then tap Stop.

To time laps, tap Lap each time the runner or swimmer or bicycle rounds the bend.

The large numbers continue giving a cumulative time; the smaller numbers above show the time of the lap.

When you tap Lap, the laps are listed below with each lap's time, as shown in Figure 2-19. If you tap Start again, the count resumes from where it left off.

Tap Reset to zero the count and erase the lap times.

Counting down to zero with Timer

While the Stopwatch starts counting from zero, the timer counts down to zero. You can set the time from one minute up to 23 hours and 59 minutes, after which, you're better off setting an alarm. After you set the timer, you can go on to do things with other apps, even press the Sleep/Wake button. The timer continues to countdown in the background and sounds when the time's up. To set the timer:

Figure 2-19: Time laps with the Stopwatch.

1. **Tap Clock on the Home screen.**

2. **Tap the Timer button in the lower right corner.**

3. **Turn the rotor to set the length of time you want to pass before the timer sounds.**

4. **Tap When Timer Ends to choose the "time's up" sound.**

   Scroll through the When Timer Ends list and tap the sound you want. Tap Buy More Tones at the top of the list to go to iTunes and buy additional sounds.

5. **Tap the Set button in the upper right corner.**

6. **Tap the green Start button on the Timer screen.**

To use the Timer as a Sleep Timer with your iPod, as shown in Figure 2-20:

1. **Tap When Timer Ends.**

2. **Scroll to the very bottom of the screen and tap Sleep iPod.**

3. **Tap Set.**

   The Time screen appears.

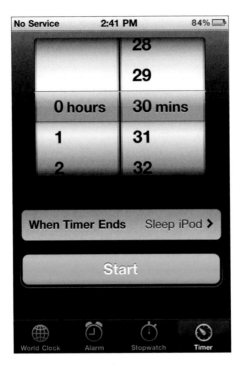

Figure 2-20: The Timer works as a regular timer on its own or as a sleep timer with iPod.

4. **Tap Start.**

   The countdown begins.

5. **Double-click the Home button.**

   The recent apps bar opens at the bottom of the screen.

6. **Flick to the far left screen to open the iPod controls.**

7. **Tap the play button if the song you want to hear is already going.**

   Or

   Tap the iPod button to open iPod and select what you want to listen to or watch.

8. **Whatever you are listening to or watching is turned off when the timer stops.**

Remembering with Reminders

If alerts and alarms aren't enough to keep you on time, you can rely on Reminders to keep track of your deadlines and commitments and remind

you when they're due. Reminders is a listmaker's electronic dream come
true. Reminders is a catch-all for your To Do lists, neatly divided into Home
and Work, and any other categories you want to add. There's a Completed
list so you have the satisfaction of seeing things checked off your list. And,
Reminders automatically syncs with iCloud, iCal, and Outlook, so if you jot
down a reminder on your iPhone, it appears in the calendar app on your
computer. (Turn Reminders On in Settings⟳iCloud.)

Creating New Reminders

You can ask Siri to create a reminder for you (see Book I, Chapter 3) or you
can create them by yourself. Make lists of tasks and assign the dates you
want Reminders to remind you of the tasks. If you have an iPhone 4 or 4S,
you can set up Reminders to remind you of your task when you leave or
arrive at a location, such as home or work. Here's how to create new
Reminders:

1. **Tap Reminders on the Home screen.**

   The Reminders screen opens as shown in Figure 2-21.

Figure 2-21: Reminders keeps track of your tasks
and deadlines.

2. **Tap on the lined piece of "paper" or tap the plus sign in the upper right corner.**

   The keyboard appears.

3. **Type the task you want to remember and tap return.**

   The task appears in the list with a check box to the left and an arrow to the right.

4. **Tap the arrow.**

   The Details screen opens. Tap Show More to see the Details screen shown in Figure 2-22.

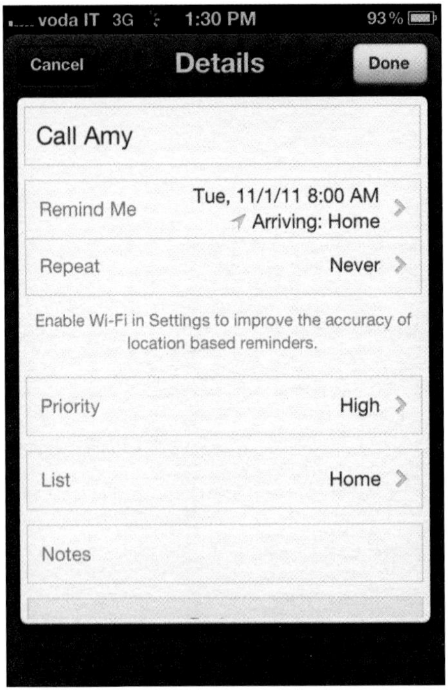

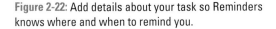

Figure 2-22: Add details about your task so Reminders knows where and when to remind you.

5. **Tap each item to specify how you want Reminders to help you remember this task.**

   • *Remind Me* gives you further choices to specify a date and location for the reminder, refer to Figure 2-23. Tap on Day On and tap the date to open a rotor that allows you to specify the date and time. Tap Location On. If you want to be reminded of the item when you leave or arrive at a specific location, tap either When I Leave or When I Arrive, and then tap Done. If you want to use a different location, tap Current Location and tap Home (which Reminders uses from your card in Contacts) or tap Choose Address. Contacts Opens and you can choose an address there. Tap Remind Me in the upper left corner after you choose the location. You return to the Remind Me screen. Tap Done after you have specified a Day or Location (or both) to return to the Details screen. The Location option only works with iPhone 4 and 4S and works better if you use a street address.

- *Repeat* lets you choose to repeat this reminder. Tap to set the interval.

- *Priority* lets you set the task as a low, medium, or high priority.

- *List* gives you the option to specify in which list you want to keep the reminder. See the next section, "Using Reminders lists."

- *Notes* is where you can type in any additional details about the reminder.

Figure 2-23: Specify the day and location for when you want to be reminded of your task.

6. **Tap Done when you finish with each item to return to the previous screen.**

7. **Go to Settings⇨Sounds and Settings⇨Notifications to choose the alert tone and style you want Reminders to use.**

You can edit a task at any time by tapping the arrow to the right of the task to open the Details screen. Tap Delete at the bottom of the Details screen to eliminate a task.

Using Reminders lists

Reminders comes with four lists: Reminders, Home, Work, and Completed. You can add other lists (and delete any or all of the first three) and then create new Reminders on the lists you want. To view the existing lists, tap the List tab at the top of the screen and then swipe left and right to move from one list to the next. Or, tap the list button in the top left corner (it looks like three horizontal lines) and then tap the list you want to see. To add or delete a list, follow these steps:

1. **Tap Reminders on the Home screen to open Reminders.**

2. **Tap the Lists tab at the top of the screen if you aren't in List view.**

3. **Tap the List button in the top left corner to open the Lists screen.**

4. **Tap Edit in the upper right corner.**

5. **To create a new list, tap Create New List.**

   The keyboard opens.

   Type in the name of the list and then tap Done.

6. **To delete a list, tap the red and white minus sign to the left of the list name in the list.**

7. **Drag the list button to the right of the items to rearrange their order.**

8. **Tap Done to return to the Lists screen and then tap Done again to return to the specific lists (refer to Figure 2-21).**

When you complete a task, tap the check box to the left of the task on the list and the task moves onto the Completed list. You can also view completed tasks for a specific list by tapping Completed at the top of the list. You may have to scroll up to see Completed if you have more than seven items on your list.

Viewing by Date

If you want to see all your tasks for one day, as shown in Figure 2-24, tap the Date tab at the top of the screen. Do one of the following to view a certain day's tasks:

- Tap Today in the upper right corner, to see today.

- Swipe from right to left to go from one day to the next or to a previous day.

- Drag the time slider at the bottom of the screen to the date you want to see. The dot at the far left of the time slider reveals your Completed list.

- Tap the calendar button in the upper left corner and then tap the date you want to see.

Figure 2-24: Date view combines your tasks for one day from every list.

Book IV
Chapter 2

Managing Your
Time with Calendar,
Clock, and Reminders

Search in Reminders by tapping Date and then tapping the Calendar button. Type a few words of the task you're looking for in the search field or use Spotlight Search from the Home screen. Or if you have an iPhone 4S, just ask Siri to find a reminder for you.

Chapter 3: Tapping into Maps, Compass, Weather, Calculator, and Stocks

In This Chapter

✏ **Adjusting iPhone's location settings and services**

✏ **Seeking, finding, and sharing points of interest**

✏ **Getting directions**

✏ **Orienting yourself with Compass**

✏ **Talking about the Weather**

✏ **Doing the math with Calculator**

✏ **Tracking investments with Stocks**

*Y*our iPhone comes with more than 20 apps installed. Some, like Phone, Mail, and Messages, help you communicate. Others, like Music, Video, and the Camera are about doing things for fun or leisure. The apps we talk about in this chapter are best described as tools. Tools can help you do something you already do, but with more ease and sometimes better performance.

Each app we cover in this chapter has a corresponding real-life counterpart in the non-iPhone world, and iPhone's version works in a similar way — as soon as you open the app, it feels familiar. For example, you can find your way using a paper map, although you need a degree in origami to refold it when you reach your destination. With Maps, just type in beginning and ending points and a mapped out route appears — no folding necessary.

Sailors and farmers have relied on the sky, sun, and stars to get their bearings and predict weather patterns, but for the rest of us, the web is our favorite way of finding our way around the world. Closer to home (as in your pocket), the Compass app can be a handy ally when you want to know which way is north by northwest. The Weather app can help you decide whether you ought to tote an umbrella when you leave for work tomorrow morning.

Whereas Barbara relaxes by doing calculations in her head (a family trait), numbers make Joe tremble, which is why the Calculator app is one of his personal favorites (and maybe yours, too). Getting back to our real-life counterparts metaphor, you can check the daily newspaper for once-a-day stock quotes. But as anyone who really plays the market will tell you, having close to real-time information about your stocks can spell the difference between knowing whether you can afford that new sailboat or if you're better off keeping your canoe (because you already have a trusty Compass to guide you). Like we said, apps are like real-life tools, only better.

Because the apps we cover here are stand-alone tools, don't feel obliged to read this chapter from start to finish (although we're always happy if you do). We go through them one by one and give you all the ins and outs, tips, and tricks so you get the most out of each app. We begin with Maps and Compass, and then talk about the Weather. We cover both Calculators (yup, there are actually two), and then explain Stocks. At the end of the chapter, we tell you about a couple of other handy apps you may want to consider downloading from the App Store.

Adjusting iPhone's Location Settings and Services

Before we go into using Maps and Compass, we want to show you how to turn Location Services on. Without Location Services, Maps can give you directions from one address to another and the Compass can give you magnetic north. However, if you want to know where you are, or want true north, you have to turn on Location Settings. Maps uses your location to give you the best local information available, whereas the Compass uses your location to identify true north. We give you a simple explanation about the difference between true north and magnetic north when we talk about Compass.

Other apps use Location Services too. For example, the Camera adds where the photo was taken to the date and time of the photo. (Everything about the Camera is explained in Book V, Chapter 1.) The first time an app wants to use Location Services, a notification message appears asking if you want to allow the app to use your location. You can choose yes or no. If you don't want the Camera to put your location on your photos, just tap no when Camera asks to use your Location. You can change these settings at any time, as explained in the third step here:

1. **Tap Settings on the Home screen.**

2. **Tap Location Services, and then tap the toggle switch On.**

   The Location Services list, as seen in Figure 3-1, opens and displays all apps that can use your location in one way or another.

   When Location Services is on, its icon appears in the status bar. This is good to know because it consumes battery power, so don't leave it on if you're not using it.

3. **Turn Location Services on or off for each app.**

   Apps with the Location Services icon next to them have accessed your location in the last 24 hours.

Location Services must be on for Find my iPhone to work. This should be a strong incentive to use a passcode to lock your iPhone. Otherwise, whoever "finds" your iPhone could just turn off Location Services and render Find My iPhone useless.

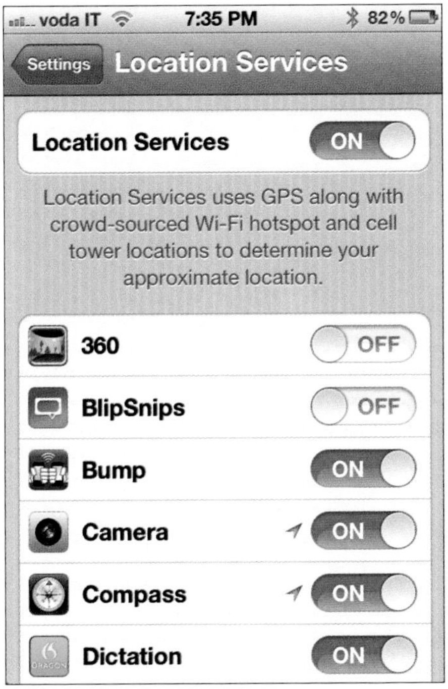

Figure 3-1: You can turn Location Services on for specific apps.

Getting There from Here with Maps

With Maps, you can do normal things that maps do — like find out where you are, if you're curious (or lost); or homing in on a street address you want to go to. Or you can use Maps to accomplish loftier goals, like charting a course from your home to your vacation destination. What's more, with Maps, you can find rest stops, outlet malls, historic sites, and hotels along the way.

In this section, we tell you how to find your present location and how to find an address you know. Then we'll show you how to find a service, such as a restaurant or bookstore, near a location. We talk about how to get directions from one place to another, and finally, how to share or save the locations and directions you use.

Finding yourself

With Location Services on, Maps can tell you where you are. Tap Maps on the Home screen to open Maps, and then tap the Location Services button in the lower left corner. If you have Location Services turned off, a notification message gives you the option of turning it on so Maps can find you.

Your exact location is the blue dot on the map, like you see in Figure 3-2. If there is a pulsing circle around the blue dot, your location is approximate; the smaller the circle, the more precise your exact (or nearly exact) location. If you're walking or driving, the blue dot moves along the map as you move along the road (or hiking trail or beach surf — you follow our point).

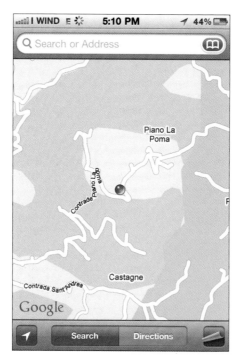

Figure 3-2: The blue dot indicates your present location and follows your every move.

 Double-tap the Tracking button and a flashlight beam shines from the blue dot, lighting the way your iPhone is oriented. The Tracking button at the bottom of the screen changes to a flashlight icon, as in Figure 3-3.

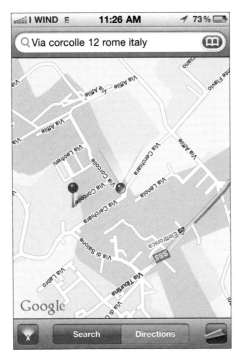

Figure 3-3: Tap the Location Services button to determine the direction you're facing.

Maps combines the GPS (Global Positioning System), Wi-Fi, and cellular network data to determine your location and then uses Google Maps to display locations and calculate routes.

Seeking and finding locations

Instead of finding a street name on a list, and then flipping a large unwieldy piece of thin, easily ripped paper, otherwise known as a map, to look for quadrant K-5, Maps lets you type in the address you seek. As fast as your Internet connection allows, the equivalent of quadrant K-5 appears on your iPhone screen. You can also find addresses from Contacts and from bookmarks that you set up in Maps. Follow these steps to map-folding freedom:

1. **Open Maps from the Home screen.**

2. **Tap the Spotlight search field at the top of the screen.**

    The keyboard opens. If you don't see the Spotlight search field, tap Search at the bottom of the screen.

3. **Type in the address you're searching for.**

4. **Tap the blue Search button in the bottom right corner.**

   A red pin on the map indicates the address you seek. The address is written on a flag attached to the pin.

To find an address from Contacts, follow this sequence:

1. **Open Maps from the Home screen.**

2. **Tap in the Spotlight search field.**

   The keyboard appears.

3. **Begin typing the name of the person or business you want.**

   As you type more letters, your search narrows.

4. **When you find who or what you're looking for, tap it.**

   Maps automatically opens to that address.

If two addresses exist for your chosen contact, the Info screen opens for that contact. Tap the address you want to find, and Maps opens to that address. To view and use an address you've recently used or select one from a Maps bookmark (see the next section for how to set up bookmarks), do the following:

1. **Open Maps from the Home screen.**

2. **Tap the Spotlight search field at the top of the screen.**

3. **Tap the Bookmarks button on the right of the Spotlight search field.**

 4. **Tap the Bookmarks button at the bottom left of the screen to use a bookmarked location.**

   A list of bookmarks opens.

   Or

   Tap the Recents button at the bottom in the center of the screen to use an address you've recently accessed.

   A list of recently used addresses opens.

5. **Tap the address you wish to use.**

   A map opens and a red pin indicates the address or location you're looking for.

You can blunder around an unfamiliar city looking for a place to eat until you stumble upon an appealing restaurant, or you can rely on Maps. Follow these steps to find sites and services quickly and easily:

1. **Open Maps from the Home screen.**

2. **Tap the Spotlight search field at the top of the screen.**

The keyboard opens so you can type what you're looking for, say, pizza.

3. **Type** pizza **in the Search field.**

   As you begin typing, Spotlight opens Contacts. Just ignore that and type the whole word **pizza**.

4. **Tap the Search button in the bottom right corner.**

   Red pins appear on the pizza parlors in your vicinity.

5. **Tap one of the pins.**

   A flag opens, giving the name and address of the location.

6. **Tap the arrow on the right end of the flag.**

   An info screen opens that shows information like the phone number and address of the selected site, or the site's web address, as seen in Figure 3-4.

   Tap the web page address to find out more about the pizza parlor (to see if they offer an online menu, for instance), or tap the phone number to call the pizza parlor so you can place your take out order or make a reservation.

Figure 3-4: The Info screen shows information about a location you select.

If you have an iPhone 4S, press and hold the Home button and ask Siri to find a restaurant — or whatever you're looking for — for you.

Marking, saving, and sharing points of interest

Often you may find yourself using a couple of locations repeatedly as your starting point or destination. Instead of retyping the address each time you want to use those locations, you can set up bookmarks in Maps for those locations.

Maps bookmarks make it easy to return to frequently used addresses. Or, you may find a great restaurant that you want to add to Contacts and send to a fellow foodie friend. Here's how to bookmark, save, and share locations:

1. **Tap the flag attached to the pin, which indicates the address you want to bookmark, add to Contacts, or share with someone.**

   If there's no flag, tap the pin to open one.

2. **Tap the arrow on the right end of the flag.**

   An Info screen opens (refer to Figure 3-4).

3. **Tap one of the buttons at the bottom of the screen.**

   * **Add to Contacts** gives you the option of creating a new contact or adding the information to an existing contact. Choose the task you wish to do. See Book IV, Chapter 1 for complete details on using Contacts.

   * **Share Location** lets you send the information about this location to someone via e-mail, MMS, or Twitter (you must be logged in to your Twitter account). Tap the corresponding button that appears and a New Message screen opens. See Book I, Chapter 4 to learn about Twitter settings, Book III, Chapter 2 to learn about sending MMS and Book III, Chapter 4 to learn about e-mail.

   * **Add to Bookmarks** brings up an Add Bookmark screen where you type in a name for this location's bookmark, and then tap Save.

If there's no pin on the location you want to save or share, tap the curled page button and tap Drop Pin. A purple pin shows up on the map with a flag that reads *Dropped Pin*. Why would you want to do that? Say you find yourself in front of a closed bookstore that has a first edition a friend of yours has been looking for, and you want to remember or tell your friend where this store is. Tap the Tracking button, the blue dot shows where you are. Drop a pin on your location; a flag shows the address of the pin. If the pin isn't exactly where you want it, zoom in on the map (double-tap with one finger), drag the pin and then let go on the exact spot you want to mark. Tap the blue arrow button to display options you can tap to do things with the bookstore's location, like add the location to your Contacts or Bookmark the location, get directions, or share the location with your friend via e-mail or MMS. To remove the pin, tap Remove Pin. That's exactly what happens when you return to the Map screen — out of sight, out of mind.

If you still prefer your maps on paper, tap the curled page button and then tap Print. See Book I, Chapter 2 for details about printing.

Getting directions

We showed you how to find your present location or a single location with Maps but, more often than not, you want detailed instructions for going from one place to another. Follow these steps for getting directions:

1. **Search for an address in one of the four ways detailed previously.**

   The pin with the flag indicates the sought-after address.

2. **Tap the arrow on the right end of the flag.**

   An Info screen opens.

3. **You can obtain directions to and from this location by tapping one of the buttons:**

   Directions to here: The Directions screen opens as seen in Figure 3-5. Current Location is the default for the starting point.

   Directions from here: The Directions screen opens; however, Current Location is the default ending point or destination.

   Swap the Start and End points of the Directions by taping the Swap button.

4. **If you want to use your Current Location as your starting or ending point, tap the Route button in the bottom right corner or tap in the field that contains Current Location.**

   Current Location is highlighted.

   1. **Tap the circled x on the right end of the field to clear the field.**

   2. **Type in the address you wish to use.**

   3. **Tap the Next button on the bottom right.**

      The cursor moves to the other field, which has the previously established address. You can change it with the keyboard if you want.

Figure 3-5: Fill in the starting point and destination you want on the Directions screen.

4. **Tap the Route button in the bottom right corner.**

Or

Click on the Bookmarks button to the right of the field where Current Location appears.

A screen opens as shown in Figure 3-6.

1. **Tap one of the buttons at the bottom:**

   • **Bookmarks** to use an address you've bookmarked in Maps.

   • **Recents** to choose an address you've recently used.

   • **Contacts** to choose an address from Contacts.

2. **Tap the address you want to use.**

3. **Tap the Route button in the bottom right corner.**

5. **The screen displays a map showing the route from your starting point to your destination, or from your destination back to your starting point, if you prefer.**

   The distance and estimated travel time are displayed above the map. If more than one route is available, Maps displays alternate routes, assigning a number to each. Tap the route you want to follow.

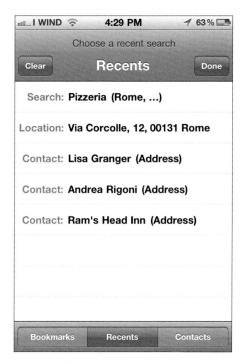

Figure 3-6: You can choose an existing address from Bookmarks, Recents, or Contacts.

6. **Tap the curled page button to select and change how you see the map.**

   You see the screen shown in Figure 3-7.

7. **Choose one of the following views:**

   • **Standard** shows you a map. This is the default view.

   • **Satellite** shows a satellite view. The accuracy of this view depends on when the images you're viewing were last updated by Google Maps.

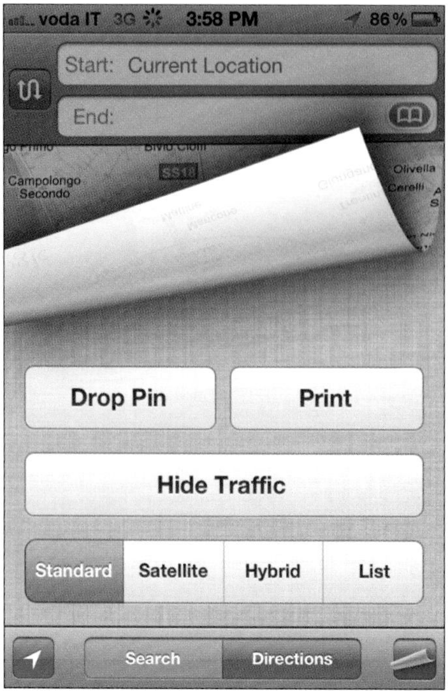

![Screenshot of iPhone Maps showing map view options]

voda IT 3G 3:58 PM 86%

Start: Current Location

End:

Campolongo Secondo   Olivella Carelli

Drop Pin   **Print**

Hide Traffic

Standard | Satellite | Hybrid | List

Search   Directions

Figure 3-7: You have four map views to choose from.

- **Hybrid** shows the street names on a satellite view.

- **List** gives you a list of directions, as seen in Figure 3-8. If you tap on one of the steps, the map opens to that portion of the route.

A fifth map view called Street view shows you what you see if you're walking down the street — or what you might have seen at some point in the past few years, since you see the view from whenever Google filmed the area. If Street view is available, an orange button with a person icon inside appears on the left side of the pin's location information flag. Tap that button and Street view appears, as seen in Figure 3-9. A round map thumbnail with the flashlight beam aimed in the direction appears in the bottom right corner. Flick your finger left or right in the center of the street view screen to rotate your view in 360 degrees; tap arrows that appear on the street to move up or down the street and continue your up close and more personal Street view stroll. Tap the circular map button in the lower right corner to return to the map.

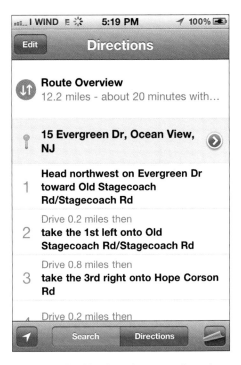

Figure 3-8: The List view shows you the written directions from your starting point to your destination.

Figure 3-9: Street view shows what you see as you walk down the street.

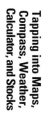

8. **Tap Show Traffic.**

The roads on the map pulsate with red, yellow, green, or gray highlights to show you traffic conditions.

- **Red** shows where traffic is heavy and stop and go.

- **Yellow** means traffic is moving below the posted speed limit.

- **Green** indicates traffic is moving at the posted speed limit.

- **Gray** means there's no traffic information available for that street.

9. **Tap the Start button in the upper right corner.**

In Map, Satellite, or Hybrid view, Maps zooms in to the first step of the list. Tap List to see the indications from starting point to destination. Tap any item in the list to see that point on the map. Tap Route Overview to return to the whole map.

10. **Tap the right arrow in the upper right corner to go to the next indication.**

A circle indicates the intersection of the turn or road change at each step.

11. **If you want to change your starting point or destination or the whole route, tap the Edit button in the upper left corner.**

The Directions screen opens with the keyboard.

12. **Tap the field you want to edit or tap the Clear button in the upper left corner to start over completely.**

Double-tap on the map to zoom in. Tap once with two fingers to zoom out. Repeat either tap to zoom in or out more. You can also use the pinch and spread technique to zoom in and out.

Traveling by car, bus, or hoofing it on foot

In these days of high-priced fuel, public transportation and walking are looking better and better all the time. (Plus it's the greener thing to do!) By tapping the buttons at the top of the screen, you can choose your mode of transportation. The distance and estimated travel time change to reflect the mode you choose.

 Tap the car button to display driving directions to your destination.

 Tap the bus button to display public transit routes and schedules (not always available or current in all areas). Tap the clock button to set your departure or arrival time and choose an appropriate schedule.

 Tap the pedestrian button to display a walking route.

On the Info screen, fields that appear arc active and information that's available on your iPhone is filled in. For example, if an address you arc using is associated with a person in Contacts for whom you also have a phone number and e-mail, those fields appear. If the location is unknown, only the Directions to Here and Directions from Here buttons appear, along with the Add to Contacts, Share Location, and Add to Bookmarks. Activate these options by tapping on the associated button:

- **Phone numbers:** Places a call to the phone number.

- **Addresses:** Returns you to the Maps screen.

- **Web page addresses:** Opens the webpage in Safari.

- **E-mail:** Creates a new Mail message.

- **Directions to Here and From Here:** Displays the Directions screen.

- **Add to Contacts:** Displays option to Create New Contact or Add to Existing Contact.

- **Share Location:** Displays option to create a new E-mail or MMS message containing the location.

- **Add to Bookmarks:** Displays the Add Bookmark screen so you can save the address in Maps' bookmarks.

Orienting Yourself with Compass

iPhone uses a built-in magnetic field sensor — a magnetometer — to give compass readings. Compass is subject to magnetic interference; that is something that inhibits its capacity to correctly indicate the direction. The first thing we explain is how to calibrate the Compass to cancel the interference and get Compass back on course. We show you how to read the Compass, and explain the difference between true and magnetic north and how to select one or the other.

Calibrating your iPhone for greater accuracy

When you first open Compass, a notification message appears indicating that you should calibrate your iPhone. If iPhone detects some interference, usually something with a magnetic field or an electronic device like a cell phone or stereo, you may see a message asking you to calibrate your phone. Simply move your iPhone in a big figure eight pattern a few times until the Compass itself appears.

Getting your bearing

Whether to determine the direction you're facing or find the direction you want to go, Compass is a great tool. After the Compass is calibrated, hold your iPhone (face-up, of course) so the back of your hand is parallel to the ground.

The red arrow on the Compass points north, the direction your iPhone is pointing is written in white above the compass. Move around, and the compass rotates and the headings change. When you have Location Services turned on, your geographic coordinates are displayed below the compass, as shown in Figure 3-10.

What's really helpful is that Compass links to Maps. If you want to see where you are on a map, tap the Location Services button in the bottom left corner. Maps opens and the blue dot indicates your location.

Double-tap the Location Services button to open the flashlight beam that shows you the direction you're facing. If you want to know the address, drop a pin and the address appears in the attached flag.

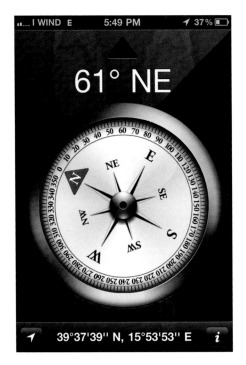

Figure 3-10: The Compass shows both the heading and the geographic coordinates for your location.

Choosing between true north or magnetic north

Compass gives accurate readings of both true north and magnetic north, and both are valid indications. True north, which is a GPS bearing linked to the geographical location of the North Pole, works when Location Services is turned on.

Magnetic north, on the other hand, depends on the Earth's natural magnetism, which changes based on your physical location. It works when Location Services is both on and off. Because magnetic north changes at different latitudes, it can be a few to many degrees different than true north and even south of your latitude. This difference is called *declination*. In some places, declination is less than one degree so it barely alters your bearings. Keep in mind, however, if you're hiking in the wilderness on a trail with 10 degrees of declination, those seemingly minor ten degrees can result in you being miles off course after several hours of continuous hiking. Technically speaking, to achieve the most accurate results, you have to know the actual declination degrees you're traversing for your current location to calculate the difference between magnetic north and true north. Localized trekking maps often have declination degrees on them, so you can adjust the orientation of your map when using true north. To choose between the two:

1. **Tap Compass on the Home screen.**

   The Compass opens (refer to Figure 3-10). When Location Services is on and GPS is available, you see your coordinates at the bottom of the screen.

2. **Tap the Information button in the lower right corner.**

   The screen flips and you have the choice of True North (dimmed if Location Services is off) and Magnetic North.

3. **Tap your preferred north, and then tap Done in the upper right corner.**

   The Compass screen returns.

Talking about the Weather

As much as our lives are conducted indoors, in offices, restaurants, shopping malls, cars, buses, and homes, we haven't completely lost interest in Mother Nature. Weather forecasts occupy a portion of every newscast, and there are countless weather websites, not to mention the numerous all-weather cable channels.

iPhone's Weather app is updated hourly and gives you the current temperature and the forecast for six days for cities across the country and around the world.

Tap the Weather button on the Home screen and the weather forecast for Cupertino, California — Apple's hometown — opens. The first thing you want to do is add cities that are important to you, unless you happen to live in Cupertino. We show you how to do that first and then look at the forecast options.

**Book IV
Chapter 3**

Tapping into Maps,
Compass, Weather,
Calculator, and Stocks

Adding, removing, and reorganizing cities

You probably want to add your hometown, but you may want to add other cities and locales too. Say you have to go on a multi-city book tour and want to know what the weather will be like in each city. You can add the cities you'll be going to and then quickly flip through each day to see whether to expect sunny skies in your upcoming stop. Follow these steps:

1. **Tap Weather on the Home screen.**

2. **Tap the Information button in the bottom right corner.**

   The screen as shown in Figure 3-11 opens.

3. **Tap the F or C button at the bottom of the page if you want to switch between Fahrenheit and Celsius temperature readings.**

4. **Tap the plus sign in the upper left corner.**

5. **A screen opens with a search field and keyboard.**

6. **Type in the name or ZIP code of the city you want to add.**

   A list opens with possible matches.

Figure 3-11: Add, delete, and reorder the cities you want Weather forecasts for.

7. **Tap the name of the city you want to add.**

   The city now appears in your list.

To delete a city from your list:

1. **Tap Weather on the Home screen.**

2. **Tap the Information button in the bottom right corner.**

3. **Tap the minus sign to the left of the name.**

   A Delete button appears to the right of the name.

4. **Tap the Delete button.**

   The city disappears from the list.

   If you tapped the minus sign by mistake, tap it again to cancel.

5. **Tap the Done button in the upper right corner.**

   The weather screen returns.

You can also determine the order you want to view the forecasts for each city. For example, you want to put the cities in the order that you'll be visiting them on your multi-city book tour. Touch and hold the reorder button, and then drag the city to the position on the list. Drag the names of the cities around until they are in the order you like.

Viewing current and upcoming conditions

After you've added and organized the cities and tapped Done, the weather screen returns, as shown in Figure 3-12. Each city on your list has its own weather forecast screen.

Flick left or right to move between screens. The white dots at the bottom of the screen tell you how many cities you have forecasts for. The background is blue when it's daytime in that city and black when it's nighttime. The current temperature is the biggest number at the top of the page; then you see a six-day forecast with the weather symbols we're used to: sunny, partly sunny, cloudy, thunderstorms, and so on.

If you want more information, tap the Yahoo! button in the bottom left corner. This opens the Yahoo weather page in Safari and gives you more detailed weather information such as humidity, wind, and sunrise and sunset times along with links to websites with news and other information about that city.

**Book IV
Chapter 3**

Tapping into Maps, Compass, Weather, Calculator, and Stocks

Figure 3-12: Weather gives you the current temperature and a six-day forecast.

Doing the Math with Calculator

The Calculator app on your iPhone is really two calculators: a basic four-function calculator that you use for addition, subtraction, multiplication, and division, and a scientific calculator that is capable of performing trigonometric calculations, expressions, square roots, and percentages.

Doing basic addition, subtraction, multiplication, and division

Even if you remember your times tables, there are times when you reach for a calculator and you don't have to reach any farther than your iPhone. The basic four-function calculator opens when you tap Calculator. Follow these steps:

1. **Tap Calculator on the Home screen or you might find it in the Utilities folder on the Home screen.**

   The Calculator opens as shown in Figure 3-13.

2. Tap the numbers and operations you want to perform.

A white outline appears around the operation key you tap to remind you which operation is active.

Figure 3-13: The four-function Calculator adds, subtracts, multiplies, and divides.

You can copy and paste numbers from the Calculator results display to another app by pressing and holding on the display until the Copy/Paste button appears. You can also paste a number from another app into the calculator display to use it in a calculation. See Book I, Chapter 3 to learn about editing functions and commands.

The four buttons just below the display are for memory commands:

- **mc** clears any numbers you have in memory.

- **m+** adds the number on the display to the number in memory.

- **m-** subtracts the number on the display from the number in memory.

- **mr (memory replace)** uses the number you put in memory in your current calculation. The button is outlined in white when a number is stored.

Switching to a scientific view

Most cell phones have calculators today, but iPhone offers a full-function scientific calculator too. To open the scientific calculator, turn your iPhone to landscape view, as seen in Figure 3-14. (If you have locked your iPhone in Portrait view, this won't work until you unlock it: double-tap the Home button and swipe right to find the Orientation Lock button.)

You may not need the trigonometric and parenthetical expression functions; however, the percentage function, which can quickly calculate discounts and markups, is useful even for non-astrophysicists.

If you have two vendors vying for your business and Vendor A offers a 3.475 percent discount over Vendor B's offer, you can quickly determine how much that percentage means in dollar and cents savings.

Type in the total amount and then the minus sign, followed by the amount of the percentage off and the percent sign. A quick press of the equals sign, and you have the final, discounted price: for example, 45000 — 3.475% = 43,436.25.

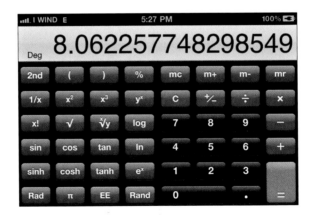

Figure 3-14: Turning your iPhone to landscape view opens the Scientific calculator.

Tracking Investments with Stocks

Whether you have a single mutual fund or a sizeable portfolio managed by a financial advisor, keeping an eye on your investments is usually a good idea. And that's exactly the idea behind iPhone's Stocks app, a simple yet powerful tool you can tap into to display and track activity for the stocks and funds you're interested in for the time interval you want. First we show you how to add the companies you want to watch and put them in an order that you like. Next, we show you how to manage the viewing options Stocks offers.

Adding, deleting, and reordering stocks, funds, and indexes

Stocks comes with the U.S. (Dow Jones, NASDAQ, S&P 500) and foreign (FTSE/UK, DAX/German, HSI/Hong Kong, N225/Japan) index listings along with Apple, Google, and Yahoo! share activity already specified, as seen in Figure 3-15.

Figure 3-15: Stocks shows market activity for U.S. and foreign indexes as well as individual corporate share prices.

The first thing you want to do is add your personal stock or fund holdings or those that you're interested in watching for potential investments and delete any loaded ones that don't interest you. Here are the steps to follow:

1. **Tap Stocks on the Home screen.**
2. **Tap the Information button in the bottom right corner.**

   The Stocks screen opens.
3. **Tap the plus sign button in the upper left corner.**

   A search field opens with a keyboard.
4. **Type a company name or a stock identification code.**

   Stocks searches and a list of possible matches appears.
5. **Tap the stock you wish to add to your list.**

   The screen returns to the list. The stock or fund you chose is added to the bottom of the list.
6. **Tap the Done button in the upper right corner.**

   The current price screen returns.

To delete a stock or index from your list:

1. **Tap Stocks on the Home screen.**
2. **Tap the Information button in the bottom right corner.**
3. **Tap the minus sign to the left of the name.**

   A delete button appears to the right of the name.
4. **Tap the Delete button.**

   The stock or index disappears from the list.

   If you tapped the minus sign by mistake, tap it again to cancel.
5. **Tap the Done button in the upper right corner.**

   The current price screen returns.

You can arrange the stocks and indices in any order you want, such as putting those you're most interested in at the top.

Touch and hold the reorder button, and then drag the stock to the position on the list. Drag the names of the stocks around until they are in the order you like.

The three buttons at the bottom of the Stocks information page let you choose how you view market fluctuations: by percentage changes, by price changes, or by market capitalization.

The market fluctuations appear on a green background if there's been a price increase and on red if there's been a decrease. The information lags about 20 minutes behind actual market activity.

Scrolling through views and news

After you establish the stocks and indices you want to follow, you may want to look at some historic data or see what the press has said about that company today.

Referring to Figure 3-15, the screen is divided into two zones: The top holds the list of stocks and indices you follow (six appear at a time, but you can scroll to see the other companies on your list). Below that, you see Apple's activity that day.

The lower zone shows information about whichever stock or index you select from the upper zone. This zone scrolls left to right. After the price activity section, there's a graph that shows historic activity from one day up to two years. Scroll to the next screen to see a vertically scrollable list of news stories related to the stock or index highlighted in the upper zone. That's one information-packed screen!

Monitoring investment performance over time

But wait, there's more. Go back to the graph that shows historic activity. There are seven time intervals at the top. Tap any of those intervals and the graph expands or contracts to show price fluctuations from today back to the date that corresponds with the interval you chose.

To display a more detailed view, turn your iPhone to landscape view, as in Figure 3-16. The graph for the interval you were viewing in portrait view appears with the greater detail that increased landscape size allows. This screen is interactive. For example, if you choose the one week view, touch on a day and a yellow vertical line shows the price for the day you are on.

Touch and drag the yellow line left and right and you see price fluctuations at intervals throughout the day. If you knew an announcement was made at a certain time on a certain day, you could see how soon after the announcement a change in the share price appeared. In the three month, six month, and one year views, the detail gives the daily closing price; in the two year view, the daily closing price is given for every other day.

Touch and hold on the screen to bring up the yellow line, and then drag left and right to see the price for different days. If you put two fingers on the screen at once, two vertical, yellow lines bracket a time interval and the share price change in that period is shown.

Move your fingers in and out to shorten and lengthen the time interval. In landscape view, when you flick from left to right, you see the graph for the same interval for each of the stocks and indexes on your personalized list.

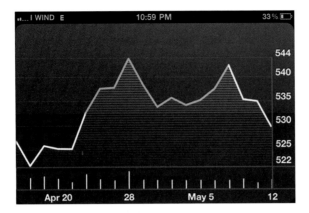

Figure 3-16: Turn Stocks to landscape view and the share price fluctuation graph becomes interactive.

Chapter 4: Creating and Sharing Notes and Voice Memos

In This Chapter

✏ Creating, viewing, managing, and sharing notes

✏ Adjusting Notes settings

✏ Syncing existing Notes with iTunes and e-mail accounts

✏ Recording, playing, and managing and sharing voice memos

✏ Syncing Voice Memos with iTunes

*A*re you the note-taking type who goes through little yellow sticky notes faster that a chimp in a peanut factory? Do ideas pop into your head that you don't remember later because those sticky notes and a pen aren't within reach? And even if they were close at hand, you wouldn't be able to use them anyway because you're doing something like driving or working out?

If you answered yes to any or all of those questions, you're in good company. This chapter is all about using two of your iPhone's most useful apps — Notes and Voice Memos. Using this dynamic duo, you can capture your every thought on the fly, as neatly typed out notes, or as recorded audio files captured using your iPhone's built-in mic (or your stereo headphone's mic) that you can listen to later.

In this chapter, we talk about syncing your notes and voice recordings with your computer using iCloud or iTunes, and we describe which computer programs you can use to access and edit those notes or voice recordings.

Taking Note of Notes

Notes is a super-simple app you can use to keep track of lists, ideas, and any other kind of note you'd normally scribble down on a sticky pad or cocktail napkin. Notes you create are stored on your iPhone and, optionally, synced with any e-mail accounts you have set up on your iPhone.

To get started, tap the Notes app icon on the Home screen to launch Notes. The main Notes screen shows a list of any notes already saved in Notes, as shown in Figure 4-1.

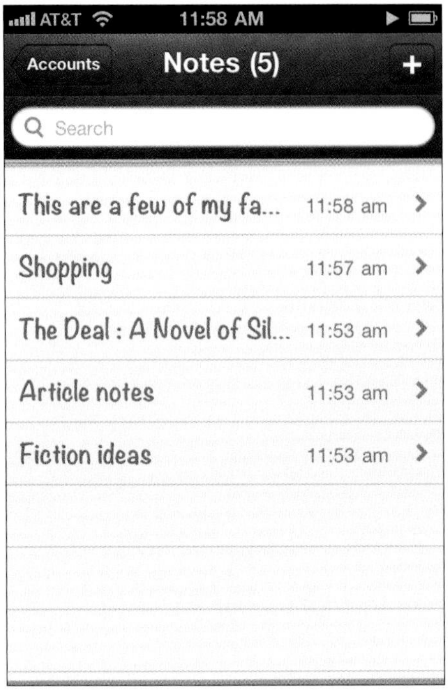

AT&T 🔋   11:58 AM   ▶ 📶

| Accounts | **Notes (5)** | ＋ |

🔍 Search

This are a few of my fa...   11:58 am   ❯

Shopping   11:57 am   ❯

The Deal : A Novel of Sil...   11:53 am   ❯

Article notes   11:53 am   ❯

Fiction ideas   11:53 am   ❯

Figure 4-1: A list of notes you have saved in the Notes app.

You may see one or more notes listed even if you hadn't previously created notes using the Notes app. That's because Notes displays any notes that are copied to your iPhone when you sync your iPhone with iTunes (if you have that option turned on). Notes can also come from any e-mail accounts set up on your iPhone if you've turned on the Notes option in those e-mail accounts' settings. When the Notes option is turned on, you see an Accounts button appear in the upper left corner of the Notes window. We write about syncing Notes and e-mail accounts in the section "Evaluating Your Note Sync Options" later in this chapter.

Creating a new note

Tap the plus sign (+) button to create a new note. The keyboard appears, ready to capture your brilliant thoughts, as shown in Figure 4-2.

Figure 4-2: Typing with a narrow focus, or a wider point of view.

Turning your iPhone sideways displays the landscape mode keyboard, which can help increase your typing speed and accuracy. If the wider keyboard doesn't appear when you turn your iPhone sideways, double-click the Home button and flick the bottom of the screen to the right, and then tap the orientation lock button to unlock the orientation lock feature.

Tap Done to save your note and hide the keyboard.

Tap Notes to return to the notes list.

You can tap the dictation key and dictate your notes instead of typing, if you have an iPhone 4S with Siri turned on.

Searching and managing your Notes list

Notes are listed in chronological order, with the newest (or most recently edited) note appearing at the top of the list, and the least recently modified note relegated to the bottom of the list. Notes titles are automatically generated based on the first 30 characters of each note's first line; if you enter a return in the first line, only the word (or words) before the return appear in the title.

When viewing the Notes list, you can do the following:

✔ Swipe left or right across a note title to display the Delete button, and then tap Delete to delete the note.

✔ Tap Accounts, (refer to Figure 4-1), to display any of your e-mail accounts for which you turned on the Notes sync setting in Settings⇨ Mail, Contacts, Calendars. When viewing the Accounts list, as shown in Figure 4-3 you can do the following:

• Tap All Notes to display a list of all of your notes saved and synced with all of your e-mail accounts.

• Tap an e-mail account name to display only the notes stored and synced with that specific e-mail account.

• Tap the plus sign (+) to create a new note that will be saved in your default e-mail account's Notes data when you press Done to save the note.

✔ Tap plus sign (+) to create a new note.

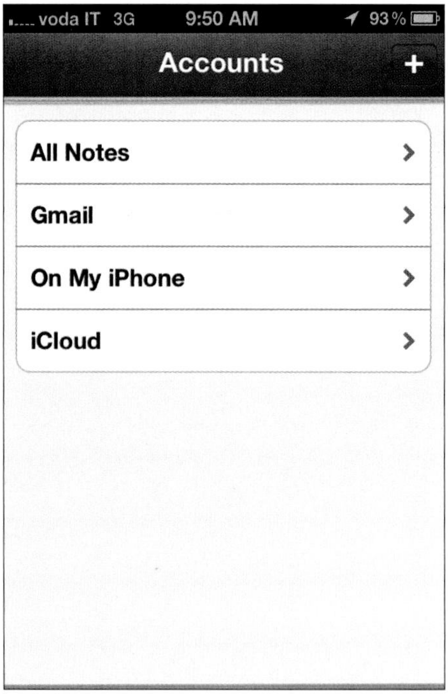

Figure 4-3: Accounts displays e-mail accounts for which you have Notes turned on.

✔ Tap a note to view the note or do other things with the note.

✔ Tap the status bar at the top of iPhone's screen or drag your finger down the list to reveal the Search field (as shown in Figure 4-4), and then type in the first few characters of whatever you're looking for to display the titles of any notes matching your search criteria; tap the note title to view that note.

If you have selected Notes in Settings➪General➪Spotlight Search, any searches you perform from the Spotlight Search Home screen will search in Notes too. (Refer to Figure 4-4.)

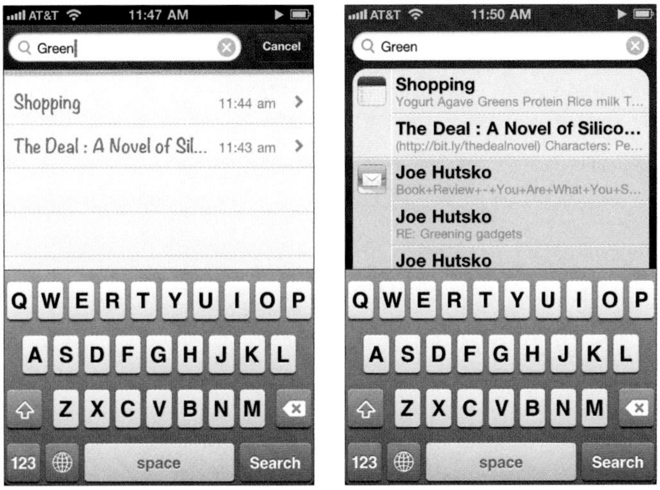

Figure 4-4: Tap the status bar to reveal the Search field.

Browsing, editing, deleting, and e-mailing Notes

Notes you create can contain regular and accented letters, numbers, and symbols (in other words, any of the alphanumerical stuff you can type with the keyboard), but not pictures, audio clips, videos, or other non-alphanumeric information.

When viewing a note, as shown in Figure 4-5, you can do the following:

✔ To add more text or edit a note, tap where you want to begin typing or editing, and then type or edit to your heart's content. (See Book I, Chapter 3 for editing tips.)

**Book IV
Chapter 4**

Creating and
Sharing Notes and
Voice Memos

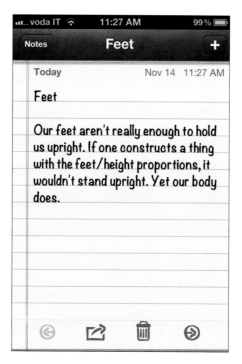

Figure 4-5: Edit, print, e-mail, or delete your note.

✔ Shake your iPhone when the keyboard is displayed to display the Undo Typing message; tap Undo to, well, undo what you just did. Shake again to display the Redo Typing option and tap Redo to redo what you undid.

✔ Tap the left and right arrow buttons to flip to the previous or next note.

✔ Tap the trash button to delete your note.

✔ Tap the action button to print your note or create an e-mail message containing the contents of your note, as shown in Figure 4-6, and then

   • Begin typing the name of the person you want to send the note to; a list of suggested recipients saved in Contacts appears. Tap the one you want to select, or continue typing in the intended recipient's e-mail address if it isn't one you have saved in Contacts.

   • Add any additional recipients to the To: or Cc/Bcc fields if you want to send your note to more than one person.

   If you've set up more than one e-mail account on your iPhone, tap the Cc/Bcc: to display the hidden From: field. Tap the From: field to display a list of all your e-mail accounts, and then tap the one you want to use to send your message.

- Edit or add any additional text to the Subject field and/or in the body of the e-mail message if you want.

- Tap Send to send your e-mail message.

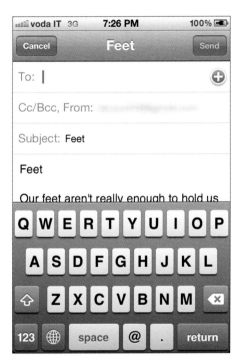

Figure 4-6: E-mail the contents of your note.

Changing the Notes font

To change the Notes font, tap Settings (from the Home screen), and then tap Notes to display your font choices (three at the time of this writing), as shown in Figure 4-7. Tap the choice you like the most.

If the Default Account option appears beneath the Font list, that means at least two (or more) of your e-mail accounts are already configured to sync with Notes. Tap Default Account to display those e-mail accounts, then choose the account you want Notes to use to sync new notes you create.

You won't see the Default Account option if none or only one of your e-mail accounts is configured to sync with Notes.

We write about syncing your notes with your e-mail accounts, and with e-mail programs on your computer, in the next section.

**Book IV
Chapter 4**

**Creating and
Sharing Notes and
Voice Memos**

Evaluating your Notes sync options

Notes you choose to sync with your e-mail accounts appear on both your iPhone and on your computer's e-mail program (Mail, Outlook, Google Mail, or Yahoo!).

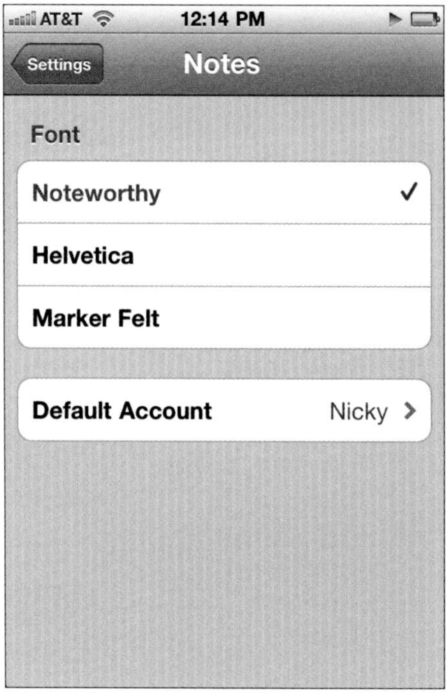

Figure 4-7: Choose a Notes font that's more your type.

You can sync your iPhone's notes a few different ways, and understanding these different ways can help you choose the best method for you.

The three ways you can sync Notes include

- Using iCloud to sync Notes to all your devices including your iPhone, your computer, and any other iOS 5 devices like iPad or iPod touch. Go to Settings➪iCloud and tap the switch by Notes to On.

✔ Using iTunes to shuttle notes back and forth between your computer's e-mail program, which you activate by checking the Sync Notes With option in the Info pane of iTunes, as shown in Figure 4-8. On Macs, notes appear under the Reminders heading in the left column of the Mail program that comes with every Mac. On Windows PCs, notes appear in the Notes section of Microsoft Outlook.

We write about using iCloud or iTunes to sync your Notes and other information in Book II, Chapter 1.

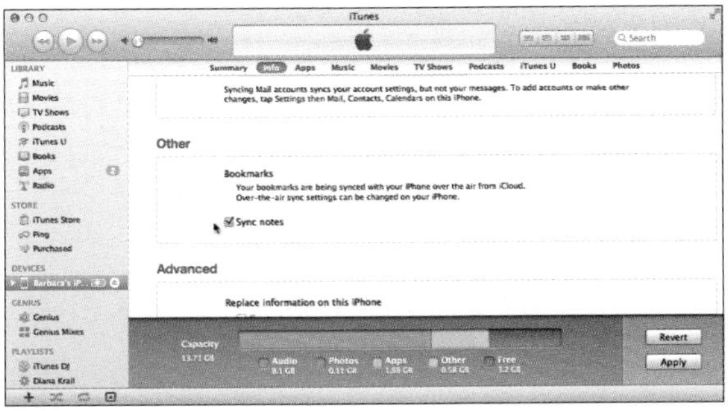

Figure 4-8: Sync iPhone notes with your Windows or Mac using iTunes.

✔ Syncing Notes with your e-mail accounts. Go to Settings⟹Mail, Contacts, Calendars, and then tap the account you want to sync Notes with. Tap the switch next to Notes ON (see Figure 4-9) to automatically sync your notes over-the-air. AOL, Gmail, Yahoo!, and Hotmail e-mail accounts all offer the option to turn on the Note sync option, but syncing with any of them is a one-way way affair. When you log in to each respective e-mail service's website, you see notes you created on your iPhone; however, notes you create on those websites don't get synced back to your iPhone. We write about configuring e-mail accounts in Book III, Chapter 4.

TIP

If you take taking, juggling, and syncing notes as seriously as we do, your best option may be to skip iPhone's Notes app altogether and use a more powerful notes app for iPhone like Evernote. For a look at other notable note-taking apps, check out the online bonus content, Bonus Chapter 1.

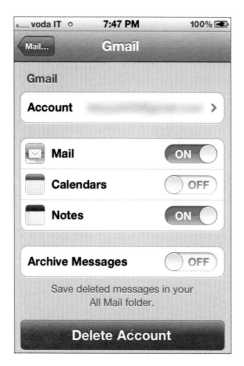

Figure 4-9: Notes can sync with your iPhone's e-mail accounts.

Speaking of Voice Memos

Once upon a time, people carried portable cassette tape recorders to capture the spoken word and other audible stuff like interviews, live music events, and baby's first words ("Mama?" "Dada?" "iPhone?"). Thanks to iPhone's Voice Memos app, you can quickly and easily record, listen to, edit, and share those kinds of out-loud sounds without the hassle of juggling clunky cassette tapes.

And so, as a big believer in the adage "actions speak louder than words," rather than listening to more introductory words by yours truly, why don't you act on recording and listening to *your* spoken words and other sounds with Voice Memos?

Speaking of your first action: Tap Voice Memos on the Home screen (it may be in the Utilities folder) to launch the app, as shown in Figure 4-10.

Figure 4-10: Step up to the mic.

Recording voice memos

Although that big silver thing that takes over most of the main Voice Memos screen *looks* like a mic, it doesn't actually record your voice or other sounds.

That function is handled by your iPhone's built-in mic, or by the mic built into the stereo headphones that came with your iPhone if you have those plugged in.

Other mic-enabled options for recording audio with Voice Memos include external mics designed to plug into your iPhone's headset jack or Dock Connector, and wireless Bluetooth headsets and headphones that let you cut the proverbial cord altogether (thus freeing your hands for flailing, gesticulating, or whatever).

At bottom center of the Voice Memos screen is the sound level meter; the needle twitches in response to any sounds the mic picks up, whether you're actually recording those sounds. (Go on, don't be shy, say "hello" or "testing one, two, three" to your iPhone right now to see the meter in action.)

**Book IV
Chapter 4**

Creating and
Sharing Notes and
Voice Memos

For optimal recording quality, Apple recommends a recording level between the -3 and 0-decibels (dBs) zone. Translation: As you're speaking, move your iPhone (or headphone mic) closer or farther from your mouth, or lower or raise your voice, or use a combination of both, to try to keep the recording level meter needle in or as close to that optimal-quality sweet spot between the black 3 and the red 0.

On the meter's left is the record button, and on the right, the voice memos list button. Both buttons change to other buttons when you begin recording, as you will see in the next breath.

To record, pause, continue, and stop recording a voice memo:

✔ Tap the record button to begin recording your voice memo.

When you begin recording, four things happen at once to let you know your live recording session is underway: A single-chime sound plays, the record button changes to a pause button, the voice memos list button changes to a stop button, and a pulsing red banner with a recording length timer appears at the top of the screen, as shown in Figure 4-11.

Figure 4-11: Live, from New York! (Or wherever are!)

TIP

If you go to the Home screen, or switch to another app, or lock your iPhone while you're recording a voice memo (or you pause a memo you're recording), the red banner stays stuck at the top of the screen so you don't forget about your recording, as shown in Figure 4-12. Tap the red banner to return to Voice Memos.

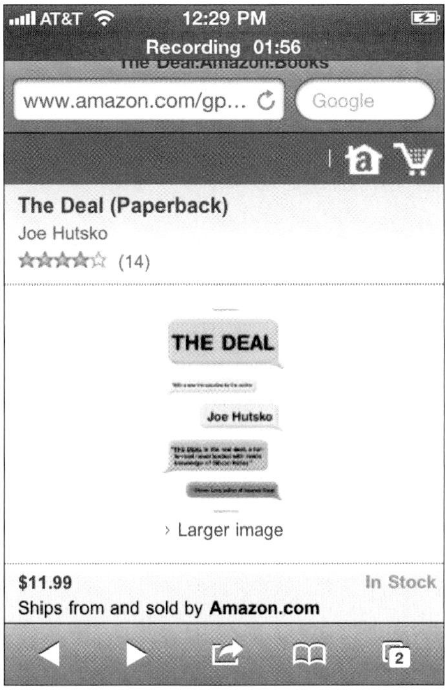

Figure 4-12: Voice Memos can keep recording even if you switch apps or lock your iPhone.

To stop or pause recording, do one of the following:

- Tap the stop button to stop recording.

    A double-chime sound plays, the left and right buttons return to their original functions, and the red banner and recording length timer disappear.

- Tap the pause button to pause recording.

    The red banner stops pulsing and the recording length timer freezes in time, the left button changes to the record button, and the right button changes to the memo list button.

✔ To resume or stop a paused recording, do one of the following:

• Tap record to resume recording your voice memo.

Recording resumes, as in the very first bullet of this section; you can repeat this process of pausing and resuming your recording as many times as you want until you decide to tap stop to end your recording session.

• Tap the voice memos list button to stop recording your voice memo.

A double-chime sound plays, and then the voice memos list appears and your newly recorded voice memo begins playing — and what lucky timing, at that. The voice memos list is what we tell you about in the next section.

TECHNICAL STUFF

You *shouldn't* hear the chime and double-chime sound effects that play when you start and stop recording a memo if iPhone's ring/silent switch is switched to silent mode. We say *shouldn't* because in some countries or regions, the recording sound effects play even when the ring/silent switch is set to silent. Our guesstimate as to why those sound effects may still be heard even when iPhone is set to be quiet? To offer some kind of audible warning to anyone within earshot that you may be recording anything they say. (However, whether anything hypothetical persons may say can or will be held against them in a court of law, is not for me to say. We can only speculate.)

Listening to voice memos

The voice memo list displays your voice memos in chronological order, from newest to oldest, as shown in Figure 4-13.

TIP

To access the voice memo list from the main Voice Memos screen, tap the voice memo list button (refer to Figure 4-10). To return to the main Voice Memos screen, tap the Done button.

Voice memos are automatically titled with the time the voice memo was recorded. Beneath the title, you'll see the voice memo's recording date, and the recording length number to the right is the voice memo's length.

The > button to the far right takes you to Info screen, which displays additional information about the voice memo, and options to do other things with the voice memo, which we tell you about in the next section. Ditto for the Share button at the bottom of the screen memo list screen.

To listen to, pause, and control play of a voice memo:

✔ Tap a voice memo in the list to select the voice memo, and then tap the Play button that appears to the left of the voice memo's title.

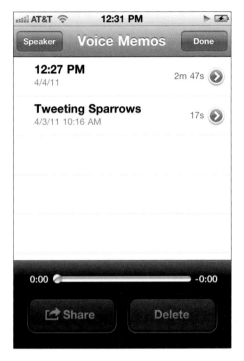

Figure 4-13: The voice memos list.

As your voice memo begins playing, the scrubber bar with a scrolling playhead button appears, and the play button turns into a pause button.

✔ Tap the Pause button to pause listening to your voice memo, as shown in Figure 4-14, and then press Play to resume.

✔ Drag the playhead left or right in the scrubber bar while the voice memo is playing or paused to move backward or forward.

✔ Tap the Speaker button if you want to hear your voice memos out loud through your iPhone's built-in speaker. (By default, your voice memos play through your iPhone's receiver speaker, or through your headphones, if you have those plugged in.)

✔ To select another voice memo, tap the one you want to listen to, and then use the play, pause, and scrubber playhead button as previously described to listen to your selected voice memo.

To delete a voice memo:

1. Tap a voice memo to select it, and then tap the Delete button.

**Book IV
Chapter 4**

Creating and
Sharing Notes and
Voice Memos

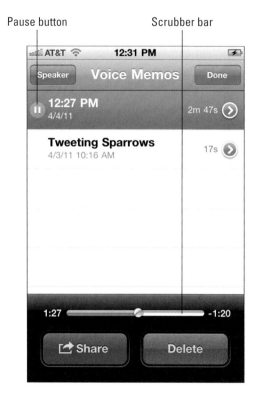

Pause button   Scrubber bar

Figure 4-14: Pausing a voice memo.

The Delete Voice Memo and Cancel buttons shown in Figure 4-15 appear, giving you a moment to consider whether you really want to delete your selected voice memo.

2. **Tap Delete Voice Memo to say goodbye to your selected voice memo, or tap Cancel if you've had a sudden change of heart and you want to keep your voice memo.**

Deleting a voice memo instantly erases the voice memo from your iPhone. But that doesn't necessarily mean the voice memo is gone forever — if you've turned on the voice memos sync option in iTunes, which copies all of your recorded voice memos to your computer's iTunes library and stores them there even if you later decide to delete those synced voice memos from your iPhone. Of course, voice memos you record and then delete before syncing with iTunes are gone forever. We tell you how to sync your voice memos with iTunes later in this chapter.

Figure 4-15: To delete or not to delete? That is the question.

Naming, trimming, and sharing voice memos

The > button accompanying each voice memo in the voice memos list is your gateway to the Info screen.

Tap the > button on a voice memo in the voice memo list to display the Info screen for your selected voice memo, as shown in Figure 4-16.

To close the Info screen and return to the voice memos list, tap the Voice Memos button.

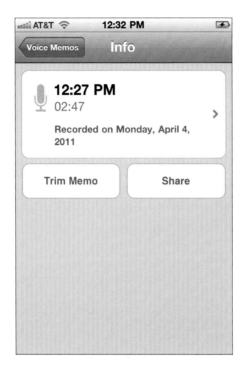

Figure 4-16: The Info screen lets you do more with your voice memos.

The Info displays the full date you recorded your voice memo, and buttons you can tap to do the following things with your selected voice memo:

- Tap the big wide button surrounding your voice memo's name to display a list of ready-made labels, and then tap the label that best describes your voice memo, as shown in Figure 4-17. To create a label of your own, tap Custom, type a descriptive name for your voice memo like "Lovely Linda Interview" or "Tweeting Sparrows," and then tap the Label button to save your custom label name. Tap Info to return to the Info screen.

- Tap Trim Memo to display the trim tool, and then drag the left or right edge of the guide toward the center to set the length you want to trim from either (or both) end, as shown in Figure 4-18. Tap the tiny play button to the left of the trim tool to hear a preview of your selection, and then make any necessary adjustments to your selection. When you're pleased with your cutting work, tap Trim Voice Memo button to save your edited selection (or tap Cancel if you change your mind and you don't want to trim your voice memo after all).

Figure 4-17: Assigning a descriptive label to a voice memo.

Figure 4-18: Trimming a voice memo down in size.

✔ Tap Share, and then tap Email or Message to choose your preferred method of delivery. A new e-mail or MMS or iMessage containing an audio file icon of your voice message appears in the body of your new e-mail or MMS or iMessage, as shown in Figure 4-19.

If a message saying your voice memo file is too large to send appears, you need to trim your voice memo using the trim tool (see the previous bullet) before you can try sending your message again.

Fill in the To: field with the name of the person (or persons) you want to send your voice memo to. You can type a greeting or other text in the body of your message if you want, and if you're sending your voice memo as an e-mail, feel free to type a description in the Subject: line. (If you chose to send an MMS or iMessage, the camera icon is grayed out because you can't include a picture with your voice memo in the same message.) Tap Send to send your voice memo message.

Selecting a voice memo and then tapping the Share button on the voice memos list screen takes you to the same options we describe previously for sending your voice memo as an e-mail or MMS or iMessage.

Figure 4-19: Send your voice memo in an e-mail or MMS message.

Syncing voice memos with iTunes

Capturing voice memos on the fly is handy for remembering things you don't want to forget. After you've dealt with whatever your voice memos remind you to do, you can then delete those voice memos from your iPhone.

Other voice memos, like a gang of friends and family singing "Happy Birthday" at your mom's 80th, or an interview with a fast-talking politician you recorded for an article you're writing, may be ones you want to (or must) keep for personal or professional reasons.

But you probably don't need to keep those kinds of audio files on your iPhone, where they consume storage space you'd rather free up to store other stuff like every song ever sung by your favorite musical artist (or perhaps voice memos of *you* singing every song ever sung by said favorite artist).

The solution? Sync any voice memos you want to keep with iTunes on your computer, and those voice memos remain safe and sound, so to speak, until you want (or need) to hear them anew.

Because we give you the full lowdown on how to pick and choose the kinds of information and files (including voice memos) you want to sync between your iPhone and your computer using iTunes in Book II, Chapter I, we won't repeat ourselves here. Not completely, anyway. We would be remiss if we didn't take a moment to at least mention a few points worth knowing about when you're thinking about syncing your voice memos with iTunes, including

- ✎ iTunes automatically creates a playlist named (drum roll, please . . .) Voice Memos on your computer, and that's where you can track down new, not so new, and downright ancient voice memos you recorded and synced with iTunes syncs.

- ✎ Voice memos you delete from your iPhone remain safely backed up in your iTunes library.

- ✎ If you delete a voice memo from iTunes that you have saved on your iPhone as well, that voice memo is deleted from your iPhone the next time you sync with iTunes.

- ✎ You can sync the iTunes Voice Memos playlist to the Music app on iPhone using the Music pane in iTunes.

- ✎ To copy a voice memo from iTunes that you previously deleted from your iPhone, connect your iPhone, launch iTunes on your computer, click the Voice Memos to view your saved voice memos, and then drag and drop the voice memo (or memos) you want to your iPhone, as shown in Figure 4-20. iTunes copies your chosen voice memo (or memos) to iPhone's Voice Memos, ready for you to play again, Sam (or Sally, Dick, or Jane).

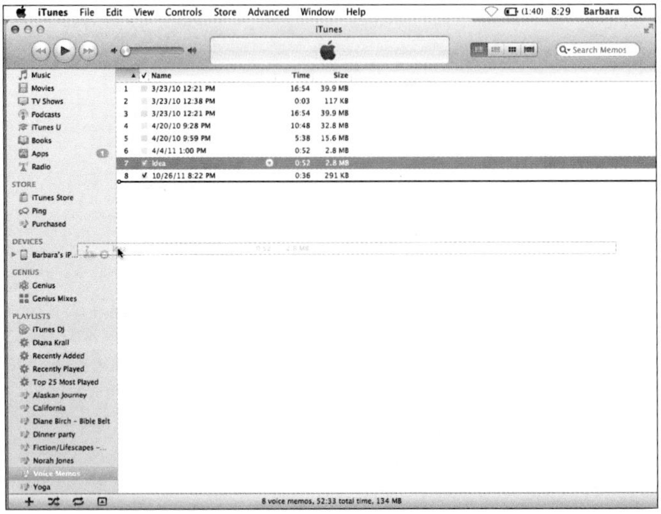

Figure 4-20: Drag and drop your way to voice memo restoration.

Book V

Letting iPhone Entertain You: Photos, Video, Music, and More

The 5th Wave   By Rich Tennant

"In fact it does come with a compass."

When it comes to photos, music, and videos, your iPhone is a hands-down winner. This minibook is chock full of how-tos for capturing, viewing, listening, and sharing media. Chapter 1 focuses on using the front and back cameras for taking still photos and videos. We give you tips for using the flash and digital zoom and explain the iPhone's photo and video editing options. Chapters 2 and 3 are all about music and audio. Chapter 2 takes you through the iTunes Store, where you can shop for music, movies, audiobooks, podcasts, and more. In Chapter 3, we present your iPhone as an iPod — using your iPhone to listen to and manage your music and audio collection. We move through video and YouTube in the last chapter, explaining how to watch videos from both the iTunes Store and YouTube on your iPhone.

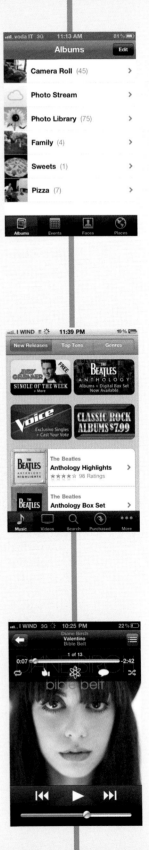

Chapter 1: Capturing and Sharing Photos and Videos with Camera

In This Chapter

✔ Snapping a picture with Camera

✔ Focusing, flashing, and zooming

✔ Turning the lens on yourself

✔ Recording a video with Camera

✔ Editing photos and trimming videos

✔ Viewing and sharing photos and videos

The Camera app on your iPhone is really three digital cameras in one: an 8 megapixel still camera (iPhone 4S; 5 megapixel on iPhone 4) and a high definition video camera, both with LED flash, on the back of your iPhone; a 640X480 pixel still and video camera on the front of your iPhone so you can take self-portraits and use FaceTime, your iPhone's video chat app. All three work in both portrait and landscape position.

In this chapter, we explain how to use all three cameras. We talk about focusing, using the flash, and zooming in on your subject. After you capture photos and videos, you probably want to edit them, so we show you how to enhance the photo quality, crop photos, trim videos, and cure that terrible red-eye disease. At the end of the chapter, we give you all your options for sharing your photos and videos via e-mail, text messages, Twitter, YouTube, and good old-fashioned slideshows and printing.

Camera Features and Controls

The first time you open Camera, a message appears asking if Camera can use your location. Tapping OK lets Camera geotag your location. A geotag uses GPS (Global Positioning System), Wi-Fi, and cellular access to add the longitude and latitude of the location of the photos and videos you shoot. (In some situations, say, if you're standing in a lead-walled bunker, your iPhone may not be able to activate geotagging.) Like the date and time, a geotag is a piece of information about your photo that's kept in the metadata; that is, data you don't see that describes your data. You can then sort and search for photos based on the location — more about that later in this chapter.

If at some point you want to turn geotagging off, tap Home⇨Settings⇨ Location Services. You can turn Location Services off completely or turn Location Services off for specific apps, such as Camera.

Previewing through the viewfinder

We think the easiest way to learn about taking photos and videos with your iPhone is to snap a few shots or capture a few minutes of video. First, we show you the three simple steps for taking a photo, and then we explain the basics of capturing video. Because the tools are the same for both photos and videos, we go through the options that help perfect your photo and video skills.

The two basic "parts" of any camera that you need to know are the view-finder and the shutter button. Unlike traditional cameras where you close one eye and put your open eye up to the viewfinder to see and frame your subject, your iPhone — like most new digital cameras — doesn't have a viewfinder. Instead, you point your iPhone at your subject and then look at the screen to see how it will be framed.

As for the shutter button, your iPhone actually has two:

- ✔ **Camera button:** Tap the button on the bottom of the screen in the center to snap a photo. The button is a red circle when you switch to video mode.

- ✔ **Volume Up button:** Press the volume up button on the left side of your iPhone to snap a photo or to start and stop video recording.

If your iPhone is locked, double-click the Home button. A Camera button appears to the right of the Slide to Unlock slider bar, as shown in Figure 1-1. Tap the Camera button to open the Camera app, and then take photos or video as explained next.

Taking photos with the back camera

Here's how to take a photo with the back camera:

Figure 1-1: When your iPhone is locked, double-tapping the Home button brings up a Camera button by the unlock slider.

1. **Tap Camera on the Home Screen or, if your iPhone is locked, double-click the Home button and then tap the Camera button.**

   A shutter opens, revealing a screen as shown in Figure 1-2.

2. **Point your iPhone at whatever you want to photograph.**

3. **Tap the Camera button or press the Volume Up button.**

   A clicking noise lets you know the photo was taken. You can mute the shutter sound by moving the ring/silent switch to silent.

   If you have a hard time holding the phone still, you can press on the shutter button, steady the camera, and then remove your finger.

4. **A thumbnail image of the photo you took appears in the lower left corner (in landscape mode, the lower right or upper left corner depending on which direction you rotate your phone).**

LED flash   Switch point of view

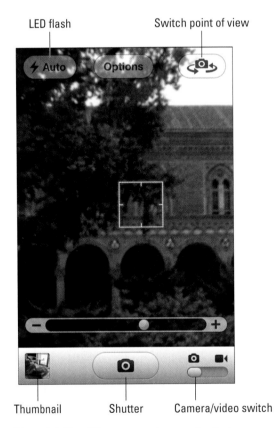

Thumbnail   Shutter   Camera/video switch

Figure 1-2: Your iPhone screen is your viewfinder.
The buttons on the bottom shift to the right side
in landscape view.

Shooting video with the back camera

iPhone 4S shoots video in high definition, up to 1920x1080 pixels (iPhone 4 shoots Hd up to 1280x720 pixels) and 30 frames-per-second. This means you can make smooth, clear full-motion videos. Each video can be up to an hour long, although one minute of video takes about 80 MB of memory or close to 5 GB for an hour of video.

To capture video:

1. **Tap Camera on the Home Screen or, if your iPhone is locked, double-click the Home button and then tap the Camera button.**

2. **Tap under the video icon of the Camera/Video Switch to move the button to Video.**

   The "shutter" has to open before you can flick the switch.

3. **Point your iPhone at the action you want to capture.**

4. **Tap the Video button, which is the red dot in place of the Camera button, or press the Volume Up button.**

   The button blinks while the video is recording.

5. **Tap the Video button or press the Volume Up button to stop recording.**

   You can also press the center button on iPhone's earphones to start or stop recording.

6. **A thumbnail of your video's keyframe appears in the lower left corner in portrait orientation. In landscape, it will be at the upper left if the volume buttons are on top, or the lower right if they're on the bottom.**

Turning the lens on yourself

The Switch Camera button in the upper right corner of the screen switches the active objective from the back of your iPhone to the front so you see yourself on the screen. The front camera has lower resolution, no flash or zoom, but it can take advantage of the Backside Illumination Sensor and takes both still photos and video. It's handy for self-portraits (or if you find yourself without a mirror and some lettuce in your teeth) and FaceTime.

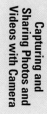

The Backside Illumination Sensor perceives low light conditions and makes adjustments to compensate. You can tap on areas that are too dark or too bright to adjust the lighting. The sensor corrects the contrast of the image as a whole. Figure 1-3 shows the difference between two photos.

Figure 1-3: The Backside Illumination Sensor perceives areas that are too dark or too light and corrects the contrast.

To use the front camera — that's the one above the screen:

1. **Tap Camera on the Home Screen.**
2. **Tap the Switch button in the upper right corner.**

   You see yourself on the screen.

3. **Use the Camera or Video button to take a photo or shoot video of yourself, as explained in the two previous procedures.**

Setting the exposure and focus

The buttons, as shown in Figure 1-2, appear when you open Camera. Tap the screen if you don't see them. The first thing you want to do is choose where you want Camera to focus its attention. Your iPhone's default autofocus is the center of the image on the screen, where you see the white box.

iPhone 4S uses face detection and focuses on the most prominent face. Face detection balances exposure across up to ten faces. If you want the Camera to focus on a subject that isn't in the center, tap that area on the screen. You see the focus and exposure change to put your chosen subject in the best light. (Unless you want the subject in the center, in which case, move your iPhone until you see the subject in the center of the screen.)

You can change the exposure (that is, the amount of light that is allowed through the lens) and then focus on a different area. Tap and hold on the area on the screen that has the amount of light you want the photo to have. A blue box blinks to indicate that the exposure lock is on and the words "AE/AF Lock" (Auto Exposure/Auto Focus) appear at the bottom of the screen. Move iPhone to the subject you want to photograph, and then tap the Camera button. Tap elsewhere on the screen to unlock the AE/AF Lock.

For example, if you point your iPhone out a sunny window and activate the AE/AF lock, the natural light needs less exposure. Then point your iPhone at a subject indoors, and take the photo. The exposure needed for the natural light is applied to the indoor setting and the photo comes out dark, even if the room seems well-lit.

Lighten up

Your iPhone has an LED light next to the objective lens on the back camera that functions as a flash. You see the flash button at the top left of the screen. Auto is the default position, meaning your iPhone turns the light on if it senses there's not enough light for the photo. Tap the flash button to turn the flash on or off manually, as shown in Figure 1-4.

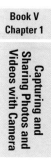

Figure 1-4: Tap the Flash button to show the options: Auto, On, or Off.

Focus, flash, and the Backside Illumination Sensor work in both still photo and video mode.

To zoom or not to zoom

To zoom in on a portion of the subject you want to photograph, use the pinch and spread technique. iPhone's zoom is a digital zoom, which means it zooms by enlarging the image, not by getting closer to the subject. Digital zooming compromises the quality of the final image, so physically moving closer to your subject is by far the better choice. Try taking zoomed and normal photos to see if you can live with the compromise.

Macro mode kicks in automatically when you're about two inches away from the person or object you want to photograph. Tap the object you are focusing on to create a special effect where the main object is crisp and the background is blurry, as shown in Figure 1-5.

Figure 1-5: Camera activates Macro mode when the subject is closer than two inches.

Using Grid

The Grid feature puts a three-by-three grid overlay on your screen, which divides the screen into nine sections. This helps you visualize the distribution of objects in your photo and is useful if you use the photographer's rule of thirds. To activate the grid:

1. **Tap the Options button at the top center of the screen.**

2. **Tap On next to Grid to turn the grid overlay on (see Figure 1-5).**

3. **Tap Done.**

Turning on iPhone's HDR

Digital photography is terrific in bright to shady situations, but in overly bright or very low light conditions, the quality can be poor and result in overexposed or underexposed photos. Tapping the Options button opens the switch to turn iPhone's high dynamic range, or HDR, option on and off. HDR is off by default.

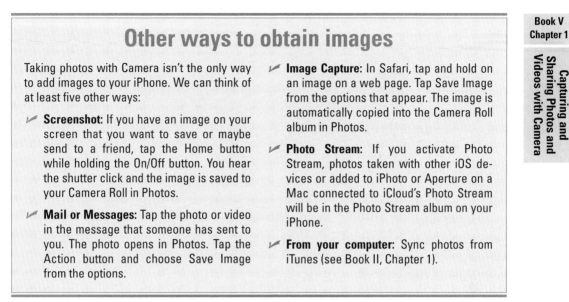

Other ways to obtain images

Taking photos with Camera isn't the only way to add images to your iPhone. We can think of at least five other ways:

✔ **Screenshot:** If you have an image on your screen that you want to save or maybe send to a friend, tap the Home button while holding the On/Off button. You hear the shutter click and the image is saved to your Camera Roll in Photos.

✔ **Mail or Messages:** Tap the photo or video in the message that someone has sent to you. The photo opens in Photos. Tap the Action button and choose Save Image from the options.

✔ **Image Capture:** In Safari, tap and hold on an image on a web page. Tap Save Image from the options that appear. The image is automatically copied into the Camera Roll album in Photos.

✔ **Photo Stream:** If you activate Photo Stream, photos taken with other iOS devices or added to iPhoto or Aperture on a Mac connected to iCloud's Photo Stream will be in the Photo Stream album on your iPhone.

✔ **From your computer:** Sync photos from iTunes (see Book II, Chapter 1).

WARNING!

The LED flash doesn't work when HDR is on.

When High Dynamic Range is on, Camera takes three photos with different exposures and superimposes them to create a better image. Taking images with HDR takes a few seconds longer than shooting normal photos, so try to hold iPhone steady and ask the subject to remain still.

You can save both a normal version and an HDR version. In Settings⇨ Photos, tap Keep Normal Photo on. If you turn this off, only the HDR version is saved.

Browsing and Editing Photos and Videos

After you've taken some photos and videos, you probably want to see them and maybe make a few adjustments. You view your photos and videos in the Photos app. The thumbnail view gives you access to the photos stored on your iPhone. As soon as you tap the Camera or Video button, the photo or video is stored in the Photos app in the album called Camera Roll. When you import photos from your computer to your iPhone, they're placed in an album called Photo Library. You can create albums directly in Photos using photos from any album, Camera Roll, Photo Library, or Photo Stream.

You can open Camera Roll from the Camera app by tapping the preview button on the lower left corner, but you access other albums from Photos.

When you open Photos, you see a list of your Albums. At the bottom of the Albums screen, as shown in Figure 1-6, are browse buttons that give you options to view your photos in four ways:

- **Albums:** Shows Camera Roll, Photo Stream, Photo Library, and any albums that you create on your iPhone. Tap on an album to open a thumbnail view of the photos in the album.

- **Events:** Shows collections of photos divided by event, as set up on your computer. Tap on an event to see thumbnails of those photos.

- **Faces:** Supported only by photos imported from iPhoto or Aperture on a Mac. Sorts photos by identifying people in the photo.

- **Places:** Takes advantage of geotagging. Pins on a map indicate where photos were taken. Tapping a pin opens a thumbnail view of photos taken in that location.

You see Events and Faces only if you imported photos to your iPhone from a Mac using iPhoto or Aperture.

Figure 1-6: The browse buttons at the bottom of the screen give you sorting and searching options.

You can tell the difference between photos and videos in the thumbnail view because videos have a video icon and the playing time on the thumbnail.

Creating albums

If you take a lot of photos, you can organize them in albums on your iPhone. The original photos remain in Camera Roll, Photo Library, or the existing album that you copy them from. Albums lets you put related photos together for easier viewing. To create a photo album, follow these steps:

1. **Tap the Photos icon on the Home screen to open Photos.**

   The Albums list appears. Tap Albums at the bottom of the screen if you don't see the Albums list.

2. **Tap the Edit button in the upper right corner.**

3. **Tap the Add button that appears in the upper left corner.**

   The New Album dialog opens.

4. **Type in a name for your new Album.**

5. **Tap Save.**

   The Add Photos screen opens.

6. **In the list of albums, tap Camera Roll, Photo Library, or an existing album, wherever the photos you want in the new album reside.**

7. **The thumbnail view of the photos in the album opens.**

8. **Tap all the photos you want to include in the new album, and then tap Done.**

9. **Your new album appears in the Album list.**

10. **(Optional.) To add more photos to the album, tap the album in the Album list to open the thumbnail view. Then tap the Action button in the upper right corner. Tap the Add button at the bottom and repeat steps 6 through 8.**

11. **(Optional.) To delete an album, tap Albums at the bottom of the Photos screen. Tap the Edit button, and then tap the red and white minus sign to the left of the album name.**

12. **(Optional.) To change the order of albums on the Album list, tap the Edit button, and then drag the Rearrange button to the right of the album name to move it to the position you want in the list.**

Editing photos

If you use the iPhoto application on the Mac, the edit options in Photos will be familiar. Here's how to use them:

1. **Tap Photos on the Home screen.**

2. **Tap Camera Roll.**

3. **Tap the photo you want to edit.**

4. **Tap the Edit button.**

   Four buttons appear at the bottom of the screen, refer to Figure 1-7:

Figure 1-7: You have three photo-editing options in Photos: Auto-Enhance, Red-Eye Removal, and Crop and Rotate.

Rotate: Tap to rotate 90 degrees at a time. Tap Save when you like the orientation.

Auto-Enhance: Tap to adjust the sharpness and contrast of the photo, and then tap Save.

Red-Eye Removal: Tap the tool then tap the red eye to correct the were-wolf effect of your subject's eyes.

Crop/Constrain: Use your fingers to zoom, pan, and rotate the image until it appears as you wish. Drag the corners of the crop grid to set the area you want to crop or tap the Constrain button to choose one of the pre-set aspect ratios. Tap Crop to see the edits, and then tap Save. Your image is saved with the changes you made.

5. Tap Camera Roll or Albums to return to your Photos albums.

The online bonus content, Bonus Chapter 4 suggests photo enhancement apps that you can download to your iPhone.

Viewing and trimming videos

Watching a video is as simple as browsing your photos. Open Photos, and then tap the album where your video is stored. The video icon and playing time stamped on the thumbnails distinguish videos from photos. Tap the video you want to watch, and then tap the Play button (the triangle at the bottom center of the screen). The Play button becomes a Pause button when the video is playing, but after a few seconds, the controls disappear to give you a cleaner viewing screen.

Double-tap on the screen to switch between fill-screen or full-screen modes.

Photos gives you the possibility of trimming your video:

1. Tap the screen to make the controls visible.

A bar across the top of the screen displays the video frame by frame.

2. Tap and hold an area of the frame bar.

The frames become longer, making it easier to decide where to trim.

3. Use the slider on the bar to move through the video in slow motion.

4. Tap the left or right end of the bar.

The yellow trim button appears in the upper right corner and the bar is highlighted in yellow, as shown in Figure 1-8.

5. Drag the end brackets toward the center to trim off the beginning or ending of the video.

6. Tap the Trim button when you have the bracket positioned where you want.

You have the option to Trim Original, which overrides the original video, or Save as New Clip, which keeps the original and saves the trimmed video as an additional video in the Camera Roll album.

7. Tap Cancel at any time if you want to start over.

Figure 1-8: Trim removes frames from the beginning and end of your video.

If you want more editing options on your iPhone, you can purchase Apple's iMovie app at the App Store.

Ready, Action

After you're happy with your photos and videos, you can share, copy, and print photos singly or in batches. You can also delete photos and videos that you've shot on your iPhone and that are stored in the Camera Roll or an album you created on your iPhone.

Tap on a photo from the thumbnail view and flick left or right to move from one photo to the next and back again.

You can copy, print, and send photos and videos to others as e-mail attachments or multimedia messages (MMS or iMessage), or upload them to Twitter or YouTube. You can take these actions with a single photo or video or with batches of photos. First, we look at how to do things with a single photo or video, and then we explain managing batches of photos.

To take an action on a single photo or video:

1. **Tap Photos on the Home screen.**

2. **Tap the album where the photo or video you want to share, copy, or print resides.**

   The thumbnail view opens.

3. **Tap the photo or video you want to use.**

4. **Tap the screen to reveal the controls, as shown in Figure 1-9.**

   At the top of the screen, you see

   • **Camera Roll or "Album Name" button (Pizza in the figure):** In the upper left corner, it shows where this photo resides. Tapping this button takes you back to the album where you began.

   • **Photo number:** Indicates where in the lineup this photo or video falls.

5. **Choose the action you want to take from the buttons at the bottom of the page:**

Figure 1-9: The controls on the photo or video let you share images.

↙ **Action button:** Up to eight choices appear when you click it:

- **E-mail Photo/Video:** The photo is pasted into a new message. Type in the address and a message if you wish, and tap Send. (See Book III, Chapter 4.) You are asked to choose what size file you want to send: Small, Medium, Large, or Actual Size. The approximate megabyte size is indicated; if your e-mail service has size limits for attachments, choose an image that is about half the size of the limit.

- **Message:** Pastes the photo in a New Message, which will be sent as an MMS or iMessage. Type in the phone number and tap Send. (Refer to Book III, Chapter 2.)

- **Send to YouTube (video only):** Uploads video to your YouTube account. See Book V, Chapter 4 to learn how to do this.

- **Assign to Contact (photo only):** Assigns the photo to a person or entity in Contacts. See Book IV, Chapter 1 for complete details.

- **Use as Wallpaper (photo only):** Uses the photo as the background for your lock or Home screen. We explain how to do this in the section "Using a Photo as Wallpaper" later in this chapter.

- **Tweet (photo only):** Sends your photo to your Twitter account. You must be signed in to Twitter to use this feature.

- **Print (photo only):** Prints the photo to a printer on your wireless network. See Book I, Chapter 2 for details about wireless printing.

- **Cancel:** Tap to return to the thumbnail view.

↙ **Play Slideshow:** Opens a slideshow of the images in the album or begins playing the video.

↙ **Trashcan (Camera Roll only):** Tap to delete the photo or video. This option is available only for photos and videos shot directly on your iPhone. You can't delete photos or videos imported from your computer; you have to deselect those photos in iTunes and sync again.

Many sites make uploading photos as easy as sending an e-mail, both Flickr and Facebook assign a specific e-mail to your account; send an e-mail with a photo attached to that address and the image is posted to your account.

Batches

Sometimes you have more than one photo that you'd like to print or e-mail, or even delete. Photos lets you choose a group of photos and then take the same action for all of them at once. While in the thumbnail view of an album, do the following:

1. Tap the action button in the upper right hand corner.

In the Camera Roll album or albums you created on your iPhone, you see four buttons at the bottom on the screen: Share, Copy, Add To, Delete (Remove in created albums).

In the Photo Library album, you see three buttons: Share, Copy, Add To.
You can't delete photos imported from your computer from your
iPhone, you have to re-sync the photo library with iTunes and not sync
the photos you want to remove.

2. **Tap the photos you want to act on; they don't have to be consecutive.**

   A white checkmark in a red circle appears on the photo, as seen in
   Figure 1-10.

Figure 1-10: Batching lets you take an action
on a group of photos.

3. **The actions that can be taken have active buttons. Tap the button of
   the action you want to take:**

   • **Share:** The choice of E-mail, Tweet, Message, or Print opens; choose
     which you want to use. For e-mail or message, fill in the address or
     phone number of the recipient as explained in Book III, Chapters 2
     and 4. You must be signed in to your Twitter account (Settings⟿
     Twitter); type your Twitter message in the Twitter form that opens,
     and then tap Send. You can print as many photos as you like, e-mail
     up to five photos at a time, message up to two photos at once, and
     tweet one photo. Tap Print and the Printer Options screen opens.

Select the Wi-Fi printer you are connected to and print the number of copies you want.

- **Copy:** Places a copy of the images in the clipboard of your iPhone. You can then paste the images in another app, such as Notes.

- **Add To:** Tapping this button gives you two options:

  Add to Existing Album: The album list opens and you tap the one you want to add the photos to.

  Add to New Album: The New Album dialog appears where you type in a name and tap Save).

- **Delete/Remove:** Deletes the batch of photos from the Camera Roll. Removes the batch of photos from a created album but the original photos remain in Camera Roll.

Using a photo as wallpaper

You can customize the wallpaper, or background image, that appears on your lock screen and your Home screen. We explained how to do this from Settings in Book I, Chapter 4. Here we explain how to assign wallpaper directly from Photos:

1. **Select the photo you want to assign from any of the albums on Photos.**

2. **Tap the Action button in the bottom left corner.**

3. **Tap Use as Wallpaper.**

   The Move and Scale screen opens.

4. **Pinch and spread the photo to zoom to the size you want and pan, or move, the photo around until the image is just how you want it on the screen.**

5. **Tap the Set button.**

6. **Choose one of the options that appear:**

   - **Set Lock Screen:** To use the image for the Lock screen.

   - **Set Home Screen:** To use the image for the Home screen.

   - **Set Both:** To use the image for both the Lock and Home screen.

   - **Cancel:** If you decide to leave things the way they are.

Viewing slideshows

Gone are the days of 35 mm slides and overstuffed guests falling asleep while you try to figure out which way to put the slide in the projector so it doesn't display upside-down and out of focus. With its crystalline display, your iPhone shows off your photos beautifully. You can also connect to a television or monitor to play your slideshow, which we explain in Book I, Chapter 2. To view a slideshow on your iPhone, follow these steps:

1. **Open the photo or album where you want the slideshow to begin.**

2. **Tap the slideshow button: It's the triangle between the Forward and Backward buttons.**

   The Slideshow Options screen opens.

3. **Tap Transitions.**

   Choose the type of transition you want from the list. A transition is what happens on the screen between one photo and the next.

4. **Tap Play Music On or Off.**

   If you want music to accompany your slideshow, tap On. Start a song from the iPod app and then return to Photos and begin a slideshow.

5. **Tap Start Slideshow.**

   The slideshow plays from the photo where you begin through to the end of the album.

The Slideshow settings give you a few viewing options. Tap Settings⟳Photos. In the Slideshow section, set the following:

- **Play Each Slide For:** Choose the duration of each image on the screen, from 2 to 20 seconds.

- **Repeat:** Plays the slideshow in a continuous loop.

- **Shuffle:** Plays the images in a random order.

Importing Photos and Videos to Your Computer

We talk about syncing in Book II, Chapter 1, where we mention that moving photos from your iPhone to your computer is handled by your photo management software. On a Mac, this might be Image Capture, iPhoto Aperture, or another application that you prefer. On Windows, you may use Photoshop Elements (3 or later), Live Photo Gallery, or Pictures Library.

Essentially, when you connect your iPhone to your computer with the USB connector cable, the photo management application you use recognizes your iPhone as it would any other digital camera. If import photo choices don't appear automatically, you may have to go to a command such as File⟳ Import and choose to import all the photos or select only some of the photos you want to import.

Photo Stream

Photo Stream is an alternative to connecting your iPhone to your computer with the USB connector cable and is part of Apple's iCloud remote storage service. Photo Stream automatically uploads new photos in Camera Roll to iCloud (up to 1,000 photos that are less than 30 days old) from your various iOS 5 devices, such as your iPhone, iPad, or iPod touch. Then, Photo Stream downloads them to the other devices and your computer. It also uploads photos from the last 30 days from your computer. For example, if you take photos with a digital camera then move them to your computer, those photos are uploaded to Photo Stream and downloaded to your iOS devices.

Photos are then permanently stored on your computer and on your iPhone for as long as you keep them there; the most recent 1,000 are stored on iCloud for 30 days. As you take new photos, the oldest ones are deleted.

Turn Photo Stream on in Settings⇨Photos. You must be connected to Wi-Fi for Photo Stream to function.

iCloud comes with Mac OS X 10.7.2 Lion, or later. The iCloud Control Panel for Windows is available to download at `support.apple.com/kb/DL1455`.

Chapter 2: Acquiring and Browsing Music, Videos, Movies, and More

In This Chapter

- Copying media you already own to iTunes
- Changing import settings
- Browsing, sampling, and buying media with iTunes
- Exploring iTunes U, books, and podcasts
- Managing and transferring purchases
- Making friends with Ping
- Tracking down free iTunes promotional music and other goodies

By now, you know that your iPhone isn't just a great phone: It's also a fabulous web browser, contact manager, calendar, alarm clock, and a terrific media player. Music, movies, TV shows, podcasts, and audiobooks sound and look crisp and clear on your iPhone. You can use HomeSharing to listen to and watch media on your iPhone, or you can copy media onto your iPhone, which we explain in this chapter.

In this chapter, we first consider media you already own, which you copy to iTunes so that you can then sync it to your iPhone. We then take a closer look at the iTunes store, both on your iPhone and on your computer, and show you the ins and outs of browsing, sampling, and buying media. If you think iTunes is just for music, think again. We explore iTunes' other offerings including iTunes U, audiobooks, podcasts, and free promotional music. In case you're wondering, Chapter 3 of this book is all about the Music app.

Moving Your Media to iTunes

With the advent of iOS 5, syncing became a Wi-Fi act. What's more, for a yearly fee of $24.95, iTunes Match "matches" any song you have that's available from the iTunes Store and puts it in your iTunes library as an iTunes item. You might ask why you do such a thing if you already own the song. Because anything in your iTunes library is also in iCloud, with iTunes Match, even songs you didn't purchase through iTunes are available in iCloud. After the media is in iTunes, and you activate iCloud, you're just a syncing step away from having everything in your iTunes library on your iPhone.

Media that's already on your computer

You may have media that you downloaded from another site like Amazon (www.amazon.com) or GoMusic (www.gomusic.com). You simply drag those files into your iTunes library. To make that task even easier, choose the Automatically Add to iTunes folder when selecting the destination for saving a downloaded file, and the file shows up in your iTunes library. If you subscribe to iTunes Match, those files go into iCloud even though they were purchased through another source (so long as they are items available in the iTunes Store).

---

iTunes encoding music settings

When iTunes imports music, it automatically compresses the file with the iTunes Plus encoder, which plays at 256 Kbps in stereo (128 Kbps in mono). However, iTunes also gives you the option of using a different encoder to compress music you import. Click Import Settings at the bottom right of the iTunes screen to change your settings for the active import (set your own default import settings by going to iTunes⇨Preferences⇨General and clicking the Import Settings button). You have five choices, each of which has an Auto setting, and four have custom settings.

Considering that CD quality audio is around 44,000 KHz per second with 16 bits of data over two channels for stereo listening, one minute of music requires 10 MB of storage. Compressing makes the file smaller so you can fit more songs on your personal listening device;

that is, your iPhone. AAC and MP3 encoders compress the data by removing audio you wouldn't be able to hear unless you have bionic ears. AIFF, WAV, and Apple Lossless Encoders transform the data without removing any audio so it can be played on your computer or iPhone.

Here's a brief explanation of the settings to help you choose if you decide to change the encoder you use to import music:

- **AAC (Advanced Audio Coding) Encoder:** Offers better sound quality and more flexibility at the same bit rate as MP3. The Custom settings are iTunes Plus, High Quality (128 Kbps in stereo and 64 Kbps in mono), and Spoken Podcast (64 Kbps in stereo and 32 Kbps in mono). Files are compressed and tags identify information about the song, such as artist, CD, and title.

✓ **AIFF (Audio Interchange File Format) Encoder:** Custom settings let you choose a Sample Rate between 8,000 and 48,000 KHz; a Sample Size of 8 or 16 bit, and mono or stereo channels. AIFF and WAV offer the highest listening quality but don't copy tag information, such as the name of the artist, CD, or song (although iTunes does track that in its database, it won't show up if you burn to another CD), and the files are large because they aren't compressed. AIFF files can be read and created on iTunes on both the Mac and Windows, but they are more commonly used in the Mac environment.

✓ **Apple Lossless Encoder:** Offers only an automatic setting. Apple Lossless compresses files without removing (or losing) any audio so you have audio quality similar to AIFF/WAV but with slightly smaller files. It also sets tags like AAC and MP3 encoders. The downside is that most non-Apple devices don't support Apple Lossless.

✓ **MP3 Encoder:** Choose Good Quality at 128 Kbps, High at 160, or Higher at 192. Custom settings offer Stereo Bit Rates between 16 and 320 Kbps; seven settings for Variable Bit Rate (VBR) encoding, ten choices for the Sample Rate between 8,000 and 48,000 kHz, mono or stereo channels, and normal or joint stereo mode. You also have an on/off option for Smart Encoding and Filter Frequencies Below 10 Hz. Files are compressed and tagged. This is the choice to make for non-iOS MP3 players or if you want to burn an MP3 CD to play in a portable CD player or car stereo.

✓ **WAV Encoder:** Offers the same custom settings as the AIFF encoder. iTunes on both Mac and Windows reads and creates WAV files. They are widely used with Windows and other operating systems.

To convert a song from one format to another, click on the song and then click Advanced⇨Create Version, where the version will be what you established in the Import Settings. Keep in mind there's no sense converting a lower quality file to a higher quality, for example, converting an MP3 file to AIFF. The encoder can't add in audio that was removed. You can go from one encoder to another of similar quality, such as AIFF to WAV or Apple Lossless to MP3 with good results, albeit slight additional detail loss.

You choice depends on how sensitive your ears are and what kind of output device you'll be using to listen to your music.

Media on a CD

To import media from a CD, follow these steps:

1. **Open iTunes.**

2. **Insert the CD you want to copy into the disc drive on your computer.**

   The CD appears under Devices in the iTunes source list on the left, as shown in Figure 2-1.

   If the CD doesn't appear under Devices or it begins playing, go to iTunes⇨Preferences⇨General. Towards the bottom of the screen you see the When You Insert a CD pull-down menu. Choose Show CD to see the CD under Devices. If you are planning to copy many CDs, you can select Import CD and Eject and skip the following steps. You can also change the default Settings here.

Figure 2-1: The iTunes source menu shows your libraries, devices, and playlists.

3. **Click on the CD in the Devices list on the left of the iTunes screen.**

   The songs are listed and selected by default. If you only want to import some of the songs, deselect those you don't want.

4. **(Optional) Click Import Settings to change the default settings for this import. (See the sidebar for details about import settings.)**

5. **Click Import CD.**

6. **The status display at the top of the screen displays the songs that are being copied and the time remaining.**

   When finished, the songs are stored in the Music library. You see aliases of the songs in the Recently Added playlist.

7. **Click the Eject button to remove the CD from your drive.**

If you have an active Internet connection when you copy a CD to iTunes, iTunes will automatically scan the Gracenote Internet music database for any information related to the CD and copy it into the Info about that CD. You can do this later by clicking Advanced⇨Get Track Names. After copying a CD to iTunes, download any album artwork that's available in iTunes by clicking Store⇨Get Album Artwork. You have to have an Internet connection and sign in to your Apple ID account to use this feature.

Converting media files so they can play on your iPhone

You can convert audio and video files in iTunes, so we think it's worth mentioning here. iPhone can play AAC (8 to 320 Kbps), Protected AAC (from iTunes Store), HE-AAC, MP3 (8 to 320 Kbps), MP3 VBR, Audible (formats 2, 3, 4, Audible Enhanced Audio, AAX, and AAX+), Apple Lossless, AIFF, and WAV media. That's probably more than enough for your listening pleasure.

Your iPhone also supports these video formats: H.264 video up to 720p, 30 frames per second, Main Profile level 3.1 with AAC-LC audio up to 160 Kbps, 48kHz, stereo audio in .M4V, .MP4, and .MOV file formats; MPEG-4 part 10 video, up to 2.5 Mbps, 640X480 pixels, 30 frames per second, Simple Profile with AAC-LC audio up to 160 Kbps per channel, 48kHz, stereo audio in .M4V, .MP4, and .MOV file formats; Motion JPEG (M-JPEG) up to 35 Mbps, 1280X720 pixels, 30 frames per second, audio in ulaw, and PCM stereo audio in .AVI file format. Whew! If you have an audio or video that is in a different format, you can convert it with the following procedure:

1. **In iTunes, choose the library where the song, video, podcast, or iTunes U lecture you want to convert resides, and then select the audio or video file.**

2. **Click the Advanced menu and see which format is listed in the Create Version command.**

   For audio: Your choices may be AAC, AIFF, Apple Lossless, MP3, or WAV.

   For video: Choose between Create iPod or iPhone Version (probably the one you want) or Create iPad or Apple TV Version.

3. **If the format you want to convert to is displayed, click Create Version.**

   iTunes automatically creates a copy of that song or video in the new format.

4. **If the audio format you want isn't displayed, open Preferences.**

   Mac: iTunes⇨Preferences

   Windows: Edit⇨Preferences

5. **Click General.**

6. **Click Import Settings.**

   The Import Settings dialog box opens.

7. **From the Import Using pop-up menu, choose the encoder you want to use — AAC, AIFF, Apple Lossless, MP3, or WAV.**

8. **Click OK to close Import Settings.**

9. **Click OK to close Preferences.**

10. **Select the audio file or files you want to convert.**

11. **Click Advanced⇨Create Version.**

    The format should reflect the setting you chose in Preferences.

12. **The new file is placed in the same library as the old file and has the same name. Look at the Info for the audio or video file to see which version is which.**

For formats that iTunes can't read, you can use Handbrake (`handbrake.fr/`), an open source video transcoder.

Browsing, Sampling, and Buying Music, Movies, and More at the iTunes Store

Have your Apple ID handy when you want to use iTunes because that's what you use to sign in. If you haven't yet created an Apple ID, see Book II, Chapter 1 for instructions.

When you first open the iTunes Store, it can seem overwhelming, and in a way it is: It offers more than 14 million songs. (Barbara did a rough calculation and came up with the figure of 80 years of non-stop listening to hear every song!). Besides all the music, iTunes also carries more than one million podcasts and thousands of movies and TV shows. Whew!

Luckily, the iTunes Store, on your computer and iPhone, is organized to help you narrow your choices. If you're familiar with the App Store, which we covered in Book II, Chapter 1, you'll recognize the iTunes Store setup.

On your computer

The window is divided into sections that offer suggestions for music, movies, and TV shows to download, rent, or purchase. See Figure 2-2.

Figure 2-2: The iTunes Store lets you browse for music, movies, TV shows, and more.

At the top, you see rotating banner ads for songs, television shows, and movies. Below the ads are sections (you can only see the first one in the figure) divided by: Music, Genius Recommendations, Ping Artists and Music, Movies, TV Shows, Special Offers, and Free on iTunes along with special iTunes offers. Clicking any of the ads or icons in this smorgasbord of offers takes you to an information screen about that item.

In each section, you see two rows of icons. You can use the scroll bar underneath the selection to scroll horizontally, or click See All to see the entire selection from that section.

Across the top of the window are tabs for each type of media: Music, Movies, TV Shows, App Store (refer to Book II, Chapter 2), Books, Podcasts, and iTunes U. (There's also a tab for Ping, the iTunes social network, which we explain later in this chapter.) To the far right, you see your Apple ID, which is a tab, too. (The Apple ID in Figure 2-3 is barbaradepaula.) When clicked, each tab opens a pull-down menu, as shown in Figure 2-3. The menu choices take you to selections of new releases, special offers, or specific categories or genres available in that type of media. The pull-down menu from your Apple ID tab gives you account management options.

Apple ID

Figure 2-3: Click a media tab to open a pull-down menu with direct links to specific types of selections, such as new releases or those in a category or genre.

Down the right side, you see two sections:

✔ **Quick Links:** This section is divided into two parts — the top part lists options for searching, browsing, and buying; the lower part is related to your iTunes/Apple ID account so you can see your wish list, recent activity, and Genius recommendations, which we explain in the "Playlists" section later in this chapter.

✔ **Top Charts:** This section is divided into Singles, where you can view songs or music videos; and Albums, Movies, and TV Shows, which can be viewed by episode or season. Each has a See All option to view the top 200 in the category. Except for Songs, each See All selection can be sorted by Name, Bestseller, or Release Date.

When you click on a song or album icon or name from anywhere in the iTunes store, the album information window opens. Click on a TV show and the season information screen opens. Click on a movie and a movie information screen opens. Figure 2-4 shows an example. These are the parts of an information screen:

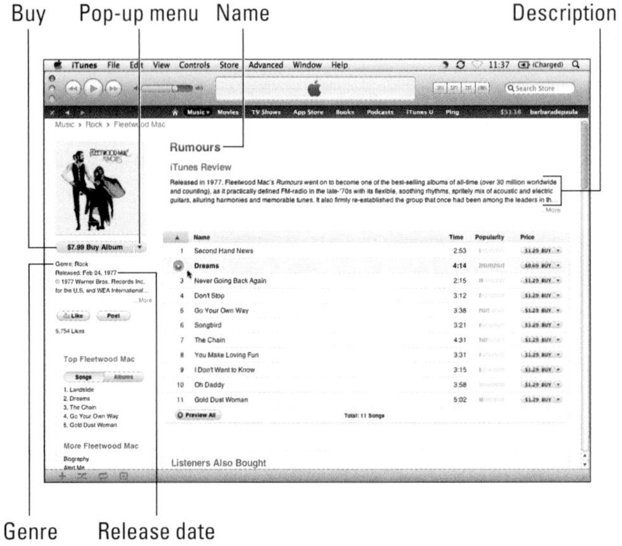

Figure 2-4: Information about the media item is displayed in iTunes.

✔ **Name**

✔ **Genre**

✔ **Release date**

✔ **Buy button:** Click to download the media. Each option, for example rent or buy, standard or high-definition, has its own button. Songs can be purchased singly by clicking the Buy button in the Price column or you can purchase the whole album by clicking the Buy button under the album; TV shows can be purchased singly or by season.

✔ **Pop-up menu:** Click the triangle next to the album price for a pop-up menu that has options to gift the app to a friend, add it to your own wish list, tell a friend about it, copy the link, or share the app info via Facebook or Twitter.

You can't use a store credit to pay for a gift, you must pay with a credit card or PayPal account.

> ✔ **Ratings:** For movies only. The ratings are the usual G, PG, PG-13, R, and so on for US markets. Foreign films may have different ratings.

> ✔ **Description:** The first few lines of the description are visible. If the description is longer, click More on the right to expose the complete description.

> ✔ **Reviews:** Users can give a simple star rating, from zero to five, or write a review. Reviews help your downloading or purchasing decisions.

At the bottom, lists show items by the same performers and other items purchased by people who bought that particular item.

Finding music when you know what you're looking for

If you have a specific song or movie in mind, you can skip the rotating banner ads and lists of recommendations and search for the media you seek.

Type the name or a couple key words in the Search field at the top right of the window, and then press return. A list of matching results appears. The results are culled from the entire iTunes Store but are divided by category. If you click Movies or TV Shows in the Filter by Media Type section, you'll only see that type of media.

Click See All next to the media title to see all the items found that meet your search criteria. If you want to narrow your search, click the Power Search button.

Power Search lets you narrow your search by providing more detailed criteria like an actor's name or a genre. Adjust the criteria and click the Search button to come up with more precise search results.

You can also click one of the media type tabs at the top of the screen — Music, Movies, TV Shows — to see a greater selection in just one type of media. Click and hold to open the pull-down menu that displays genres or categories within a type of media.

Downloading media from iTunes

When you find something you like, click the Buy (or Rent) button and it's downloaded to iTunes. Of course, when you buy, you have to pay from your Apple ID account. This happens two ways:

> ✔ **Credit Card:** Insert your credit card information into your Apple ID account. You did this either when you opened it, or you can do it by going to Store⇨View My Account, and then clicking Edit to the right of Payment Information. A window opens where you can choose the type of credit

card you want to use (or PayPal) and type in the necessary information: account number, expiration date, billing address, and so on.

✓ **Redeem:** You can redeem Apple or iTunes gift cards, gift certificates, or allowances. (You can set up a monthly allowance for yourself or some-one else. A set amount is charged to your credit card or PayPal account and credited to the designated iTunes account.) Click your Apple ID⇨Redeem. Type in the code from the card or certificate. The amount of the card or certificate is added to your account and appears to the left of the Apple ID account tab.

After you download the item, close the iTunes store by clicking the X in the upper left side. You return to iTunes Visualizer, which is non-store iTunes on your computer. In the Source list that runs down the left side of the iTunes window, click the Library category for the type of media you downloaded (Music, Movies, and so on) to see the media you have, as in Figure 2-5. You can also check in the Recently Added playlist to confirm that the items you rented or purchased were downloaded.

Figure 2-5: The Music section of the Library shows which songs, albums, and music videos you have in iTunes.

 You can select Automatic Downloads so that whenever you download some-thing on your computer or device, it's automatically downloaded to other computers or devices using the same Apple ID. On your computer, in iTunes, go to iTunes⇨Preferences and click the Store tab. Check the boxes next to the media you want automatically downloaded to other devices: Apps, Music, and/or Books. On your iPhone, tap Setting⇨Store and tap the switches next to Music and/or Apps On. While you're there, you can choose to use the cellular network to download purchases by tapping the switch by Use Cellular Data On, although there are size limits for downloading on the cellular network. Use a Wi-Fi connection to download larger files.

Weighing renting versus buying options

Because video rental stores have just about gone the way of the dinosaurs, online rentals have become the way to watch movies and television shows. You also have the option of buying movies and television shows to expand your video library.

Two things you have to consider when deciding whether to rent or buy a video or TV show from the iTunes Store:

- **How often do you want to watch the video:** If you think you'll only want to watch it once, renting is probably fine. At the time of publication, movie rentals cost between $3.99 and $4.99 and $.99 for TV shows. You have thirty days to begin watching the movie and 24 hours (48 hours for TV

shows) to finish watching once you begin. If you think it's a classic or a keeper, you probably want to buy.

- **How much do you want to spend:** Rentals are $3.99 for a standard version and $4.99 for high definition. iTunes runs specials to purchase films for as low as $4.99 and new releases in high definition go for around $14.99.

Keep in mind that you can only watch movies rented on your iPhone (from 4 on up) on your iPhone, whereas movies rented on iTunes can then be transferred to your iPhone. We explain viewing video on your iPhone in Book V, Chapter 4.

You can view your media in several ways by clicking the view buttons at the top of the screen:

List: Shows the content in list without images. Click the heading of any part of the list and the list is sorted by that heading; for example, Name sorts alphabetically by artist name. Click the triangle to the right of the name to sort in the opposite direction.

Album List: Shows an album cover or movie or TV show icon, along with a list of tracks on albums or episodes of TV shows.

Grid: Displays album covers, which can then be further sorted by album, artist, genre, or composer, or shows movie or TV show icons, which can be sorted by name, genre, and unwatched.

Cover Flow: Displays the album cover or show icon in the top half of the screen and a list of the details in the bottom half (like the List view). Move from one item to another by clicking the item on the list or using the scroll bar or the directional arrows at either end of the scroll bar. Tap the full-screen button to see the cover flow display on your entire screen.

When you are browsing your Music Library in any of the lists — List, Album List, or the list in Cover Flow — you can change the columns you see by opening the library you want and then clicking View⇨View Options. Select the check box next to the columns you want to see and deselect those you want to hide, and then click OK.

Other media

iTunes isn't just about music and movies: You can also find podcasts, audiobooks, and even university courses and K-12 lessons. Here we take a brief look at what each category offers, but don't just take our word for it. Take a look for yourself at the vast assortment of media available.

iTunes U

Divided into 13 faculties, iTunes U features audio and video lectures from seminars and courses at universities around the world. This means you can get an Ivy League education (but not the degree) without writing any term papers and without the Ivy League cost — the lectures are free!

The opening screen is organized like the Music and Movies sections. Banner ads scroll across the top, Noteworthy and Categories sections follow, and Quick Links and Top Charts run down the right side. You can search by institution, by faculty, or, with the power search function, by description, institution, or title. The lectures aren't limited to universities and colleges. You find lectures from conferences and professional organizations in the Beyond Campus category and K-12 offers basic subjects.

When you find a course you want to watch or listen to, subscribe to the entire course by clicking the Subscribe button or download one lecture from the course by clicking on the name of the course, which opens the information screen and shows a list of lectures to choose from.

Books

The layout is familiar by now: banner ads, sections by category, and top charts down the right side. The iTunes top downloads are divided into paid and free; *New York Times* bestsellers are divided by fiction and nonfiction. The Books section of iTunes comprises electronic books, which you can download and read on your iPhone and also on your iPad or iPod touch, and audiobooks, which you listen to via iTunes on your computer, your iPhone, iPod, or iPad. To switch between electronic books (iTunes refers to them just as "books") and audiobooks, click on one of the subheads in the Books or Audiobooks section to open that department of the iTunes Store.

Podcasts

iTunes offers both audio and video podcasts for free in 16 categories (at the time of publication) and you can view the podcasts by audio or video only, by category, or by new releases. Apple's recommendations show up under the Staff Favorites link, and the Top Charts lists the most popular episodes. You can *stream* a podcast — that is, listen to it while it's downloading. If you want to download and listen later, click the Pause button; the podcast will download into the Podcast library and you can play it at a later time. Choose a single episode of a podcast or subscribe, in which case iTunes automatically downloads new episodes to your podcast library.

Ping

The last tab is Ping, iTunes' social network. The first time you click the Ping tab, you use your Apple ID and password to activate it, and then fill out the information requested: name, gender, hometown. The photo and personal description are optional. Choose three genres of music from the check boxes shown to give Ping an idea about what you like. Click Continue and then select the privacy options you want from those offered, as in Figure 2-6.

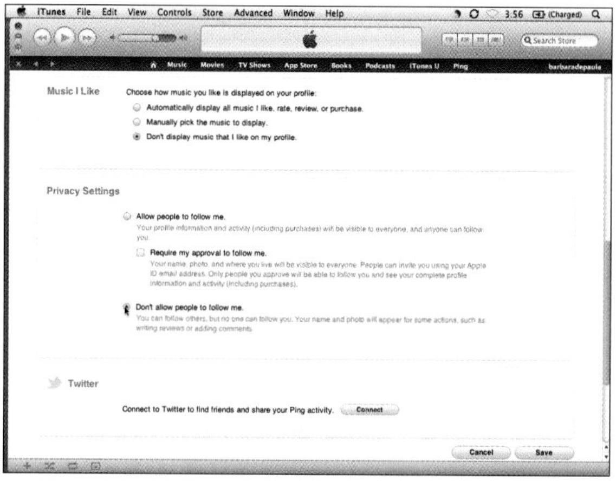

Figure 2-6: Choose who sees what about you in the Ping privacy settings.

After you activate Ping, you can choose artists to follow, which means that when you open Ping, you'll see the latest activity about those artists, new releases, upcoming concert dates, and the like. You can also follow other people whose musical interests interest you.

At any time, you can click on My Profile and make changes to your information or privacy settings. Refer to Figure 2-7 for Ping on iTunes. To turn Ping off, choose account from the pull-down menu that appears when you click on your account name, the tab on the far right of the window. Click Turn Off to turn Ping off. You can also reach your Ping profile from here by clicking on Edit Profile.

In the iTunes Visualizer Music library, click once on an item and a Ping button appears. Click this button to open a menu that gives you

   ✓ **Ping options:** Click Like to add a thumbs-up to the song, album, or artist, or Post to add a review or comment. People who follow you will see your likes and posts.

Figure 2-7: The Ping screen on iTunes.

✔ **Show Artist Profile:** This takes you to the iTunes store and displays information about the artist.

✔ **iTunes:** Clicking this gives you four choices that you can click to take you to a destination in the iTunes store: the first takes you to the song itself, the second, to the artist; the third, to the album; and the fourth, to other albums in that genre.

Authorizing iTunes to play your purchased music, videos, books, and apps

When you open an iTunes account or Apple ID, you automatically authorize that computer to open videos, books, and apps purchased from the iTunes Store with your account. The media and the computer have to have the same authorization. You can authorize up to five computers, which means you can access your iTunes account from each of those five computers. Follow these steps to authorization:

1. **From iTunes, click Store➪Authorize This Computer.**

   A pane opens asking you to type in your Apple Account name and password. That's what you established when you set up your account on iTunes.

2. **Click Authorize.**

   A message appears telling you how many computers are authorized with this account.

At some point, you may want to deauthorize an account, say, if you buy a new computer and donate your old one to the local homeless shelter.

Instead of clicking Authorize This Computer, click Store⊅Deauthorize This Computer. Type in your Apple Account name and password, and then click Deauthorize. Any videos, books, or apps associated with that computer are no longer available.

TIP

If you turn on Home Sharing, the five computer limit is moot because you essentially put your iTunes collection on your home network and can access it from any number of computers on that network. iOS devices don't count.

On your iPhone

iTunes on your iPhone is a streamlined version of the iTunes Store. The listening part of iTunes is found on the Music app on your iPhone, which we cover in the next chapter. The recommendations are all there, but because of the smaller screen space, you see less of it at once — which might be a good thing. You have to have a Wi-Fi or cellular data connection to use iTunes on your iPhone. When you tap the iTunes button on the Home screen, the screen shown in Figure 2-8 opens. The first time you open iTunes, the Music section appears, but if the last time you looked in iTunes you were browsing videos or podcasts, when you re-open, that's what you'll see.

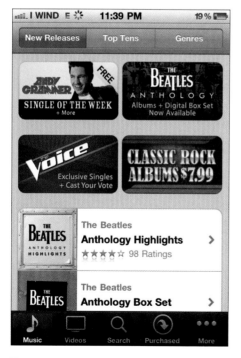

Figure 2-8: The iTunes screen on your iPhone.

Tapping any of the buttons in the browse bar at the bottom of the screen takes you to the corresponding section of iTunes. Tap More to open a list of sections that aren't displayed in the browse bar. Within each section, there are lists of recommendations sorted by most recent releases, most downloaded, and category. Here we go through each section briefly:

✔ **Music:** Across the top of the screen, you have three choices: New Releases, Top Tens, and Genres.

- **New Releases:** Shows four banner ads and then a list of new releases. Scrolling down to the bottom reveals two more banner ads and two buttons.

- **Complete My Album:** If you purchased a few songs from one album, complete my album downloads the remaining song(s) at a discounted price.

- **Redeem:** Opens a screen where you enter the code from any gift card or iTunes codes you have; the amount is added to your Apple ID account.

- **Top Tens:** Opens a list of music categories. The first choice is iTunes, which shows the week's ten most popular songs across all iTunes content. Tapping on any of the categories displays the top ten bestsellers in that category for the week. You can view the Top Songs or Top Albums in each category.

- **Genres:** Lists 50 or so of the newest releases in each genre.

Join a Starbucks Wi-Fi network (in the U.S.) and the Starbucks icon appears at the bottom of the iTunes screen. Preview and purchase the song currently playing along with other songs from featured Starbucks Collections.

✔ **Videos:** The three choices across the top are Movies, TV Shows, and Music Videos. Tapping any of the tabs displays a list of New releases. Scrolling down to the bottom of the screen reveals two or three more buttons:

- **Top Tens:** Takes you to a list of genres; tapping one of the genres opens a list of the top ten movies or TV shows in that genre.

- **Genre:** Shows the newest movie or TV show releases in that genre.

- **Redeem:** Opens a screen to let you type in a gift card or iTunes code. Music Videos doesn't have this button because music videos are free.

✔ **Podcasts:** What's Hot, Top Tens, and Categories are the buttons across the top.

- **What's Hot:** Lists the most popular podcasts across all categories.

- **Top Tens:** Shows the most popular podcasts sorted by category.

- **Categories:** Displays a list of categories. Tapping on a category opens a list of more than 30 recent podcasts for that category.

✔ **Audiobooks:** The opening screen shows featured audiobooks; these are the New and Notable additions to iTunes' audiobooks assortment. You can access lists sorted by Top Tens and Categories from the opening screen as well.

If you're looking for e-books, you find them as in-app purchases in the iBooks app.

✔ **iTunes U:** Three buttons across the top open links to lectures sorted by

- **What's Hot:** Forty new and noteworthy offerings across all categories.

- **Top Tens:** The top ten most downloaded lectures divided by category.

- **Categories:** Displays a list of categories. Tapping on a category opens a list of new, noteworthy, and hot items.

✔ **Ringtones:** Offers ringtones that you can use on your iPhone as the default ring or assigned to a contact. Ringtones usually cost $1.29. Like the other types of media, ringtones are sorted in three ways:

- **Featured:** More than 40 options.

- **Top Tens:** The top ten ringtones, displayed by category.

- **Genres:** Each genre has a list of 30 ringtones.

Tap the ringtone once to hear a preview; double-tap to open an info screen.

From the More screen, tap the Edit button to rearrange the buttons you see at the bottom of the screen and those that appear in the secondary More screen. Just drag the icon of the button you want on the bar over the one you want to replace and they exchange places.

Downloading to your iPhone

When you reach the center of the iTunes vortex and find the song, video, podcast, or whatever it is that you want to download, tapping the item opens an information screen. On items that have more than one component, such as an album that comprises songs or a TV show that has multiple episodes, the information screen shows a list of each component, as shown in Figure 2-9.

To preview an item:

1. **Tap the item that interests you.**

2. **Tap the Preview button to the left of the name.**

   The Preview button transforms to a loading button and then a piece of the song or video plays.

Figure 2-9: An iTunes information screen on your iPhone.

 You can preview video via Airplay or on Apple TV by tapping the Airplay button.

To download an item:

1. **Tap on the price or Free button to the right of the item.**

   The price button transforms to read Buy Now; Free becomes Download.

2. **Tap Buy Now or Download.**

   If you tap Buy Now by mistake, tap somewhere else on the screen, and it disappears.

   To purchase items, you must have credit or credit card information in your Apple ID account. Free items begin downloading immediately.

 Items that are larger than 10 MB cannot be downloaded over the cellular network; you must connect to Wi-Fi to download large files or you can download them on your computer. Rented Movies or TV shows begin playing after the download is complete.

Bonus songs and video download to your iPhone; iTunes Extras, iTunes LP, and digital booklets can only be downloaded to your computer. In iTunes, choose Store⟳Check for Available Downloads to retrieve these items.

3. **Downloaded items appear in the Purchased section of both the iTunes and Music apps on your iPhone and in the associated media library in Music.**

> **TIP**
>
> Access your Apple ID account information on your iPhone by scrolling to the bottom of any media list screen in iTunes and tapping Apple ID. Alternatively, go to Settings⟳Store⟳View Apple ID.

Those other browse buttons

You'll see a few other options for iTunes on your iPhone. The default browse bar has two:

- **Search:** Tapping the Search button opens a search field. Tap in the field to open the keyboard. Tap type in the title or subject of the item you want to find, and then tap the Search button. iTunes searches its entire media database and displays matches by category, as shown in Figure 2-10.

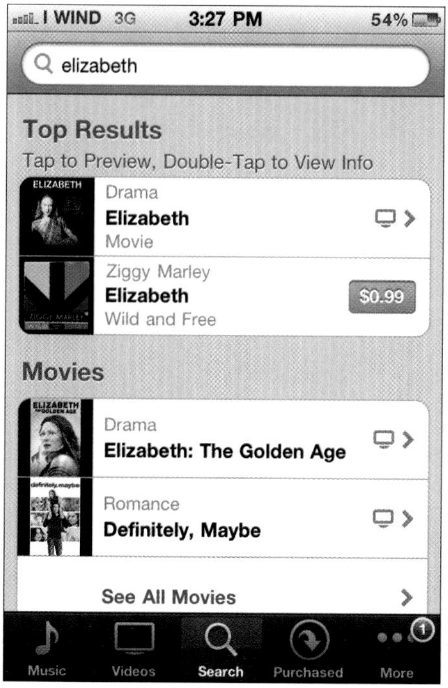

Figure 2-10: Search looks through iTunes' entire media database to find matches.

✔ **Purchased:** Displays by All, which is everything you've purchased on iTunes, or Not On This iPhone, where iTunes compares the media you've purchased and the media on your iPhone and shows you things that haven't been synced to your iPhone yet. Click the download button to download those items to your iPhone.

The other three options are found on the More screen:

✔ **Genius:** Genius makes recommendations based on your iTunes purchasing history. To use Genius, tap iTunes⟳More⟳Genius. Tap the media you want recommendations for Music, Movies, or TV Shows. Genius gives you a list of results it thinks you'll like. Tap any of the results to go to the information screen. Purchase and download as instructed earlier in this section.

✔ **Ping:** iTunes' social network lets you follow your favorite artists and see what your friends are listening to or watching.

✔ **Downloads:** Shows a status list of pending and in-progress downloads. Tapping the Pause button pauses the download until you start it again. If you lose your Internet connection, iPhone starts the download when the connection re-opens, or iTunes on your computer completes the download the next time you sign-in to iTunes. Pre-ordered items remain in the list until they are available and you download them. Tap the item for release date information. When it's available, tap the item and then tap the Download button. Pre-ordered items do not download automatically.

Ping

The Ping social network connects artists and friends with similar music interests. After you activate your Ping account on iTunes via your computer, you can access Ping from your iPhone. You see three options across the top of the Ping screen, as shown in Figure 2-11:

✔ **Activity:** Shows the latest likes and comments from, and information about, people you follow.

✔ **People:** Displays who you follow and who follows you. From here, you can search for artists and/or friends.

✔ **My Profile:** View and change your profile info.

We certainly don't condone stalking, but following someone on Ping is a great way to learn about music you might not otherwise be exposed to. When you follow artists and friends, you see their likes and comments in the Activity section of Ping. You also get information about new releases, upcoming concerts, and biographic information about artists or bands. There are three ways to follow someone:

✔ **While searching:** Search by an artist's or friend's name in the People section. Tap the name of the person who interests you, and then tap Follow.

✔ **While browsing iTunes:** Tap the Profile button at the bottom of an album info screen, and then tap Follow on the Profile screen.

✔ **While browsing Ping:** Tap on a person's name, and then tap Follow on the Profile screen.

Leave your comments or simply "like" a song, artist, or album when you're browsing iTunes. Tap the Concert button to see information about an artist's upcoming concert dates. You can access a link to purchase tickets, see who's going, and tap the I'm Going button to let others know you'll be there.

Your likes and comments are automatically linked to your Ping activity. People who follow you see your activity if you let them. You can set your privacy settings in Ping on iTunes (as explained earlier in this chapter) or by tapping My Profile in Ping on your iPhone.

Figure 2-11: Access Ping from iTunes.

Managing and Transferring Purchases

Now that you've purchased and downloaded different types of media, you probably want to put them in a useable order. iTunes, on its own, puts the media into libraries so the songs and music videos are in the music library, movies are in the movie library, and so on.

One way you can organize your media is with playlists, which we explain here. You can also create folders to put your playlists in.

Change the media type of an item by clicking on the song or video and going to File➪Get Info➪Options. Choose a different media type from the Media Kind pop-up menu. This is handy, for example, if a podcast from another site ends up in your Music library.

Playlists

Playlists used to belong to the realm of wedding planners and DJs. With iTunes, you can create your own playlists, which are groups of songs that you want played together in a certain order. Playlists are nice for listening to music on your iPod, but they're great for putting together a sequence of songs for your yoga practice or a dinner party — no more running to the stereo to change the CD or listening to the same CD repeat for an entire evening. Instead, just connect your iPhone to your stereo, plug it into the dock of your iPhone speakers, or connect to remote speakers with AirPlay. (We tell you about these kinds of accessories in Book II, Chapter 3.) To create a playlist,

1. **Open iTunes.**

2. **Click the plus sign button in the lower left corner.**

    Or click File➪New Playlist. Either way, an untitled playlist appears under the Playlist on the Source menu.

3. **Type the name of your playlist.**

    The words *Untitled Playlist* are highlighted and are replaced by whatever name your type.

4. **Drag songs you want in the playlist from the list of songs over the name of the playlist.**

5. **Click and drag the songs up and down to rearrange the order.**

Your playlists are copied to your iPhone when you sync.

You can also let iTunes do the work for you. There are three types of playlists that iTunes creates. iTunes DJ is an ever-changing playlist that you can interact with using the Remote app on your iPhone. Smart Playlists are based on criteria you set, whereas Genius playlists are created with songs iTunes thinks go well together. Genius also suggests new songs it thinks you'll like based on your purchase history and what you have in your library. Here's how to create these three types of playlists:

- **iTunes DJ:** Click iTunes DJ in the Playlist section of the Source pane. (If you don't see it, go to iTunes⇨Preferences⇨General and check iTunes DJ.) Select the Source you want iTunes DJ to use to play a random selection, such as the Music library or a playlist. Click the Settings button to choose the number of songs in the playlist and to establish criteria for controlling iTunes DJ with the Remote app (available free at the App Store) on your iPhone. Connect your iPhone to the same Wi-Fi network that your computer is on, and then tap the Remote app on the Home screen to access iTunes and "request" songs from iTunes DJ or other playlists.

- **Smart Playlists:** Click File⇨New Smart Playlist and set the criteria for the type of media, songs, videos, and podcasts you want put together in a playlist. iTunes creates a playlist based on that criteria. When you add a new song or video to iTunes, if it meets the criteria of an existing smart playlist, the new song or video is automatically added to the appropriate smart playlist. You can edit the criteria of an existing smart playlist (including those in iTunes such as Recently Added or Recently Played) by clicking the playlist, and then clicking File⇨Edit Smart Playlist (or Control+playlist name).

- **Genius:** Click Store⇨Turn Genius On. iTunes accesses the iTunes Store so it can review your interests in music, movies, and TV shows and make informed suggestions about media you might like. Click a song you like and then click the Genius button in the bottom right corner. A playlist is created from your music library with songs that iTunes thinks go well with the song you selected. In addition, a list of suggested songs from iTunes appears in the sidebar, as shown in Figure 2-12. Click the triangle next to the Genius button to open the sidebar. If you use Ping, the iTunes social network program, you'll see what your friends' favorite artists are listening to, too, in the sidebar.

Click to open the Genius sidebar.

Figure 2-12: Genius creates a playlist based on a song you select from your music library.

If you've created many playlists, you can organize them into folders. Click File⇨New Playlist Folder. A folder appears in the Playlist library. Name that folder and then click and drag the playlists you want into the folder.

Tracking purchases

One of the nice things about iTunes is how it keeps a history of everything you ever downloaded, free or paid. This is really useful if your computer is stolen or irreparably damaged. You can transfer media directly from iTunes to a new computer, without having to re-purchase items you already bought.

Follow these steps to retrieve items you already downloaded:

1. **Open iTunes.**

2. **Click Purchased in the Quick Links list.**

3. **Click Not In My Library in the upper right section.**

   A list of the items that you purchased in the past but that aren't on your device appears with a little cloud Download button next to them, as shown in Figure 2-13.

4. **Click the Download button for the item you want to retrieve or click Download All at the bottom of the screen.**

5. **The items are downloaded to the appropriate iTunes library.**

Click to download.

Figure 2-13: Download past purchases to the same device.

You can view purchased and free items you've downloaded by clicking Purchase History on the Account Information screen of iTunes.

On your iPhone, tapping Purchased in the browse bar opens a list of the media you purchased. You can view all or only those that haven't yet been added to your iPhone.

Getting the Goods for Free

You probably noticed the word "free" floating around on iTunes. Some things, like lectures from iTunes U and podcasts, are always free. Other things are iTunes promotions. You can find them in different places:

- **iTunes Store Home page:** Take a look around. There's usually at least one link to something free in the banner ads. Scroll through the other sections. Free and discounted items are marked with a yellow triangle on the upper right corner of the icon. At the very bottom of the page, there's a section called Free on iTunes. Tap See All to view the entire selection.

- **Music and TV Shows:** Click the Free link under Quick Links on the upper right section of the page. Pilot episodes of new television series are often free.

- **Books:** Click the free button in the Top Charts section on the right side. Only electronic books are offered; audiobooks don't have a free section.

Chapter 3: Listening to Music and Audio

In This Chapter

✒ **Meeting and mastering the Music App**

✒ **Searching Music for media**

✒ **Creating Playlists**

✒ **Controlling music, audiobook, and podcast playback**

✒ **Customizing Music's settings**

*W*e're not anthropologists, but even before humans began to speak, they probably made rhythmic sounds with sticks and rocks or hand clapping. Music seems to be part of our DNA and with your iPhone along, you never find yourself without something to listen to.

With iOS 5, the iPod app on your iPhone became Music and Video apps just like on the iPod touch and iPad. In the previous chapter, we wrote about getting media onto your iPhone, either via your computer, from iCloud, or the iTunes Store. In this chapter, we talk about Music, the app you use to listen to music, audiobooks, and podcasts. In Book V, Chapter 4 we explore video.

Meeting and Mastering the Music App

Now that you have media on your iPhone, you have the joy of listening to your favorite singers, authors, and commentators whenever you have your iPhone with you. First, we take you through the general layout of Music and then show you the basic commands for listening to music and creating playlists.

Tap Music on the Home screen and you see a screen as shown in Figure 3-1. You see five browse buttons across the bottom of the screen:

Professor Brian Cox, OBE, the pres of the hugely popular BBC2 seri Wonders of the Solar System, appe at the Apple Store in Covent Garde 17th November 2010 to talk about book, which accompanied the ser Professor Cox was interviewed wit Radio 6 Music DJ Shaun Keaver

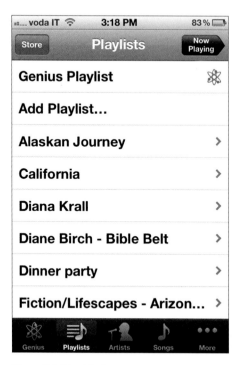

Figure 3-1: The Music screen.

✓ **Genius:** Shows a list of Genius playlists you synced from iTunes or created on your iPhone, if you have Genius turned on.

✓ **Playlists:** Displays a list of playlists you have either created on your iPhone or synced from iTunes.

✓ **Artists:** Displays an alphabetical list of artists. The first item in the list reads All Albums. Tapping All Albums opens a list of the albums on your iPhone. The first item in that list is All Songs, which takes you to the alphabetical list of songs.

✓ **Songs:** Shows a list of songs in alphabetical order by song title, as shown in Figure 3-2. Tapping the Shuffle button at the top of the screen begins playing all the songs on your iPhone in a random order.

✓ **More:** Brings up a list of additional viewing options:

 • **Albums:** Takes you to the Album view.

 • **Audiobooks:** Opens a list of audiobooks you have on your iPhone.

 • **Compilations:** Shows a list of compilations, which are often songs from different albums or artists put together as one.

- **Composers:** Displays an alphabetical list of composers. Tapping the name of the composer opens a list of songs written by that composer.

- **Genres:** Shows a list of genres. Tapping the genre opens a list of media in that genre, which can also include spoken podcasts.

- **iTunes U:** Opens a list of items you downloaded from iTunes U.

- **Podcasts:** Displays a list of audio podcasts you have on your iPhone.

••••• voda IT 🛜	**3:18 PM**	83% 🔋

| Store | **Songs** | Now Playing ▸ |

Shuffle ⤨

A

All I Want
Blue - Joni Mitchell

Almost Blue
The Girl In The Other Room - Diana Krall

Amado Mio
Bambina Impertinente - Carmen Consoli

Among the Living
Ophelia - Natalie Merchant

Amor de loca juventud
Buena Vista Social Club - Buena Vista...

Amore di Plastica
Bambina Impertinente - Carmen Consoli

The Ancient Shepherd and th...

Q A B C D E F G H I J K L M N O P Q R S T U V W X Y Z #

Genius Playlists Artists **Songs** More

Figure 3-2: Tapping the Songs button in the browse bar opens an alphabetical list of songs.

Tapping the Edit button in the top left corner of the More screen opens a Configure screen. Tap and drag a button from the main part of the screen over one of the browse buttons and the two buttons exchange places. This lets you put the buttons you use most in the browse bar.

Finding songs

Sometimes you want to hear a particular song, other times, a particular artist or album. You can play the song or album you want to hear from different views.

In Songs

Tap the Songs button in the browse bar; tap More if you don't see it there, and choose it from the list that appears. Now you have three choices:

- ✓ **Flick up to scroll through the list until you find the song you want to hear.**

- ✓ **Tap the letter of the first word of the song in the alphabet that runs down the right side of the screen.** "The", "A", and "An" don't count as first words.

- ✓ **Type the name of the song in the search field at the top of the screen.** If you don't see the search field, tap the status bar at the very, very top of the screen or the magnifying glass at the top of the alphabet that runs down the right side.

In Artists

Tapping Artists in the browse bar opens an alphabetical list of artists, sorted by first name. Find the name of the artist you want by using the search field, flicking through the list, or going to the letter with the alphabet that runs down the right side. Tap the name of the artist to see a list of songs by that artist.

In Albums

Tapping Albums in the browse bar or from the More screen opens a list of albums. Tap the album that has the song you want to hear and you see a list of the songs on that album, as shown in Figure 3-3. The name of the artist and the album name appear to the right of the album cover image. The number of songs and album playing time are shown as well. The playing time for each song appears to the right of the song name.

With Search

From a screen in Music in any category, you can open Search and look for a song or other audio media. Tap the status bar at the very top of the screen and the Search field appears. Tapping in the Search field opens the keyboard. Begin typing the name of the artist, album, song, podcast, whatever type of audio you want to find, and a list appears divided by category: artist, album, song, or audio podcast. The more letters you type, the narrower your search results. Search looks at all the words in a title, not just the first word.

You can find media from outside Music too. Open Spotlight Search, the farthest left screen of the Home screens, and type in a few letters or a word of the song or artist you seek. The results appear by App, so if a match is found in Music, it appears in the results list under the Music app.

Figure 3-3: Tapping an album name in Albums view opens information and a song list for the album.

Playing songs

When you find the song you want to hear, tap the song. The song begins playing and you see the Now Playing screen as shown in Figure 3-4. If you have any other songs in your library that are from the same album, those subsequent songs play until they're finished or you tap the pause button.

The main controls — Play/Pause, Previous/Rewind, Next/Fast Forward, and Volume — are at the bottom of the screen.

✐ **Play/pause:** Tap to begin playing the song or to pause. When the song is paused, it stays at that paused point even if you do other things on your iPhone. When you return to the song that was playing, it picks up where it left off.

✐ **Previous/rewind:** Tap to jump to the beginning of the playing song, unless you are in the first three seconds of the song, in which case you jump to the previous song. The numbers above the scrubber bar tell you which song in the lineup you're listening to. Tap and hold to rewind.

Repeat Artist/Song title/Album

Back Ping Like Ping post Track list

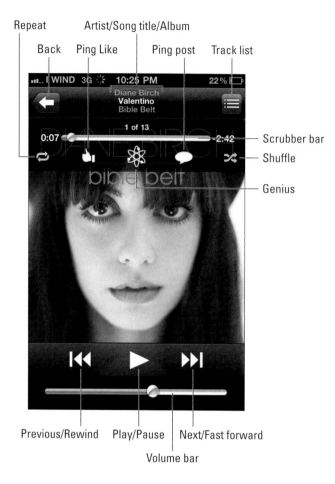

Scrubber bar

Shuffle

Genius

Previous/Rewind Play/Pause Next/Fast forward

Volume bar

Figure 3-4: The Now Playing screen shows the album cover of the song that's playing along with the Music controls.

↙ **Next/fast forward:** Tap to jump to the next song. Tap and hold to fast-forward the song you are listening to.

You can also fast-forward or rewind in a song by dragging the playhead (the ball on the bar) along the scrubber bar. Slide your finger down to use half-speed scrubbing or keep your finger on the scrubber bar for high-speed scrubbing.

Tap the album image to bring up other control buttons. Lyrics or podcast information appear if you have that option turned on in Settings, which is explained at the end of this chapter. You see three or five buttons under the scrubber bar, which are

✔ **Repeat:** Tap once to repeat the entire album continuously (the button turns blue), tap a second time to repeat only the song that's playing (a number one in a circle appears on the button), and tap a third time to stop repeating (the button turns white again).

✔ **Shuffle:** Tap once and music plays the songs of the album in a random order (the button turns blue); tap again to turn off shuffle and hear the songs in the order they appear on the album (the button is white again). You can also shake your iPhone to Shuffle, unless you've deactivated that function in Music settings, which are explained a little later in this chapter.

If you turn on Ping and/or Genius in iTunes on your computer and then sync your iPhone with iTunes, you see one, two, or three of these buttons:

✔ **Genius:** Tap once while you're listening to a song and Music creates a playlist that goes well with the song you're listening to. (Go to iTunes on your computer and select Store➪Turn Genius On.)

✔ **Ping Like:** Tap to let your Ping followers know you like the song (the button turns blue). (Go to iTunes on your computer and click Ping in the source list. Follow the onscreen instructions to create a Ping profile or log in.)

✔ **Ping Post:** Tap to make a comment about the song.

Tap Repeat album and Shuffle together (both will be blue) to hear the album continuously in a random order.

The Back button at the top left of the screen returns you to the spot where you chose the song, which could be the album itself, the Songs list, the Artists list, and so on. You can also swipe to the right to go back.

The Track List button switches between the Song Playing view, as shown in Figure 3-4, and the Album Playing view, as seen in Figure 3-5.

In the Album Playing view, you can assign a rating of one to five stars to each song. iTunes can then use your ratings to create a playlist based on your ratings, for example, a playlist of songs that have four or five stars. A blue triangle indicates the song that's playing and the controls at the bottom work the same way as in Song Playing view. Tap the Album/Song button again to return to the Song Playing view.

Figure 3-5: The Album Playing view shows a list of the songs on the album and a rating for the song that's playing.

Playing albums

You can go directly to an album by tapping Albums in the browse bar (tap More in the browse bar if you don't see it) and then choosing the album you want to hear from the list. Tap the first song and the album begins playing. You can also start the album from another song or tap the shuffle button to let Music choose a random playing order.

You can also play an album from the songs list. When you tap any song from an album, the Now Playing screen opens. Tap the Previous/Rewind button to return to the first song of the album or tap Shuffle to play the album in a random order.

From the Now Playing screen, turning your iPhone to a horizontal position opens the Album view, as seen in Figure 3-6. Flick from left to right to scroll through your album collection. Tap on an album cover to open the track list. Tap a song to begin playing. You can tap the Play/Pause button in the lower left corner to use those two control; however, you have to turn your iPhone to the vertical position to use the other playback controls.

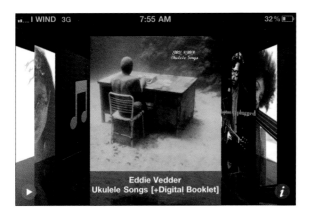

Figure 3-6: The Album view in Music.

Playlists

We explain creating playlists in iTunes in the previous chapter. Playlists are sort of like creating your own personal radio station that plays songs you like all the time. You mix and match the songs you want to listen to together, in the order you want to hear them, and save it to listen to again and again.

Tap the Playlists button in the browse bar. The first two items in the list are Genius Playlist and Add Playlist. A playlist that iTunes creates for you using the music in your collection is a Genius playlist. A simple playlist is one you create yourself. A few default playlists come with Music, such as 90s Music and Classical. Under the Playlists category, you also find the Purchased, Recently Played, and Top 25 Most Played playlists, which you find in iTunes on your computer. At the bottom of the list, you see the Playlists or Genius Playlists that you and iTunes created.

Creating Genius playlists

Make sure Genius is turned on in iTunes on your computer (select Store⇨ Turn On Genius) and then sync your iPhone with iTunes as explained in Book II, Chapter 1. To create a Genius playlist, you select a song and iTunes creates a playlist of songs it thinks go well with the song you selected. To create a Genius playlist, follow these steps:

1. **Tap Playlists from the browse bar.**

2. **Tap Genius Playlist.**

   The Genius Playlist screen opens, as shown in Figure 3-7.

3. **Tap New to create a new Genius playlist.**

   The Songs screen opens.

4. **Scroll through to select the song you want iTunes to use as the basis for the playlist.**

5. **Tap the song you want to be the basis of the playlist.**

   The song begins playing.

6. **Tap the Genius button.**

   If you don't see the Genius button, tap the album image on the screen to bring up additional controls.

7. **Tap the Back button to see the Genius playlist iTunes created.**

   The playlist plays until you pause the song.

8. **Tap Save to save the playlist.**

   The name of the playlist is the name of the song you chose at the beginning. It appears at the bottom of the playlist list and the Genius icon is next to the name.

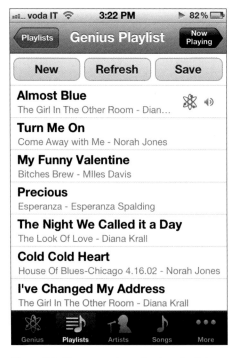

Figure 3-7: iTunes creates a Genius playlist based on a song you select; the Genius Playlist screen shows the songs in the playlist.

If you add more songs to your iTunes collection, you can update an existing Genius playlist. Tap the playlist to open it, and then tap the Refresh button. iTunes looks at your content and creates an updated playlist that may include songs you've added since the playlist was created, if any of those new songs meet the criteria of the old playlist.

To delete a Genius playlist, tap the playlist and then tap the Delete button.

You can create a Genius playlist directly from a song while you're listening to it — just tap the Genius button and iTunes creates a new playlist.

Creating your own playlist

If you already have a playlist in mind, you can create one yourself:

1. **Tap Playlists in the browse bar.**

2. **Tap Add Playlist.**

   A New Playlist box appears as shown in Figure 3-8.

3. **Type a name for your playlist in the Title field.**

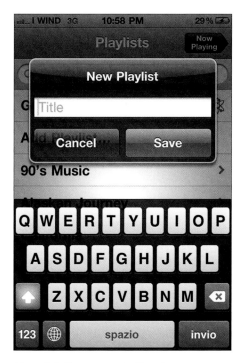

Figure 3-8: Name your playlist when you tap Add Playlist.

4. **Tap Save.**

   The Songs list opens.

5. **Tap the songs you want in your playlist.**

   You can also go to other views such as artist or album to choose songs.

6. **Tap Done when you're happy with your selections.**

   Your playlist appears on the screen, as shown in Figure 3-9.

Figure 3-9: You can edit playlists you create.

7. **Tap the Edit button to do the following:**

   - Drag the reorder buttons up and down to move the songs around in the order you want to play them. You can also let Music randomly reorder the sequence by playing the playlist with the Shuffle button.

   - Delete songs if you decide some don't fit in with the playlist.

   - Tap the plus sign to add more songs. The songs list opens and you select songs to add as in the initial steps.

8. **Tap Done when you are finished.**

9. **Tap the first song to begin playing your playlist or tap the Shuffle button to hear the playlist in a random order.**

If you want to change or delete your playlist at a later time, tap the playlist and follow step 7 above to add, delete, or reorder songs. Tap Clear to clear the songs on the playlist and start over with the same title. Tap Delete to eliminate the playlist entirely.

Playlists created on your computer, including Smart Playlists, or your iPhone are synced one to the other the next time you perform a sync.

Playing Audiobooks and Podcasts

Music isn't just for listening to music any more than iTunes is just for buying tunes. Audiobooks have been around for decades. When audiobooks came on the scene, giving commuters something to do with their commute time, it took a dozen cassette tapes (or, later, CDs) to listen to a whole book. Now, you can download an entire book on your iPhone and listen at your leisure without worrying about carrying around all those tapes or CDs. Podcasts, available in both audio and video formats, are flourishing as a way to communicate.

To play an audiobook or podcast, the procedure is the same as for songs:

1. **Tap Music on the Home screen.**

2. **Tap More, and then tap Podcast or Audiobooks.**

3. **Tap the item you want to listen to (or watch if it's a video podcast).**

    A list of the podcast episodes or the audiobook chapters appears.

    If you want additional episodes of the podcast, tap Get More Episodes. iTunes opens automatically to that podcast and any episodes you haven't yet downloaded have a Free button next to them. Tap Free, and then tap Download. (You may be asked to type in your Apple ID password.) The new episodes are added to Music.

    When a file is larger than 20 MB, you have to connect to a Wi-Fi network or download the file to your computer and then sync.

4. **Tap the episode or chapter you want to hear.**

    The podcast or audiobook begins playing and you see the Now Playing screen as in Figure 3-10. The text across the image is podcast information, which is explained in the "Customizing Music Settings" section at the end of this chapter.

Figure 3-10: The playback and additional controls for podcasts and audiobooks.

5. **The playback controls — Previous/Rewind, Play/Pause, Next/Fast Forward, and the scrubber bar — are the same as for songs. The additional commands, those you see below the scrubber bar, are slightly different and you see Ping only if you turned it on in iTunes and then synced your iPhone with iTunes:**

  - **E-mail:** Tap to send an e-mail link to this podcast or audiobook.

  - **Ping Like:** Tap to like this podcast or audiobook.

  - **30-second repeat:** Tap to replay the last 30 seconds.

  - **Ping Post:** Tap to post a comment about this podcast or audiobook.

  - **Playback Speed:** Tap to change the speed — 1X is normal (the button is white), 1/2X plays at half speed, and 2X plays at twice the speed (both are blue).

Controlling Audio Playback

As with so many things iPhone, there are multiple ways and places to access the same information or controls. The playback controls are no exception. In addition to the playback controls in Music on the Now Playing screen, there are three other ways to control playback: from the multitasking bar, using the headset remote, and with Voice Control.

Using the Playback Controls in the Multitasking bar

Your iPhone is capable of multi-tasking, so you can listen to music and write an e-mail at the same time. Instead of opening Music and going back and forth to another app, try this:

1. **Double-click the Home button.**

   The Multitasking bar appears at the bottom of the screen, showing which apps are open.

2. **Flick from left to the right to open the playback controls, as shown in Figure 3-11.**

   The icon for the media app that was most recently open appears, such as Music, Video, or YouTube, next to the playback controls for Rewind, Play/Pause, and Fast Forward, as well as the orientation lock button.

3. **Tap the button for the action you want to take.**

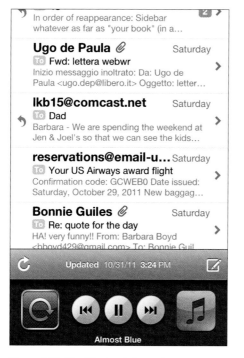

Figure 3-11: The Playback Controls.

If you double-click the Home button when your iPhone is locked but you are listening to audio, the playback controls appear on the lock screen.

Using the headset remote to control playback

You likely listen to music or other media with the headset. The headset that comes with your iPhone has a microphone and a center button that you press to answer incoming calls and up and down buttons to control the volume of the incoming call. These three buttons work when your iPhone is locked and, while listening to music, control playback. Here's how to use them:

- **Volume:** Press the up or down buttons to increase or lower the volume.

- **Pause:** Press the center button; press again to resume playing.

- **Next song:** Press the center button twice quickly.

- **Fast forward:** Press the center button twice quickly and hold.

- **Previous song:** Press the center button three times quickly.

- **Rewind:** Press the center button three times quickly and hold.

If someone calls while you're listening to something, your iPhone rings both in the headset and from iPhone's speaker, unless you have the Silent/Ring button switched to Silent. You have these command options:

- **Answer the call:** Press the center button.

- **Decline the call:** Press and hold the center button for a couple seconds; two low beeps indicate you successfully declined the call.

- **Put a call on hold to answer another incoming call:** Press the center button; press again to return to the caller you left on hold.

- **Answer an incoming call but hang-up on the current call:** Press and hold the center button for a couple seconds; two low beeps let you know you ended the first call.

- **Hang up:** Press the center button. After you hang up, the music or audio you were listening to resumes playing where you were before the call came in.

Using Voice Control or Siri to control playback

We think Voice Control and Siri are great, especially when used along with the headset for an almost hands-free command center. Remember to speak slowly and clearly. If you find that Voice Control or Siri misunderstands you, try moving to an area with less ambient noise and if there are still problems, turn your iPhone off, wait a few seconds, and then turn it back on. To control playback with Voice Control or Siri:

1. **Press and hold the Home button until the Voice Control screen appears and you hear a beep or Siri asks how she can help you.**

   If you're wearing the headset, press and hold the center button until you hear the beep, and then speak the commands.

2. **Say one of the following commands:**

   - **"Play" or "Play Music"**

   - **"Pause" or "Pause Music"**

   - **"Next Song" or "Previous Song"**

   - **"Play album/artist/playlist," and then say the name of the album, artist, or playlist you want to hear**

   - **"Shuffle"** to shuffle the playlist or album that's playing

   - **"Genius" or "Play more like this" or "Play more songs like this"** to create a Genius playlist

   - Ask **"What's playing?," "What song is this?," "Who sings this song?," or "Who is this song by?"** to hear information about the song you're listening to

   - **"Cancel" or "Stop"** to pause the song that's playing

Using the Clock app to put Music to sleep

After a particularly stressful day, getting to sleep can be a challenge. Listening to relaxing music or ambient sounds like rainfall or ocean waves can be more effective than counting sheep. By using the Clock app in conjunction with Music, your iPhone can play music for a set period of time so you can fall asleep and not worry about turning the music off. We recommend you listen with iPhone's speaker or connect your iPhone to external speakers rather than listening with the headset.

To use the Timer as a Sleep Timer with your iPhone:

1. **Tap Clock on the Home screen.**

2. **Tap Timer from the browse buttons at the bottom of the screen.**

3. **Tap When Timer Ends.**

4. **Scroll to the very bottom of the screen and tap Sleep iPod.**

5. **Tap Set.**

   The Time screen appears.

6. **Flick through the rotors to set the amount of time you want Music to play before automatically turning off.**

   The countdown begins.

7. **Double-click the Home button.**

   The open apps bar opens at the bottom of the screen.

8. **Flick to the far left screen to open the Music controls.**

9. **Tap the play button if the song you want to hear is already going.**

   Or

   Tap the Music button to open Music and select what you want to listen to.

10. **Whatever you are listening to is turned off when the timer stops.**

Customizing Music's Settings

You control a few of your listening options in Settings. These options affect everything in Music, not just one individual song. Tap Settings on the Home screen and then scroll down to tap Music (it's in the section that begins with General). Refer to Figure 3-12 and consider these options:

- **iTunes Match:** A paid subscription ($24.95/yr) where iCloud stores the music and playlists you have in iTunes on your computer. Even songs in your iTunes library that you didn't purchase through iTunes but that exist in the iTunes store are accessible through iCloud. Songs you have that aren't available in iTunes are uploaded. iCloud then pushes the songs to your iPhone if you turn on this feature. With iTunes Match, Genius Mixes and Genius Playlists on your iPhone are disabled.

- **Shake to Shuffle:** Just shake your iPhone to immediately change the current song.

- **Sound Check:** Often media from different sources plays back at different volume levels. Sound Check corrects so that everything plays at the same volume, saving you from turning the volume up and down with each media change.

- **EQ:** Tap to open a list of equalizer settings. Choose one that is best associated with the type of media you listen to most. You may have to try a few different ones to see which you like best, but be warned that EQ will drain the battery a bit faster than usual.

- **Volume Limit:** Set a maximum limit for music and video volume, but not phone calls. The limit applies to the earphones, iPhone speaker, and external speakers. Tap Lock Volume Limit to enter a code that must be used to change the volume limit.

✔ **Lyrics & Podcast Info:** If this setting is on, any lyrics or podcast information available from iTunes is displayed when you tap the album cover or image on the Now Playing screen.

✔ **Group by Album Artist:** By default, this option is on and it groups artists by the information listed under Album Artist instead information in the Artist field.

...ıl. voda IT 🤏	3:25 PM	▶ 81 % 🔋
◀ Settings	**Music**	

iTunes Match	⬤ OFF
Shake to Shuffle	⬤ OFF
Sound Check	ON ⬤
EQ	Vocal Booster ❯
Volume Limit	Off ❯
Lyrics & Podcast Info	ON ⬤
Group By Album Artist	ON ⬤

Home Sharing

| **Apple ID** | barbaradepaula |

Figure 3-12: The iPod settings give you options for your listening pleasure.

You can play music from your iPhone on AirPlay-enabled speakers. See Book II, Chapter 3 for details.

Chapter 4: Watching Videos and YouTube

In This Chapter

✓ **Watching movies and videos**

✓ **Controlling playback**

✓ **Playing video on a bigger screen**

✓ **Watching video with Home Sharing**

✓ **Finding and watching YouTube videos**

✓ **Displaying info, commenting, rating, and flagging videos**

✓ **Tuning in to other video, media, and sharing apps**

*Y*our iPhone is not only great for listening to music and podcasts, but it's also great for watching music videos, video podcasts, movies, and television shows, not to mention for watching the home movies you make with the video recorder built in to your iPhone.

Apple developed pixels that are 78 micrometers wide, which means four times as many pixels fit on the 3.5-inch screen as before, a pixel density of 326 pixels per inch. The Retina display uses in-plane switching (IPS) that offers a wider viewing angle and an 800 to 1 contrast ratio, which means brighter whites and darker blacks. LED backlighting and the ambient light sensor adjusts the image to let you see it best in the light available. If you're worried about scratches and fingerprints — don't be. The Retina display is made of super-durable, scratch-resistant, oleophobic (fingerprint-resistant) glass. To you, all this means crisp, clear images and type.

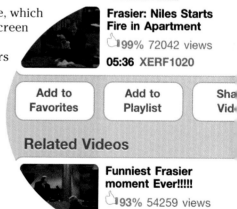

Frasier: Niles Starts Fire in Apartment
👍99% 72042 views
05:36 XERF1020

| Add to Favorites | Add to Playlist | Sha Vid |

Related Videos

Funniest Frasier moment Ever!!!!!
👍93% 54259 views
00:56 starcry100

In Chapters 1 through 4 of this minibook, we explain using the video camera, sharing videos, and downloading music and videos from iTunes. We close this minibook with this chapter on watching videos that you make, download, or stream from YouTube. First, we go through getting video onto your iPhone, which could be in the form of home movies, rented or purchased movies, television shows, podcasts, or music videos and how to convert the video if it's in a non-iPhone format.

One by one, we give details of the video controls of the Video app, and how to hook up your iPhone to a television so you can watch your videos on a bigger screen. We also include a section on using the YouTube app on your iPhone.

Getting and Watching Videos on Your iPhone

We use the term "video" as a generic term to mean a multimedia file, which combines audio with moving. Video can be a music video, a movie, a television show, a podcast, a home movie, or pretty much anything that you watch, and you can watch most of them on your iPhone. The first thing you have to do is get the video to your iPhone. You have three ways to do that:

- ✔ **Camera app:** Make a video directly on your iPhone, as explained in Chapter 1 of this minibook.

- ✔ **iTunes Store:** Download a rented or purchased video from the iTunes Store on your iPhone. You need a Wi-Fi connection to download movies, television shows, and videos.

- ✔ **Your computer:** Sync the videos on your computer to your iPhone via iTunes as explained in Book II, Chapter 1.

Your iPhone supports H.264 video up to 720 pixels and MPEG-4, part 10 video at 640 by 480 pixels, both at 30 frames per second with stereo audio in .m4v, .mp4, and .mov file formats. Motion JPEG (9M-JPEG) is supported at 1,280 by 720 pixels with stereo audio in .avi format. Although the popular Adobe Flash format is not supported directly, in September 2011, Adobe released a product that allows website designers to offer Flash streaming for their online videos, so you will probably begin to see videos that perhaps you couldn't see before.

If you copy a video to your iPhone and it doesn't open automatically, chances are it isn't in one of the supported formats. To see a video's format, go to iTunes and select the video from the list in Movies, TV Shows, Podcasts, or iTunes U. Click File ⇨Get Info. Click the Summary tab. Look under Kind, as indicated by the arrow in Figure 4-1.

To save the video in an iPhone-readable format, click once on the video in the list in iTunes. Click Advanced⇨Create iPod or iPhone Version. The file is saved in the MPEG-4 format with the same name as the original, so you'll want to rename it so that when you sync the file to your iPhone, you sync the one in the correct video format. (To rename the file, click on the name. When it's highlighted, type in a new name or add something like "iP" so you know it's iPhone's version.)

Pass the Potatoes Ethel Merman

| Summary | Info | Video | Sorting | Options | Lyrics | Artwork |

Pass the Potatoes Ethel Merman (25:20)
That Girl
That Girl, Season 2
© Daisy Productions (1966–1971)

That Girl

Kind: Protected MPEG–4 video file
Size: 293.7 MB
Bit Rate: 102 kbps
Date Modified: 5/19/11 1:49 AM
Plays: 1
Last Played: 5/19/11 6:29 PM
Volume: Not available
Rating: TV–G

Profile: Low Complexity
Channels: Stereo
Purchased by: Barbara Jane Boyd
Account Name: barbaradepaula
FairPlay Version: 2
Purchase Date: 5/19/11 1:42 AM
Total Bit Rate: 1574 kbps
Video Dimensions: 640x480

Where: /Users/Babs/Music/iTunes/iTunes Music/TV Shows/That Girl/Season 2/01 Pass the Potatoes Ethel Merman.m4v

(Cancel)   (OK)

Figure 4-1: Determine the video format in Get Info on iTunes.

If you have a video that iTunes can't handle, you can try converting the file with a video transcoder utility such as Handbrake (`handbrake.fr/`).

Controlling playback

After you have a video on your iPhone, tap Videos on the Home screen, and then tap the video you want to watch from the list, as shown in Figure 4-2. If it's a television or an iTunes U series, a list of series' episodes opens. Tap the episode you want to watch.

The videos are divided by category, like they would be in iTunes: Movies, TV Shows, Podcasts, iTunes U. The movie or TV show has to be completely downloaded before you can begin watching it; you can, however, pause during the download and finish it later.

The video begins playing as soon as you open it. Ideally, you watch the video in landscape view. You can see the video in portrait view, but it will generally be quite small, the exception being if video was recorded with the front-camera on iPhone in portrait view.

In the first few seconds, you see the playback controls on the screen, which disappear after about six seconds. To open the playback controls, tap the screen. Refer to Figure 4-3 for the controls explained here:

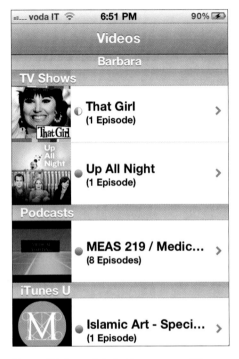

Figure 4-2: See a list of videos on your iPhone from the Videos app.

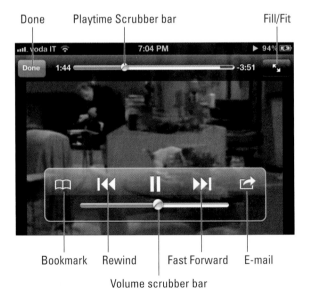

Figure 4-3: The video playback controls.

- **Rewind:** Tap and hold to rewind; tap once to return to the beginning of the episode. If you're watching a movie that has chapters, tap twice to go back one chapter.

- **Fast forward:** Tap and hold to fast forward; tap twice to go to the next chapter.

- **Volume Scrubber Bar:** Drag the white ball on the volume scrubber bar to raise or lower the volume. You can also use the volume buttons on the side of your iPhone.

- **Playtime Scrubber Bar:** The time on the left is the time the video has played; the time on the right is the time remaining. Drag the white ball, known as the playhead, right and left on the scrubber bar to move forward and backward in the video. Slide your finger down as you drag the playhead to adjust the speed at which the video moves.

- **Fill/Fit:** Tap the Fill/Fit button to toggle between two ways you can view video.

  - **Choose Fit** to see videos in their original ratios, although you will see black vertical bands on television shows and horizontal bands on movies, called *pillarboxing* and *letterboxing,* respectively.

  - **Choose Fill** to fill the whole iPhone screen but lose some of the edges of the original version.

- **Done:** Press when you want to stop watching and return to the Videos list. If you stop watching before a video is finished, when you start again, it picks up where you left off. You can also press the Home button to stop watching and return to the Home screen.

You see a few control buttons only under certain circumstances:

- **Bookmark:** When watching a YouTube video, the bookmark button lets you add the video to your favorites. Tap once. The video doesn't stop playing, but you find it on your YouTube favorites list. (We explain YouTube in the second half of this chapter.)

- **E-mail/Twitter:** While watching YouTube, tap this button to send someone a link to the video via e-mail. The video pauses and a New Message screen opens. Fill in the recipient's address and tap Send. You return to video you were watching. Your other choice when you tap this button is to tweet the link. A Twitter message opens, as shown in Figure 4-4. Type your message then tap Send.

You have to download the Twitter app and sign in to your Twitter account to use the Twitter option. Tap Settings⇨Twitter.

- **Language:** Some movies have subtitle or language options. This button appears when they are available. Tap to see your options.

- **Audio Output:** Set the output device you want to use to view your video on another monitor.

If you're wearing the earbuds, you can use the volume buttons on the microphone. You can also click twice on the center part to skip to the next chapter, or three times to go back a chapter.

Figure 4-4: Use Twitter to send links to videos you find on YouTube.

Video settings

You have control over a few Video settings. Tap Settings⟹Video and the Video settings open, as shown in Figure 4-5. These are your options:

- ✔ **Start Playing:** Determines where your video picks up when you stop viewing midway through a video. Where Left Off is the default and it's what we refer to in this chapter — stop a video and when you restart, you pick up where you left off. The other choice is to start a video from the beginning when you restart. Tap Start Playing and check From Beginning if you prefer that choice.

- ✔ **Closed Captioning:** When closed captioning is available, if this switch is on, you see captions. If the switch is off, even when captions are available, you won't see them.

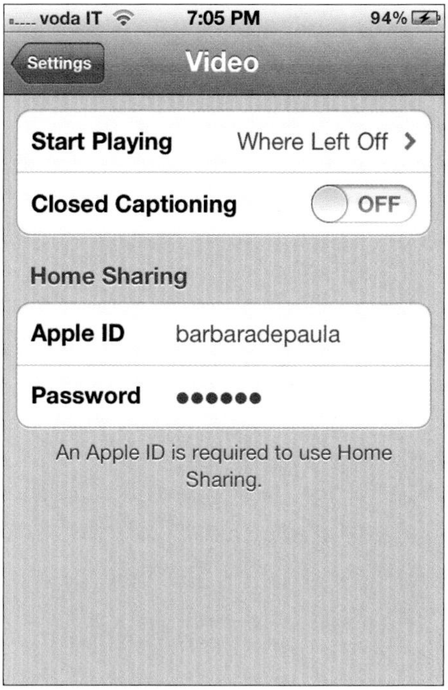

Figure 4-5: Choose where you want to begin when you resume playing your video.

Watching videos on your TV or display

Your iPhone, especially if you have a version with 32 or 64 gigabytes of memory, is a portable video warehouse. You can watch the movies and television shows that are stored on your iPhone, on your iPhone, or you can connect your iPhone to a television or monitor and watch on a bigger screen. We explain the connection procedure in Book I, Chapter 2, so here is just a quick review.

To attach your iPhone to a television, you need one of the following cables:

- **Apple Component AV Cable:** This connects to your iPhone dock at one end and your television's component ports on the other.

- **Apple Composite AV Cable:** This connects to your iPhone dock at one end and your television's composite ports on the other.

- **Apple Digital AV Adapter and an HDMI cable (iPhone 4):** Attach the adapter to your iPhone and then connect an HDMI cable from the adapter to your television.

- **Apple VGA Adapter and a VGA cable:** This setup connects your iPhone to a VGA-compatible television, monitor, or projector.

To play your movie or television show:

1. **Connect the cable to both your iPhone and your television or monitor.**

2. **On your television, select the input device.**

   Refer to the instruction booklet for your television if you don't know how to do this.

3. **Play the video from Videos as you normally would on your iPhone.**

   You see the images on your television.

Playing video with Airplay

To play video wirelessly using Airplay, you have to have an Airplay-enabled device, such as Apple TV, and your iPhone. Follow these steps:

1. **Tap Videos on your Home screen.**

2. **Open the video you want to watch.**

3. **Tap the Play button.**

4. **Choose Apple TV from the list.**

   If Apple TV doesn't appear on the list of AirPlay devices, check that both your iPhone and Apple TV are on the same wireless network.

Home Sharing

If someone in your household is using your computer but there's a video stored on iTunes that you would like to watch, you can access the video from your iPhone with Home Sharing. You have to have iTunes 10.2 or later and both the computer and your iPhone have to be on the same Wi-Fi network. You also need an Apple ID and password. Follow these instructions:

1. **On your computer, in iTunes, click Advanced⇨Turn On Home Sharing.**

2. **Enter your Apple ID and password, and then click Create Home Share.**

3. **On your iPhone, tap Settings⇨Video.**

4. **In the Home Sharing section, type in the same Apple ID and password (refer to Figure 4-5).**

   You see Home Sharing only if you have an active Wi-Fi connection.

5. **Open the Videos app from the Home screen or the multitasking bar.**

   The Shared screen opens with two choices: My iPhone and your user name.

6. **Tap your user name.**

7. **A list of the videos stored on your computer appears on your iPhone.**

8. **Tap the video you want to watch and follow the previous instructions for playback control.**

9. **To return to the content on your iPhone, tap Shared and then tap My iPhone.**

Finding and Watching YouTube Videos

YouTube is a window on the world — the good, the bad, and the ugly. With literally millions of videos, and new ones posted each day, you can find instructional and entertaining videos, news clips, political campaigns, and old television episodes. People from all over the world post videos — we call them "posters" here for lack of a better word. Just this week we learned how to make an apartment-sized hydroponic growing system, watched a video from Japan of a man who taught his dog to catch a ball in the air with his paws, saw a clip of a speech by a Hamas leader who the poster suggested was really George Clooney, and an excerpt from an episode of *Oprah*. Barbara was addicted to the brit-com *As Time Goes By* for a while and found all nine seasons' episodes posted by a young man in Greece! Your viewing options are limited only by the time you have to search.

Your iPhone comes with Apple's YouTube app installed, which is different than the mobile YouTube viewing page (`www.m.youtube.com`). When you watch a video on YouTube, you are streaming video (that is, watching it online), so you must have a cellular or Wi-Fi connection to view anything on YouTube.

You can browse and search the YouTube video collection in several ways; refer to Figure 4-6 for a list from the Featured browse mode. Tap YouTube on the Home screen and look at the browse buttons at the bottom of the page. You see four of the following buttons and a More button on the right; tap More to see the other browse options, as shown in Figure 4-7. The first four in this list are YouTube generated, while the last five are lists made by you:

- **Featured:** Displays a list of videos selected by the YouTube editors.

- **Most Viewed:** Choose between the videos that have been most viewed today, this week, or in all of YouTube history.

- **Most Recent:** A list of the most recently added videos.

- **Top Rated:** Ratings are based on viewers "liking" or "disliking" the video; lists are available for today, this week, or all.

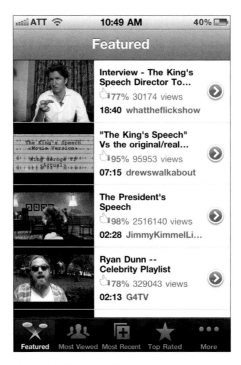

Figure 4-6: Featured videos are chosen by YouTube's editors.

✔ **Search:** Tap in the search field to open the keyboard; type in a few key words and tap Search. Results appear in the list based on video titles, descriptions, tags, and user names.

✔ **Favorites:** This is a list of your favorites. You add videos to this list by tapping the bookmark button while the video is open.

✔ **History:** Shows the videos that you've watched.

✔ **My Videos:** Displays a list of videos that you've uploaded to YouTube.

✔ **Subscriptions:** You can subscribe to a site so you'll be notified when a new video is posted.

✔ **Playlists:** Shows a list of your playlists; refer to the section below for setting up playlists and adding videos to them.

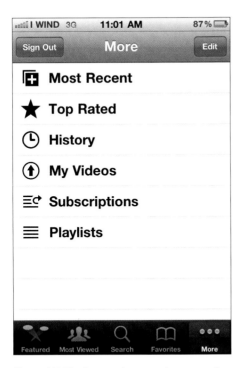

Figure 4-7: The browse buttons give you options for finding videos in YouTube.

You can change the browse buttons you see on the bottom by tapping More and then tapping the Edit button in the top right corner. A Configure screen opens. Touch and drag the button you want to move from the top over the one you want to replace in the browse bar, as shown in Figure 4-8. Their positions will reverse.

Tapping on one of the first four browse buttons described opens a list of videos. The videos you see in any of the lists have the same information:

- **Video image**
- **Name of the video**
- **Rating:** Shows the percentages of all the people who voted either like or dislike for the video.
- **Views:** The total number of views.
- **Time:** How long the video runs.
- **Author:** The user name of the person who posted the video.

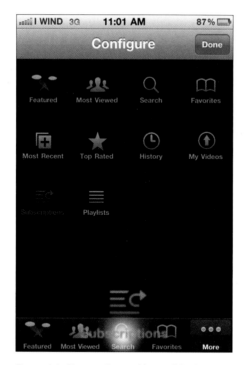

Figure 4-8: Change the positions of the browse buttons by dragging one over another.

Tap on the video image and the video begins playing immediately if you're on a Wi-Fi network. With a slower cellular connection, you see the YouTube logo as the video loads. It will begin playing after enough of the video has begun streaming.

Tap the blue and white arrow to the right of the list entry, and a screen opens that shows a slightly expanded version of the list entry. Three buttons appear across the middle of the screen:

- ✔ **Add to Favorites:** Tapping this button adds the video to your favorites, but the screen remains the same. If you come back to this video after you've made it a favorite, the Add to Favorites button disappears.

- ✔ **Add to Playlist:** Takes you to the Add to Playlist screen.

- ✔ **Share Video:** An e-mail message opens with the cursor blinking in the To field and the keyboard is ready for typing the recipient's address. Tap Send to send a link to this video.

Tap the blue and white arrow on the right of the video at the top of the screen to open expanded information about the video:

- ✔ **Info:** Tap to see the poster's comments, the date the video was added, the category in which it was posted, and any tags that were attached. Scroll down to see the Rate, Comment, or Flag button (more about that in just a section) and comments by other views.

- ✔ **More Videos:** Opens a list of other videos by the same poster.

Tap the video itself to play it.

You can only watch videos when you have a cellular or Wi-Fi connection. All lists are empty if opened without an Internet connection.

YouTube features

You don't need a YouTube account to watch videos on YouTube, but if you want to post videos of your own, subscribe to another account (to easily find videos by the same poster), add favorites, write comments, or rate videos, you do need an account. If you have a Gmail account, you can link your YouTube account to it: Although your YouTube account will have a different ID, the password will be the one you use for your Google account.

Subscriptions

You have to have an account to post a video on YouTube. Most members who post videos don't post just one; they post many. Some even post on a regular basis. If you like one video from a poster, chances are you'll like others that he posts. You can subscribe to the account and, rather than search for new videos by that poster, you can just click on the account in your subscription list and see all the videos by that poster. To subscribe to an account, do the following:

1. **In any list view, tap the blue and white arrow to the right of the video that is part of the account you want to subscribe to.**

   The first info screen opens, as seen in Figure 4-9.

2. **Tap the blue and white arrow to the right of the video at the top of the screen.**

   The More Info screen opens, as seen in Figure 4-10.

3. **Tap the More Videos button.**

   A list of other videos posted by the same author appears.

4. **Scroll down to find the Subscribe button and tap it.**

   You are automatically subscribed to that account's postings. You have to enter your YouTube ID and password if you aren't signed in.

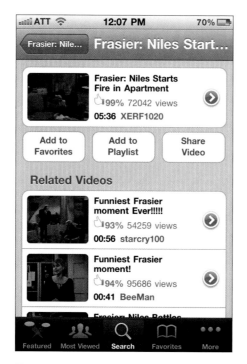

Figure 4-9: The first info screen shows the video you tapped on at the top, three buttons for actions you can take, and a list of related videos.

To unsubscribe, follow the same steps but tap the Unsubscribe button that appears where the Subscribe button was.

Playlists

Whereas a subscription takes you to a list of videos posted by one author, a playlist comprises videos that you like and want to keep together in one group. Refer to Figure 4-11 to see a Playlists screen. Here we explain how to create and delete a playlist and how to add and delete videos to a playlist.

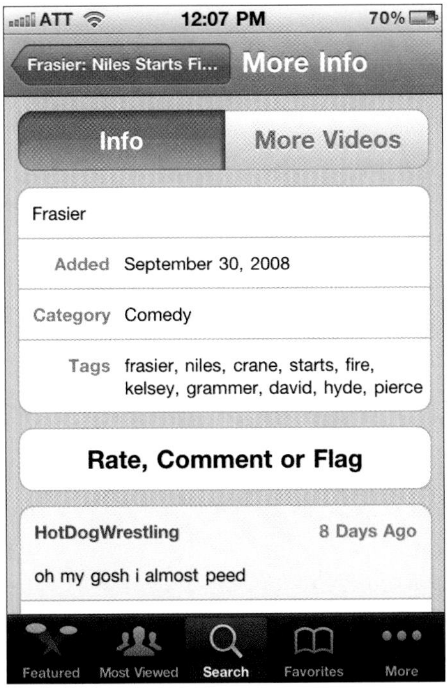

Figure 4-10: The More Info screen displays the title, Added date, Category, Tags, and comments about a video. You can add a rating, comment, or flag from here or tap More Videos to see other videos posted by the same author.

To create a playlist:

1. **Tap Playlist from the browse bar.**

   If it's not there, tap More and choose Playlist from the list.

2. **Tap the Edit button.**

3. **Tap the plus sign in the upper left corner.**

4. **Type in a name for the playlist you want to create.**

5. **Tap Done.**

   The name you typed appears in the list of playlists.

To delete a playlist, open Playlist from the browse bar. Tap Edit. Tap the minus sign that appears next to the playlist you want to delete, and then press the delete button that appears on the right.

Figure 4-11: The Playlists screen shows your playlists, which are groups you create of related videos.

To add a video to a playlist:

1. **Tap the blue and white arrow to the right of the video you want to add to a playlist.**

   The first info screen opens.

2. **Tap the Add to Playlist button.**

   The Playlists screen opens.

3. **Tap the name of the playlist where you want to add the video.**

4. **If you want to create a new playlist for this video, tap the plus sign in the upper left corner to add a new playlist to your playlists.**

   The video is added to the new playlist.

To delete a video from a playlist:

1. **Tap the playlist from the list.**

   A list of videos in that playlist appears.

2. **Tap Edit in the top right corner.**

3. **Tap the minus sign to the left of the video you want to delete.**

4. **Tap the Delete button.**

Commenting, rating, and flagging videos

With so many videos on YouTube, ratings and comments are critical to the success and popularity of a video. You can add your two cents by giving a rating — like or dislike — adding a comment, or flagging a video as inappropriate. To add your rating, comment, or flag:

1. **Go to the More Info screen (tap through two screen levels with the blue and white arrow).**

2. **Tap the Rate, Comment, or Flag button.**

3. **You have three choices, as shown in Figure 4-12:**

   • **Rate or Comment:** Opens a screen where you can choose like or dislike to rate; add a comment in the Comments field if you want to express your opinion of the video.

   • **Flag as Inappropriate:** If you find the video has inappropriate content. Of course, inappropriate is subjective, and YouTube defines inappropriate as material that violates their Terms of Use. If you flag a video as inappropriate, you must give a reason. Flags are reviewed by YouTube staff before the video is removed.

   • **Cancel:** If you hit the button by mistake or change your mind.

Sharing YouTube videos

Some videos are so good, you don't want to keep them to yourself. You can share them in two ways:

✓ **Send a YouTube Video to Someone Else:** While watching a video, tap the screen, and then tap the e-mail button to send a link to that video to someone. A New Message opens with a link already pasted in the text field; you need only address the message and tap Send.

✔ **Post Your Video on YouTube:** You can shoot a video from your iPhone camera app (see Book V, Chapter 1 to read all about shooting video) and then post it directly from your iPhone to YouTube. You have to have a YouTube account. To post a video to YouTube from your iPhone:

Figure 4-12: Add your rating, comment, or flag to a video.

1. **Tap Photos on the Home screen.**

2. **Tap the Album where your video is stored.**

3. **Tap the video to open it.**

4. **Tap the Action button on the lower left side.**

5. **Tap Send to YouTube.**

   A Publish Video screen opens, as seen in Figure 4-13. You have to sign into your YouTube account to post a video to YouTube.

6. **Tap in the Title field.**

   The cursor appears in that field and the keyboard opens.

7. **Fill in the Title and Description fields.**

   Tap return to move from one field to the next.

8. **Choose to post the video in Standard Definition or HD (high definition) video format.**

   The approximate size of your video is shown in parentheses. You must have a Wi-Fi connection to post in HD.

9. **Add any tags you want to identify the video.**

   Tags are words that describe the video and are used as part of the search criteria.

10. **Tap Category to choose a category.**

    A rotor with a selection of categories opens. Tap the category you want to assign to the video.

11. **Tap the level of access you want to assign to the video: Public, Unlisted, Private.**

12. **Tap Publish in the upper right corner.**

Sometimes you run into trouble if the video is too long, either for your cellular data service limits or for YouTube limits. In the first case, try with a Wi-Fi connection or sync to your computer and post from there. In the second case, you have to edit your video down or divide it into multiple parts.

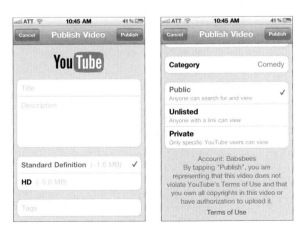

Figure 4-13: Post your videos to YouTube from your iPhone. The image on the left is the top of the screen; scroll down to reach the section shown on the right.

Index

D